Perl Graphics Programming

Perl Graphics Programming

Shawn Wallace

O'REILLY®

Beijing · Cambridge · Farnham · Köln · Paris · Sebastopol · Taipei · Tokyo

Perl Graphics Programming
by Shawn Wallace

Published by O'Reilly & Associates, Inc., 1005 Gravenstein Highway North, Sebastopol, CA 95472.

O'Reilly & Associates books may be purchased for educational, business, or sales promotional use. Online editions are also available for most titles (*safari.oreilly.com*). For more information, contact our corporate/institutional sales department: (800) 998-9938 or *corporate@oreilly.com*.

Editor:	Nathan Torkington
Production Editor:	Emily Quill
Cover Designer:	Ellie Volckhausen
Interior Designer:	David Futato

Printing History:

December 2002:   First Edition.

ISBN: 0-596-00219-x

[M]

Table of Contents

Preface

Welcome to *Perl Graphics Programming*! This book is kind of a second, expanded edition of *Programming Web Graphics*, which was published in 1999. That book focused solely on the PNG, JPEG, and GIF image formats, and was intended more for web applications programmers than for Perl programmers. This book still has a heavy slant toward web applications, but it has been rewritten to fit in better with the other "applied Perl" books. The scope has also been expanded to include the SVG and SWF vector image formats. Intermediate-level Perl users will probably get the most out of this book, though hopefully it will demystify the manipulation of graphics files for newcomers as well.

Perl Graphics Programming takes a practical, resource-based approach to the material. Each section starts with a tour of the internals of the file format in question, followed by a tutorial and reference for one of the popular free Perl libraries or applications that implement the format. The reference sections are more than a generic rehash of the perldoc pages. In some cases, the reference material supplements existing documentation, and in some cases it provides help where the existing documentation is inadequate. Throughout, I have tried to anticipate the questions that a newcomer to the material might ask.

The software covered in this book includes:

- GD and GD::Graph, for creating indexed raster graphics
- ImageMagick, for handling a wide range of image formats
- The Gimp, for specialized image manipulation tasks and filters
- Various Perl XML tools, for SVG files
- Ming, for creating SWF (Flash) movies
- Ghostscript and the PostScript modules, for PostScript files
- The PDF::API2 module, for PDF documents

The focus is always on free software, when it is available. Some fine software has been prominently overlooked (PDFlib in particular) because it is not available under a free license. Some software (such as Ghostscript) offers both free and proprietary versions.

Most of the topics in this book are applicable to any platform (Windows, *nix, Mac OS). You may, however, detect a slight bias toward the Unix world, since most of the book's development was done on a Linux-based system, and some of the tools (such as the Gimp) started their lives in the Unix world (just like Perl).

The book is divided into three sections that correspond to three types of images and application areas: raster images and web graphics; vector images and animations; and documents and printing.

Creating Raster Images and Web Graphics

Part I covers raster image formats and several popular libraries for manipulating them. Since most people will be using these tools to generate graphics for the Web, this section is supplemented by Appendix A, which presents the standard ins and outs of creating CGI scripts that generate dynamic images. Appendix A also takes a look at the HTML tags that embed images in web pages.

In Chapter 1, *Creating Graphics with Perl*, the "black box" of the three predominant web graphics formats (GIF, JPEG, and PNG) is opened, explored, and accompanied by a discussion of web graphics concepts such as transparency, compression, interlacing, and color tables.

In Chapter 2, *On-the-Fly Graphics with GD*, we discover the GD module, a collection of functions for reading, manipulating, and writing simple raster images. GD is great for CGI scripts and for building other modules (such as GD::Graph; see Chapter 4).

In Chapter 3, *Graphics Scripting with Image::Magick*, we are introduced to ImageMagick and its Perl interface. ImageMagick is a collection of functions and a transparent interface for reading and writing over 40 different graphics file formats. It is a great "Swiss army knife" for image conversions, scaling, cropping, and color management. It can handle file formats that contain multiple images in a single file such as GIF89a. ImageMagick is (of necessity) a bit bulky, and may not be suited for all CGI programming tasks, but it certainly can be used for a lot of them. This chapter is supplemented by Appendix C, a table of the various file format capabilities of ImageMagick.

In Chapter 4, *Charts and Graphs with GD::Graph*, we use GD::Graph to create graphs from data. GD::Graph is a Perl module that extends the GD module by offering a number of functions for creating eight types of graphs and charts. In the early days of the Web, almost all of the financial graphs or web server load graphs were generated by CGI scripts using GD::Graph (actually, its precursor, GIFGraph) to generate the images.

In Chapter 5, *Scripting the Gimp with Perl*, we learn how to use the Gimp-Perl module to create custom plug-ins for the GNU Image Manipulation Program. The Gimp is a poster child for the free software movement; it's a platform (similar to Adobe's Photoshop) for manipulating raster images. The Gimp has a sophisticated scripting interface (several, actually). In this chapter we use the Gimp-Perl interface to write Gimp plug-ins. Chapter 5 is supplemented by Appendix B, which provides a reference guide for the Gimp.

Creating Vector Images and Animations

Part II focuses on the Scalable Vector Graphics (SVG) format and Macromedia's SWF (Shockwave/Flash) format. Vector images differ from raster images in that the image data is stored as a series of points and instructions for connecting those points. The strength of vector graphics is that the same image can be represented at any scale without a loss of quality or information.

In Chapter 6, *SVG: The Scalable Vector Graphics Format*, we describe SVG, an XML file format designed to tightly integrate with the other document standards of the World Wide Web.

Chapter 7, *Creating SVG with Perl*, expands on the SVG discussion in Chapter 6, providing recipes for SVG animation, scripting, and manipulation using the XSLT XML transformation language.

In Chapter 8, *SWF: The Flash File Format*, we introduce the Shockwave/Flash file format, a compact format for web animations used by Macromedia's popular Flash tool. Although many web purists claim to despise the spread of "Flash-enabled" web sites, SWF is too prevalent to ignore. Flash can actually be used constructively, even if you just think of it as a stop-gap until SVG catches on!

In Chapter 9, *Using Ming*, we present the Ming library, an API for making SWF files from Perl. This chapter is supplemented by Appendix D, an ActionScript reference. While there are many fine books about ActionScripting, they are all geared toward users of Macromedia's Flash software. The needs of a Ming developer are slightly different, and Appendix D fills those needs.

Creating Documents and Printing

Although PostScript and PDF are fundamentally vector drawing formats, they are more accurately described as document encoding formats. PostScript is the standard page description language used by most laser printers and printing devices. It is also the foundation on which the PDF document encoding format is built. Part III describes how both can be utilized from Perl programs.

In Chapter 10, *Printing with Postscript and PDF*, we are introduced to the PostScript language and the Portable Document Format (PDF).

In Chapter 11, *Using the PostScript Modules*, we develop a framework for easily generating PostScript text blocks, graphics, and documents from Perl.

In Chapter 12, *Creating PDF Documents with Perl*, we explore the PDF::API2 module, an object-oriented interface for building PDF documents from Perl.

Conventions Used in This Book

The following typographic conventions are used in this book:

Italic
> Used for email addresses, URLs, directory names, filenames, program names, and new terms where they are defined.

`Constant Width`
> Used for code listings and for keywords, variables, function names, command options, module names, parameters, attributes, and XML elements where they appear in the text.

`Constant Width Bold`
> Used to highlight key fragments of a larger code example or to show the output of a piece of code.

`Constant Width Italic`
> Used as a general placeholder to indicate terms that should be replaced by actual values in your own programs.

How to Contact Us

Please address comments and questions concerning this book to the publisher:

> O'Reilly & Associates, Inc.
> 1005 Gravenstein Highway North
> Sebastopol, CA 95472
> (800) 998-9938 (in the United States or Canada)
> (707) 829-0515 (international/local)
> (707) 829-0104 (fax)

There is a web page for this book, which lists errata, examples, or any additional information. You can access this page at:

> *http://www.oreilly.com/catalog/perlgp/*

To comment or ask technical questions about this book, send email to:

> *bookquestions@oreilly.com*

For more information about books, conferences, Resource Centers, and the O'Reilly Network, see the O'Reilly web site at:

http://www.oreilly.com

The examples and other resources are also available at:

http://shawn.apocabilly.org/PGP/

Acknowledgments

This book is dedicated to my wife, Jill, to my parents, Bob and Paula, to my sister Erin, and to Grammy Alice.

Thanks to everyone at O'Reilly, especially editor Nathan Torkington, editorial assistant Tatiana Diaz, and illustrator Jessamyn Read. Thanks also to Brian Jepson, who was instrumental in goading me to start (and finish) writing books.

I'd like to thank all my friends and co-workers at AS220, including Jonathan Wisehart. Several artists allowed me to use their work in some of the examples herein: thanks to Jill for the characters and Pam Murray for the photos in Chapter 1, Sue Riddle for the illustrations in Chapter 3, Scotty "Blue Bunny" Grabell for photos in Chapters 5 and 12, Bob Arellano for the "The first time I rode into Providence…" project, Keith Munslow for various drawings, and Jonathan Thomas for letting me use his head throughout.

A prestigious group of technical reviewers took a lot of time to help us remove all of (well, most of) the typos, technical goofs, and boldfaced lies from the text: Gregory Baumgardner, Aaron Straup Cope, Ben Evans, David Hand, Steve Jenkins, Joe Kline, Steve Marvell, and Simon Wistow. Thanks to Steve Marvell in particular for his thorough and pointed criticism. A number of people took the time to offer suggestions, corrections, and patches to the previous edition of this book. They are: Harmen Bussemaker, Jeremy Fowler, Shane Geiger, Susan Malveau, Ricardo Muggli, Faisal Nasim, Maurits Rijk, Greg Roelofs, Ron Savage, Dan Smeltz, and Bob Walters. Thanks also to Tom Cross, Jay Gramlich, Steven Harris, Chris Krum, Johnathan Kupferer, Erik LaBianca, Joakim Lemström, Tom Riemer, Vinay Samudre, Simon Twigger, Johan Vromans, and Erasmus Zipfel for offering patches and improvements to the PostScript module (even if I didn't use them all).

## PART I

Raster Images and Web Graphics

## CHAPTER 1

Creating Graphics with Perl

Almost every modern application goes beyond plain text. Graphics appear in the form of logos, icons, charts, animations, or even as a "Save as PDF" option. These graphics can be images (static pictures), animations (moving pictures, possibly interactive), and documents (formatted pages of text and images).

You have several choices of representation for each type of graphic. For example, images are often kept as JPEG or GIF files. But the JPEG format and the GIF format are quite different, and impose different restrictions on the types of images you can store. This chapter explains the different file formats; their characteristics, advantages, and disadvantages; and what each is capable of. This information will help you to select an appropriate format for your graphics.

Introduction to File Formats

Over time there have been many different file formats for representing graphics. Most are footnotes to history, with only a few ever becoming wildly popular. In this book we talk about the image formats PNG (Portable Network Graphics), JPEG (Joint Pictures Expert Group, the committee that designed the format), and GIF (Graphic Interchange Format); the animation formats SVG (Scalable Vector Graphics), SWF (used by Macromedia Flash), and to a lesser extent GIF again; and the document formats PostScript and PDF (Portable Document Format).

All of these formats fall into one of two camps: *raster* or *vector*. A raster image is composed of dots, called *pixels*. Almost every image on a web page is a raster image, and the PNG, JPEG, and GIF formats are raster formats. The alternative to representing a picture as a series of dots is to represent it as you might draw it, with lines, curves, and filled colors. This is a vector image. The most noticeable difference between raster and vector images is how they scale. If you zoom in on a raster image, each pixel simply becomes a larger and larger spot, which leads to chunky images. A vector image, in contrast, gives infinite magnification.

Each raster file format represents an image's pixels differently. These formats vary in how much color information they store, whether they can handle transparency in an image, and whether you have to pay to use them. For this reason, not all graphics formats are suited for all jobs. JPEG is generally much better for photos because it has good compression, for example, and GIF is the only raster image format that can handle animated sequences.

The limitations of a file format highlight its design goals. The flexible PNG format, for example, has a maximum size of approximately 2 Gigapixels × 2 Gigapixels. At a standard screen resolution of 72 pixels per inch, could store an image of approximately 470 miles × 470 miles. This would allow you to save a 1:1 life-sized image of most of New England in a single PNG file! By comparison, a GIF file has a maximum size of 75 feet × 75 feet, which would let you store a 1:1 image of a good-sized house. So, the next time you need a life-sized image of Rhode Island, you'll know which file format to use.

Table 1-1 gives you some of the important details of the file formats covered in this book.

Table 1-1. File format details

Format	Type	Max. color depth	Alpha channel	Max. image size (pixels)	Multiple images	Toolkits
PNG	Raster	8-bit indexed 16-bit grayscale 48-bit RGB +16 bits w/alpha	16 bit	2Gig x 2Gig	No	GD, GD::Graph, ImageMagick, Gimp; can be embedded in SWF, SVG
JPEG	Raster	12-bit grayscale 36-bit RGB 32-bit CMYK	No	64K x 64K	No	ImageMagick, GD, Gimp; can be embedded in SWF, SVG
GIF	Raster	8-bit indexed	1-bit transparency	64K x 64K	Yes	ImageMagick, Gimp
SVG	Vector	24-bit	Limited by user agent	Limited by user agent	Yes	ImageMagick, Gimp
SWF	Vector	24-bit	8-bit	1Gig x 1Gig (twips)	Yes	Ming library
Post-Script	Document	Limited by display device	No	Limited by display device	Yes	PostScript module, ImageMagick, Gimp
PDF	Document	Limited by user agent	Limited by user agent	Limited by user agent	Yes	PDF::API2, ImageMagick

Let's now nail down a few definitions that are used for all graphics formats, starting with color.

Color

Several color models (or *color spaces*) have been created over the years for different applications. For our purposes, they can be divided into two areas: *additive* color spaces (e.g., RGB) and *subtractive* color spaces (e.g., CMYK). Because many of the toolkits used to manipulate graphics expose the underlying color model, it pays to know your way around RGB and CMYK before you delve into graphics programming.

The RGB Color Space

The vast majority of computer graphics applications use the RGB (Red, Green, Blue) additive color space because cathode ray computer monitors generate colors using those three components. In the RGB space, the light spectra of varying fractions of the three primary colors, red, green, and blue combine to make new colors ("peach puff," for example, or "grassy knoll"). These primaries are referred to as *channels*.

The actual color generated by an RGB display device never exactly matches the perfect model because of differences between devices and variations in the software that controls those devices. However, most graphics display devices are calibrated to be within an acceptable tolerance of each other.

The RGB model is generally represented as a three-dimensional cube, where each axis is one of the three primary colors. In the abstract model, we typically look at a unit color cube, where each axis has intensity values from 0 to 1. The RGB unit cube is shown on the left side of Figure 1-1.

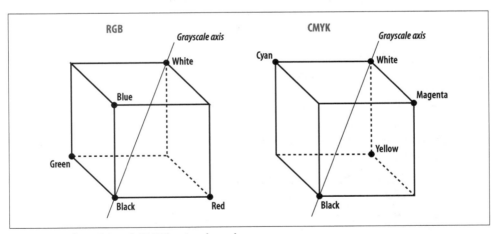

Figure 1-1. The RGB and CMYK unit color cubes

This unit cube is scaled by the number of bits used to represent each component; e.g., a 24-bit color cube would have components in the range 0–255. Each color in the color space can be represented as a three-value coordinate (or *vector*), for example (255, 127, 54). In HTML and in many of the Perl graphics modules described in this book, we represent an RGB color as three 8-bit hexadecimal values concatenated together. Bright purple, for example, would be:

```
#FF00FF
```

The diagonal of the color cube running from black (0, 0, 0) to white (1, 1, 1) contains all of the gray values. This lets you manipulate color with vector math. For example, you can perform a simple grayscale conversion by taking the dot product of the RGB and grayscale vectors:

```
# Where $r, $g, $b are values in the range 0..255

my $gray_value = int(255 * (abs(sqrt($r**2 + $g**2 + $b**2)) /
                    abs(sqrt(255**2 + 255**2 + 255**2)))));
print int(100*$gray_value/255), "% gray\n";
```

The CMYK Color Space

The most common subtractive color space is CMYK (Cyan, Magenta, Yellow, and Black), which is used in offset printing. It is called a subtractive model because the resulting color is composed of those frequencies that are *not* absorbed as light reflects off of a surface. Cyan ink absorbs red light, magenta absorbs green, and yellow absorbs blue. Thus, the combination of magenta and yellow ink reflects red, the combination of cyan and yellow reflects green, and cyan and magenta produce blue.

In an ideal mathematical world, you can convert from the RGB color space to the CMYK color space by subtracting each of the components from the maximum value of that component (in this case, each component is 8 bits):

```
my ($c, $m, $y) = map {255-$_} $r, $g, $b;
```

In the real world, certain practical issues make this more complicated. For one, a black component is usually added to the mix. This is because black is a common color, especially for text. It is much more economical to print one coat of black ink than to print three layers of cyan, magenta, and yellow in perfect registration (it also makes the paper less soggy). And anyone who paints will tell you how difficult it is to mix a true black from primary colors.

The "1 minus RGB" method of converting to CMYK is fine for tasks where exact colors are not necessary. To achieve good color matching, though, you can't treat CMYK as a completely subtractive model because the translucency of inks, the interaction between inks, and differences in substrates make the conversion nonlinear.

Good color matching schemes require various corrections that are determined by experimentation. Unfortunately, a lot of the study and work on the subject is not in the public domain; most of the information is patented by companies that create "color systems" like Pantone or TRUMATCH. That's the primary reason why a lot of public domain software (such as the Gimp, described in Chapter 5) lacks the CMYK capabilities of proprietary graphics software.

Color Depth

The average human can distinguish between about 7 million different colors, which can be easily represented in 24 bits. An image with a color depth of 24 bits per pixel (or more) is known as a *truecolor* image. Each pixel in the image is saved as a group of three bytes, one for each of the red, green, and blue elements of the pixel: 8 red bits + 8 green bits + 8 blue bits = 24 bits. Each of the R, G, and B elements can be represented as one of 256 (2^8) values, which gives us 256^3 or 16,777,216 possible colors. This also means that a 200×200 pixel truecolor image saved in an uncompressed format would take up 120 KB for the image data alone, and a 500×500 pixel image would take up 750 KB. Both of these images would be too large to put on a web page, which is why the image formats used on the Web are compressed file formats (see the section "Compression" later in this chapter).

The PNG format allows you to save color images with a depth of up to 48 bits per pixel, or grayscale images at 16 bits per pixel. This is actually beyond the display capacity of most consumer video hardware available today, where 24-bit color is the standard. JPEG also lets you store images with a color depth of up to 36 bits. GIF does not handle truecolor images.

A *bitmap* is an image with a color depth of 1. That is, each pixel is either the foreground color or the background color. The XBM format is an example of a bitmapped image format. Other images represent colors in less than 24 bits, usually by storing a collection of color values in a separate color table.

Color Tables

An image with a color depth of 8 bits is sometimes called a *pseudocolor* or *indexed color* image. Pseudocolor allows at most 256 colors through the use of a *palette*, which is sometimes also referred to as a *color table* or a Color Lookup Table (CLUT). Rather than storing a red, green, and blue value for each pixel in the image, an index to an element in the color table (usually an 8-bit index) is stored for each pixel. The color table is usually stored with the image, though many applications should also provide default color tables for images without stored palettes.

To save a truecolor image as a pseudocolor image, you must first *quantize* it to the size of the palette (256 colors for a GIF or an indexed PNG). Quantization alone usually gives you an image that is unacceptably different from the source image, especially in images with many colors or subtle gradients or shading. To improve the quality of the final image, the quantization process is usually coupled with a *dithering* process that takes the available colors and tries to approximate the colors in the original by combining the colors in various pixel patterns.

Figure 1-2 shows a 24-bit image (left). That image must be quantized to an optimal 256 colors (the 256 colors that occur most frequently in the image) to save it as an 8-bit indexed image (middle). Dithering is applied with the Floyd-Steinberg dithering process to improve image quality (right).

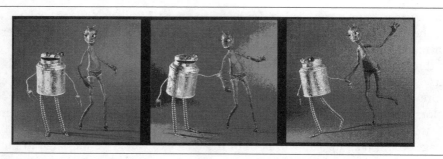

Figure 1-2. A 24-bit image (left) quantized to 256 colors (middle) and dithered (right)

The GIF file format is an indexed color file format, and a PNG file can optionally be saved as an indexed color image. A GIF image always has at most 256 colors in its palette. Animated GIFs (multiple images in one file) can have a new palette for each image, so the 256 color limit is applicable to only one image of a multi-image sequence. A PNG may also have a 256 color palette. Even if a PNG image is saved as a 24-bit truecolor image, it may contain a palette for use by applications on platforms without truecolor capability.

You can use the Image::Magick interface described in Chapter 3 for color reduction. Example 1-1 reads in a 24-bit JPEG image and converts it to an indexed GIF. Two output images are created for comparison: a 16-color dithered version, and one without dithering.

Example 1-1. Converting a truecolor image to 16 colors, with and without dithering

```
#!/usr/bin/perl -w

use strict;
use Image::Magick;

my $image = new Image::Magick;

my $status = $image->Read('24bitimage.jpg');
die "$status\n" if $status;

my $image2 = $image->Clone();

# Reduce to 16 colors with and without dithering

$image->Quantize(colorspace => 'RGB',
                 colors => 16, dither => 1
                 );
```

```
$image->Write('gif:4bitimage.gif');

$image2->Quantize(colorspace => 'RGB',
                  colors => 16, dither => 0
                  );
$image2->Write('gif:4bitimagenodither.gif');

undef $image;
undef $image2;
```

Transparency and Alpha

Transparency in graphics allows background colors or background images to show through certain pixels of the image. Often, transparency is used to create images with irregularly shaped borders (i.e., non-square images). The three primary file formats have varying degrees of support for transparency.

Transparency is not currently supported in JPEG files, and it will most likely not be supported in the future because of the particulars of the JPEG compression algorithms and the photography niche at which JPEG is aimed.

The GIF file format handles transparency by allowing you to mark one index in a color table as the transparent color. The display client uses this transparency index when displaying the image; pixels with the same index as the transparency index are simply "left out" when the image is drawn. Each image in a multi-image sequence can have its own transparency index.

The PNG format allows for better transparency support by allowing more space for describing the transparent characteristics of the image, although the full range of its capabilities are not necessarily supported by all web clients. PNG images that contain grayscale or color data at 8 or 16 bits per channel may also contain an *alpha channel* (also called an *alpha mask*), which is an additional 8 to 16 bits (depending on the image color depth) that represent the transparency level of each pixel. An alpha level of 0 indicates complete transparency (i.e., the pixel should not be displayed), and an alpha value of $2^n - 1$ (where n is the color depth) indicates that the pixel should be completely opaque. The values in between indicate a relative level of translucency.

Figure 1-3 shows PNG and GIF transparency. Both images are rectangular, but use transparency to give the impression of a circle. The GIF image (on the left) can only have a well-defined border to the circle because GIF only permits pixels to be drawn or transparent, with no gradation. The PNG image (on the right) has a fuzzy border because PNG permits levels of transparency.

Figure 1-3. GIF's 1-bit transparency (left) versus PNG's full alpha channel (right)

Raster File Formats

A raster image is one that is described by a grid of colored pixels. Even though particular image formats may use compression algorithms to store the image data differently, or alpha channels to create the illusion of non-rectangular shapes, all raster graphics translate into a rectangular grid of pixels.

Two techniques have been developed to make raster images easier to transfer over the Internet. Each image format has its own compression system, where advanced mathematics or data structures are used to exploit regularity in the image data so that the full image can be reconstructed from a smaller number of bytes. Many raster image files are arranged so that they may be displayed while partially downloaded (a technique called *interlacing*).

Table 1-2 gives you an idea of the relative effectiveness of each compression mechanism and the interlacing styles used by each format.

Table 1-2. Raster graphic compression and interlacing comparison

Format	Compression ratio	Compression algorithm	Method	Progressive display	Interlacing style
PNG	4:1 to 10:1	Deflate	lossless	Yes	Adam7
JPEG	5:1 to 100:1	JPEG	lossy	Yes	PJPEG
GIF	3:1 to 5:1	LZW	lossless	Yes	Scan line

The rest of this section describes compression and interlacing styles. The three raster image formats are then described in greater detail.

Compression

Image transmission is always a tradeoff between two limiting factors: the time it takes to transfer the image over the network and the time it takes to decode the image. JPEG, for example, is a highly compressed format that allows for small files and quick transmission times but requires longer to decode and display. The format works very well because generally the network is the bottleneck, with the average desktop computer perfectly able to perform the necessary decoding operations in a reasonable amount of time. The ideal is to achieve a very small file that can be very easily decoded. In practice, it is always a tradeoff.

Files can be compressed using "lossy" or "lossless" compression. People generally interpret the term "lossy" compression to mean that information is lost in the translation from source image to compressed image, and that this information loss results in a degraded image. This is true to a point. However, you could also argue that information is lost in the process of creating a GIF (a so-called "lossless" storage format) from a 24-bit source image, since the number of colors in the image must first be reduced from millions to 256. A more accurate definition of lossy would be something like "a compression algorithm that loses information about the source image during the compression process, and repeated inflation and compression results in further degradation of the image."

JPEG is an example of a lossy compression format. PNG and GIF are both examples of "lossless" compression. A lossless compression algorithm is one that does not discard information about the source image during the compression process. Inflation of the compressed data exactly restores the source image data.

The distinction between these two methods of compressing image data affects the way you do your everyday work. For example, assume you have created a number of images for a web site, to be served as JPEGs (a lossy format) because they contain nice gradients that would look terrible as GIFs (and you haven't explored the possibility of PNG yet). You create all these images in Photoshop (or even better, the Gimp) and save them as JPEGs, but neglect to save the original source files. What if your client wants the images cropped slightly differently? You have to re-open those JPEGs, edit the images, and re-save them. This would be a very painful way to learn the meaning of lossy compression, because the resulting images would be less smooth and the artifacts would make them less pleasing than the originals.

Generally a JPEG can be decoded and re-encoded, and, as long as the quality setting is the same, the image is not visibly degraded.* If you change any part of the image, however, the changed part loses even more information when it is re-encoded (see Figure 1-4). If an image is cropped or scaled to a different size, the entire image loses more information.

The GIF format uses a type of compression called LZW (Lempel-Ziv-Welch), which is also used by the Tagged Image File Format (TIFF). The enforcement of the patent on LZW has caused a lot of controversy, as we shall see in the later section "GIF Animation for Fun and Profit."

The PNG file format was developed as an alternative to GIF. The compression algorithm used by PNG is actually a version of the Deflate algorithm used by the pkzip utility. Deflate is, in turn, a subset of the LZ77 class of compression algorithms (yes,

---

* Actually, there is a form of lossless JPEG, but it has not been widely implemented.

Figure 1-4. Repeated decoding and encoding of JPEGs can result in information loss

that's the same L and Z as in LZW compression). PNG's compression method does not use any algorithms with legal restrictions, however. This is one of its major selling points.

The JPEG file format uses a custom compression system called JPEG compression. It works on completely different principles from GIF and PNG, and is explained in the JPEG section later in this chapter.

Interlacing

All three of the standard web graphics formats provide for the progressive display of an image as it is downloaded. The rationale for the further complication of an image file to support progressive display is that there is perceived to be a major improvement in download speed. Partial information about an entire image may be shown and the display refined as the image downloads, rather than displaying the final image one row at a time.

This capability is achieved by saving the pixels in a non-consecutive order. If the pixels are drawn in the order that they are decoded from the stream, the image is drawn as a grid of pixels that is progressively filled in with more information. Images with this sort of pixel ordering are said to be *interlaced*. Interlacing is implemented differently by different file formats.

Interlaced files tend to be slightly larger than non-interlaced files (except for progressive JPEGs, which tend to be slightly smaller). This is because most compression schemes make certain assumptions about the relationships of adjacent pixels in an image, and the interlacing process can disrupt this "natural" ordering of pixels that work well with compression algorithms. Interlacing can more than make up the slight difference in file size with a perceptual download speedup, however.

Scanline (GIF) interlacing

The image data for a GIF file is stored by the row (or *scanline*), with one byte representing each pixel. A non-interlaced GIF simply stores each scanline consecutively in the image data field of the GIF file. An interlaced GIF still groups pixels into scanlines, but the scanlines are stored in a different order. When the GIF file is encoded, the rows are read and saved in three passes; the even-numbered rows (using a 0-based counting system) are saved in the first four passes, and the odd-numbered rows are saved in the final pass. The interlacing algorithm looks like this, with each pixel coordinate labeled with the pass on which it is saved and rendered:

```
Row 0 11111111...
Row 1 44444444...
Row 2 33333333...
Row 3 44444444...
Row 4 22222222...
Row 5 44444444...
Row 6 33333333...
Row 7 44444444...
```

When the image is later reconstituted, the display client (e.g., web browser) usually temporarily fills in the intervening rows of pixels with the values of the nearest previously decoded rows, as you can see by looking at the progressive stages in an interlaced GIF display shown in Figure 1-5. The interlacing approach taken by the GIF format allows us to view a 1/8 vertical resolution version of the entire image after one pass of the display, 1/4 after two passes, 1/2 after three, and the complete image after the fourth. In many cases the user can interpret the image after only the first or second pass.

Figure 1-5. Interlacing provides a perceptual increase in download speeds by presenting a distribution of pixels as the image comes across the network

Adam7 (PNG) interlacing

PNG uses a slightly different interlacing scheme than GIF does. GIF completes the interlacing in four passes, where the first three passes count even scan lines. PNG uses a seven-pass scheme called Adam7 (named after its creator, Adam M. Costello), where the first six passes contribute to the even rows of pixels, and the seventh fills in the odd rows. Because PNG files do not necessarily have to store pixels in a scan-line together, each pass contains only certain pixels from certain scanlines.

Graphically, this looks like the grid below, where each pixel in an 8×8 block is labeled with the pass on which it appears on the screen:

```
1 6 4 6 2 6 4 6
7 7 7 7 7 7 7 7
5 6 5 6 5 6 5 6
7 7 7 7 7 7 7 7
3 6 4 6 3 6 4 6
7 7 7 7 7 7 7 7
5 6 5 6 5 6 5 6
7 7 7 7 7 7 7 7
```

This scheme leads to a perceptual speed increase over the scanline interlacing used by GIF. After the first pass, only 1/64 of the image has been downloaded, but the entire image can be drawn with 8×8 pixel resolution blocks. After the second pass, 1/32 of the file has been transferred, and the image can be drawn at a 4×8 pixel block resolution. Small text in an image is readable after PNG's 5th pass (25% of the file downloaded), which compares favorably with GIF's interlacing gains, where small text is typically readable after the 3rd pass (50% of the file downloaded).

Progressive JPEGs

JPEG files may also be formatted for progressive display support. Progressive JPEG (PJPEG) is considered an extension of the JPEG standard, and the progressive display of PJPEGs is not fully implemented by all web clients.

The scanline interlacing techniques used by GIF and PNG are not applicable to JPEG files because JPEGs are a more abstract way of storing an image than a simple stream of pixels (it is more accurate to call a JPEG file a collection of DCT coefficients that describe a pixel stream, but that's probably too much information). Essentially, a Progressive JPEG that is displayed as it is transferred over the network would first show the entire image as if it had been saved at a very low quality setting. On successive passes the image would resolve into the complete image, with the quality level at which it was saved.

Progressive JPEGs are not yet the most efficient means of progressive display, as the entire image must be decoded with each subsequent pass. The JPEG format can offer such high levels of compression, however, that progressive display is not as important as for other file formats.

PNG: An Open Standard for Web Graphics

In the "GNU's Not Unix" tradition of self-referential acronyms, PNG may unofficially be taken to stand for "PNG's Not GIF." PNG was designed as an open standard alternative to GIF, and it plays that role very well. However, PNG will not completely replace GIF because PNG can store only one image per file,* and there are millions of web pages out there that are full of GIF images.

Because of patent issues, most Perl modules abandoned support for GIF in the late '90s and retrofitted their code to support the PNG standard. For example, GIFgraph became PNGgraph (and eventually GD::Graph, documented in Chapter 4), and the GD library (see Chapter 2) starting using PNG, amongst other formats. ImageMagick (see Chapter 3) had always supported PNG and GIF, but stopped writing LZW-compressed GIFs by default. All of this helped to contribute to PNG's popularity.

PNG is a well-written and flexible format. It supports indexed color images as well as 24-bit color images. It can also save a full alpha channel. It is best used as a GIF replacement, for images with text or spot colors, or for saving photographs without losing information. In general, however, JPEG allows a better balance between compression ratio and image quality for photographs. 24-bit photographic images in PNG are much larger.

JPEG: The P Stands for Photographic

JPEG stands for the Joint Photographic Experts Group (*http://www.jpeg.org*), which is the committee set up by the International Standards Committee that originally wrote the image format standard. The JPEG committee has the responsibility of determining the future of the JPEG format, but the actual JPEG software that makes up the toolkit used in most web applications is maintained by the Independent JPEG Group (*http://www.ijg.org*).

The JPEG standard actually defines only an encoding scheme for data streams, and not a specific file format. JPEG encoding is used in many different file formats (TIFF Version 6.0 and Macintosh PICT are two prominent examples), but the file format used on the Web is called JFIF. JFIF stands for JPEG File Interchange Format, which was developed by C-Cube Microsystems (*http://www.c-cube.com*) and placed in the public domain. JFIF became the de facto standard for web JPEGs because of its simplicity. When people talk about a JPEG web graphic, they are actually referring to a JPEG encoded data stream stored in the JFIF file format. In this book we refer to JFIF as JPEG to reduce confusion (or to further propagate it, depending on your point of view).

To create a JPEG you should start with a high-quality image sampled with a large bit depth (from 16 to 24 bits) for the best results. You should generally use JPEG encoding only on scanned photographs or continuous-tone images.

---

* Multiple-image Network Graphics (MNG), a PNG variant capable of storing multiple images, has been in the works for years.

JPEG encoding takes advantage of the fuzzy way the human eye interprets light and colors in images by getting rid of certain information that is not perceived to create a much smaller image that is perceptually faithful to the original. The degree of information loss may vary so that the size of an encoded file may be adjusted at the expense of image quality to gain the optimum compression for your application. The quality of the resulting image is expressed in terms of a Q factor that may be set when the image is encoded. Most applications use an arbitrary scale of 1 to 100, where the lower numbers indicate small, lower quality files and the higher numbers larger, higher quality files. Note that a Q value of 100 does not mean that the encoding is completely lossless (although you won't lose much). Also, the 1 to 100 scale is by no means standardized (the Gimp, for example, uses a 0 to 1.0 scale), but this is the scale used by the IJG software.

GIF Animation for Fun and Profit

The GIF file format is widely used, usually out of habit rather than for any technical virtues. In fact, the primary reason for not using GIFs is legal, not technical.

"What's the deal with GIF—do I have to pay licensing fees?" is one of the more frequently asked questions about the GIF file format. In a nutshell, GIF is not free and unencumbered because CompuServe, the creators of GIF, used the LZW codec (algorithm) to implement its data compression. The Unisys Corporation owns the patent for the LZW algorithm (United States Patent No. 4,558,302) and requires a licensing fee for any software that uses the LZW codec.

The GIF file format does not allow the storage of uncompressed data or data compressed by different algorithms, so if you use GIF, you must use LZW. There is some confusion as to exactly what uses are covered by the patent, but Unisys has taken the matter to court a number of times. So most developers have moved to JPEG or PNG formats.

Unfortunately, neither PNG nor JPEG allows you to store multiple images in a single file, a capability that allows you to create efficient little animations. GIF is still good for this kind of animation, patents or no patents.

GIF animation can be thought of as flip-book animation. Just as a flip book is not an appropriate format for *Fantasia*, GIF animation is not an appropriate format for long works, large images, or sequences that require many frames per second to be effective. Also, any sort of presentation that necessitates interaction with the user requires another solution based in SWF, SVG, or a language like JavaScript or Java. GIF animation does have its strengths—for example, all browsers can display animated GIFs. Users don't have to reconfigure their browsers or install a new plug-in as they might have to for SWF or SVG.

A full discussion of creating GIF animations with ImageMagick is found in Chapter 3.

Vector Graphic File Formats

Vector graphics are not represented by a fixed matrix of pixels, but by a collection of points and instructions for connecting those points. Whereas raster graphics cannot be scaled without losing or resampling the image data, vector graphics may be rendered at any scale without a loss of quality.

When we talk about vector graphics, we are actually referring to vector graphic *file formats*. Vector-based display devices (such as oscilloscopes or the old Vectrex video game console) are rare these days. All of the images that we cover in this book become rasterized in the end, whether it is by the display software, video card, or printer.

The two vector image formats that are of interest to us here are the open standard SVG format (Scalable Vector Graphics) and Macromedia's SWF format (Shockwave/Flash). You might argue that PostScript and PDF are also vector formats, since each typically defines lines and curves as a series of points and control points. However, nothing in the PostScript language description restricts it to using only vector graphics. You could, for example, craft a well-formed PostScript document in which each page is represented as a raster graphic. PostScript and PDF are more properly defined as high-level document formats, as we shall see later in the chapter.

At first glance, you might think of SVG (described in Chapter 6) and SWF (described in Chapter 8) as competing graphics formats. The two are very different beasts, actually. The overriding design goals of the SWF format have always been efficiency and widespread availability. Today, the best reasons for using SWF are that it is fast and prevalent. Tomorrow, you may find yourself using SVG for many tasks because SVG was designed as the standard way of incorporating vector graphics into XHTML documents. Let's take a closer look at how you would go about generating SVG and SWF files from Perl.

SVG for XML Images

SVG's biggest strength is that it is based on XML and can be tightly integrated into XHTML web pages. A graphic representation of a typical XHTML document is shown in Figure 1-6. Let's say that you want to implement a rollover button in this document, where the text or the outline of the button changes in response to mouse click or mouseover events. Usually this is handled by creating static PNG or GIF images, one for each state of the button. These images are then swapped using JavaScript to handle the mouse events. The problem with using static raster images for each button is that they quickly become difficult to maintain. If the site needs a redesign or if the button text changes, you have to change each of the static files. With an SVG solution, the appearance and the text of the button can be directly changed by the rollover script.*

---

* Unfortunately, this is more promise than practice as of this writing; most web browsers still only support SVG with external plug-ins.

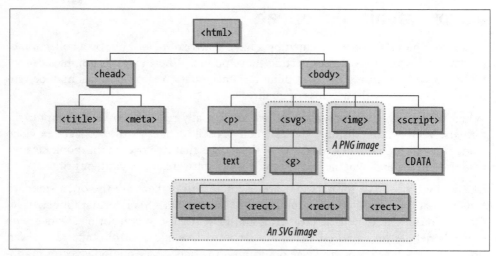

Figure 1-6. The document tree of a simple XHTML document

An SVG element is a collection of XML tags that describe the lines, curves, text, colors, and shading of the image. An SVG image can even encapsulate raster image data. Chapters 6 and 7 describe the tags that make up the SVG specification in depth, but a simple SVG element (four colored squares rotated at a 45 degree angle) looks like this:

```
<svg width="2in"
     height="2in"
     xmlns="http://www.w3.org/2000/svg">
  <g transform="translate(144,0) rotate(45) scale(.70)">
    <desc>A blue square</desc>
    <rect width="1in" height="1in" fill="#0000FF"/>
    <desc>A red square</desc>
    <rect x="0in" y="1in"
          width="1in" height="1in" fill="#FF0000"/>
    <desc>A yellow square</desc>
    <rect x="1in" y="0in"
          width="1in" height="1in" fill="#FFFF00"/>
    <desc>A green square</desc>
    <rect x="1in" y="1in"
          width="1in" height="1in" fill="#00FF00"/>
  </g>
</svg>
```

Because it is plain text, SVG can be generated from Perl using simple print statements. The following produces an equivalent SVG document on STDOUT:

```
#!/usr/bin/perl -w

use strict;
```

```
my @colors = qw(blue red yellow green);

print qq(<svg width="2in" height="2in"
        xmlns="http://www.w3.org/2000/svg">);

print qq(<g transform="translate(100,0) rotate(45) scale(.70)">);

foreach my $i (0..3) {
        print "<desc>A $colors[$i] square</desc>";
        print '<rect x="'.int($i/2).'in" y="'.($i%2).'in"'."\n";
        print qq(width="1in" height="1in" fill="$colors[$i]"/>);
}

print "</g></svg>";
```

One of the fringe benefits of using an XML-based format like SVG is that you can draw upon the library of existing XML parsing and writing tools. Some of the more popular XML Perl modules are:

XML::Writer and XML::Parser
Writing and reading interfaces to the Expat XML parser.

XML::Simple
A simplified interface to XML::Parser.

XML::Twig
An extension of XML::Parser that returns the XML document as a tree structure.

XML::SAX
A framework for building event-driven SAX (Simple API for XML) parsers, filters, and writers. Other modules, such as XML::SAX::Writer, build on this framework.

AxKit
A suite of mod_perl-based tools for integrating XML generation with the Apache web server.

XML::LibXML
An interface to the Gnome libxml2 library.

If you've installed the Image::Magick library (see Chapter 3) with XML support, you can easily rasterize SVG files and convert them to other formats. If you run the following code on the previous SVG image, you will notice that it is cropped because ImageMagick does not yet recognize the scaling attribute:

```
#!/usr/bin/perl -w

use strict;
use Image::Magick;

my $image = new Image::Magick;
```

```
my $status = $image->Read('image.svg');
die "$status\n" if $status;

$image->Write('png:image.png');

undef $image;
```

Many vector graphics drawing programs such as Adobe's Illustrator and the free
Sketch program (*http://sketch.sourceforge.net*) support SVG as an interchange format. It is also becoming more accepted on the web, but it is still not as prevalent as
the SWF format.

SWF for Flash Animation

The SWF format is Macromedia's contribution to the Web. Unlike SVG, SWF files
are stored in a proprietary binary format. An SWF file is a sequence of opcodes that
describe single or multi-frame animations called *movies*. Movies can be embedded
within other movies as *sprites*, and all elements of the document are scriptable with
the ActionScript language. SWF's strength lies in the size of its installed user base, its
efficient use of bandwidth, and its powerful scripting language. SWF is the most
powerful and common animation format currently on the Web.

Most people generate SWF files using Macromedia's Flash tool; in fact, many Flash
developers don't even know that they're generating SWF files. But there's no reason
you can't make SWF files from Perl or any other scripting language. In fact, the Ming
module provides a high-level API for doing so from Perl, PHP, C, and Java.

The Ming API is most useful as a supplement to the Flash tool, for automating certain tasks, or for creating dynamic SWF movies on the fly. One of the sample Ming
applications in Chapter 9 is a program that assembles previously created Flash movies into a new composite movie according to an XML description:

```
<movie filename="index.swf" width="400" height="400">
    <sprite url="sprite2.swf">
        <scaleTo x="2" y="8"/>
        <moveTo x="100" y="100"/>
    </sprite>
    <sprite url="sprite2.swf">
        <scaleTo x="5" y="5"/>
        <moveTo x="200" y="200"/>
    </sprite>
    <sprite url="sprite2.swf">
        <moveTo x="300" y="300"/>
        <rotateTo degrees="45"/>
    </sprite>
    <nextFrame/>
</movie>
```

See Chapter 9 for the full example.

Document File Formats

The document file formats covered in this book are PostScript and PDF. PostScript is a programming language for representing two-dimensional graphics. It was one of the many innovations of the late '70s to come out of the Xerox Palo Alto Research Center (PARC) and have a significant impact on the way people think about and use computers today. PostScript was the brainchild of John Warnock, who used the language to research graphic arts applications of computers. In 1982, Warnock and Chuck Geschke formed Adobe Systems, and the language that they developed at PARC was redesigned and packaged as PostScript.

The PDF format came along in the early '90s, also from Adobe. PDF builds on the capabilities of PostScript but is aimed at becoming a truly portable platform for the electronic interchange of files. PostScript and PDF are described in detail in Chapters 10 through 12.

PostScript: A Language for Page Representation

PostScript has become the standard programming language for printing.[*] Over the course of a couple of decades, it has gone through several revisions, referred to as PostScript Level I, Level II, and Level III. There are several other page description formats in the PostScript family, each with its own application niche:

Encapsulated Postscript (EPS)
> Encapsulated PostScript is a standard format for including a PostScript page description in other page descriptions. An EPS file is simply a one-page PostScript file (representing any combination of text or graphics) that strictly follows the Document Structuring conventions (see Chapter 10) and is self-contained to the point that it does not depend on the existence of external graphics states.

EPSI and EPSF
> An EPSI (Encapsulated PostScript Interchange) file is simply an EPS file that is bundled with a bitmapped preview image. An EPSF is an EPSI formatted for older versions of the Macintosh operating system, where the PostScript code is stored in the data fork of the file and a PICT format preview image is stored in the resource fork.

Display PostScript
> Display PostScript is a variant of PostScript intended for drawing graphics on raster displays.

---

[*] Arguably, the one exception to this statement is in the field of mathematics publishing, where TeX still dominates the serious journals.

Chapter 11 presents a new module for generating PostScript text blocks, drawing primitives, and documents from Perl. The PostScript module presents an easy-to-use interface to place blocks of text on a page:

```perl
#!/usr/local/bin/perl -w

use strict;
use PostScript::TextBlock;

my $tb = new PostScript::TextBlock;

$tb->addText( text => "The Culinary Dostoevski\n",
              font => 'CenturySchL-Ital',
              size => 24,
              leading => 100
            );
$tb->addText( text => "by Ms. Charles Fine Adams\n",
              font => 'URWGothicL-Demi',
              size => 18,
              leading => 36
            );

open IN, "example.txt";
my $text;
while (<IN>) {
    $text .= <IN>;
}
close IN;
$tb->addText( text => $text,
              font => 'URWGothicL-Demi',
              size => 14,
              leading => 24
            );

open OUT, '>culinarydostoevski.ps';
my $pages = 1;

# create the first page

my ($code, $remainder) = $tb->Write(572, 752, 20, 772);
print OUT "%%Page:$pages\n";
print OUT $code;
print OUT "showpage\n";

# Print the rest of the pages, if any

while ($remainder->numElements) {
    $pages++;
    print OUT "%%Page:$pages\n";
    ($code, $remainder) = $remainder->Write(572, 752, 20, 772);
    print OUT $code;
    print OUT "showpage\n";
}
```

The Image::Magick module relies on the free Ghostscript interpreter to handle its PostScript output. Image::Magick does a nice job rasterizing specific pages of Post-Script documents:

```perl
#!/usr/bin/perl -w

use strict;
use Image::Magick;

my $image = new Image::Magick;

# Rasterize the first two pages

$image->Set(density => "300x300");    # Default is 72x72

my $status = $image->Read('document.ps[0,1]');
die "$status\n" if $status;

$image->Write('png:document.png');

undef $image;
```

PDF: Toward a Truly Portable Document

PDF files have become a common format for the electronic distribution of documents originally created as print documents in PostScript. PDF files are meant to be printed or viewed on a screen with a viewer such as Adobe's Acrobat Reader. PDF seems to have a bright future as the document storage format of choice; printers and graphic artists have found that the PDF format offers everything needed by a professional service bureau. On the raster display side of things, PDF is being used in such applications as Quartz, the Mac OS X rendering engine, which is based on the PDF imaging model.

The PDF::API2 module described in Chapter 12 is useful for generating PDF documents. This example creates a 20-page PDF with three lines of text in the upper left corner of each page:

```perl
#!/usr/bin/perl -w
use strict;
use PDF::API2;

my $pdf=PDF::API2->new();
my $font = $pdf->corefont("Times-Roman", 0);

foreach my $p (1..20) {
    my $page = $pdf->page();
    my $text = $page->text();
    $text->font($font, 72);
    $text->translate(20,700);
    $text->text("Page $p, line 1");
    $text->cr(-80);
```

```
    $text->text("Page $p, line 2");
    $text->cr(-80);
    $text->text("Page $p, line 3");
}

print $pdf->stringify();
```

References

The Encyclopedia of Graphics File Formats
James D. Murray and William van Ryper (O'Reilly). A tome covering over 100 file formats.

http://www.wotsit.org
Wotsit is a comprehensive collection of file format specifications.

## CHAPTER 2

On-the-Fly Graphics with GD

The GD Perl module reads, manipulates, and writes PNG and JPEG files. Although it is more limited in scope than the ImageMagick package (described in Chapter 3), its size and speed make it well suited for dynamically generating graphics in CGI scripts. GD has become the de facto graphics manipulation module for Perl; other modules such as GD::Graph (described in Chapter 4) extend the GD toolkit to easily accommodate specific graphics tasks such as creating graphs and charts.

Versions of GD older than 1.20 produce GIFs as output. In 1999 this was changed so that only PNGs and JPEGs were produced, due to Unisys's unfriendly licensing scheme for software that supports the GIF format. If you really need a library that will produce GIFs, you'll have to find an older copy of GD and libgd (such as Version 1.19). Additionally, versions of GD prior to 2.0 could handle only 8-bit indexed images, even when generating PNGs and JPEGs.

The GD module was written by Lincoln D. Stein, author of the CGI modules. GD is actually an interface to Thomas Boutell's *gd* graphics library, a collection of C routines created for manipulating PNGs for use in web applications; this library is required by the GD module. The GD::Convert module provides additional methods for reading and writing xpm and ppm images, which can be useful when writing Perl/Tk applications.

GD is distributed under similar terms as is Perl itself—the Artistic License or the GPL, at the user's discretion. The *gd* C library on which GD is based is covered by a separate copyright held by the Quest Protein Database Center, Cold Spring Harbor Labs, and Thomas Boutell. See the COPYING file that comes with the standard GD distribution for more specific copyright information.

GD Basics

The GD module is available on every platform where Perl is available. Several versions of Perl come with GD as a standard part of the Perl distribution, such as the ActiveState Win32 port and the MacPerl port. Installation methods vary from platform to platform, but if you've ever successfully installed a Perl module on your system, you shouldn't have a problem installing GD.

GD requires several components, all of which are freely available. They are:

The GD module
> To download the latest version of GD, check CPAN first via *http://www.cpan.org*. The latest version of GD.pm should also be available at *http://stein.cshl.org*.

Thomas Boutell's libgd C library
> This can be found at *http://www.boutell.com/gd/*. Version 1.8.3 or higher is required.

Support libraries
> - The PNG graphics library, available at *http://www.libpng.org/pub/png/*
> - The zlib compression library, available at *http://www.gzip.org/zlib/*
> - Version 2 of the FreeType font rendering library for TrueType fonts, available at *http://www.freetype.org*
> - Version 6b or later of the JPEG library, available at *http://www.ijg.org*

Most of these packages use the GNU *autoconf* tools for configuring and compiling the source code. The order of installation should be:

1. Install the supporting libraries. Be sure to install the include files as well as the libraries themselves. All of the support libraries except *libpng* are optional.
2. Install *libgd*. You need to edit some options in the Makefile if you want to include support for TrueType fonts.
3. Install the GD Perl module.

The GD module gives you access to all of the methods and constants of the GD::Image, GD::Font, and GD::Polygon classes:

GD::Image
> The Image class provides the means for reading, storing, and writing image data. It also implements a number of methods for getting information about and manipulating images.

GD::Font
> The Font class implements a number of methods that store and provide information about fonts used for rendering text on images. Each of the fonts are effectively hard-coded; they are described as a number of bitmap matrices (similar to XBM files) that must be compiled as part of the source during installation on your system. Limited support for drawing with TrueType fonts is also provided.

GD::Polygon

The Polygon class implements a number of methods for managing and manipulating polygons. A polygon object is a simple list of three or more vertices that define a two-dimensional shape.

GD supports five input file formats: PNG, JPEG, XBM (black and white X-bitmaps), XPM, WBMP (Wireless Bitmap), and GD files. A GD file is an image that has been written to a file using the gd( ) method. To read in the image data from a file, use newFromPng( ), newFromJpeg( ), newFromXbm( ), newFromWMP( ), or newFromGd( ), depending on the format of the stored file.

Scripts that use the GD module to create graphics generally have four parts that perform the following functions: creating the image, allocating colors in the image, drawing on or manipulating the image, and writing the image to a file, pipe, or web browser. Each application in the next section follows this structure.

Sample GD Applications

In the larger scheme of things, there are some applications for which GD is best equipped, and some for which you may want to use ImageMagick, a more specialized tool like GD::Graph, or the Gimp. Three application areas where GD shines are:

- Images that require simple drawing commands
- Simple images created from user input
- Situations where the small size of the *gd* library is an advantage

The first part of this chapter explores these three application areas in more detail. The remainder is a more detailed description of the GD methods and constants.

Simple Drawing: Hello World

The first example will show how to draw simple text and shapes, in this case, "Hello World" in a rectangle on a random field of red polka dots (see Figure 2-1). With GD you have the option of creating 24-bit or 8-bit color images. In both cases you will allocate colors in the image the same way, with the colorAllocate( ) method. By default, GD will create 8-bit indexed PNGs, which are limited to 256 colors but will end up being smaller than 24-bit images. Use the trueColor( ) method to work on a 24-bit image, or trueColorToPalette( ) to convert a 24-bit image to an 8-bit image.

If you are not reading in an image from a previously created file, use the new( ) method to create a new Image object. The format of this image will be determined upon output, based on the output method that you select (in this case, we're making a PNG with the png( ) method).

The size of the image in this example is 401×201 pixels, so that the x values run from 0 to 400 and the y values from 0 to 200. The GD drawing primitives can draw off the edge of the canvas, but the first point of the shape (in this case, the center of

Figure 2-1. Hello world in GD

the circles) must always fall within the bounds of the canvas. The origin of the canvas is in the upper left corner. Example 2-1 shows the code.

Example 2-1. Hello World on a field of polka dots

```perl
#!/usr/bin/perl -w
# Example 2-1. Hello world in GD

use strict;
use GD;

my $image = GD::Image->newPalette (401,201);

my $gray = $image->colorAllocate(200, 200, 200);
my $red = $image->colorAllocate(255, 0, 0);
my $black = $image->colorAllocate(0, 0, 0);

# Draw a field of polka dots with random diameters

foreach my $i (0..10) {
    foreach my $j (0..5) {
        my $d = rand(50)+1;
        $image->arc($i*40, $j*40, $d, $d, 0, 360, $red);
        $image->fill($i*40, $j*40, $red);
    }
}

# Draw the text in black

my ($x1, $y1, $x2, $y2,
    $x3, $y3, $x4, $y4) = $image->stringFT($black,
        "/home/shawn/arial.ttf", 48, 0, 40, 120, "Hello World");

# Outline the text with a black box

$image->rectangle($x1-10, $y1+10, $x3+10, $y3-10, $black);

print $image->png;
```

Circles are drawn with the arc( ) method, which draws an arc between two angles centered at a specific point on the canvas. The arc( ) method actually takes two diameter parameters (one for the width and one for the height) so that you can draw ellipses.

The text in this example is drawn using a 48 pt TrueType font. It is drawn at an angle of 0 degrees (it may be rotated to other angles), with the left margin of the text's baseline positioned at the point (40, 120). You must specify the full path to TrueType fonts; if you don't have TrueType fonts available, you can use GD's built-in bitmapped fonts (see the "Strings and Fonts" section later in this chapter).

The stringFT( ) method returns the four coordinates of the bounding box of the text, counterclockwise starting with the lower left corner. The rectangle( ) drawing primitive uses this information to draw a black box with a 10-pixel margin around the text.

The next example provides a little more detail on the use of some of these methods.

Images from User Input: A Customized Billboard

The second example is a modified version of a script that was part of a site-specific installation during the Convergence Festival in Providence, Rhode Island. Artist Bob Arellano solicited the citizens of RI to complete the phrase "When I first rode into Providence..." The answers were collected and displayed on various billboards throughout town. Part of the project included a web page interface that would collect phrases and return an image of a billboard with the phrase stamped on it.

Example 2-2 is a CGI script that takes a string from an HTML form and draws text on a blank billboard. The original billboard image was not completely square within the frame, so the script takes this into account by drawing the text along slanted baselines. To achieve a crude illusion of perspective—the text is not truly in perspective because the height of the characters does not vary as the text recedes in the frame—the slope of each baseline is also varied with each line of text.

First the script imports GD, then initializes variables and parses the CGI input. The variable $dy is the slope (rise/run) of the first line of text, which was determined manually from the source image. The variable $ddy is the amount that the slope changes as each line of text is drawn.

Example 2-2. Generating a customized billboard image from user input

```perl
#!/usr/bin/perl -w
# Example 2-2. Make a billboard from user input

use strict;
use CGI;
use GD;

# The maximum number of characters allowed in the input string
```

Example 2-2. Generating a customized billboard image from user input (continued)

```perl
my $maxchars = 220;

my $filename = 'blankbillboard.png',
my ($x1, $y1) = (50,60);              # starting point
my ($cx, $cy) = ($x1, $y1);          # The current point
my ($width, $height) = (213,56);     # dimensions of the drawing area
my $dy = -.0657;                     # initial slope of the baseline
my $ddy = .0003214;                  # change in slope with each line

# Extract the CGI parameters

my $q=new CGI;
my $string = $q->param('string');

# Replace all space-like characters with spaces

$string =~ s/\s+/ /g;

# Check length of the string

if (length($string) > $maxchars) {
    print "Content-type: text/html\n\n";
    print <<ENDHTML;
    <HTML>
    <HEAD>
    <TITLE>There is a problem with your submisison...</TITLE>
    <BODY>
    <CENTER>
    <H1>Sorry, can't be more than $maxchars chars...</H1>
    </BODY>
    </HTML>
ENDHTML
    exit;
}
```

The maximum length of the string was determined by estimating the area taken up by a longish string at the smallest point size. GD supports two types of fonts: a limited collection of fixed-width bitmapped fonts, and TrueType fonts (if the external FreeType library is installed). This script chooses the biggest font that fits the text within the drawing area.

```perl
# The text is displayed in one of three fonts, depending
# on the number of characters in the string.

my @fonts = (gdLargeFont, gdSmallFont,gdTinyFont);

# Pick the font to use, based on a guesstimate of whether the
# string fits within the block at a particular size.

my $font = gdTinyFont;

LOOP: foreach my $f (@fonts) {
```

```
        if (length($string) <= 750/$f->width()) {
            $font = $f;
    last LOOP;
        }
    }
```

To make a new image, you can create a new, empty image object of a given width
and height, or you can read an image from a file or raw data. All image creation
methods return undef on failure. If the method succeeds, it returns an Image object.
This object can contain only one image at a time. The script starts by reading in the
previously created PNG image of a blank billboard:

```
# Open the background image

open (IMG, $filename) or die "Couldn't open image...\n";
my $img = newFromPng GD::Image(\*IMG);
close IMG;
```

If you will be doing any drawing or manipulation of the image, you need to get information about the colors available in the image. You must allocate colors in the image
whether you are working with an indexed image or not. You may need to add new
colors to an image's color table, or you may need to get color indices of existing colors. Use the colorAllocate() method with a list of integer red, green, and blue values (in the range 0 to 255) to add a new color to the image. This method returns the
index of the color, which you should store for use with drawing methods requiring a
color index:

```
# Allocate a color in which to draw text

my $white = $img->colorAllocate(255,255,255);

# Split the string into individual words

my @words = split ' ', $string;

my $w = 0;              # Initialize the cumulative width
my $starty = $y1;       # Initialize the starting y coordinate

WORD: while (@words) {
    my $word = shift (@words);

    # First take care of the case where a single string is longer
    # than the width

    if (($font->width() * length($word)) > $width ) {

        # Divide the string in two and push the two words
        # back on the list

        my $length =  int($width/$font->width());
        my $front = substr($word, 0, $length);
        my $remainder = substr($word, $length+1,
                                length($string)-1);
```

```perl
        $word = $front;
        unshift @words, $remainder;
    }

    if ((($font->width( ) * length($word)) + $w) > $width ) {

        # Start a new line

        $cx = $x1;
        $cy = $starty + $font->height( );   # Move the current y pt
        $starty = $cy;

        $dy = $dy + $ddy * ($cy - $y1);
        $w = 0;

        # Move to next word if the line starts with a space

        if ($word eq ' ') {
            next WORD;
        }
    }

    # Now draw each character individually

    my @chars = split '', $word;
    push @chars, ' ';                  # Push a space on the end

    foreach my $char (@chars) {
        $img->char($font, $cx, $cy, $char, $white);

        # Move the current point

        $w = $w + $font->width( );
        $cx = $cx + $font->width( );
        $cy = $starty + int($w * $dy);
    }
}
```

When you are finished drawing on the image, you can write it to a file or to STD-OUT. To ensure platform independence, be sure that you are writing in binary mode by calling the binmode( ) method first. To write the data as a PNG file, call the png( ) method, which returns the image data in the PNG format:

```perl
# Write the image as a PNG

print $q->header(-type => 'image/png');
binmode(STDOUT);
print $img->png;

exit;
```

The source image (left) and some sample billboards are shown in Figure 2-2. Note that the script has drawn the text to fill an irregular area, changing the size of the font to fit the text within the drawing area.

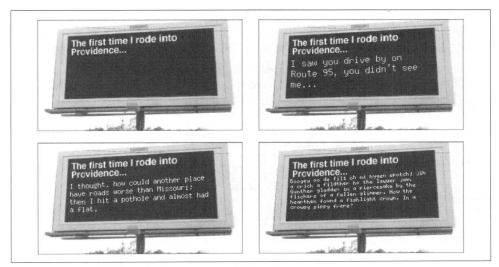

Figure 2-2. Sample billboards drawn with the billboard script

Image Generation Modules: The BrokenImage Module

A web page that accesses a dynamically generated image runs the risk of displaying uninformative "broken" images if the script that generates the image fails to successfully complete its operation. The fact that an <IMG> element that calls a script from its SRC attribute expects a valid stream of image headers and data can make it somewhat difficult to debug tricky image generation scripts. It would be nice to be able to return an informative error message rather than that generic "broken image" icon. GD provides a lightweight toolkit to implement the module.

It is easy to write a Perl module that may be used to generate this new kind of broken image icon. The script below can be used like any other Perl module; it is especially useful within CGI scripts that expect a valid stream of PNG image data as their output. The BrokenImage module implements two methods that return two different styles of broken image icons, black_box( ) and icon( ). The black_box( ) method takes a string of arbitrary length and returns a PNG with the text rendered in yellow on a black box. The icon( ) method takes an error number and returns a PNG with the error number in a gray shadowed box. They may be called from a Perl script like this:

```
#!/usr/bin/perl -w
use CGI;
use BrokenImage;
my $q = new CGI;
if ($q->param('divisor') == 0) {
    BrokenImage->black_box("This is the black box method",
                           "yellow on black...");
}
```

or:

```
# Return error #9327
BrokenImage->icon(9327);
```

These examples return the PNG images in Figure 2-3. Different styles may be added to the BrokenImage module by adding subroutines to draw different kinds of images using the GD module.

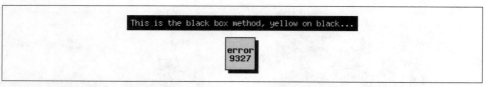

Figure 2-3. The BrokenImage module provides methods for returning meaningful error messages

The code for the BrokenImage module is shown in Example 2-3.

Example 2-3. The BrokenImage module

```
# Example 2-3. The BrokenImage module

package BrokenImage;

use strict;
use GD;            # use GD to draw the image

# Define some different styles of broken images

sub black_box {

    # A black box with text in yellow
    # Takes a string of text as a parameter.

    my $self = shift;
    my $text = shift;

    my $image = new GD::Image(6 * length($text) + 10, 20);
    my $black = $image->colorAllocate(0, 0, 0);
    my $yellow = $image->colorAllocate(255, 255, 0);
    $image->string(gdSmallFont, 5, 3, $text, $yellow);
    print_image($image);
}

sub icon {

    # An icon with an error code.
    # Takes a short string as a parameter.

    my $self = shift;
    my $code = shift;
```

Example 2-3. The BrokenImage module (continued)

```
    my $image = new GD::Image(43,48);
    my $white = $image->colorAllocate(255, 255, 255);
    my $black = $image->colorAllocate(0, 0, 0);
    my $gray = $image->colorAllocate(213, 213, 213);
    $image->filledRectangle(4, 4, 42, 47, $black);
    $image->filledRectangle(0, 0, 38, 43, $gray);
    $image->rectangle(0, 0, 38, 43, $black);
    $image->string(gdMediumBoldFont,
                  3, 10, "error", $black);
    $image->string(gdMediumBoldFont,
                  int(20-3.5*length($code)), 21, $code, $black);
    print_image($image);
}

sub print_image {

    # Print the image

    my $image = shift;
    use CGI;
    my $query = new CGI;
    print $query->header(-type    => "image/png",
                         -expires => '0s');

    print $image->png;
}

1;    # Modules should return true
```

Reading and Writing Methods

GD was originally designed to handle files in the GIF format, but has been modified to read and write more flexible formats such as PNG and JPEG instead. Additional methods are available to read X Bitmap files and read and write files in the uncompressed GD file format. Image reading and writing can be done through the use of filehandles, which allows for a great deal of flexibility in managing the flow of image data. It is simple to write an image to a file or STDOUT, or to pipe image data between processes.

The following methods are available from the GD::Image class for reading images.

---

new( ), newPalette( ), newTrueColor( )

```
$image = GD::Image::new([width, height])
$image = GD::Image::new(\*filehandle | filename)
$image = GD::Image::new(raw_data)
$image = GD::Image::newPalette([width, height])
$image = GD::Image::newTrueColor([width, height])
```

The new( ) method returns an empty image object of class GD::Image. If the width and height parameters for the starting dimensions of the image are not provided, a default value of 64×64 is used. If the method fails, it returns undef. In this case you should signal an error:

```
my $image = new GD::Image(25, 25) ||
    die "Can't create empty image! $!";
```

Alternatively, you can create an image from a PNG, JPEG, XPM, or GD2 file by providing a filename or filehandle as an argument, or you can create an image from the raw image data.

By default, all new image objects are created as 8-bit indexed images with the new( ) method. If you want to create 24-bit images by default, use the trueColor( ) method to change this default behavior or use the newTrueColor( ) method. The newPalette( ) method will always create an 8-bit indexed image object.

All truecolor images are filled with a black background when they are created.

newFromJpeg( ), newFromJpegData( )

```
$image = GD::Image::newFromJpeg(\*filehandle)
$image = GD::Image::newFromJpegData(raw_data)
```

These methods create an image from a JPEG file or raw data. The result will always be a 24-bit truecolor image.

newFromGd( ), newFromGdData( )

```
$image = GD::Image::newFromGd(\*filehandle)
$image = GD::Image::newFromGdData(raw_data)
```

The newFromGd( ) method reads in image data from a file in the same way as newFromPNG( ). A GD formatted file is a special file format that was created by GD author Tom Boutell as a means of quickly saving data to disk. It is an uncompressed storage format with little overhead in the actual reading and writing of the data stream, but the image files that are created can be quite large. You should use the GD storage format only within your script; its lack of image compression makes it unsuitable as a permanent storage format.

newFromGd2( ), newFromGd2Data( )

```
$image = GD::Image::newFromGd2(\*filehandle)
$image = GD::Image::newFromGd2Data(raw_data)
```

These methods create a new image from a file in the GD2 format, an improvement on the GD format that stores the image as chunks of compressed data and makes it easier to extract specific portions of the image.

newFromGd2Part( )

```
$image = GD::Image::newFromGd2Part (\*filehandle, x, y,
                                     width, height)
```

This method creates a new image from a file formatted in the GD2 format. Any arbitrary rectangular piece of the file may be extracted by providing the geometry of the bounding box. The following is an example of extracting a 64×64-pixel region from the upper left-hand corner of an image file:

```
open (GDFILE, "kerouac.gd2") or die "Couldn't open file!";
my $image = newFromGd2Part GD::Image(\*GDFILE, 0, 0, 64, 64) ||
    die "Not a valid GD file! ";
close GDFILE;
```

newFromPng( ), newFromPngData( )

```
$image = GD::Image::newFromPng(\*filehandle)
$image = GD::Image::newFromPngData(raw_data)
```

The newFromPng( ) method reads data from a PNG file. If the original PNG file was a true-color image, then the resulting image is a truecolor image. If the original was a grayscale PNG or a PNG with a palette, then the resulting image is an 8-bit indexed image. For true-color images, each red, green, and blue component will be represented internally in 8 bits. If the original PNG had an alpha channel, it will be represented in 7 bits. PNG is capable of handling truecolor images with more than 24 bits, but some information may be lost if you are dealing with 48-bit truecolor images or 16-bit grayscale images.

This method requires that the filehandle parameter be a handle to a previously opened file, giving you the option of reading the PNG data either from a file or (on Unix systems) from a previously opened pipe. The method automatically reads the data in binary mode (if your operating system makes that distinction), but you must explicitly close the filehandle when you are through with it.

If the method succeeds, it returns an Image object. If it fails (usually if the data is not actually a valid PNG file), it returns undef, in which case you should signal an error with die( ). For example:

```
open (PNGFILE, "burroughs.png") or
    die "Couldn't open file!";
my $image = newFromPng GD::Image(\*PNGFILE) or
    die "Not a valid PNG file!";
close PNGFILE;
```

A side note on Perl syntax—the generally approved method for passing a filehandle to a function is as a reference to a typeglob, as in:

```
somefunction(\*filehandle)
```

Passing the filehandle as a reference is preferable to passing it as a bare typeglob in that the former method does not complain if the use strict or use strict refs pragmas are in effect.

The newFromPngData( ) method expects an argument containing the binary data of a PNG file. This allows you to accept an image from sources other than a file, such as the results of an HTTP request. Example 2-4 uses the LWP module to grab a PNG image from a particular URL via HTTP. A new GD image is created from the data using the newFromPngData( ) method. The outline of the image is traced with a 4-pixel-wide red outline, and the image is written to STDOUT as a PNG.

Example 2-4. Using GD and LWP to process image data from the Web

```perl
#!/usr/bin/perl -w

# Example 2-4. Download an image from the web, outline it in red

use strict;
use GD;

# The LWP::UserAgent module provides all sorts of convenient
# methods for retrieving content via HTTP

use LWP::UserAgent;

# Create an HTTP request and use the UserAgent object to parse
# the response and extract the content from the response.

my $ua = LWP::UserAgent->new();
my $request = new HTTP::Request('GET',
    'http://apocabilly.org/images/foo.png');
my $response = $ua->request($request);
my $image_data = $response->content();

# $image_data now contains the raw binary image data

my $image = GD::Image->newFromPngData($image_data) or
    die("Couldn't create image!");

# Query the width and height of the result

my ($w, $h) = $image->getBounds();

# Create a 4x4 red brush to outline the image

my $brush = new GD::Image(4, 4);
$brush->rectangle(0, 0, 4, 4, $image->colorAllocate(255, 0, 0));

# Assign the brush to the image and draw a rectangle

$image->setBrush($brush);
$image->rectangle(0, 0, $w, $h, gdBrushed);

# Print to STDOUT as a PNG

print $image->png;
```

newFromXbm( )

```
$image = GD::Image::newFromXbm(\*filehandle)
```

The newFromXbm( ) method allows you to read from a black and white X Bitmap file. Note that pixmaps (XPMs) are not supported, nor can you write back out to an XBM. This method is used in the same manner as newFromPng( ):

```
open (XBMFILE, "corso.xbm") or
    die "Couldn't open file!";
my $image = newFromXbm GD::Image(\*XBMFILE) or
    die "Not a valid XBM file!";
close XBMFILE;
```

The following methods are available from the GD::Image class for writing images.

gd( ), gd2( )

```
$image->gd
$image->gd2
```

These methods return the image in the GD uncompressed storage format. They can be
used for writing to a file in the same way as the png( ) method:

```
open OUTFILE, ">neatniks.gd" or
    die "Couldn't open file!";    # Open the file for writing
binmode OUTFILE;                  # Make sure we're in binary mode
print OUTFILE $image->gd;         # Print GD data to the file
close OUTFILE;
```

jpeg( )

```
$image->jpeg([quality])
```

The jpeg( ) method returns the image as a JPEG. The quality parameter is a number in the
range 0–95, with higher numbers producing a larger, higher quality image. If a negative
quality value is indicated, the default quality setting of the underlying IJG JPEG library will
be used.

png( )

```
$image->png
```

The png( ) method converts an image into the PNG format and returns it. If your platform
makes a distinction between text files and binary files, ensure that you are writing in binary
mode by calling binmode( ) first. You can then write the image to the previously opened file:

```
open OUTFILE, ">beatniks.png" or
    die "Couldn't open file!";    # Open the file for writing
binmode OUTFILE;                  # Make sure we're in binary mode
print OUTFILE $image->png;        # Print PNG data to the file
close OUTFILE;
```

On Unix systems, you can pipe the image data to an image viewer, such as xv or the display
utility that comes with ImageMagick:

```
open (DISPLAY, "| display -") or
    die "display not installed!";
```

```
print DISPLAY $png_data->png;      # Pipe PNG data to image viewer
close DISPLAY;                     # Close the pipe
```

wbmp( )

`$image->wbmp([`*`foreground_color`*`])`

This returns the image formatted as a wireless bitmap (WBMP) file. WBMPs are only black and white. A color index should be supplied to indicate which of the colors in the color table should be considered the foreground color (black). If more than two colors are in the color table, all colors besides the specified foreground color will be considered the background (white).

Getting and Setting General Information

As we will see in the next chapter, Image::Magick has a large battery of methods for gleaning information about images. GD provides a few basic ones, including the useful compare( ) method for determining the similarities and differences between two images.

compare( )

`$result = $image->compare(`*`image2`*`)`

The compare( ) method compares two images pixel by pixel, and returns a bitmap of values that describe the differences between the two images (or 0 if the images are identical). The bitmap of return values must be logically ANDed with one or more of the following constants:

GD_CMP_BACKGROUND
: The two images have different background colors.

GD_CMP_COLOR
: The two images have different palettes.

GD_CMP_IMAGE
: The two images are visibly different. The differences may be in content, color, or size.

GD_CMP_INTERLACE
: The two images are interlaced using different methods.

GD_CMP_NUM_COLORS
: The two images have different numbers of colors in their color tables.

GD_CMP_SIZE_X
: The two images are not the same width.

GD_CMP_SIZE_Y
: The two images are not the same height.

GD_CMP_TRANSPARENT
   The images have different transparent colors.

These constants are not imported by default. Including the :cmp tag:

    use GD qw(:cmp);

imports the constants into your script's namespace:

    unless ($image->compare($image2) & GD_CMP_IMAGE) {
        print "These images are visibly the same.";
    }

getBounds( )

@bounds = $image->getBounds( )

The getBounds( ) method returns a list containing the width and height of the image in pixels. For example:

    my ($width, $height) = $image->getBounds( );

interlaced( )

$image->interlaced(*boolean*)
$isinterlaced = $image->interlaced( )

The interlaced() method indicates that the image is to be saved in an interlaced format (if true) or not (if false). Calling interlaced( ) without a parameter queries whether the image is currently interlaced.

isTrueColor ( )

$image->isTrueColor( )

This method returns 1 if the image is a 24-bit color image, 0 if it is 8-bit.

Color Table Manipulation Methods

When a new image is created, a temporary color table is created with it. If the image is an 8-bit indexed image (the default behavior), the color table will be limited to 256 colors. If the image is truecolor, you can add as many colors as you want to the color table (you can think of the color table as more of a color library, if that helps).

GD provides a number of methods for retrieving information about an image's color table and for manipulating entries in the table. In addition, several special color constants can be used to implement different-shaped brushes and line styles.

colorAllocate( )

`$index = $image->colorAllocate(`*`red, green, blue`*`)`

The `colorAllocate( )` method is an object method that takes three decimal integers in the range 0–255 for the three color channels and allocates a space in the image's color table. The method returns the index of the color in the color table if successful, or –1 if it fails. The first color that is allocated with this method becomes the background color for the image.

`colorAllocate( )` does not check to see if the color is already in the colormap; it is possible to have the same color allocated multiple times within a colormap. Another quirk is that GD always keeps the number of entries in the colormap to a multiple of two. Thus, if eight colors are currently in a colormap and you allocate a ninth, the colormap is expanded to include 16 colors, the ninth of which is the color you just allocated and the remainder of which are random colors. If you are working with an 8-bit indexed image, you cannot allocate more than 256 colors in an image. In this case, you must first use `colorDeallocate( )` to remove indices from the color table before adding new ones.

To use the color later in your script, store the returned index value. For example:

```
$blue = $image->colorAllocate(0, 0, 255);
```

colorDeallocate( )

`$image->colorDeallocate(`*`color`*`)`

The `colorDeallocate( )` method makes the color referred to by the color parameter available for reallocation with the `colorAllocate( )` method. The color must be an index in the color table that was returned by one of the other color manipulation methods. Note that the color is actually removed from the colormap until another color is allocated. The number of colors in the colormap is not reduced by this method.

colorClosest( )

`$index = $image->colorClosest(`*`red, green, blue`*`)`

This method returns the color table index of the color that best matches the color specified by the given red, green, and blue values, or –1 if the table has no colors allocated.

colorClosestHWB( )

`$index = $image->colorClosestHWB(`*`red, green, blue`*`)`

This method returns the color table index of the color that best matches the color specified, using the Hue-White-Black color space to make this determination. The HWB representation of colors tends to more closely match human perceptual patterns. The method returns –1 if the table has no colors allocated.

colorExact( )

$index = $image->colorExact(*red, green, blue*)

The colorExact( ) method returns the color table index of a color that matches exactly the color specified by the given red, green, and blue values. It returns −1 if the color is not in the image's color table.

```
$DodgerBlue = $image->colorExact(30,144,255);
print "DodgerBlue is in the color table.\n" if $DodgerBlue >= 0;
```

colorResolve( )

$index = $image->colorResolve(*red, green, blue*)

This method combines the colorExact( ) and colorAllocate( ) method calls. It returns the index of the specified color if it is already in the table; if it is not (and there is room), the color is allocated and its index is returned. It returns -1 if the color could not be allocated. This method always succeeds for a truecolor image.

colorsTotal( )

$ncolors = image->colorsTotal( )

This method returns the number of colors that are allocated in the color table of an image.

getPixel( )

$index = $image->getPixel(*x,y*)

The getPixel( ) method returns the color table index of the color at the specified pixel. As with all functions that return a color index, you can use the rgb( ) method to convert the index to a list of the integer red, green, and blue values.

rgb( )

@rgb = $image->rgb(*color*)

The rgb( ) method returns a list with the red, green, and blue values that correspond to the color to which the color index parameter refers. It can be used like this:

```
($red, $green, $blue) = $image->rgb($someindex);
```

setPixel( )

$image->setPixel(*x, y, color*)

The setPixel( ) method sets the color of a given pixel to the color referred to by the color parameter. Use a brush associated with the image (gdBrushed or gdStyledBrushed) to stamp the shape of the brush onto the image at the given center point.

transparent( )

`$image->transparent([colorindex])`

The `transparent( )` method makes any pixels of color *colorindex* in an image transparent. Only one color may be transparent at a time; a second call to `transparent( )` overrides the first call, and returns pixels that were previously transparent to their original color. To turn off transparency in an image, give *colorindex* a value of −1. To find the index of the transparent color in an image, call `transparent( )` without a parameter.

To make the color that is closest to white in an image transparent, use:

```
$close2white = $image->colorClosest(255,255,255);
$image->transparent($close2white);
```

This function can be used with `setBrush( )` to create irregularly shaped brushes. See the `setBrush( )` method for an example of this.

trueColor( )

`GD::Image->trueColor(boolean)`

By default, all new, empty image objects are created as 8-bit indexed images. Call this class method to change the default behavior. If passed a true value, 24-bit images will be created when the `new( )` method is called.

trueColorToPalette( )

`$image->trueColorToPalette([dither], [max_colors])`

This method will convert a 24-bit color image to an 8-bit color image. The *dither* parameter is a Boolean value that indicates whether dithering should be used when reducing the number of colors. The *max_colors* parameter specifies how many colors should be in the palette of the resulting image. The algorithm used is virtually identical to the `Quantize( )` method of the Image::Magick module.

Brushes, Styles, and Tiles

GD defines four alternatives to drawing or filling shapes with simple solid colors. These special "color" variables are:

```
gdBrushed
gdStyled
gdStyledBrushed
gdTiled
```

The following three methods allow you to define the behavior of these special colors.

setBrush( )

$index = $image->setBrush(*image*)

The drawing commands available through GD can be called with either a solid color or with a special brush that is accessed via the gdBrushed constant. This brush is simply an image that must be created or read in from another image. The setBrush( ) method assigns a particular image as the current brush for drawing within another image. To draw with a brush, follow these steps:

1. Create a new image object for the brush, or read the brush from a PNG file. Here we create a new square 20 × 20 pixel brush:

    ```
    my $brush = new GD::Image(20, 20);
    ```

2. If you are creating a new brush with the GD drawing commands, allocate a color for the brush and draw the brush shape. In this case, the brush is a red circle:

    ```
    my $red = $brush->colorAllocate(255, 0, 0);
    $brush->arc(10, 10, 20, 20, 0, 360, $red);
    ```

3. If you are creating an irregularly shaped brush, set the background color of the brush with the transparent( ) method so that the brush does not overwrite its own path:

    ```
    my $white = $brush->colorAllocate (255, 255, 255);
    $brush->transparent($white);
    ```

4. Assign the brush to the image you want to draw on:

    ```
    $image->setBrush($brush);
    ```

5. Call a drawing command with gdBrushed as the *color* parameter to use the brush.

    ```
    $image->line(0, 0, 50, 50, gdBrushed);
    ```

Figure 2-4 illustrates some examples of different brushes.

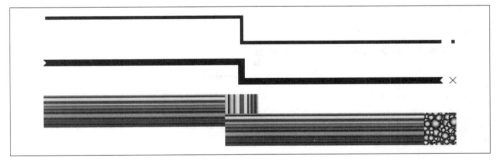

Figure 2-4. Drawing with different brushes

setStyle( )

$image->setStyle(@*colorindices*)

Dotted and dashed lines can be drawn using the GD drawing commands with the gdStyled line style instead of the *color* parameter. The setStyle( ) defines a line style for an image. Follow these steps to create a styled line:

1. Allocate the colors you wish to use in the line style, or get their color indices with one of the methods described previously:

```
$blue = $image->colorAllocate(0, 0, 255);    # allocate blue
$red = $image->colorAllocate(255, 0, 0);     # allocate red
```

2. Create a list of color indices. Each element of the list represents one pixel in a sequence that is repeated over the length of the drawn line. To indicate a blank space in a dashed line, use the gdTransparent constant instead of a color index. If a color index has already been marked as transparent for the image, it is transparent in the drawn line. To indicate a blue and red dashed line that repeats blue for two pixels, red for three pixels, and then a two-pixel break, use the following for the color list:

```
@linestyle = ($blue, $blue, $red, $red, $red,
              gdTransparent, gdTransparent);
```

3. Assign the style to the image:

```
$image->setStyle(@linestyle);
```

4. Draw with a drawing method and the gdStyled special color. If the gdStyledBrushed constant is used, the brush pattern is drawn for those pixels that are not set to gdTransparent. To draw a dashed rectangle, use:

```
$image->rectangle(0, 0, 100, 100, gdStyled);
```

Use setStyle( ) when you need to draw a line or a shape with an arbitrary dotted or dashed line. Use the gdStyledBrushed to combine the properties of the gdStyled and gdBrushed special colors. Figure 2-5 shows some examples.

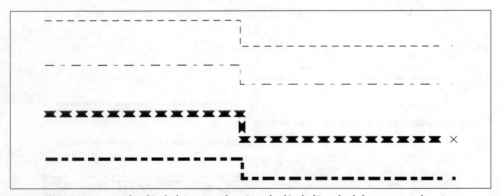

Figure 2-5. Drawing with gdStyled (top two lines) and gdStyledBrushed (bottom two lines)

setTile( )

$image->setTile(*image*)

Use the setTile( ) method to assign an image as a tileable pattern for use when drawing filled shapes within an image. First call setTile( ) with an image object, then draw using the gdTiled special color constant instead of the drawing command's color parameter. In the following example, we must use the trueColor( ) method (or the newTrueColor( ) method) when creating the new empty image. This is because the image to be tiled is read in as a 24-bit PNG, and the destination image and tile image color depths must match. For example:

```perl
#!/usr/bin/perl -w

use strict;
use GD;

# Read in a pattern from a PNG file

my $wallpaper = GD::Image->newFromPng('monkey.png')
    or die "Couldn't open wallpaper!";

# The wallpaper is truecolor; make sure the image is truecolor!

GD::Image->trueColor(1);
my $image = GD::Image->new(600,400);

# Set $wallpaper as the current tilable pattern

$image->setTile($wallpaper);

# Draw a 600x200 rectangle tiled with the wallpaper pattern

$image->filledRectangle(0, 0, 599, 399, gdTiled);
$image->rectangle(0, 0, 599, 399, $image->colorAllocate(0,0,0));

print $image->png();
```

Figure 2-6 shows an example.

Figure 2-6. Drawing with gdTiled

Copying and Transforming Images

Several methods are provided for copying rectangular regions between images. When copying between images with different color tables, the table of the destination image is filled with as many unique colors from the source image as can fit. In an 8-bit indexed image with a full color table, the rest of the colors are intelligently matched to colors already in the destination image.

clone( )

```
$image2 = $image->Image::clone( )
```

This method returns a copy of the image. The copy is a new, distinct Image object with the same properties as the original. For example:

```
my $image = new GD::Image( );              # Create a 64x64 image
$image->colorAllocate(255, 255, 255);      # Allocate a background
my $image2 = $image->clone( );
```

However, the exact indices of the colors in the cloned image may not match the original. Color indices allocated in the source image should not be used to refer to colors in the cloned image.

copy( )

```
$destimage->copy(srcImage, destX, destY, srcX, srcY,
                 width, height)
```

The copy( ) method copies all pixels within the *width* × *height* region, starting at the coordinate *srcX*, *srcY* of the image *srcImage*, to a similarly sized region of the destination image at *destX*, *destY*. The source and destination images may be the same if you wish to copy from one part of an image to another, but the source and destination regions should not overlap or terrible things will happen.

copyMerge( )

```
$destimage->copyMerge(srcImage, destX, destY, srcX, srcY,
                      width, height, percent)
```

This method behaves the same as the copy( ) method, except that when the region is added to the new destination image, it is overlaid using the *percent* argument (an integer between 0 and 100) as a kind of alpha channel. If *percent* is 50, each pixel in the source image region is merged with each pixel of the destination region such that the result is half of each component of the two values. Using a value of 100 has the same effect as doing a straight copy( ).

copyMergeGray( )

```
$destimage->copyMergeGray(srcImage, destX, destY, srcX, srcY,
                          width, height, percent)
```

This method is similar to copyMerge( ) except that the destination image region is first converted to a grayscale. When the grayscale is combined, only the intensities of the two images are merged.

copyResized( )

```
$destimage->copyResized(srcImage, destX, destY, srcX, srcY,
                        destWidth, destHeight, srcWidth, srcHeight)
```

The copyResized( ) method copies a region from one image to another, with the option to scale the image region to fit the target region. The following code copies a region from $image2 to $image1 and shrinks it to fit:

```
# create the image objects
$image1 = new GD::Image(20, 20);
$image2 = new GD::Image(200, 200);

# This assumes we draw or read in something to copy
# ...
# copy the upper left quadrant of $image2 to $image and scale it

$image1->copyResized($image2, 0, 0, 0, 0, 20, 20, 100, 100);
```

copyResampled( )

```
$destimage->copyResized(srcImage, destX, destY, srcX, srcY,
                        destWidth, destHeight, srcWidth, srcHeight)
```

This is a more intelligent version of copyResized( ), where each pixel in the region is sampled from a selection of surrounding pixels. The result is more accurate and has less jaggy transitions between pixels, but may be a little blurrier than copyResized( ) for some images.

copyRotate90( ), copyRotate180( ), copyRotate270( )

```
$image = $sourceimage->copyRotate90( )
$image = $sourceimage->copyRotate180( )
$image = $sourceimage->copyRotate270( )
```

These methods behave the same as the copy( ) method, except that when the region is added to the new destination image, it is rotated by 90, 180, or 270 degrees.

flipHorizontal( ), flipVertical( ), rotate180( )

```
$image->flipHorizontal( )
$image->flipVertical( )
$image->rotate180( )
```

The first two methods flip the image horizontally or vertically. The rotate180( ) method is equivalent to performing a flipHorizontal( ) followed by a flipVertical( ). These transforms are all done in-place, altering the image the methods were called on.

Image Drawing and Manipulation Methods

For all the drawing methods, the coordinate system is defined with (0, 0) as the upper left corner of the image and the x and y values increasing to the right and down. In general, when a method takes a color as a parameter, you should pass the index of a color previously allocated with one of the methods described in the earlier section "Color Table Manipulation Methods," or use one of the special color constants.

The drawing and manipulation methods are as follows.

arc( )

```
$image->arc(x, y, width, height, start, end, color)
```

The arc( ) method allows you to draw arcs, circles, and ellipses on an image, centered at the coordinate given by *x* and *y*. The *height* parameter indicates the maximum vertical diameter of the arc, and the *width* parameter is the maximum horizontal diameter. For a circle, both the height and width are equal to the diameter of the circle; you can vary either value to produce ellipses.

The *start* and *end* parameters are the starting and ending angles (in degrees) that the arc should sweep through. These angles are measured from the horizontal axis and increase in the clockwise direction, with 0 degrees at 3 o'clock, 90 degrees at 6 o'clock, and so on.

To draw a circle centered at (100,100) with a radius of 25 pixels, you would use:

```
$image->arc(100, 100, 50, 50, 0, 360, $red);
```

To draw the right half of an ellipse, use:

```
$image->arc(100, 100, 100, 50, 270, 90, $red);
```

The *color* parameter may be a color index or any of the special colors gdBrushed, gdStyled, or gdStyledBrushed.

fill( )

`$image->fill(x, y, color)`

The `fill( )` method flood-fills an area with a given color. The area to fill is defined by all those pixels neighboring the pixel at *x*, *y* that are of the same color as the pixel and are connected by pixels of the same color. The operation is the same as the paint-bucket tool in paint programs. The *color* can be either a color index, or the `gdTiled` special color if you want to fill the area with a tiled pattern.

The `fill( )` method can be used to draw filled shapes with different colored borders, as in:

```
# Draw a green-filled circle with a red border

$image->arc(100, 100, 50, 50, 0, 360, $red);
$image->fill(100, 100, $green);
```

filledPolygon( )

`$image->filledPolygon(polygon, color)`

The `filledPolygon( )` method is used the same way as the `polygon( )` method, except that the area defined by the polygon is filled with the given *color*. To draw a filled polygon with the lines stroked in a different color, use `polygon( )` with the `fill( )` method or draw a second non-filled polygon on top of the filled polygon. The *color* may be either:

A color index
> The polygon is filled with the specified color. If the color has been marked as transparent, the pixels become transparent.

gdTiled
> The polygon is filled with the pattern previously assigned as the current tile pattern with `setTile( )`. If the polygon is larger than the tile pattern, the tile pattern is repeated to fill the polygon.

See also the later section "Polygon Methods."

filledRectangle( )

`$image->filledRectangle(x1, y1, x2, y2, color)`

The `filledRectangle( )` method draws a rectangle with one corner at *x1*, *y1* and one corner at *x2*, *y2*, and filled with the specified *color*. The *color* parameter can be either:

A color index
> The rectangle is filled with the specified color. If the color has been marked as transparent, the pixels become transparent. Note that no mechanism is provided for stroking the border of the rectangle with a different color than the fill color. To do this you must draw a second rectangle on top of the filled rectangle with the desired border color, or use the `fill( )` method.

gdTiled

The rectangle is filled with the pattern previously assigned as the current tile pattern with setTile(). If the rectangle is larger than the tile pattern, the tile pattern is repeated to fill the rectangle.

fillToBorder( )

$image->fillToBorder(*x, y, bordercolor, color*)

The fillToBorder() method operates in the same way as the fill() method, except that it fills the area defined as all pixels neighboring the pixel at *x, y* and bordered by the color given by *bordercolor*. This can be useful when dealing with images with shapes that are filled with dithered colors, or areas where all the pixels are not of exactly the same color. Note that the *color* must be a color index, not one of the special GD color constants.

line( )

$image->line(*x1, y1, x2, y2, color*)

The line() method draws a single-pixel-wide line from *x1, y1* to *x2, y2*. The *color* parameter can be a color index, gdBrushed, gdStyled, or gdStyledBrushed. To create dashed lines, use the setStyle() method and gdStyled constant.

polygon( )

$image->polygon(*polygon, color*)

This is a drawing method that allows you to draw a polygon defined by a GD::Polygon object onto an image. You must first create a polygon object and define its points with the addPt() method; a polygon must have at least three points, the first and last of which are automatically connected when they are drawn to the image.

To create a four-sided red parallelogram, for example, use:

```
use strict;
use GD;
my $image = new GD::Image(101,101);
my $white = $image->colorAllocate(200,200,200);
my $red = $image->colorAllocate(255, 0, 0);    # Allocate red
my $parallelogram = new GD::Polygon;           # Create the polygon
$parallelogram->addPt(20, 0);                  # Add the 4 vertices
$parallelogram->addPt(0, 100);
$parallelogram->addPt(80, 100);
$parallelogram->addPt(100, 0);
$image->polygon($parallelogram, $red);         # Draw the polygon
print $image->png();
```

openPolygon() may be used as an alias for polygon(). To draw a filled polygon, use this method followed by a call to fill(), or use the filledPolygon() method. The *color* parameter can be a color index, gdBrushed, gdStyled, or gdStyledBrushed. See also the later section "Polygon Methods."

rectangle( )

`$image->rectangle(x1, y1, x2, y2, color)`

The rectangle( ) method draws a rectangle with its upper left corner at *x1, y1* and its lower right corner at *x2, y2*. The *color* parameter can be a color index, gdBrushed, gdStyled, or gdStyledBrushed.

Strings and Fonts

When you load the GD module the five built-in fonts are imported into your script's namespace as the global variables gdGiantFont, gdLargeFont, gdMediumBoldFont, gdSmallFont, and gdTinyFont (see Figure 2-7). They are all fixed-width fonts with 256 characters in their character sets. The dimensions of each can be determined with the width( ) and height( ) object methods, or by consulting Table 2-1.

Table 2-1. The dimensions of the five standard GD fonts

Font name	Width (pixels)	Height (pixels)
gdTinyFont	5	8
gdSmallFont	6	12
gdMediumBoldFont	7	12
gdLargeFont	8	16
gdGiantFont	9	15

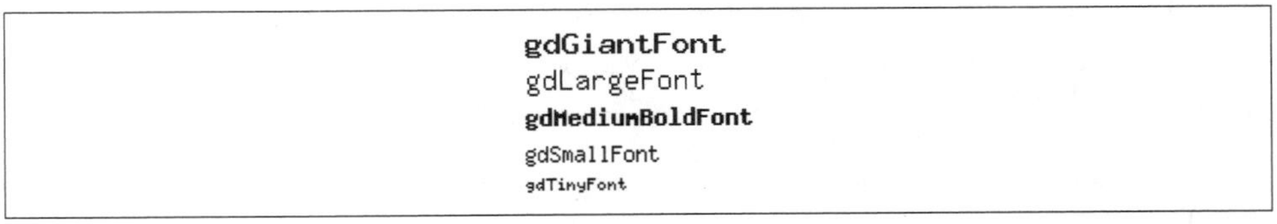

gdGiantFont
gdLargeFont
gdMediumBoldFont
gdSmallFont
gdTinyFont

Figure 2-7. The built-in bitmapped GD fonts.

To draw a string with the bitmapped fonts, use the char( ), charUp( ), string( ), or stringUp( ) methods. To use a TrueType font, use the stringFT( ) method.

char( )

`$image->char(font, x, y, char, color)`

The char( ) method draws a single character at the coordinate *x, y*. This method is for use only with the built-in bitmapped fonts.

charUp( )

$image->charUp(*font, x, y, char, color*)

The charUp( ) method draws a character rotated 90 degrees counterclockwise, with the lower left corner of the text block at the coordinate *x, y*. This method is for use only with the built-in bitmapped fonts.

nchars( )

gdFontName->nchars

This method returns the number of characters in the font. All of the standard GD fonts have 256 characters in their character sets. This function is provided for future expandability.

offset( )

gdFontName->offset

This method returns the ASCII value of the first character in the font. All of the GD fonts have an offset of 0.

string( )

$image->string(*font, x, y, string, color*)

The string( ) method draws the *string* onto the image with the upper left corner of the text box starting at the coordinate *x, y*. The *font* must be one of the six GD fonts: gdTinyFont, gdSmallFont, gdMediumBoldFont, gdLargeFont, or gdGiantFont.

Because of its limited font support, GD does not interpret escaped linefeeds (or other special characters) in the same way that ImageMagick does. Multiple lines of text must be drawn as separate strings, with the space between lines computed using the height( ) object method. You may want to consider using ImageMagick for creating text-intensive graphics, as its font support is more robust than GD's.

An example:

```
$image->string(gdTinyFont,10, 10,
            "A way a lone a last a loved a long the", $red);
```

stringUp( )

$image->stringUp(*font, x, y, string, color*)

The stringUp( ) method draws a *string* rotated 90 degrees counterclockwise, with the lower left corner of the text block at the coordinate *x, y*. The stringUp( ) method has no corresponding stringDown( ) method; it is really only useful for tasks such as labeling axes on a graph.

This method is for use only with the built-in bitmapped fonts. Consider using the ImageMagick package if you need to use other fonts or have greater control over the positioning of your text.

stringFT( )

`$image->stringFT(color, font_path, size, angle, x, y, string)`

The stringFT( ) method draws the *string* onto the image using the specified TrueType font, at the specified *angle*. To use TrueType fonts you must install GD with TrueType support, as previously described, and you must have the fonts installed on your system. The *font_path* argument should be the absolute pathname to a TrueType font file.

The string can be any UTF-8 sequence, so non-Western character sets may be used. The text is drawn using antialiased letterforms at the given point size, which may be a fractional value. The *angle* argument should be provided in radians, though you can use the deg2rad( ) function of the Math::Trig module if you want to work with degrees.

The function returns an eight-element list containing the coordinates of the bounding box of the text (see getBounds( ) under "Getting and Setting General Information"). The coordinates of the return array start at the lower left corner and continue counterclockwise. To calculate the bounding box without actually drawing the text, call stringFT( ) as a class method:

```
my @bounds = GD::Image->stringFT(0, "/home/shawn/arial.ttf",
    48, 0, 40, 120, "Hello World");
```

width( ), height( )

```
gdFontName->width
gdFontName->height
```

These methods return the width and height of the font, in pixels. For example, the following returns 5 and 8:

```
($width, $height) = (gdTinyFont->width, gdTinyFont->height);
```

Polygon Methods

Just to make life a little easier, the GD package now includes a number of polygon manipulation routines that were not part of the original library. All coordinate points are defined with (0, 0) being the upper left corner of the image. To create a shape, add points to the polygon with the addPt( ) method and draw it to the image with the polygon( ) or filledPolygon( ) method. The script in Example 2-5 draws a hobo symbol meaning "man with gun." The image generated is shown in Figure 2-8.

Example 2-5. Drawing paths with polygons

```perl
#!/usr/bin/perl -w
#
# Example 2-5. Drawing with polygons

use strict;
use GD;

my $image = new GD::Image(280,220);

# Create two new polygon objects

my $polygon1 = new GD::Polygon;
my $polygon2 = new GD::Polygon;

# Set up the points as a space-delimited string,
# compatible with the SVG polygon format

my $points1 = "140,140 220,60 220,10 270,60 220,60 ".
              "140,140 60,60 60,10 10,60 60,60 ";

my $points2 = "140,40 260,200 20,200";

# Add the points to each polygon

add_points($polygon1, $points1);
add_points($polygon2, $points2);

# Allocate colors; white is the background

my $white= $image->colorAllocate(255,255,255);
my $black = $image->colorAllocate(0,0,0);

# Draw the two extended triangles

$image->polygon($polygon1, $black);

# Draw the center triangle, filled

$image->filledPolygon($polygon2, $white);

# Stroke the center triangle

$image->polygon($polygon2, $black);

# Print the image

print "Content-type: image/png\n\n";
print $image->png( );

exit;
```

Example 2-5. Drawing paths with polygons (continued)

```
# Split a space-delimited string of coordinates

sub add_points {
    my ($poly, $pts) = @_;
    foreach my $pair (split /\s/, $pts) {
        $pair =~ /(\d+),(\d+)/;
        $poly->addPt($1, $2);
    }
}
```

Figure 2-8. "Man with gun" hobo symbol, drawn with polygon methods

addPt( )

$polygon->addPt(*x, y*)

A polygon is constructed one point at a time with this method, which adds a new vertex to a polygon object. A polygon must have at least one point added to it before it is drawn.

bounds( )

@bounds = $polygon->bounds

This method returns a list of values that describe the smallest rectangle that completely encloses the polygon. The return values are in a list of the form (*left, top, right, bottom*), where *left* is the x value of the left side of the rectangle, *top* is the y value of the top, *right* is the x value of the right side, and *bottom* is the y value of the bottom. The following draws a red box around a previously defined polygon:

```
my @boundingBox = $poly->bounds;      # $poly is a polygon object
$image->rectangle(@boundingBox, $red);
```

deletePt( )

`$polygon->deletePt(`*index*`)`

This method deletes the vertex at the given index and decrements the index of vertices after the deleted vertex. The deletePt( ) method returns a list containing the coordinates of the deleted point, or undef if there was no point at that index.

getPt( )

`@coord = $polygon->getPt(`*index*`)`

This method returns a list with the x,y coordinate of the given point of a polygon object. The first point added to a polygon has an *index* of 0, the second has an index of 1 and so on. If a point is removed from somewhere in the middle of the list with deletePt( ), all points added after the removed point will have their indices decremented by 1. The method returns undef if the point does not exist.

```
# Retrieve the fourth point in the polygon
my ($x, $y) = $polywolly->getPt(3);
```

length( )

`$l = $polygon->length`

This method returns the total number of vertices in a polygon.

map( )

`$polygon->map(`*srcLeft, srcTop, srcRight, srcBottom,*
`                destLeft, destTop, destRight, destBottom`)

This method scales an existing polygon to fit a region, changing the values of all of the vertices within the polygon. The first four parameters define the bounding box of the source area, and the last four define the bounding box of the destination area. Example 2-6 draws a triangular polygon, then repeatedly calls map( ) to create the image in Figure 2-9.

Example 2-6. Calling map() repeatedly on a triangle

```
#!/usr/bin/perl -w
# Example 2-6. Using map( )
use strict;
use GD;

my $image = new GD::Image(280,280);

# Create a new polygon and add three points

my $polygon = new GD::Polygon;
$polygon->addPt(140,20);
```

Example 2-6. Calling map() repeatedly on a triangle (continued)

```
$polygon->addPt(260,260);
$polygon->addPt(20,260);

# Allocate colors; gray is the background

my $gray= $image->colorAllocate(200, 200, 200);
my $black = $image->colorAllocate(0,0,0);

# Draw the largest triangle first, then map it into progressively
# smaller bounding boxes

for my $i (0..20) {
    my ($x1, $y1, $x2, $y2) = $polygon->bounds();
    $polygon->map($x1, $y1, $x2, $y2,
                  $x1, $y1, $x2-$i, $y2-$i);
    $image->polygon($polygon, $black);
}

# Print the image to STDOUT as a PNG

binmode(STDOUT);
print $image->png();
```

Figure 2-9. Using the polygon map() method

offset( )

$polygon->offset(*dx, dy*)

This method moves every vertex in a polygon *dx* pixels horizontally and *dy* pixels vertically. Positive numbers indicate that the offset should be in the right and down directions.

scale( )

$polygon->scale(*hFactor, vFactor*)

The scale( ) method shrinks or enlarges a polygon by the given horizontal and vertical factors. Use a decimal factor to shrink a polygon and a positive multiple to enlarge it. For example, $poly->scale(2, 2) enlarges the polygon's area by 400%, and $poly->scale(.5, .5) shrinks it by half.

setPt( )

$polygon->setPt(*index, x, y*)

This method allows you to change the coordinates of a particular point that has already been added to a polygon object. The method returns undef if the point with the given index does not exist.

toPt( )

$polygon->toPt(*dx, dy*)

This method allows you to specify the points of a polygon relative to a starting point. Use addPt( ) to define the first point in the polygon; subsequent calls to toPt( ) will create new points by adding the *dx* and *dy* parameters to the x and y values of the previous point. Note that the polygon object still stores only the absolute values of the coordinates, so getPt( ) returns the same value as if you had added the point with addPt( ).

To draw a parallelogram whose vertices are at (10,10), (20,20), (30,20), and (20,10), use:

```
my $parallelogram = new GD::Polygon;

$parallelogram->addPt(10, 10);
$poly->toPt(10, 10);
$poly->toPt(10, 0);
$poly->toPt(-10, -10);
$image->polygon($parallelogram, $black);
```

transform( )

$polygon->transform(*scaleX, rotateX, scaleY, rotateY, x, y*)

This method applies a *transformation matrix* to each vertex in a polygon. A transformation matrix is a way of mapping one coordinate system onto another; the transform( ) method provides a means for managing multiple coordinate systems while creating images. Each polygon can be defined in terms of its own coordinate space, for example, and then later mapped to that of the final image.

The transform( ) method takes the following as parameters (note their order, above):

scaleX, scaleY
> The horizontal and vertical scaling factors within the current coordinate system (i.e., before rotations or offsets). These factors are expressed in multiples of the current polygon size, so a scale factor of 4 indicates a 400% increase in size. Use a fractional value to reduce the size.

rotateX, rotateY
> The rotation factor, in degrees, to be applied to each vertex.

x, y
> The horizontal and vertical offset that should be applied to each vertex.

vertices( )

```
@vertices = $polygon->vertices( )
```

This method returns all the vertices as a list. Thus, for a list of returned vertices called @vertices, then $vertices[0][0] refers to the x value of the first point, and $vertices[1][1] refers to the y value of the second point.

## CHAPTER 3

Graphics Scripting with Image::Magick

Image::Magick is an object-oriented Perl interface to the ImageMagick image manipulation libraries. It is a more robust collection of tools than GD—in addition to PNGs and JPEGs, it can read and write to many file formats including GIF, PDF, EPS, TIFF, and Photo CD. In fact, Image::Magick is a goldmine of acronyms, with over 60 different file formats supported (see Appendix C for a full accounting).

ImageMagick can handle graphics formats with multiple frames, such as animated GIFs. It can be used effectively in CGI applications, but its real strength is as an off-line workhorse for the batch conversion and manipulation of images. This chapter illustrates both uses and provides a complete overview of the functions available within Image::Magick.

What Is ImageMagick?

ImageMagick is a C library written by John Cristy. As of this writing, the current version is 5.3.x, with minor version numbers incrementing every few months. Image::Magick is the Perl interface to the library. It acts as a transparent API for manipulating a wide range of image file formats from Perl. As of ImageMagick v.4.0, Image::Magick comes with the standard distribution.

The official ImageMagick web page is *http://www.imagemagick.org*. Image::Magick is also available via CPAN. ImageMagick compiles and runs on virtually any Unix system, Linux, Windows, Mac OS, and VMS.

An ImageMagick installation requires between 3 MB and 12 MB of disk space, depending on the platform, and you need 80 MB of virtual memory to work effectively. If you are using ImageMagick to dynamically generate web graphics, you should probably have at least 128 MB of physical RAM free to handle multiple simultaneous requests. Because ImageMagick was designed as a robust and versatile package, it does have additional overhead that a specialized package like GD does not have. Keep this in mind when selecting which toolkit to use.

ImageMagick also requires a number of freely available graphics libraries in order to support certain graphics formats. Current versions of many of these libraries are available from the main FTP site, and some distributions (e.g., Windows) come packaged with the latest source for many of these libraries. The requirements are detailed in Appendix C.

Installing ImageMagick

If you have any experience with building and installing software from source, you should have no problem installing ImageMagick. For those who don't like to get their hands dirty or who don't have the proper tools, precompiled binaries are available for most platforms.

Before you build the software, you may want to change a few of the default settings, particularly if you are planning to create GIF files. Because of the legal issues involved with the patented LZW compression scheme used in GIF files, support for LZW is turned off in the default distribution. The authors did this intentionally to encourage a migration from GIF to PNG usage, and to enable ImageMagick to be bundled with other packages without hassle. If you want to create GIF images for the Web, you should manually enable LZW support with the --enable-lzw configure option so your files don't swell to an unusable size.

Appendix C contains a list of all the *configure* flags and their default and suggested settings.

ImageMagick's Command-Line Tools

The ImageMagick library comes with a set of utility programs that are very handy to have around; they are perfect for quick file conversions and image previewing. They also allow you to perform concise batch operations that would be much more time-consuming (if not impossible) with a GUI-based image manipulation program such as Photoshop or Paint Shop Pro. The four primary ImageMagick programs are *display*, *animate*, *convert*, and *identify*.

display
> The *display* program is a utility for displaying an image on a workstation connected to an X Server. It also offers a graphical interface to many of the ImageMagick image manipulation functions.

animate
> The *animate* program is used for displaying a list of images as an animated sequence on a workstation connected to an X Server. For example, to display all of the GIF images in the current directory as an animated sequence, use:
> ```
> animate *.gif
> ```

convert

The *convert* utility allows you to convert one image format to another. Most of the image manipulation functions may be applied during the conversion process. For instance, to convert a TIFF image of a quahog to a GIF image, use:

```
convert quahog.tiff gif:quahog.gif
```

To convert all of the GIF images in the current directory into a single infinitely-looping animated GIF named *foo.gif* with a 1/2 second delay between frames, use:

```
convert -loop 0 -delay 50 *.gif foo.gif
```

To create a GIF image using only the 216 "web-safe" colors, try:

```
convert -map netscape: alpha.gif beta.gif
```

identify

The *identify* program provides information from the header block of a graphics file. It returns the filename, width, height, image class (whether it is color-mapped), number of colors in the image, size of the image in bytes, file format, and the number of seconds it took to read and process the image. Running *identify* with the -verbose parameter produces additional information, including the internal palette associated with the image if it is colormapped. For example:

```
identify -verbose beatniks.gif
```

produces the output:

```
Image: beatniks.gif
class: PseudoClass
colors: 256
  0: (  0,  0,  0) #000000  black
  1: (  1,  1,  1) #010101  ~black
  2: (  2,  2,  2) #020202  ~gray1
  3: (  3,  3,  3) #030303  gray1
  4: (  4,  4,  4) #040404  ~gray1
  ... (content cut for brevity)
  254: (254,254,254) #fefefe  ~white
  255: (255,255,255) #ffffff  white
matte: False
runlength packets: 15215 of 29100
geometry: 150x194
depth: 8
filesize: 9525b
interlace: None
page geometry: 150x194+0+0
format: GIF
```

import, mogrify, montage, combine

ImageMagick comes with a number of other utilities, most of which have overlapping functionality with methods available through the Image::Magick module. The *import* program captures an image from any visible window of an X client and writes it to an image file. The *mogrify* program applies any of the image manipulation routines to an image. The *montage* program duplicates the functions of the Montage( ) method, and *combine* is very similar to the Composite( ) method.

You can use the RemoteCommand( ), Display( ), or Animate( ) methods to pipe an image directly to *animate* or *display*, as shown later.

Using Image::Magick

Image::Magick provides an all-purpose graphics API for Perl. You manipulate images by reading them into an Image::Magick object and then setting attributes and calling methods on that object. Most of the file formats supported by Image::Magick have certain attributes in common, though each may implement them differently. For example, JPEG and PNG both support compression, but have different compression schemes.

Image::Magick defines a wide range of file attributes, which are listed in tables later in this chapter. Many of the image manipulation functions (as well as Read( ) and Write( )) allow you to set various attributes when calling them, or you can use Set( ) to do it directly, as in:

```
$image->Set(loop=>100);
$image->[$x]->Set(dither=>1);
```

Note that you are not manipulating the image simply by setting attributes. In the above examples, setting the loop attribute adds a looping extension to a GIF file when it is written. The second example simply sets the default value of the dither attribute. Setting the attribute doesn't dither the image, but subsequent operations, such as a call to Quantize( ), are performed using dithering.

Use Get( ) to get an attribute:

```
($w, $h, $d) = $q->Get('columns', 'rows', 'depth');
$colors = $q->[2]->Get('colors');
```

The functions GetAttribute( ) and SetAttribute( ) are aliases for Get( ) and Set( ) and may be used interchangeably.

Image::Magick provides a suite of methods for manipulating images. You can optionally add the word Image to most of the method calls (e.g., AnnotateImage( ) is the same as Annotate( )). If a method takes only one parameter, you do not have to explicitly pass the parameter name. Some examples of image manipulation method calls are:

```
$q->Crop(geometry => '100x100+10+20');
$q->[$x]->Frame('100x200');
```

In general, the geometry parameter is a shortcut for defining a region and an offset within an image; for example, geometry=>'640x800+10+10' is equivalent to width=> 640, height=>800, x=>10, y=>10. Sometimes the geometry attribute is used to specify a coordinate by including only the offsets:

```
geometry=>'+10+10'
```

All coordinates in ImageMagick are based on the origin (0, 0) being in the upper left corner, with the x values increasing to the right and the y values increasing down.

The Basic Approach

In this section we'll draw the same "Hello World" image that we drew back in Example 2-1, but this time using Image::Magick. You'll notice that the code is a bit longer than the GD implementation. The results are nicer, however; text and shapes drawn with Image::Magick can use antialiasing to smooth out the edges.

All of the Image::Magick methods and attributes are defined by the Image::Magick module. After you import the module, use the new( ) constructor to create an image object that is capable of reading, manipulating, and writing images. Creating a new, empty canvas (in this case, with a white background) is a little more involved than the equivalent in GD. First you have to set the size of the canvas (with the size attribute), and then use the Read( ) method with one of Image::Magick's special "internal file formats" for handling raw image data:

```
#!/usr/bin/perl -w

# Hello World in ImageMagick

use strict;
use Image::Magick;

# Create a new image

my $image = new Image::Magick;
$image->Set(size => '401x201');
my $status = $image->Read(filename => 'xc:white');
warn "$status" if $status;
```

The Read( ) and Write( ) methods always return undef upon success. See the next section for more on error checking.

The next step is to draw the grid of red circles using the Draw( ) method. Drawing is accomplished by using a toolbox of drawing primitives. Here we use the Circle primitive, which needs two points: the center, and a point on the edge of the circle.

```
# Draw the field of circles

my ($x1, $y1, $x2, $y2);

for my $i (0..10) {
    for my $j (0..5) {
        my $r = rand(25)+1;    # random radius

        # The center of the circle is x1,y1
        # x2,y2 is a point on the circle

        ($x1, $y1, $x2, $y2) = ($i*40, $j*40, $i*40, $j*40+$r);
```

```
        $image->Draw(
            primitive=>'Circle',
            points=> "$x1,$y1 $x2,$y2",
            stroke=>'red',
            fill => '#FF0000',
            antialias=>1,
            linewidth => 1
        );
    }
}
```

Next, the script draws the text using the Annotate( ) method. The font can be a fully qualified X11 font (e.g., "-*-helvetica-medium-r-*-*-12-*-*-*-*-iso8859-*"), a TrueType file name (e.g., "@TimesRoman.ttf"), or a PostScript font name (e.g., "Helvetica"). Image::Magick requires access to an X11 server, the FreeType library, and Ghostscript to render X11, TrueType, and PostScript fonts, respectively.

Image::Magick contacts an X Server to obtain the specified font if the name begins with a dash (-). Use the standard form for X Server fonts. Wildcards may be used instead of individual field values, as long as you provide enough information for the font server to understand which font you're looking for (e.g., "-*-lucida-medium-r-*-*-24-*-*-*-*-*-*"). In this case, the point size of the font is specified within the string.

You can also use a scalable PostScript font. To find out if you have scalable fonts installed on your Unix system, type:

```
xlsfonts -fn '*-0-0-0-0-*'
```

This returns a list of all the scalable fonts available to you. Specify the point size within the font string.

Most X11 font aliases are accepted. X-based systems use the *fonts.alias* file to define shorter aliases for the longer form of font names. On Windows-based systems, you may simply use the name of the font family and the weight.

This example uses the geometry attribute, which is equivalent to using separate x and y attributes.

```
# Draw the text

my ($x, $y) = (40, 120);
$image->Annotate(font => '@arial.ttf',
                pointsize => 64,
                stroke => '#000000',
                fill => 'black',
                text => "Hello World",
                geometry=> "+$x+$y" );
```

In Chapter 2 we saw that the text drawing functions of the GD module automatically return the bounding box of the rendered text. In Image::Magick, we must obtain the font metric information ourselves and calculate the bounding box. Use the QueryFontMetrics( ) method, which returns a seven-element array.

In order to draw the black rectangle around the text, we need to know the width and height of the rendered text. We also need the height of the descender in order to calculate the baseline of the text.

```
# Get the dimensions of the rendered text

my ($w, $h, $ascend, $descend, $text_w, $text_h, $max) =
    $image->QueryFontMetrics(font => '@arial.ttf',
                             pointsize => 64,
                             text => "Hello World");

# Calculate the bounding box

($x1, $y1, $x2, $y2) = ($x-10, $y-$text_h-$descend-10,
                        $x+$text_w+10, $y-$descend+10);
```

The rectangle is drawn using the Rectangle primitive of the Draw( ) method:

```
# Draw a black rectangle

$image->Draw(primitive => 'Rectangle',
             points => "$x1,$y1 $x2,$y2",
             stroke => 'black',
);
```

The Write( ) method outputs the image to a file or STDOUT:

```
# Write as a PNG

$image->Write('png:out.png');
```

Once you are finished with an image object, you should destroy it to conserve memory resources. Do this with undef:

```
undef $image;
```

Figure 3-1 shows the result.

Figure 3-1. Hello World using Image::Magick

Error Checking

Most Image::Magick routines return undef if the operation was successful. This allows a very simple check for success:

```
$status = $image->Transparent('#FFFFFF');
warn "$status" if $status;                # print the error message, if any
```

If an error occurs, the method returns an error string that consists of a numeric status code in the range 0–410 and an error message. An error code less than 400 is a warning that something unexpected happened; error codes of 400 or greater indicate an unrecoverable error that should probably cause a die condition, as in:

```
$status = $image->Read('beatniks.gif');
$status =~ /(\d+)/;
die "$status" if ($1 >= 400);
```

Some methods return an image when successful. In this case we should check to see if the resulting object is a reference to an image object:

```
$image2 = $image->Clone();
warn "$image2" if !ref($image2);                # print the error message, if any
```

See Table 3-1 for a list of errors and warning codes.

Table 3-1. Error and warning codes

Code	Message	Description
0	Success	The function was executed successfully
300	ResourceLimitWarning	Not enough memory
305	XServerWarning	An X Server resource is unavailable
310	OptionWarning	An input parameter was not in the correct format
315	DelegateWarning	An ImageMagick helper program returned a warning message
320	MissingDelegateWarning	A needed helper program could not be found
325	CorruptImageWarning	The image file may be corrupt
330	FileOpenWarning	The image file could not be opened
335	BlobWarning	A binary large object could not be created
340	CacheWarning	Image data could not be saved to the cache
400	ResourceLimitError	Not enough memory, unrecoverable
405	XServerError	An X resource is unavailable, unrecoverable
410	OptionError	An input parameter was malformed, unrecoverable
415	DelegateError	An error occurred while the image was being handled by a delegate program, unrecoverable
425	CorruptImageError	An image data file was not in the expected format, unrecoverable
430	FileOpenError	An image file cannot be opened, unrecoverable
435	BlobError	A binary large object could not be created, unrecoverable
440	CacheError	Image data could not be cached, probably because of a lack of memory, unrecoverable

Sample Image::Magick Applications

ImageMagick can do almost anything to an image or group of images. Some common applications are:

- Creating animated GIFs
- Creating composite images from a sequence
- Easily reducing or thumbnailing images
- Setting transparent colors
- Reducing and correcting colors
- Converting between 60+ formats (e.g., Photo CD to JPEG, PDF to GIF, BMP to PNG)
- Creating special effects and adding text to images

Examples of two of these applications are described in the following sections.

Thumbnails with Image::Magick

Suppose you have a bunch of image files (or PostScript or PDF files) for which you want to create smaller thumbnail images. The ImageMagick package provides several ways to do this. One high-level approach is ImageMagick's Visual Image Directory virtual file format. You can convert a number of image files into a Visual Image Directory with the *convert* utility:

```
convert 'vid:*.gif' png:imageindex.png
```

This command converts every GIF file in the current directory into a single image that contains thumbnails of all the images, and saves it as a PNG file called *imageindex.png*. The resulting image looks like Figure 3-2.

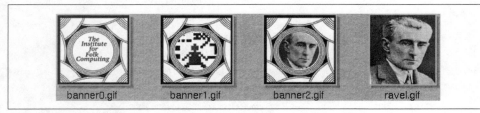

Figure 3-2. ImageMagick's Visual Image Directory allows you to create thumbnails

The Visual Image Directory is essentially a high-level function that uses some of the lower-level ImageMagick routines to read in a bunch of images, scale them into thumbnails, provide borders, labels, drop shadows, and a background, and write the resulting image out to the appropriate file. You can access all of these functions via the Image::Magick interface to ImageMagick (described later in this chapter).

The Visual Image Directory has acceptable default parameters. If you want greater control over the layout and look of your thumbnails, you can use the `Montage()` method within a Perl script, as in Example 3-1.

Example 3-1. Creating thumbnails with Montage()

```perl
#!/usr/bin/perl -w
# Example 3-1.

use strict;
use Image::Magick;
my $img = new Image::Magick;

# Read all of the images with a .gif
# extension in the current directory

my $status = $img->Read("*.gif");
if ($status) {
    die "$status";
}

# Montage() returns a new image

my $montage = $img->Montage(geometry    =>'100x100',
                            tile        =>'3x2',
                            borderwidth => 2);
$montage->Write('png:montage1.png');
```

This script produces a grid of thumbnails as a single image as in Figure 3-3.

Figure 3-3. Montage() allows you to combine several images into a single thumbnail directory

The `Montage()` Image::Magick method also allows you to set several attributes of the resulting image. Figure 3-4(a) is the result of changing the `Montage()` method call in the above example with the following statement, which sets attributes such as `pointsize` and `label` to customize the label beneath each thumbnail.

```
my $montage = $img->Montage(
    geometry=>'100x100',
    tile => '3x2',
    background => '#FFFFFF',
    pointsize => 12,
    label => "%f\n%wx%h\n(%b)",
    fill => '#000000',
    borderwidth => 2
);
```

Figure 3-4(b) shows the result of changing the statement to the following, where the mode attribute provides each thumbnail with a frame:

```
my $montage = $img->Montage(
    geometry    => "100x100+10+10",
    tile        => '3x2',
    background   => '#FFFFFF',
    label       => "%f",
    mode        => 'Frame',
    frame       => "10x10+2+4"
);
```

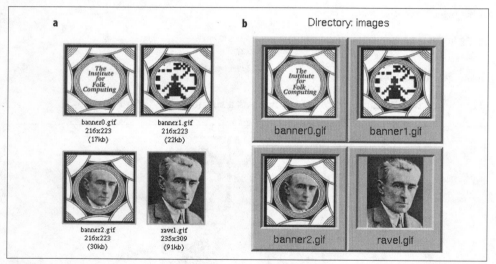

Figure 3-4. The Montage() method accepts several attributes, which change the look of the images

The tile attribute to the Montage() method controls the number of thumbnails per row and column. If there are more thumbnails than can fit within the specified tile geometry, additional images are added to the Image::Magick object. Setting the adjoin attribute of the object to 0 causes each of these groups of thumbnails to be written to a separate file when the Write() method is called. Figure 3-5 shows what happens when there are too many images for the layout specified (2×1). Here, the left two images are stored in one thumbnail file, the right two images in another.

banner0.gif   banner1.gif   banner2.gif   ravel.gif

Figure 3-5. If the number of thumbnails exceeds the specified number of rows and columns, they are grouped into separate image files

If you have a web site that distributes documents meant to be printed, you may have an archive of PostScript or PDF files. Perhaps you want to create an index of these files, with an image of the cover page serving as a link to the FTP site from which users may retrieve the original document. Example 3-2 generates just such an index; it creates an HTML document and thumbnail images of the first page of any number of PDF files.

Example 3-2. PDFconvert.pl creates thumbnails and writes out an HTML index file

```perl
#!/usr/bin/perl -w
# Example 3-2. PDFconvert.pl

use strict;
use Image::Magick;

# Retrieve the arguments provided on the command line

my @files = @ARGV;
die "You must provide a list of PDF files.\n" unless (@files);

my $img = new Image::Magick;

# To only read the first page from each PDF file we must append
# the string '[0]' to each of the file names

my @files2read = map { 'pdf:'.$_.'[0]' } @files;

print STDERR "Reading files...\n";
my $status = $img->Read(@files2read);
if ($status) {
    die $status;
}

# Create the thumbnails

my $montage = $img->Montage(geometry=>"150x150",
                            tile=>'1x1',
                            borderwidth=>2,
                            mode=> 'Frame',
                            label=>'%f',
                );
```

```
# Rather than let Image::Magick name each file, we want to
# control the naming scheme, so we'll write out each image from this loop.

for (my $i=0; $i < @$img+0; $i++) {
    print STDERR "Writing thumb$i.gif\n";
    $montage->[$i]->Write("gif:thumb$i.gif");
}

# Now create an index HTML file with links to each of the
# original documents and include the image of each first page
# as the content of each hyperlink.

print STDERR "Writing pdf_index.html\n";
open OUT, ">pdf_index.html" or
    die("Couldn't open image!\n");
print OUT "<HTML><BODY>";
for (my $i=0; $i < @files+0; $i++) {
    print OUT qq(<A HREF="$files[$i]"><IMG SRC="thumb$i.gif"></A>\n);
}
print OUT "</BODY></HTML>";
```

If you have a directory called *pdfdocs* that contains the following PDF files:

```
GimpUserManual.pdf
ImageMagick.pdf
hoosick.pdf
```

you could run the script to batch-process the files with the following command:

```
perl PDFconvert.pl *.pdf
```

This would create three image files in the directory in which the script was run called *thumb0.gif*, *thumb1.gif*, and *thumb2.gif*, as well as an HTML index of the documents called *pdf_index.html*. Note that this script is not a CGI script—it is meant as a script to batch-process the thumbnails, and may be run periodically by the web site administrator. The web page created by the script is shown in Figure 3-6.

GIF Animation with Image::Magick

Because the Image::Magick module implements the full GIF89a specification and allows us to include multiple images in a single file, we can use it to create some useful solutions to common GIF animation problems. But first, let's take a quick look at some more Image::Magick concepts.

An image object may be passed to another image object with the Clone( ) method. Several images can reside within the same image object. These individual images are referred to as *scenes* and can be retrieved by treating the object as a reference to an array. For example:

```
$image2 = $image1->[3]->Clone( );
```

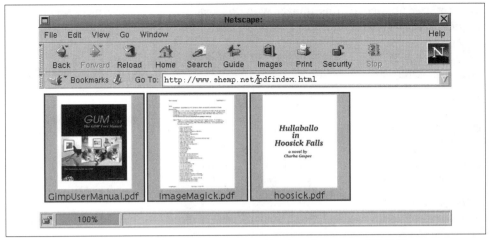

Figure 3-6. The PDFconvert.pl script creates an HTML index of a group of PDF files

Here, the image object `$image2` is assigned a copy of the fourth scene of `$image1`. The image or sequence of images is written to a file with the `Write()` method. If the `adjoin` attribute of the image object is set to 1 (the default value), the entire sequence is written as a single multi-image file (if the specified format supports multi-image files, like GIF does). If `adjoin` is 0, each image in the sequence is written to a separate file with the scene number appended to the name of the file.

The `Clone()` method can be used to piece together animations. The following script takes a single image and creates a continuous scrolling effect (right to left) through a fixed-width frame. Some frames from the resulting sequence are shown in Figure 3-7. The frame width is determined by the `$framew` variable, and the smoothness of the overall effect is set with the `$increment` variable (a larger value creates choppier movement, but a smaller file size).

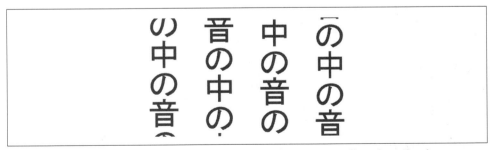

Figure 3-7. Some frames from the resulting animation of an image scrolling through a frame

To create a seamlessly scrolling image, copy the first frame's worth of rows from the original image and append those rows to the right of the image. The `Crop()` method is iteratively applied to this image, with the result saved as the next scene in the sequence. Example 3-3 does just that.

Example 3-3. Scrolling an image through a frame from right to left

```perl
#!/usr/local/bin/perl -w

# Example 3-3.

use strict;
use Image::Magick;

# The width of the frame is determined by $framew and
# the number of frames to produce is given by $frames

my ($filename, $status) ;
my $framew = 100;
my $frames = 10;

unless (defined($filename = $ARGV[0])) {
    die "Usage: perl scroll.pl filename\n";
}

my $image = new Image::Magick;        # composite source file
my $tempimage = new Image::Magick;    # used later as a temp image
my $imageout = new Image::Magick;     # final output image

$status = $image->Read("$filename");
if ($status) {
    die "$status";
}
my ($width, $height) = $image->Get('width', 'height');

# The increment of each scene shift (in pixels) is given by $increment.
# A smaller increment produces smoother action and larger files.

my $increment = 15;

print STDERR "Creating scenes...\n";
my $count = -1;

# We use Image::Magick's Roll() and Crop() functions
# to shift the image with each frame and crop to an appropriate size.

my ($rollgeometry, $cropgeometry);
for (my $x=0; $x < $width; $x+=$increment) {

   # Set up the geometry strings for the next roll and crop

   $rollgeometry = $framew."x$height+$x+0";
   $cropgeometry = $framew."x$height";

   # The Clone() method copies the content of $images
   # into the temporary image.
```

Example 3-3. Scrolling an image through a frame from right to left (continued)

```
    $tempimage = $image->Clone( );
    $count++;
    $tempimage->Roll($rollgeometry);        # Roll it
    $tempimage->Crop($cropgeometry);        # Crop it

    # Now copy the area to the next frame of the output image.

    $imageout->[$count] = $tempimage->Clone( );
    undef $tempimage;                       # Clean up
}

$imageout->Set(loop=>0);                    # Set infinite loop
print STDERR "Writing file...\n";
$imageout->Write("gif:scrolling$filename");
```

This code adds an Application Extension Block to the GIF that specifies the number of times the browser should iterate through the sequence of images when rendering the file. This extension block is sometimes referred to as the *Netscape Loop Extension* or, as it has been universally accepted as the de facto means of indicating the number of loops, just the *Loop Extension*. Note that because it's an Application Extension Block, it is not part of the GIF89a specification, and support for this information is left to the client.

With Image::Magick, you can define an *infinite loop* by setting the loop attribute of an image to 0. By setting the loop attribute, you are adding an Application Extension Block to the file with the appropriate value. The default value for loop is 1, which means the animation should play through once and end with a still final frame. The loop attribute must be set for the entire image sequence, as in:

```
    use Image::Magick;
    my $image = new Image::Magick;
    $image->Read(qw(scene0.gif scene1.gif scene2.gif scene3.gif));
    $image->Set(loop=>0);        # Setting an infinite loop for the sequence
```

The browser ignores any looping extension that is associated with only one scene within the sequence. That is, the following doesn't have the desired effect:

```
    $image->[3]->Set(loop=>0);    # Won't work: an attempt to loop a particular scene
```

The *disposal method* is a number within the Graphics Control Extension Block that indicates how an image scene is disposed of when the next image in the sequence is displayed. The Graphics Control Extension Block can appear anywhere within the file, so the disposal method may be set for individual scenes within a sequence. The default setting for the disposal method of each scene is 0 (no method specified). To implement objects moving against a static background, use a disposal method of 3 (restore to previous frame). This refreshes the area taken up by a scene with part of the last image in the sequence that was defined with a disposal method of 0 or 1. For example:

```
    use Image::Magick;
    my $image = new Image::Magick;
```

```
$image->Read(qw(scene0.gif scene1.gif scene2.gif scene3.gif));
# Set all scenes as restore to previous'
$image->Set(disposal=>3);
# Specify the first image as the static background
$image->[0]->Set(disposal=>1);
```

For the image created by this script, scenes 0 and 1 have a disposal value of 1 (do not dispose) and scenes 2 and 3 have a value of 2 (restore to background color).

You can define the amount of time that the browser should wait before displaying the next image in the sequence with the DelayTime field of the Graphics Control Extension Block. This value is always represented in hundredths of a second (i.e., 6,000 = one minute). If the delay time is set to 0, the client should display the scenes as fast as possible, with no delay between scenes. Note that this can lead to different behavior on different systems; an animation that displays properly on your test system might run too fast on a faster system. It is generally a good idea to specify a minimum delay time so that you have the maximum level of control of the end result of your efforts.

With ImageMagick, you can set the delay time with the delay attribute. Acceptable values are in the range 0 to 65,535 (an upper limit of approximately 11 minutes). The delay time can be set for the sequence as a whole or for individual scenes within a sequence:

```
use Image::Magick;
my $image = new Image::Magick;
$image->Read(qw(scene0.gif scene1.gif scene2.gif scene3.gif));
$image->Set(delay => 400);          # Set delay time to 4 sec. for every scene
$image->[2]->Set(delay => 200);     # Set delay time to 2 sec. for the third scene
```

If the User Input flag is also specified for the scene, the browser should continue to display the sequence either when the delay period is over or when input is received from the user.

The GIF89a specification allows you to specify a *local palette* that defines the colors for each individual scene in a file, or a *global palette* for all the scenes in a file. Some browsers have a problem with local palettes when the palette for the next image in a sequence is loaded before the currently displayed image is disposed. This results in a flashing effect if the two scenes have significantly different local palettes.

By default, Image::Magick creates a local palette for each image in a file. To create a global color palette, set the colors attribute of the sequence to 256 and call the Quantize( ) method to perform the color reduction (the color attribute can actually be set within the Quantize( ) method call). From the local palettes, this creates a single palette that contains all of the colors used in the file. If the total number of colors exceeds 256, the palette is intelligently reduced to 256 by the Image::Magick color reduction routines. If there are transparent colors within the image, set the colorspace attribute to Transparent first to preserve the transparency. For example:

```
use Image::Magick;
my $image = Image::Magick->new;
```

```
$image->Read(qw(scene0.gif scene1.gif scene2.gif scene3.gif));
$image->Quantize(colorspace=>'Transparent', colors=>256);
```

Currently, Image::Magick does not create a single global palette for the entire file. It actually creates a single palette based on the local palettes, and then replaces the individual local palettes with this global palette. This behavior may change in the future, but the end effect is the same as creating a single global palette.

Reading and Writing Images

The Read( ) and Write( ) methods allow you to get images into or out of an image object. Internally, images are stored in a flexible abstract data structure that may be written to any of the many different supported file formats (see Appendix C for a complete list of file formats and prefixes). The default write format is in the MIFF format (Magick Image File Format), which was created specifically for storing ImageMagick image data. If you are interested in the full specifications for the MIFF format, they are available on the CD-ROM that comes with O'Reilly's *The Encyclopedia of Graphics File Formats*.

While writing, you can set any of the attributes described in the section "Retrieving and Setting File Information" by sending it as a parameter to Write( ). For example:

```
$image->Write(filename => 'xc:white', compress => 'Zip');
```

If you are using an X Server, you can display an image directly from Perl. The Display( ) and Animate( ) methods may be used to send the image directly to the *display* or *animate* programs described at the beginning of this chapter.

Read( )

```
$image->Read(list);
```

The Read( ) method reads an image or an image sequence from the specified files (of any supported format), or reads in a new "blank" image with a background color. When an image is read, its file format is determined by the appropriate field in the image header (not by the file's extension). To force a specific image format, use the name of the format followed by a colon before the filename string. Filenames ending with a *.gz* or *.Z* extension (on a Unix system) are first decompressed using *gunzip* or *uncompress*. The *list* can be a list of strings in any of the following forms:

```
$image->Read('gif:gum.gif')           # Read a single GIF file into $image
$image->Read('foo.gif', 'gumbar.jpg'); # Read two images into $image object
                                       # guessing the file format
                                       # from their magic numbers
$image->Read('*.gif');                 # Read all of the .gif files in the
                                       # current directory into $image

open(IMAGE, 'image.gif') or
    die("Couldn't open image!\n");     # Open the file for reading
```

```
binmode IMAGE;                      # Make sure we're in binary mode
$image->Read(file => \*IMAGE);      # Read from open Perl filehandle
```

Certain file formats allow more than one image to be contained in the same file (see Appendix C), though each image in a sequence can be accessed individually. For example, to set the transparent color of only the first image in a sequence to white, use:

```
$image->[0]->Transparent('#FFFFFF');
```

You can also read in specific subimages of a multi-resolution file format such as Photo CD or MPEG. Accessing subimages can be done with the following syntax:

```
$image->Read('pcd:image1.pcd[3]');            # Read the fourth subimage
$image->Read('mpeg:image2.mpg[20-40,70-80]'); # Read the given ranges
```

ImageMagick supports a number of custom file formats that add colors or special effects to a background. They are the gradient, plasma, granite, and tile formats:

```
$image->Read('gradient:white-black');     # gradient gives a gradual trans-
                                          # ition from one shade to another.
$image->Read('gradient:#FFFFFF-#000000'); # the desired shading is the filename

$image->Read('plasma:yellow-green');      # a 'plasma fractal' pattern
$image->Read('plasma:fractal');           # A base color may be specified or
                                          # use 'fractal' for a random value

$image->Read('granite:');                 # starts with a granite texture

$image->Read('tile:images/beatniks.gif'); # tile image with a texture or file
```

To create a new image with a given background color suitable for use as a blank canvas, use the following:

```
# Note that xc is the file format type, in this case an X color

my $image = new Image::Magick;
$image->Set(size => '200x200');
$status = $image->Read(filename=>'xc:#grey80');
```

You should always check the return values of a read or write method call. If there is a problem during a read, the method continues reading and returns an error message for each file that it could not read. See the section "Error Checking" earlier in this chapter.

Write( )

```
$image->Write(list);
```

Write( ) allows you to write the data for a single image or a sequence of images to a file or standard output. When using Image::Magick in CGI applications, use the STDOUT handle to write to standard output. Calling Write( ) without a specified filename writes to the file indicated by the image's filename attribute. If there is a writing problem, Write( ) returns the number of images successfully written. Error checking is described in the section "Error Checking" earlier in this chapter.

If you have read a sequence of images into an Image::Magick object, you can write out the entire sequence as a single file if your output format supports multiple images, or you can write individual scenes from the sequence.

Here are some examples:

```perl
$button->Write('jpeg:button.jpg');      # write to button.jpg as a JPEG

$image->Write(format=>'JPEG',
            file=>\*STDOUT);            # Write to STDOUT

$image->Write(file=>IMAGE);            # Write to an open Perl filehandle

$images->[0]->Write('foobar.gif');     # write only the first image in a sequence

$image->Read('foo.gif');               # If this is the only read...
$image->Write();                       # ...this writes to foo.gif
```

Instead of writing your image to a file, you can display it to any X11 screen. Use `Display()` to display one image at a time to the screen and `Animate()` to display an image sequence.

BlobToImage( ), ImageToBlob( )

```perl
$number_converted = $image->BlobToImage(blob_list)
@blobs = $image->ImageToBlob(attribute_list)
```

These methods allow you to convert images to and from Binary Large Objects (BLOBs). In Perl, a BLOB is simply a scalar that contains the image data in a particular file format. The `BlobToImage()` method takes one or more BLOBs and returns the number of BLOBs successfully converted to images. The `ImageToBlob()` method can take a list of Image::Magick attributes as parameters and returns an array of BLOBs, one for each image in the sequence.

The following code reads in a PNG file and prints the image as a JPEG on STDOUT:

```perl
#!/usr/bin/perl
use strict;
use Image::Magick;

my $img = new Image::Magick;

my $status = $img->Read('png:monkey.png');
my @blobs = $img->ImageToBlob(magick => 'jpeg');
print $blobs[0];
```

These methods can also be used to pass images between toolkits. The following code converts an Image::Magick image object into a GD image object, draws a rectangle using GD primitives, then converts the image back to Image::Magick:

```perl
#!/usr/bin/perl
use strict;
use Image::Magick;
use GD;

# First read an image with ImageMagick

my $im = new Image::Magick;
my $status = $im->Read('monkey.png');
if ($status) {
    die "$status!";
}
```

```
# Convert to a blob and hand off to GD

my @blobs = $im->ImageToBlob();
my $gd = GD::Image->newFromPngData($blobs[0]);
my $red = $gd->colorAllocate(255, 0, 0);

# Outline in red

$gd->rectangle(0, 0, (map {$_-1} $gd->getBounds), $red);

# There and back again

my $im2 = new Image::Magick;
$im2->BlobToImage($gd->png());
$im2->Write('png:monkeyout.png');
```

Most databases support the storage of BLOBs. Once you have the image data in a scalar, you can easily save it to a database using your favorite Perl database interface.

Retrieving and Setting File Information

You can retrieve a lot of general information about an image by using the Get() method to query any of the attributes in Table 3-2. A few of the attributes (compression, interlace, filename, etc.) may also be written to with the Set() method. Setting these attributes does not immediately affect the image; they do not come into play until the image is written. Ping() is a handy function that returns information about an image's size without actually loading the image into memory.

Most of the attributes listed below can be both read and written; those with a "No" in the Write column are read-only (that is, they may be used only with the Get() method, not with the Set() method). For the methods, you can use the name of the method with the word "Image" appended to it as an alias. For example, ReadImage() is an alias for Read() and SharpenImage() is an alias for Sharpen().

Table 3-2. File information attributes

Attribute	Read	Write	Description
adjoin	Yes	Yes	Certain file formats accept multiple images within a single file. If adjoin is 1 and the image is a multi-image format, multiple reads to the same image object join the images into a single file. Set adjoin to 0 if you do not want the images output to a single file.
Base_filename	Yes	No	Returns a string that is the image's original filename.
cache-threshold	Yes	Yes	ImageMagick keeps the image data in a RAM cache and writes it out to a disk cache when it runs out of RAM. If you have a limited amount of memory available, this option allows you to set a maximum limit on the size of the RAM cache.
comment	Yes	No	Returns a string that has been saved with the image, if the image format has the ability to save comments in the file.

Table 3-2. File information attributes (continued)

Attribute	Read	Write	Description

compression	Yes	Yes	The default compression for an image is based on its original format; you can specify a compression type with the compression attribute. The type should be one of the following, based on the type of file format you plan to write:
			
			None
			  No compression
			BZip
			  BZip2 compression
			Fax
			  Fax Group 3 compression
			Group4
			  Fax Group 4 compression
			JPEG
			  JPEG compression
			LosslessJPEG
			  Lossless JPEG compression
			LZW
			  LZW compression (GIF or TIFF)
			RLE
			  Run-length encoding compression
			Zip
			  Zip compression
			
			If you indicate a compression type that is incompatible with the output file type, it is set to the original default value (e.g., a GIF file ignores a compression attribute set to JPEG, and a PNG ignores a compression attribute of Zip). Some file formats (such as PNG) are compressed by default.

delay	Yes	Yes	The delay option may be used to regulate the playback speed of an animated GIF. This integer is the number of 1/100ths of a second that should pass before displaying the next image in a sequence. The default is 0 delay, which indicates that the animation should play as fast as possible. In this case, actual speed can vary from system to system, so it is best to either specify a delay that looks good or be sure to test the results on a range of platforms. The maximum delay is 65535 (almost 11 minutes).
depth	Yes	No	Returns the bit depth of the image, either 8 or 16.
dispose	Yes	Yes	The dispose attribute sets the GIF disposal method that indicates how an image is refreshed when flipping between scenes in a sequence. You may set it to an integer between 0 and 3, which correspond to the following methods: *0* None specified (default) *1* Do not dispose *2* Restore to background color *3* Restore to previous scene

Table 3-2. File information attributes (continued)

Attribute	Read	Write	Description

filename	Yes	Yes	The default filename is the name of the file (or color) from which the image was read. When the Write( ) method is called without a parameter, it uses the image's filename attribute as the target file. For example:
			
			```\n$image->Read('gum.gif');\n$image->Set(filename => 'gum2.gif');\n$image->Write();\n```
			
			writes to the file *gum2.gif* just like:
			
			```\n$image->Read('gum.gif');\n$image->Write('gum2.gif');\n```
			
			except that in the second case, the $image object retains the original filename. If $image is a sequence of images, the default is the filename of the first image in the sequence, and changing it changes the filename for the entire sequence.

filesize	Yes	No	The number of bytes that the image takes up on disk.
format	Yes	No	The image format can be any of those supported by ImageMagick (listed in Appendix C). Remember that some image formats require additional libraries and programs to be readable and writable. Refer to the earlier "Installing ImageMagick" section for information about external libraries. The magick attribute is an alias for format.

interlace	Yes	Yes	The interlace attribute allows you to specify the interlacing scheme used when the image is written. The default value is None. The *string* can be:
			
			None
			    No interlacing.
			Line
			    Scanline interlacing (use for GIF).
			Plane
			    Plane interlacing, where each channel is interlaced separately.
			Partitioning
			    Same as plane interlacing, but each channel will be saved in its own file when written.
			
			See Chapter 1 for a description of interlacing.

loop	Yes	Yes	The loop attribute adds a looping extension to a GIF image sequence. Assigning a value of 0 to loop causes the animation sequence to loop continuously. A value other than 0 results in the animation being played for the specified number of times before stopping. The iterations attribute is an alias for the loop attribute. The default value is 1.
packetsize	Yes	No	The packetsize attribute is the number of bytes in each run-length encoded packet of image data.
packets	Yes	No	The number of run-length encoded packets in the image.
quality	Yes	Yes	The quality attribute sets the JPEG or PNG compression level; can be 0 (worst) to 100 (best). The default is 75.
signature	Yes	No	Retrieves the MD5 public key signature associated with the image, if any.

Table 3-2. File information attributes (continued)

Attribute	Read	Write	Description
taint	Yes	No	This attribute is true if the image has been modified using any of Image Magick's methods.
type	Yes	No	The image type may be any of: "bilevel", "greyscale", "palette", "true color", "true color with transparency", or "color separation".

The following methods can be used to query image files or add information to files.

Comment( )

`$image->Comment(string)`

Adds a comment to an image. You can use any of the techniques described for the Annotate( ) method. For example:

```
$image->Comment("%m:%f %wx%h");
```

creates a comment for the image with the string "beatniks:GIF 318x265" if $image is a 318 × 265 image that was read from a file titled *beatniks.gif*.

Ping( )

`Image::Magick->Ping(filename=>string)`

Ping( ) is a convenience function that returns information about a file without having to read the image into memory. It returns the width, height, file size in bytes, and file format of the image. For multi-image files, only the information for the first image in the sequence is returned.

QueryFormat( )

`$image->QueryFormat(format=>string)`

Returns a list of information about one of the supported file formats. The following fields are returned:

adjoin
    Does this format support multiple images in a single file?

blob_support
    Does this format support binary large objects?

raw
    Is this a raw file format?

decoder
    Can ImageMagick read files in this format?

encoder
    Can ImageMagick write files in this format?

description
    A short description of the format.

```
module
```
The internal module used to support this format.

This information can also be found in Appendix C.

Signature( )

```
$image->Signature( )
```

Generates an MD5 public key signature and stores it with the header information for the MIFF image format. The signature can later be used to verify the data integrity of the image. Two images with the same signature are identical.

Sizing and Transforming Images

A lot of image manipulation tasks consist of little more than resizing and cropping existing images. Table 3-3 shows the Image::Magick attributes that provide sizing and resolution information about an image. The page and density attributes may be set (with Set( )) to control the image size and resolution before reading in a Post-Script file. The size attribute can be similarly set before creating images from raw data formats.

Table 3-3. Sizing and resolution attributes

Attribute	Read	Write	Description
base_columns	Yes	No	Returns an integer that is the width of the image before any transformations have been performed.
base_rows	Yes	No	Returns an integer that is the height of the image before any transformations have been performed.
columns	Yes	No	Returns the width (integer number of pixel columns) of the image.
Density	Yes	Yes	Use this attribute to set the vertical and horizontal resolution of an image. Set the density to a string in the form '*horiz-density* x *vert-density*', e.g., '300x300'. It is most useful when reading a PostScript document.
			The default is 72 dots per inch. Increase this to 144, for example, to render the PostScript to a larger sized image.
Geometry	Yes	No	Returns the bounds of the image. The geometry string is a convenient form that allows you to specify the width and height, or a region of an image with an offset. For example:
			`geometry=>'640x800'`
			is equivalent to:
			`width=>640, height=>800`
			To refer to a 20x20 region of pixels starting at coordinate (100,150), use:
			`geometry=>'20x20+100+150'`
height	Yes	No	Returns the height (integer number of pixel rows) of the image.

Table 3-3. Sizing and resolution attributes (continued)

Attribute	Read	Write	Description
page	Yes	Yes	Declares the image canvas size and location. Typically this is useful only for the PostScript, Text, and GIF formats. *string* can be any of the page sizes in Table 3-4 or a geometry (e.g. 612x792 for Letter). The default value is Letter.
rows	Yes	No	Returns the height (integer number of pixel rows) of the image.
size	Yes	Yes	Use the size attribute before reading in an image from a raw data file format such as RGB, GRAY, TEXT, or CMYK. Images in the Photo CD format are stored at several different resolutions, so choose one of the following before reading the image: 192x128, 384x256, 768x512, 1536x1024, 3072x2048.
units	Yes	No	Returns a string describing the units in which the image's resolution is defined. The returned value may be one of: "Undefined", "pixels/inch", or "pixels/centimeter".
width	Yes	No	Returns the width (integer number of pixel columns) of the image.
x_resolution	Yes	No	Returns the *x* resolution of the image in the units defined by the units attribute.
y_resolution	Yes	No	Returns the *y* resolution of the image in the units defined by the units attribute.

Table 3-4 shows different page sizes (for use with the page attribute) and their corresponding geometries.

Table 3-4. Page sizes and their corresponding geometries

Page string	Geometry in pixels
Letter	612 x 792
Tabloid	792 x 1224
Ledger	1224 x 792
Legal	612 x 1008
Statement	396 x 612
Executive	522 x 756
A3	842 x 1191
A4	595 x 842
A5	420 x 595
B4	729 x 1032
B5	516 x 729
Folio	612 x 936
Quarto	576 x 720
10x14	720 x 1008

The following methods can be used to resize, crop, or otherwise transform images.

Chop( )

```
$image->(geometry=>geometry,
        width=>integer,
        height=>integer,
        x=>integer,
        y=>integer
```

Chop( ) removes a portion of an image starting at the offset x,y. The columns x through x+width and the rows y through y+height are chopped. If width and height are not specified, they are assumed to be the maximum width and height of the image. geometry may be used as a shortcut for width and height.

Crop( )

```
$image->Crop(geometry=>geometry,
             width=>integer,
             height=>integer,
             x=>integer,
             y=>integer)
```

Crop( ) extracts a width by height portion of the image starting at the offset x,y. The geometry parameter is shorthand for width and height. To crop a 100×100 region starting at (20,20), use Crop('100x100+20+20'). Invoking Crop( ) with the parameter '0x0' crops off excess "border color" from your image, where the border color is intelligently inferred by Image::Magick.

Flip( )

```
$image->Flip( )
```

Flip( ) creates a vertical mirror image by reflecting the scanlines around the central x axis (see Figure 3-8, left).

Flop( )

```
$image->Flop( )
```

Flop( ) creates a horizontal mirror image by reflecting the scanlines around the central y axis (see Figure 3-8, right).

Magnify( )

```
$image->Magnify( )
```

Magnify( ) is a convenience function that scales an image proportionally to twice its size. See also Minify( ).

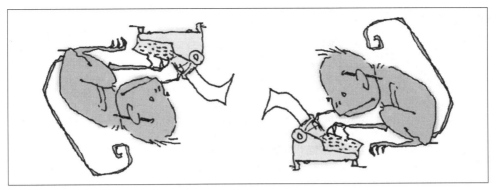

Figure 3-8. Flip( ) and Flop( )

Minify( )

`$image->Minify( )`

Minify( ) is a convenience function that scales an image proportionally to half its size. See also Magnify( ).

Resize( )

```
$image->Resize(geometry=>geometry,
            width=>integer, height=>integer,
            filter=> {Point, Box, Triangle, Hermite, Hanning,
                    Hamming, Blackman, Gaussian, Quadratic, Cubic,
                    Catrom, Mitchell, Lanczos, Bessel, Sinc},
            blur=>float)
```

Resize( ) is a convenience method that crops or scales an image to the specified dimensions with automatic filtering using the specified filter method. Use the blur attribute to control the degree of blurring; a value less than 1 is sharp, greater than 1 is blurrier.

You can also express the geometry parameter in one of the following ways:

```
$image->Resize(geometry=>'50%');        # Scale proportionally to half its size
$image->Resize(geometry=>'50%x25%');    # Scale 50% horizontally, 25% vertically
$image->Resize(geometry=>'160x160>');   # Scale so one dimension is
                                        # exactly 160 pixels
```

Roll( )

```
$image->Roll(geometry=>geometry,
            x=>integer,
            y=>integer)
```

Roll( ) offsets an image on the x or y axis by the given amount and rolls the part that is offset to the other side of the image that has been emptied. The Roll( ) method can be used to automatically create seamless tiled background patterns by "rolling" the edges into the center of the image.

Rotate( )

```
$image->Rotate(degrees=>float,
            crop=>{1, 0},
            sharpen=>{1, 0})
```

Rotate( ) rotates an image around the x axis by the number of degrees specified by the degrees parameter (0 to 360). The empty space created around the resulting parallelogram is filled in with the color defined by the bordercolor attribute. If the crop parameter is 1, the image is cropped to its original size. You may also specify whether jagged edges created by the transformation should be filtered with the sharpen parameter.

You may want to set the bordercolor to the background color of the image before calling Rotate( ) so that the end result has a consistent background color. You can then crop the excess background with the Trim( ) method:

```
# Set the border color first
$image->Set(bordercolor=>'#FFFFFF');        # a white background

# Do the rotation
$image->Rotate(degrees=>60, crop=>0, sharpen=>1);

# Now trim the excess background
$image->Trim( );
```

Sample( )

```
$image->Scale(geometry=>geometry,
            width=>integer,
            height=>integer)
```

Sample( ) scales an image to the given dimensions with pixel sampling. Unlike other scaling methods, this method does not introduce any additional colors in the scaled image.

Scale( )

```
$image->Scale(geometry=>geometry,
            width=>integer,
            height=>integer)
```

The Scale( ) method changes the size of an image to the given dimensions. The dimensions may be specified either as absolute pixel sizes:

```
$image->Scale('300x300');        # scales the image to 300 pixels by 300 pixels
```

or by percentages for proportional scaling:

```
$image->Scale('300%x300%');    # makes the image three times larger
$image->Scale('300%');         # same thing
```

Use the Resize( ) method to scale an image and automatically apply an intelligent sharpening filter that gives better results that Scale( ) in most cases.

Shear( )

```
$image->Shear(geometry=>geometry,
              x=>float,
              y=>float,
              crop=>{1, 0})
```

Shear( ) transforms an image by shearing it along the x or y axis. The x and y parameters specify the number of degrees (–179.9 to 179.9) that the image is to be sheared along that respective axis. The empty space created around the resulting parallelogram is filled in with the color defined by the bordercolor attribute. If the crop parameter is 1, the image is cropped to its original size.

Trim( )

```
$image->Trim( )
```

Trim( ) crops a rectangular box around the image to remove edges that are the background color.

Zoom( )

```
$image->Zoom(geometry=>geometry,
             width=>integer,
             height=>integer,
             filter=>{ Point, Box, Triangle, Hermite, Hanning, Hamming, Blackman,
                       Gaussian, Quadratic, Cubic, Catrom, Mitchell, Lanczos,
                       Bessel, Sinc})
```

Zoom( ) scales an image to the specified dimensions and applies one of the given filters. This generally gives a better result when enlarging images than that given by the Scale( ) method.

Copying and Composing Images

An example using the Montage( ) composition method was shown back in the "Thumbnails with Image::Magick" section. Several other methods may be used to combine multiple images into a separate file, overlay multiple images within a single frame, and create copies of images.

Append( )

```
$result = $image->Append( )
```

The Append( ) method takes a set of images and appends them to each other. All of the images must have either the same width, the same height, or both. The result is a single image, with each image in the sequence side by side if all heights are equal, or stacked on top of each other if all widths are equal.

Clone( )

`$result = $image->Clone( )`

The Clone( ) method copies a set of images and returns the copy as a new image object. The following copies all the images from $image into $image2:

```
$image2 = $image->Clone( );
```

Composite( )

```
$image->Composite(compose=>string,
                  image=>image_object,
                  geometry=>geometry,
                  x=>integer,
                  y=>integer,
                  opacity=>integer,
                  gravity=>{NorthWest, North, NorthEast, West, Center,
                            East, SouthWest, South, SouthEast} )
```

By default, Composite( ) simply replaces those pixels in the given area of the composite image with those pixels of image. The compose parameter allows you to modify the behavior of this function with the following options:

Over

Return the union of image and composite; composite obscures image in the overlap.

In

Return composite cut by the shape of image.

Out

Return image cut by the shape of composite.

Atop

Return image with composite obscuring image where the shapes overlap.

Xor

Return those parts of composite and image that are outside the region of overlap.

Plus

Add the values of the individual channels of composite and image, setting overflows to 255.

Minus

Subtract the values of the individual channels of image from composite, setting underflows to 0.

Add

Add the values of the individual channels of composite and image, applying *mod 256* to overflows. This compose option is reversible.

Subtract

Subtract the values of the individual channels of image from composite, applying *mod 256* to underflows. This compose option is reversible.

Difference

Return the absolute value of image subtracted from composite; useful for comparing two similar images.

Multiply
    Return the image multiplied by the composite; useful for creating drop-shadow effects.
Copy
    Replace the image with the composite image.
CopyRed
    Replace the red channel of the image with the red channel of the composite image.
CopyGreen
    Replace the green channel of the image with the green channel of the composite image.
CopyBlue
    Replace the blue channel of the image with the blue channel of the composite image.
CopyMatte
    Replace the alpha channel of the image with the alpha channel of the composite image.
Bumpmap
    Return image with a shading filter applied using composite as a mask.
Replace
    Return image replaced with composite.
Displace
    Return image with a displacement filter applied using composite as a mask.

The x and y parameters give the position at which to overlay the object, and gravity specifies the preferred placement of images within a larger image.

Many of the parameters described for Composite( ) are also used for the Montage( ) routine, which is a specialized variant of Composite( ) for assembling images into multi-row composites with borders and backgrounds.

Montage( )

```
$image->Montage(background=>color,
            borderwidth=>integer,
            compose=>{Over, In, Out, Atop, Xor, Plus, Minus, Add, Subtract,
                    Difference, Bumpmap, Replace, MatteReplace, Mask,
                    Blend, Displace},
            filename=>string,
            font=>string,
            foreground=>color,
            frame=>geometry,
            geometry=>geometry,
            gravity=>{NorthWest, North, NorthEast, West, Center, East,
                    SouthWest, South, SouthEast},
            label=>string
            mode=>{Frame, Unframe, Concatenate}
            stroke=>color,
            fill=>color,
            pointsize=>integer
            shadow=>boolean
            texture=>string,
            tile=>geometry,
            title=>string,
            transparent=>color)
```

The Montage( ) method is a layout manager that lets you composite several images into a single image suitable for use as a visual index of thumbnails or as an image map for a variety of applications. Montage( ) allows a good deal of control over the placement and framing of the images within the composite.

To create a montage, first read all of the images to be included into an Image::Magick object, and then apply the Montage( ) function with the appropriate parameters. Montage( ) automatically scales the images to the appropriate size and composes them into a single image (or more than one image if the number of images exceeds the number of rows and columns specified by the tile parameter). Most of the parameters sent to Montage( ) are the same as those described in the section "Retrieving and Setting File Information." The compose parameter offers the same overlay options as in the Composite( ) function.

The parameters specific to Montage( ) include:

background
> The background color of the image.

borderwidth
> The width of the border around the image (in pixels).

filename
> Name the montage with this string.

foreground
> Provide a color name for the montage foreground.

frame
> Surround the image with a frame of line width and height specified as a string of the form *widthxheight*.

geometry
> Give the geometry of the maximum tile and border size for each tile. The default maximum tile size is 120×120.

gravity
> Specify one of the eight points of the compass as the preferred layout position for a tile.

label
> Assign this string as a label for the image.

mode
> Provide one of three framing options for thumbnails: Frame, Unframe, Concatenate. The default value is Frame, which enables all of the scaling and framing parameters. Setting mode to Unframe causes the images to be montaged without frames, and Concatenate causes them to be composed into a single image with each of the subimages added at its original size.

shadow
> If 1, add a shadow beneath the tile.

texture
> Apply a tileable texture to the image background.

tile
> Give the number of tiles per row and column as a geometry string of the form *rowsxcolumns*. The default is 5×4. If the number of tiles exceeds this maximum, more than one composite image is created.

`title`
> Give this title to the montage.

`transparent`
> Make this color transparent.

Use the `directory` attribute to get a list of all the filenames of the images in a montage.

If you are montaging a group of thumbnail images, it is generally a good idea to create the thumbnails in advance with `Scale( )` or `Zoom( )` and hand them over to the `Montage( )` function to avoid memory problems.

Color and Transparency

Of the color methods, the `Quantize( )` and `Map( )` functions are the most immediately useful for adjusting the number of colors in an image and synchronizing the color maps of different indexed images. Use the `Transparent( )` or `MatteFloodfill( )` methods to add transparency to an image with an alpha channel. (ImageMagick uses the terms "matte" and "transparent" interchangeably.)

Certain of the attributes in Table 3-5 (the component primary points and `rendering_intent`, for example) are really advanced colorimetry options and are not generally used unless you are working in the specialized area of color profiling. See the International Color Consortium's ICC Profile Format Specification at *http://www.color.org* for more information on color profiles and colorimetry.

Table 3-5. Color and transparency attributes

Attribute	Read	Write	Description
background	Yes	Yes	Sets or returns the background color of an image. Remember that for a GIF multi-image sequence, every image is sized by default to the size of the largest image; the background color fills the remaining space.
bordercolor	Yes	Yes	The `bordercolor` attribute is used in functions such as `Rotate( )` and `Shear( )` where an image is transformed and "empty" background spaces are created that should be distinct from the background color.
blue_primary	Yes	Yes	Returns the chromaticity blue primary point. This is a color management option. Set the value with '`x_value,y_value`'.
class	Yes	No	A `Direct` class image is of continuous tone and is stored as a sequence of red-green-blue intensity values. A `Pseudo` class image is an image with a color-map, where the image is stored as a map of colors and a sequence of indexes into the map.
colormap	Yes	Yes	Sets or returns the color table entry at position *i*. To set a color, use a name (e.g., red) or hex value (e.g., #rrggbb). An entry is returned as a three-element list of RGB values.
colors	Yes	No	Returns the number of colors that are used in the image.

Table 3-5. Color and transparency attributes (continued)

Attribute	Read	Write	Description
colorspace	Yes	Yes	Color reduction takes place in the RGB colorspace by default, but in certain cases you may get better results with a different colorspace. *string* corresponds to one of several color models; the values we are interested in are:
			RGB Red, green, blue
			Gray *(not* Grey*)* Grayscale
			Transparent RGB with retained transparent colors (if any)
			YIQ A color model used by NTSC
			YUV Luminance, Chrominance used by MPEG
			YCbCr A variant of YUV that gives good results with skin tones
			CMYK Cyan, magenta, yellow, black
			The colorspace attribute must be followed by a Quantize( ) method call for the change to take effect. The attribute may also be set directly from the Quantize( ) call, as in: $image->Quantize(colorspace=>'Gray');
dither	Yes	Yes	Most web browsers automatically dither an image whose colors do not exactly match those in its colormap. The dither attribute allows you to apply Floyd/Steinberg error diffusion, which may help smooth out the contours produced when sharply reducing colors. Note that dithering takes effect only if the image is color-quantized, which happens in one of two ways: • Explicitly, when you set the color attribute to the desired number of colors with the Quantize( ) method to reduce the number of colors in the image • Implicitly, when an image is converted from a file format that allows many colors to one that allows fewer (converting a JPEG to a GIF, for example)
gamma	Yes	No	Returns the image gamma value. Use the Gamma( ) method to actually apply a gamma value to the image pixels.
green_primary	Yes	Yes	Returns the chromaticity green primary point.
index	Yes	Yes	Allows you to access and change individual entries in the color table of an indexed image.
matte	Yes	Yes	The matte attribute is 1 if an image has transparent colors defined.
mattecolor	Yes	Yes	Indicates the color that is to be transparent.
maximum-error	Yes	No	Reflects the normalized maximum error per pixel introduced when reducing the number of colors in an image with method Quantize( ). The maximum error value gives one measure of how well the color reduction algorithm performed and how close the color-reduced image is to the original.
monochrome	Yes	Yes	Setting the monochrome attribute makes the image black and white.

Table 3-5. Color and transparency attributes (continued)

Attribute	Read	Write	Description
mean-error	Yes	No	Reflects the normalized mean error per pixel introduced when reducing the number of colors in an image with method Quantize( ). The mean error value gives one measure of how well the color reduction algorithm performed and how close the color-reduced image is to the original.
red_primary	Yes	Yes	Returns the chromaticity red primary point.
rendering_ intent	Yes	Yes	The rendering intent should be one of the following values: Undefined, Saturation, Perceptual, Absolute, or Relative.
total_colors	Yes	No	Use this attribute to get the total number of unique colors in an image. The returned value for a colormapped image is the number of colors in the image colormap.
white_point	Yes	Yes	This attribute returns the chromaticity white point. Set the value with 'x_value,y_value'.

The following methods control the colors or transparency of an image.

Channel( )

```
$image->Channel(colorname=>string )
```

This function returns a new grayscale image representing the intensity values of the specified channel of the image. The colorname parameter should be "Red", "Green", "Blue", or "Matte."

Gamma( )

```
$image->Gamma(gamma=>float,
          red=>float,
          green=>float,
          blue=>float)
```

The Gamma( ) method may be used to "gamma correct" an image for applications in which exact color matching is critical. The same image viewed on different workstations (a Macintosh versus a PC, for example) has perceptual differences in the way the color intensities are represented on the screen. To ensure accurate color reproduction, an image should be gamma-corrected for various platforms. You may specify individual gamma levels for the red, green, and blue channels, or you can adjust all three with the gamma parameter. Values should be in the range of 0.8 to 2.3. For example:

```
# Gamma correct an image for viewing on a Macintosh
$image->Gamma(gamma=>1.8);

# Set the gamma correction for the individual channels
$image->Gamma(red=>1.8, green=>2.2, blue=>1.9);
```

Gamma( ) can also be used to eliminate channels from an image by giving that channel a gamma value of 0.

Map( )

```
$image->Map(image=>image-object,
          dither=>{1, 0})
```

This method changes the colormap of the image to that of the image given as a parameter. This may be used to "synchronize" the colormaps of different images, or used with the special NETSCAPE template format to convert an image's colormap to the 216-color web-safe palette:

```
$websafe = Image::Magick->new;
$status = $websafe->Read('NETSCAPE:');
$image->Map(image=>$websafe, dither=1);      # dither to 216-color cube
```

MatteFloodfill( )

```
$image->MatteFloodfill(geometry=>geometry,
                    x=> integer, y=> integer,
                    matte=>{0..255}, bordercolor=> integer)
```

This changes the matte value (or alpha channel) of all the pixels in a region to the specified matte value. The region is determined by all those points that are contiguous neighbors of the point x, y of the same color. If the bordercolor option is provided, all neighboring pixels that are not of the specified color are considered part of the region to be filled.

Profile( )

```
$image->Profile(filename=>filename,
             profile=>{ 'ICC' | 'IPTC'} )
```

This function attaches an existing color profile (in the specified file) to the image file. This profile contains information about the display device on which the image was created, and is used by professional graphic arts software (e.g., Photoshop) that adapts the display information across devices with different characteristics. The color profile can be in one of two formats: the format specified by the International Color Consortium, or the one specified by the International Press Telecommunications Council.

Quantize( )

```
$image->Quantize(colors=>integer,
             colorspace=>string,
             treedepth=>integer,
             dither=>{1, 0})
```

The Quantize( ) method sets the maximum number of colors in an image. If the specified number of colors is less than the number of colors in the image, the size of the colormap is intelligently reduced to the new number. Setting the dither attribute causes the image to be dithered to more accurately represent colors.

The colors attribute allows you to specify the maximum number of colors that an image has after the Quantize( ) method is called. If an image has fewer unique colors, any duplicate or unused colors are removed from the colormap. The colorspace and dither attributes also affect the results of reducing the number of colors in an image. The default colorspace for color reduction is RGB; you may get better results by first changing the colorspace to YUV or YIQ.

The following example illustrates a way to preserve the transparency of an image when reducing the number of colors by first transforming the image to the Transparent colorspace:

```perl
#!/usr/bin/perl

use Image::Magick;

my $image = Image::Magick->new;
$image->Read('dog.gif');
$image->Transparent('#FFFFFF');

# Reduce to three colors, one of which is the transparent
#
$image->Quantize(colorspace=>'Transparent', colors=>3);
$x = $image->Display();
undef $image;
```

If you want to make the image black and white, set the number of colors to 2 and the colorspace to Gray. You can also set the dither attribute if you want black and white dithered approximations of colors.

See the descriptions of the colorspace and dither attributes in Table 3-5.

QueryColor( )

$image->QueryColor(*list*)

The QueryColor( ) function accepts one or more color names and returns their respective red, green, and blue color values as a comma-delimited string:

```perl
($red, $green, $blue) = split /,/, $image->QueryColor('PeachPuff'));
```

See Appendix B for a table of valid color names.

Segment( )

```
$image->Segment(colorspace=>string,
                cluster=>float,
                smooth=>float)
```

Segment( ) separates an image by analyzing the histograms of the color components and identifying units that are homogeneous.

Transparent( )

$image->Transparent(color=>*color*)

The Transparent( ) method makes all pixels of the given color transparent within the image. To make only certain areas of color transparent, use the Matte primitive with the

Draw( ) function. If you write the image to a file format that does not support transparency, the original color is written without the transparency information.

Note that each image in the sequence can be assigned a different transparency color. To make white the transparent color for the first image and black the transparent color for the second, use:

```
$image->[0]->Transparent('#FFFFFF');
$image->[1]->Transparent('#000000');
```

Multiple colors can be made transparent with repeated calls; to set both black and white to transparent in the first image of a sequence, try:

```
$image->[0]->Transparent('#FFFFFF');
$image->[0]->Transparent('#000000');
```

Annotation and Drawing

Image::Magick still sports some powerful drawing features that you may choose to use over GD's simple drawing API (see Chapter 2). In particular, Image::Magick has better text annotation capabilities, allowing you to use TrueType, PostScript, and X11 fonts. Additionally, you can query the metrics of those fonts for information that is necessary for more complicated text layouts. Table 3-6 lists the attributes associated with drawing and annotation.

Table 3-6. Annotation and drawing attributes

Attribute	Read	Write	Description
antialias	Yes	Yes	If a true value, use antialiasing when drawing or annotating an image.
font	Yes	Yes	The text annotation methods Annotate( ) and Draw( ) require a font. This can be a fully qualified X11 font (e.g., -*-helvetica-medium-r-*-*-12-*-*-*-*-*-iso8859-*), TrueType (e.g., @TimesRoman.ttf), or PostScript (e.g., Helvetica) font name. Image::Magick requires access to an X11 server, FreeType library, and Ghostscript to render X11, TrueType, and PostScript fonts, respectively.
stroke	Yes	No	Methods Annotate( ) and Draw( ) require a stroke color.

pixel	Yes	Yes	The pixel attribute returns the red, green, blue, and opacity value (or colormap index for colormapped images) at the given coordinate as four decimal numbers separated by commas. For example, if an image has a white pixel at (20,50), the following code:
			
			`@pixel = split /,/,`
			`$image->Get('pixel[20,50]');`
			`print "Red: $pixel[0]\nGreen: $pixel[1]\nBlue:`
			`$pixel[2]\nOpacity: $pixel[3]\n";`
			
			will print the following:
			
			`Red: 255`
			`Green: 255`
			`Blue: 255`
			`Opacity: 0`
			
			If you want to change a group of pixels, use the Draw( ) method with the Color primitive.

Table 3-6. Annotation and drawing attributes (continued)

Attribute	Read	Write	Description
pointsize	Yes	Yes	The pointsize attributes determines how large to draw a PostScript or True-Type font with the Annotate( ) or Draw( ) methods.

The following methods are used for drawing on images.

Annotate( )

```
$image->Annotate(text => {string | '@filename'},
                 font => string,
                 pointsize=>integer,
                 family=>string, style=>{Normal, Italic, Oblique, Any},
                 stretch=>{Normal, UltraCondensed, ExtraCondensed, Condensed,
                           SemiCondensed, SemiExpanded, Expanded,
                           ExtraExpanded, UltraExpanded},
                 weight=>integer,
                 density=>geometry,
                 align=>{Left, Center, Right}
                 stroke => colorname,
                 stroke_width => colorname,
                 fill => colorname,
                 box => colorname,
                 x => integer, y => integer, geometry => geometry,
                 gravity => {NorthWest, North, NorthEast, West,
                             Center, East, SouthWest, South, SouthEast},
                 antialias => boolean,
                 translate => geometry, scale => geometry, rotate => float,
                 skewX => float, skewY => float
)
```

Annotate( ) adds text to an image. The text may be represented as a string or as data from a file if the string has @ as the first character. If the text is larger than the current image size when rendered at the given point size, it is truncated to fit within the dimensions of the image.

Optionally, you can include any of the following bits of information about the image in the string by embedding the appropriate special characters, as shown in Table 3-7.

Table 3-7. Special annotation characters

Character	Description
\\n	Newline
\\r	Carriage return
\0xb43c	Unicode character
%b	The image file size in bytes
%c	The comment associated with the file
%d	The directory in which the image resides
%e	The extension of the image file

Table 3-7. Special annotation characters (continued)

Character	Description
%f	The filename of the image
%h	The image height
%i	The name of the file from which this image was read
%k	The number of unique colors in the image
%l	The label associated with the image
%m	The image file format
%n	The number of scenes in the file
%o	The output filename attribute
%p	The page number
%q	The quantum depth
%s	The scene number of the image
%t	The filename of the image file without the extension
%u	The temporary filename associated with the image
%w	The image width
%x	The x resolution
%y	The y resolution

The x and y coordinates (or the geometry attribute), along with the gravity attribute, define where the text is positioned (e.g., if a gravity of NorthWest is specified, the upper left corner of the bounding box is at x,y. Use the QueryFontMetrics( ) method to obtain information about the font that can be used to help position the text on the image. For example:

```
$image->Annotate(font => 'CenturySchL-Roma',
                  pointsize => 24,
                  stroke => 'red',
                  text => "here\nkitty\nkitty",
                  align => 'Center', y => 20
);
```

See also the example in the earlier section "The Basic Approach."

ColorFloodfill( )

```
$image->ColorFloodfill(geometry=>geometry,
                       x=>integer,
                       y=>integer,
                       fill=>color,
                       borderfill=>color)
```

This function fills a region with the specified color. The region is determined by all those points that are contiguous neighbors of the point x,y of the same color. If the borderfill option is provided, all neighboring pixels that are not of the specified color are considered part of the region to be filled.

Draw( )

```
$image->Draw(primitive=>string,
           points=>string,
           method=>{Point, Replace, Floodfill, FillToBorder, Reset},
           stroke=>colorname,
           fill=>colorname,
           tile=>image_object,
           strokewidth=>float,
           antialias=>boolean,
           bordercolor=>colorname,
           affine=>float_array,
           x=>float, y=>float,
           translate=>geometry,
           scale=>geometry, rotate=>float,
           skewX=>float, skewY=>float
)
```

The Draw( ) method allows you to draw anywhere on an image with one of many graphics primitives. The points parameter indicates the position to start drawing and must be a string of one or more coordinates, depending on the primitive being used. A coordinate string can look like any of these:

```
"3,5"                    # a single point
"10,10 20,20"            # two coordinates for a line, rectangle or circle
"40,40 80,80 50,80 90,40"  # four points for a polygon
```

Choose one of the following primitive types:

Bezier

> This draws a curved line whose points are written as a cubic Bezier curve, where each curved segment is defined by two points and a single control point. For example:

```
$image->Draw(primitive=>'Bezier',
           points=> "350,475 250,475 250,400 ".
                    "250,350 325,350 325,400",
           stroke=>'red',
           antialias=>1,
           linewidth=>1
        );
```

Circle

> The Circle primitive uses the first coordinate to define its center and the second coordinate to define a point on the edge. For example, to draw a circle centered at (100,100) that extends to (150,150), use:

```
# draw a fat circle of radius 50 centered at 100,100
$image->Draw(primitive=>'Circle',
           points=>'100,100 150,150',
           linewidth=>10);
```

Color

> Use Color to change the color of a pixel or area of pixels. This primitive takes a single coordinate for points and one of the following methods:

Point

> Re-colors the pixel with the stroke color.

Replace
> Re-colors any pixel that matches the color of the pixel at the given coordinate with the stroke color.

Floodfill
> Re-colors any pixel that matches the color of the pixel and is a neighbor of the given coordinate. This can be thought of as the Paintbucket method.

Reset
> Re-colors all the pixels in the image with the stroke color.

Ellipse
> This draws an ellipse, with the points string in the form "originX,originY width,height arcStart,arcEnd". For example:
>
> ```
> $image->Draw(primitive=>'Ellipse',
>               points=>'100,100 50,100 0,360');
> ```

Image
> The Image drawing primitive is similar in functionality to the Composite( ) method in that it allows you to overlay one image on another at a given coordinate. Composite( ) offers greater control over how the two images are composed.

Line
> The Line primitive draws a line between two given coordinates with the specified stroke color and line width.

Matte
> Use the Matte primitive to make a pixel or area of pixels transparent. Matte takes a single coordinate for points and one of the following methods:

Point
> Makes the given pixel transparent.

Replace
> Makes any pixel that matches the color of the pixel at the given coordinate transparent.

Floodfill
> Makes any pixel that matches the color of the pixel and is a neighbor of the pixel transparent.

Reset
> Makes all pixels in the image transparent.

Rectangle
> The Rectangle primitive draws a rectangle between the given upper left and lower right coordinates with the specified stroke color, line width, and fill color.

Path
> This draws a line where the points parameter may use the syntax defined for SVG images. See Chapter 6 for a complete description of the SVG path syntax.

Point
> This draws a point at the single specified coordinate.

Polygon

Use the Polygon primitive to draw a polygon with the given coordinates as vertices. A line (of given width and color) is drawn between the three or more coordinates provided. The last point is automatically connected to the first point to create a closed shape.

Polyline

A polyline is just like a polygon, except the first and last points are not automatically connected.

Text

Use the Text primitive to place text on an image at a given coordinate, similar to the Annotate( ) method. The text to be drawn is appended to the coordinate string given in the points parameter; if the string has embedded spaces or newline characters, enclose them in double quotes within the string:

```
'100,100 Yowza!'                # a string without embedded spaces
'100,100 "Yowza yowza yowza!"'  # a string with embedded spaces
```

Optionally, you can include bits of information about the image in the string by embedding the appropriate special characters as described in Table 3-7. For example:

```
$image->Draw(primitive=>'Text', points=>'50,50 "%m:%f %wx%h"' );
```

annotates the image with the string "beatniks:GIF 318x265" if $image is a 318×265 image that was read from a file titled *beatniks.gif*.

If the first character of the string is @, the text is read from a file whose name is in the rest of the string.

@filename

If the first character of the primitive string is @, a sequence of text or graphics primitives is read from a file whose name is the remainder of the string. For example:

```
$image->Draw(primitive=>'Circle',
        points=>'100,100 150,150 100,100 120,120 100,100 110,110');
```

is the same as:

```
Draw(primitive=>'@circles.txt');
```

where *circles.txt* is a file in the same directory that contains the following primitives:

```
Circle 100,100 150,150
Circle 100,100 120,120
Circle 100,100 110,110
```

Label( )

```
$image->Label(string)
```

This function adds a label to an image. This is a simplified alternative to Annotate( ); the label is centered underneath the image. Optionally, you can include bits of information about the image in the string by embedding any of the special characters in Table 3-7. For example:

```
$image->Label("%m:%f %wx%h");
```

creates a label for the image with the string "beatniks:GIF 318x265" if $image is a 318×265 image that was read from a file titled *beatniks.gif*.

QueryFont( )

`$image->QueryFont(font=>`*`fontname`*`)`

This function returns a list of information about the specified font. Use it in the following way:

```
my ($family, $alias, $description,
    $format, $weight, $glyphs, $metrics, $version) = QueryFont('Times-Roman');
```

If `QueryFont( )` is called without a parameter, it returns a list of all the available fonts.

QueryFontMetrics( )

`$image->QueryFontMetrics(text=>`*`string`*`,`
`                         size=>`*`float`*`,`
`                         x=>`*`integer`*`,`
`                         y=>`*`integer`*`,`
`                         font=>`*`fontname`*`)`

This function returns an array of information about the specified string as it is rendered with the specified font and size. The return values are:

width
> The width of an individual character expressed in pixels

height
> The height of an individual character expressed in pixels

ascender
> The height of the character's ascender

descender
> The length of the character's descender

text width
> The width of the string

text height
> The height of the string

max. horizontal advance
> The x value of the rightmost extent of the string

Filters and Effects

Another common task is applying filters to images to correct blurriness or to smooth out imperfections. A `Sharpen( )` filter, for example, can be applied to an image after it is resized to clean up some of the blurring effects of resampling. Some of the methods described in this section, such as `OilPaint( )`, `Whirl( )`, or `Implode( )`, can also be used to add special effects to an image.

The `Convolve( )` method is an all-purpose filter; many of the other filters utilize the `Convolve( )` routine with built-in presets. If you know what a convolution kernel is, you may want to experiment with your own filters (or add to the built-in ones) with this function.

The Mogrify( ) method is also interesting. It acts as an alternative interface to the API, where you can specify filter or other method names with a text string. The MogrifyRegion( ) method lets you apply a filter or effect to a limited area of the image.

The two attributes in Table 3-8 may be read or set for use with certain filter methods.

Table 3-8. Filter and effect attributes

Attribute	Read	Write	Description
fuzz	Yes	Yes	The fuzz distance is used by ImageMagick functions that operate on all pixels of a certain color (e.g., the Floodfill drawing option or the Crop( ) method). If the fuzz distance is not 0, colors within the fuzz distance of each other are treated as the same color.
texture	Yes	Yes	The texture attribute assigns the filename of a texture to be tiled onto the image background.

The following filters and special effects are built-in.

AddNoise( )

```
$image->AddNoise(noise=>string)
```

This function adds random noise to the image, where *string* specifies one of the following types: Gaussian, Multiplicative, Impulse, Laplacian, Poisson, or Uniform.

Average( )

```
$result = $image->Average( )
```

The Average( ) method averages the color values in a set of images and returns a new image.

Blur( )

```
$image->Blur(radius=>real,
             sigma=>real)
```

Blurs an image, where radius is the distance that each pixel with be blurred into its neighbors, and sigma is the standard deviation used in the blurring algorithm.

Border( )

```
$image->Border(geometry=>geometry,
               width=>integer,
               height=>integer,
               color=colorname)
```

This method surrounds the image with a border of color, or with the color indicated by the bordercolor attribute if no color is explicitly given. After the transformation, the image is 2*width pixels wider and 2*height pixels taller.

Charcoal( )

`$image->(order=>percentage)`

A special-effect filter that simulates a charcoal drawing.

Colorize( )

```
$image->Colorize(color=>color,
            fillcolor=>color)
```

This method changes all pixels of the specified color to the new color fillcolor.

Contrast( )

`$image->Contrast(sharpen=>{1, 0})`

Contrast( ) enhances the intensity differences between the lighter and darker elements of the image. Setting the sharpen parameter to 1 enhances the image, and setting it to 0 reduces the image contrast.

Convolve( )

`$image->Convolve(coefficients=>[ kernel_value_list ])`

This function applies a filter to an image. It takes a list of coefficients for a convolution kernel and applies this to the image. If you know what a convolution kernel is, you could try to apply a Bartlett filter with a 5×5 kernel:

```
$image->Convolve(coefficients=>[ 1, 2, 3, 2, 1,
                                 2, 4, 6, 4, 2,
                                 3, 6, 9, 6, 3,
                                 2, 4, 6, 4, 2,
                                 1, 2, 3, 2, 1 ]
            );
```

CycleColormap( )

`$image->CycleColormap(amount=>integer)`

CycleColormap( ) shifts an image's colormap by a given number of positions. This option is popular for creating psychedelic animations.

Despeckle( )

`$image->Despeckle( )`

Despeckle( ) reduces the number of noisy extra pixels in large areas of continuous color.

Edge( )

`$image->Edge(radius=>percentage)`

Edge( ) finds the edges in an image and enhances them (Figure 3-9, left).

Emboss( )

`$image->Emboss( )`

Emboss( ) applies a filter to the image, transforming it into a grayscale image with a three-dimensional effect similar to that created by an embossing die (Figure 3-9, right).

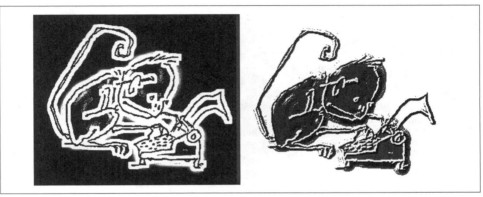

Figure 3-9. Edge (left) and Emboss (right)

Enhance( )

`$image->Enhance( )`

Enhance( ) applies a digital filter that improves the quality of a noisy image.

Equalize( )

`$image->Equalize( )`

This function performs a histogram equalization on the image. This enhances the contrast in all parts of the image, bringing out details.

Frame( )

```
$image->Frame(geometry=>geometry,
            width=>integer,
            height=>integer,
            inner=>integer,
            outer=>integer,
            color=>string)
```

Frame( ) adds a simulated 3D border around the image (see Figure 3-10). width and height specify the line width of the vertical and horizontal sides of the frame, respectively (geometry may be used as a shortcut for width and height). The inner and outer parameters indicate the line width of the inner and outer "shadows" of the frame; a wider shadow gives the effect of a deeper frame. Both the width and the height must be larger than the sum of the inner and outer values if the method is to work properly.

Note that the width and height of the frame are added to the dimensions of the image. To create a frame that maintains the original dimensions of the image, Crop( ) the image before applying the frame:

```
# Make a frame that hugs the inside border of an image,
# retaining its dimensions

my ($w, $h) = $image->Get('columns', 'rows');

# First crop the image
$image->Crop(width=>$w-20,          # width and height indicate the area
             height=>$h-20,         # to be cropped
             x=>10,                 # x and y indicate the offset
             y=>10);

# Now add the Frame
$image->Frame(width=>10,            # here width and height are the line widths
              height=>10,           # of the vertical and horizontal borders
              inner=>3,
              outer=>3,
              color=>'#FF0022');    # a reddish sort of color
```

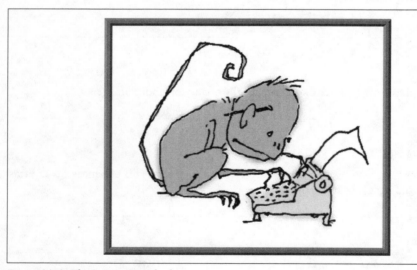

Figure 3-10. The Frame() method

Implode( )

$image->Implode(amount=>*percentage*)

Implode( ) applies a special-effect filter to the image where amount is a percentage indicating the amount of implosion. Use a negative percentage for an explosion effect (see Figure 3-11).

```
$image->Implode(.6);
```

Figure 3-11. Implode( ) with a positive value (left) and a negative value (right)

MedianFilter( )

$image->MedianFilter(radius=>*float*)

This function replaces each pixel in the image with the value of the mean average of all the pixels in the neighboring radius (Figure 3-12).

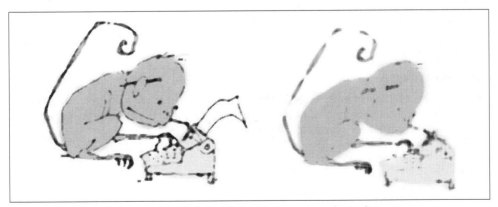

Figure 3-12. MedianFilter( ) with a radius of 2 (left) and a radius of 4 (right)

Modulate( )

```
$image->Modulate(brightness=>percentage,
                 saturation=>percentage,
                 hue=>percentage)
```

Modulate( ) lets you control the brightness, saturation, and hue of an image. Each parameter is in the form of a percentage of the current value for that parameter. For example, to decrease brightness by 10% and increase saturation by 50%, use:

```
$image->Modulate(brightness=>-10, saturation=>50);
```

Mogrify( )

```
$image->Mogrify(method_name,
                parameter_list)
```

The Mogrify( ) method is a convenience function that allows you to call any image manipulation method by giving it a method name as a string and a list of parameters to pass to the method. The following calls have the same result:

```
$image->Implode(factor=>50);
$image->Mogrify('Implode', factor=>50);
```

MogrifyRegion( )

```
$image->Mogrify(region_geometry,
                method_name,
                parameter_list)
```

MogrifyRegion( ) applies the Mogrify( ) method to the region of the image referred to by the geometry string. For example, if you wish to apply the OilPaint( ) filter to a 50×50 portion of the image starting at (10,10), you could use:

```
$image->MogrifyRegion('50x50+10+10', 'OilPaint', radius=>5);
```

Negate( )

```
$image->Negate(gray=>boolean)
```

Negate( ) flips each bit of every color in the colormap of the image, effectively negating the intensities of the three color channels (Figure 3-13, left). If the optional gray parameter is set to 1, only the grayscale pixels are inverted.

Normalize( )

```
$image->Normalize( )
```

The Normalize( ) method enhances the contrast of a color image by adjusting its colormap such that it spans the entire range of colors available.

OilPaint( )

`$image->OilPaint(radius=>`*`integer`*`)`

`OilPaint( )` applies a special-effect filter that simulates an oil painting by replacing each pixel in a circular region specified by the `radius` parameter with the most frequent color occurring in that region (Figure 3-13, right).

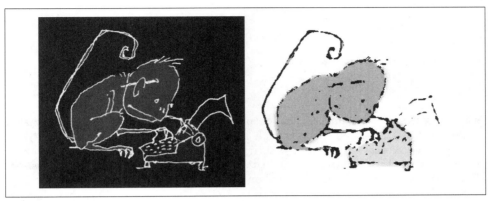

Figure 3-13. Negate( ) and OilPaint( )

Opaque( )

`$image->Opaque(color=>`*`color,`*
`            fill=>`*`color`*`)`

`Opaque( )` changes the entry corresponding to the color parameter in the image's colormap to the `fill` color. To change all the white pixels in an image to red, for example, use:

```
# Change all white pixels to red
$image->Opaque(color=>'white', fill=>'red');
```

Raise( )

`$image->Raise(geometry=>`*`geometry,`*
`            width=>`*`integer,`*
`            height=>`*`integer`*`)`

`Raise( )` creates a three-dimensional button-like effect by lightening and darkening the edges of the image (Figure 3-14, left).

```
$image->Raise('10x10');
```

ReduceNoise( )

`$image->ReduceNoise( )`

The ReduceNoise( ) method smooths the contours of an image while still preserving edge information. The algorithm works by analyzing 3×3 blocks of the image for "noisy" pixels and replacing these pixels with the best match in its surrounding 3×3 block. Use AddNoise( ) to add noise to an image.

Shade( )

```
$image->Shade(geometry=>geometry,
              azimuth=>integer,
              elevation=>float,
              color=>{1, 0})
```

Shade( ) creates an effect similar to that of Emboss( ) in that it gives the edges of the image a three-dimensional look and lights it with a distant light source (in fact, Emboss( ) is a special, enhanced case of the Shade( ) function). You may control the light source with the azimuth and elevation parameters; azimuth is measured in degrees off the x axis, and elevation is measured in "virtual pixels" on the (also virtual) z axis. The geometry parameter may be specified as a shortcut for azimuth × elevation. The Shade( ) effect is shown in Figure 3-14, right.

```
$image->Shade(azimuth => 60, elevation => 50, color => 0);
```

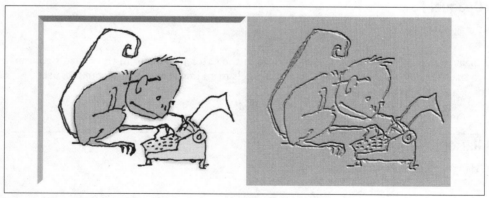

Figure 3-14. Raise( ) and Shade( )

Sharpen( )

`$image->Sharpen(factor=>percentage)`

Sharpen( ) enhances an image where factor is a percentage (0% to 99.9%) indicating the degree of sharpness.

Solarize( )

`$image->Solarize(factor=>`*`percentage`*`)`

Solarize( ) applies a special effect to the image, similar to the effect achieved in a photo darkroom by selectively exposing areas of photo-sensitive paper to light (as in the work of the surrealist photographer Man Ray). The factor attribute is a percentage (0% to 99.9%) indicating the extent of solarization.

Spread( )

`$image->Spread(amount=>`*`integer`*`)`

Spread( ) randomly displaces pixels within a block defined by the amount parameter (Figure 3-15, left).

Swirl( )

`$image->Swirl(degrees=>`*`float`*`)`

The Swirl( ) method swirls the pixels around the center of the image (Figure 3-15, right). The degrees parameter indicates the sweep of the arc through which each pixel is moved; a higher degree means a more distorted image.

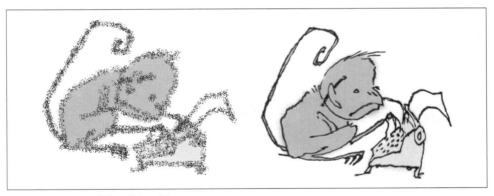

Figure 3-15. Spread() and Swirl()

Texture( )

`$image->Texture(filename=>`*`string`*`)`

Texture( ) reads an image file and applies it in a tiled pattern as a "texture" to the background of the image.

Threshold( )

`$image->Threshold(threshold=>`*`integer`*`)`

Threshold( ) changes the value of individual pixels based on the intensity of each pixel. There are two cases:

1. If the intensity of a pixel is of greater intensity than the threshold parameter, the pixel is set to the value of the maximum intensity in the image.
2. If the intensity of a pixel is of lesser intensity than the threshold parameter, the pixel is set to the value of the minimum intensity in the image.

The resulting image is a high-contrast, two-color image in the RGB colorspace. The effects of this method within different colorspaces may vary.

Wave( )

```
$image->Wave(geometry=>geometry,
             amplitude=>float,
             wavelength=>float)
```

The Wave( ) filter creates a "ripple" effect in the image by shifting the pixels vertically along a sine wave whose amplitude and wavelength are specified by the given parameters.

## CHAPTER 4

Charts and Graphs with GD::Graph

GD::Graph is a Perl module that expands on the capabilities of GD by offering an API for creating graphs and charts. For a long time, almost all the financial graphs or web server load graphs that you could find on the Web were generated by this module. GD::Graph started life as GIFGraph; the name changed when the module was modified to work with the later versions of GD that did not generate GIF files. This chapter illustrates various ways of working with GD::Graph and GD to produce charts and graphs with lines, bars, points, pies, and more.

Let's Make Some Graphs!

The GD::Graph package was written by Martien Verbruggen. It should run on any operating system on which the GD module is available. GD::Graph uses the GD module for all of its drawing and file primitives, and also relies on the GD::TextUtil package. Both packages are available from CPAN at *http://www.cpan.org/authors/id/ MVERB/*.

Graph construction with GD::Graph can be broken into three phases. First you need to gather the data, parse it, and organize it in a form that you can pass to the graph drawing routines. Then you set the attributes of the graph such that it will come out the way you want it. Finally, you draw the graph with the plot() method.

The data for the graph must be in a very particular form before you plot the graph. The plotting methods expect a reference to an array, where the first element is a reference to an anonymous array of the x-axis values, and any subsequent elements are data sets to be plotted against the y axis. A sample data collection looks like this:

```
#!/usr/bin/perl -w

use GD;         # for font names
use GD::Graph::lines;
my @data = ( [ qw(1955 1956 1957 1958
                1959 1960 1961 1962
                1963 1964 1965 1966
```

```
        1967 1968 1969 1970
        1971 1972 1973 ) ],    # timespan of data

# thousands of people in New York
[ 2,   5,   16.8,  18, 19, 22.6, 26, 32, 34, 39,
  43, 48, 49, 49, 54.2, 58, 68, 72, 79 ],

# thousands of people in SF
[ 11,   18,   29.4,  35.7, 36, 38.2, 36, 41, 45, 49,
  50, 51, 51.4, 52.6, 53.2, 54, 67, 73, 78 ],

# thousands of people in Peoria
[ 5,   8,   24,   32, 37, 40, 50, 55, 61, 63,
  61, 60, 65.5, 68, 71, 69, 73, 73.5, 78, 78.5],

# thousands of people in Seattle
[ 4.25,   8.9, 19, 21, 25, 24, 27, 29, 33, 35,
  41, 40, 45, 42, 44, 49, 51, 58, 61, 66],

# thousands of people in Tangiers
[ 2,   11,   9,   9.2, 9.8, 10.1, 8.2, 8.5, 9, 7,
  6, 5.5, 6.5, 5.2, 4.5, 4.2, 4, 3, 2, 1 ],

# thousands of people in Moscow
[ 3.5,   8,   22,   22.5, 23, 25, 25, 25, 26, 21,
  20, 19.2, 19.7, 21, 18, 23, 17, 12, 10, 5],

# thousands of people in Istanbul
[ 6.5,   12.8,   31.7,   34, 32, 29, 19, 20.5, 28, 35,
  34, 33, 30, 28, 25, 21, 20, 16, 11, 9]
    );
```

You can use the GD::Graph::Data module to help reorganize your data if it's in a different format (an example is shown later in this section). If your data set doesn't have data for each point, use undef for those points without data.

GD::Graph implements eight different types of graphs: area, bars, hbars, lines, lines and points, points, mixed, and pie graphs (see Figure 4-1 for samples of each of these graph types). To create a new graph that connects all the data points with different colored lines, start with:

```
my $graph = new GD::Graph::lines( );
```

Each graph type has many attributes that may be used to control the format, color, and content of the graph. Use the set( ) method to configure your graph:

```
$graph->set(
        title               => "America's love affair with cheese",
        x_label             => 'Time',
        y_label             => 'People (thousands)',
        y_max_value         => 80,
        y_tick_number       => 8,
        x_all_ticks         => 1,
        y_all_ticks         => 1,
```

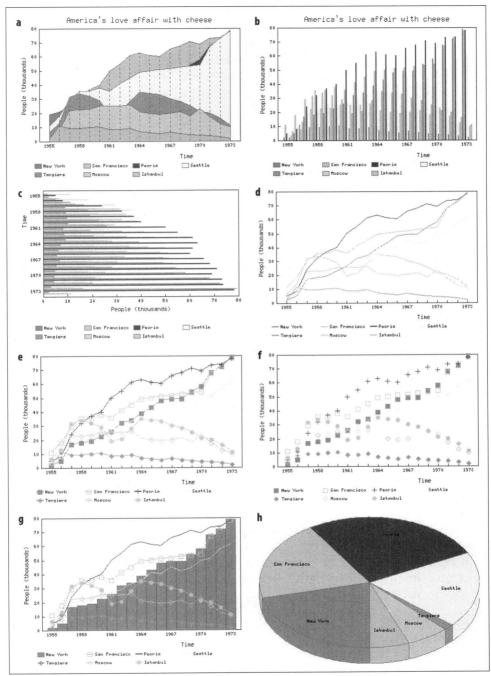

Figure 4-1. 8 kinds of graphs: a) area; b) bars; c) hbars; d) lines; e) linespoints; f) points; g) mixed; h) pie chart

```
        x_label_skip      => 3,
    );

$graph->set_legend_font(GD::gdFontTiny);
$graph->set_legend('New York', 'San Francisco', 'Peoria',
                   'Seattle', 'Tangiers', 'Moscow', 'Istanbul');
```

Finally, draw the graph with the plot( ) method, which creates a graph and returns a GD object. Use the GD object to create a PNG image:

```
my $gd = $graph->plot( \@data );

open OUT, ">cheese.png" or die "Couldn't open for output: $!";
binmode(OUT);
print OUT $gd->png( );
close OUT;
```

The mixed chart is a special type that combines different charting methods within the same frame. In the next example, we'll use a mixed area-and-bars chart to communicate a year's worth of stock activity for the fictional Shemp company. It graphs three values for each day in the year: the stock's high value, low value, and volume. Then we'll do a little graphical sleight-of-hand to make the high and low values look like one jagged line that varies in thickness to demonstrate the volatility of the price—the thicker the line, the greater the difference between the high and low. The output is shown in Figure 4-2.

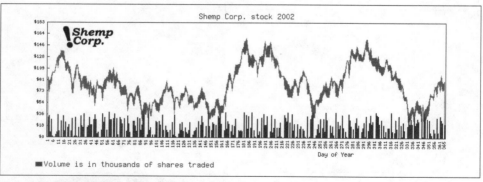

Figure 4-2. A stock graph using the mixed chart type

This example also shows the use of the GD::Graph::Data module as a cleaner alternative for specifying chart data. First we create a new GD::Graph::Data object, which can read in data from a previously created file:

```
#!/usr/bin/perl -w
#
# A mixed stock graph

use strict;
use GD;
```

```
use GD::Graph::Data;
use GD::Graph::mixed;

# Read in the data from a file

my $data = GD::Graph::Data->new( );
$data->read(file => 'stock_data.dat');
```

where the *stock_data.dat* file is in the format:

```
1       96      80      32
2       89      72      34
3       90      86      8
4       98      84      28
5       104     103     2
...etc...
```

The default delimiter between each field of this file is a tab; you can set the `delimiter` parameter to use a different delimiter string. The first field on each line is the x value, followed by the y values for high, low, and volume. Look at the documentation for the GD::Graph::Data module for more methods to help you manage data.

The next step is to create the graph and set the various attributes. The `types` attribute assigns a different chart type to each of the data sets. The `dclrs` attribute assigns a color to each data set. For an area graph, the space underneath the curve of the graph is shaded with the specified color. The daily high value is drawn first in solid red, followed by the daily low in white. The low value acts as a mask, so that only the y values between the low and the high are drawn in red. The daily volume is charted along the bottom as a blue bar graph.

```
my $graph = new GD::Graph::mixed(900, 300) or die "Can't create graph!";

# Set the general attributes

$graph->set(
        title           => "Shemp Corp. stock 2002",
        types           => [qw(area area bars)],
        dclrs           => [qw(red white blue)],
        transparent     => 0,
);

# Set the attributes for the x-axis

$graph->set(
        x_label         => 'Day of Year',
        x_label_skip    => 5,
        x_labels_vertical => 1,
);
```

The range of y-axis values is determined by a function of the GD::Graph::Data module that returns the minimum and maximum values of each data set. When plotting each y-axis label, use a special feature of the y_number_format attribute. If this attribute is set to a reference to a subroutine, each y-axis label is passed to the routine, and the returned value is used as the label. In this case, we add a dollar sign to each label and round off fractional values:

```
$graph->set(
        y_max_value       => ($data->get_min_max_y_all())[1]+25,
        y_tick_number     => 10,
        y_all_ticks       => 1,
        y_number_format   => sub { '$'.int(shift); },
);
```

The *legend* is a string that describes each of the various data sets. Here we only need to make a note about the scale used for the volume graph, so the legends for the first two data sets are assigned undef.

```
# Set the legend

$graph->set_legend(undef, undef, 'Volume is in thousands of shares traded');
$graph->set_legend_font(gdLargeFont);
$graph->set(legend_placement => 'BL');

# Plot the data

my $gd = $graph->plot( $data ) or die "Can't plot graph";
```

If you wanted to add a little graphical logo to a corner of the graph, you would typically use the `logo` attribute to assign a PNG file for the logo. However, the `copyResized()` method (used by GD::Graph to apply logos) was broken in the beta version of the GD module I was using when I wrote this book. It's easy enough to reimplement logo insertion with GD, though. Since we've already plotted the graph, we have a GD object ready for use:

```
my $logo = GD::Image->newFromPng('shempcorp.png');
my ($w, $h) = $logo->getBounds();
$gd->copy($logo, 50, 25, 0, 0, $w, $h);

# Write the PNG

print $gd->png();
```

The pie chart is a bit different from the other graph types. The next example uses pie charts as elements that are pieced together into a larger information graphic using GD. The five pie charts are drawn with GD::Chart.

We've collected data on the seven deadly sins in five New England cities, each of which will have its own pie chart showing the particular weaknesses of that community. Each pie chart will be placed near the city on the map and is sized proportionately according to the population of the city (see Figure 4-3).

To do this, we first set up a data structure that encapsulates the data for each city. A big hash works fine for this:

```
#!/usr/bin/perl -w
#
```

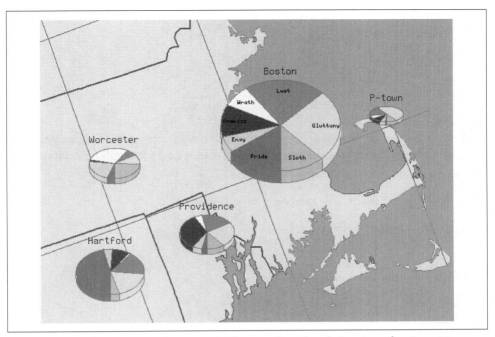

Figure 4-3. An information graphic using pie charts to show the relative vices of various cities

```perl
# Pie charts on a map

use GD;
use GD::Graph::pie;

# The sins

my $pie_labels = [ qw(Pride Envy Avarice
                      Wrath Lust Gluttony Sloth)];
my %cities = (
    'Boston' => { size => 175,
                  x => 260,
                  y => 100,
                  data => [24, 9, 18, 12, 35, 40, 19] },
    'Providence' => {
                  size => 80,
                  x => 200,
                  y => 300,
                  data => [5, 10, 60, 8, 35, 40, 19] },
    'Hartford' => {
                  size => 100,
                  x => 50,
                  y => 350,
                  data => [100, 9, 18, 2, 35, 40, 9] },
    'Worcester' => {
                  size => 75,
```

```
                    x => 70,
                    y => 200,
                    data => [2, 9, 1, 12, 3, 4, 10] },
        'P-town' => {
                    size => 50,
                    x => 475,
                    y => 140,
                    data => [2, 9, 18, 12, 35, 90, 19] },
    );
```

Next we read the previously created image of the map into a new GD image. Then, we loop through the keys of the city hash and create a new pie graph for each data set.

```
my $map = GD::Image->newFromPng('map.png');

# Loop through the cities, creating a graph for each

foreach my $city (keys(%cities)) {
    my $size = $cities{$city}->{'size'};

    my $graph = new GD::Graph::pie($size,$size)
        or die "Can't create graph!";
    $graph->set( transparent     => 1,
                 suppress_angle => 360*($size<150),
                 '3d'           => 1,
                 title          => $city,
        );
```

The suppress_angle attribute is unique to the pie chart type. If this attribute is non-zero, the label for a particular piece of pie is not drawn if the angle is less than this value. If the angle is 360, no pie labels are produced. This code suppresses labels for pie charts that are smaller than 150 pixels in diameter.

Next, we plot the pie chart, then place it on the map with GD's copy( ) method.

```
    # Plot the graph

    my $gd = $graph->plot([ $pie_labels,
                            $cities{$city}->{'data'} ])
        or die "Can't plot graph";

    # Copy the graph onto the map at the specified coordinate

    my ($w, $h) = $graph->gd()->getBounds();
    $map->copy($graph->gd(),
            $cities{$city}->{'x'},
            $cities{$city}->{'y'},
            0, 0, $w, $h);
}
```

When all five pies have been added, we print out the composite map as a PNG to STDOUT.

```
    # Print the map to STDOUT

    print $map->png();
```

The following section collects the concepts developed here into a complete working application.

A Sample GD::Graph Application

As an example of using GD::Graph, we'll implement a web-based biorhythm server. The general idea of biorhythms is that cyclic processes in nature (seasonal changes, and particularly the changing phases of the moon) are reflected in the processes of the human body. Although they have no real basis in scientific study, these cyclic patterns have captured people's imaginations for years. You can even get your biorhythm read by coin-operated machines at many rest stops on America's highways.

Here's how the biorhythm server works. First, a user enters her birth date, and a range of dates for the biorhythm report. These are submitted via a CGI script to a Perl script that creates a graph for the three primary biorhythm patterns: physical, emotional, and intellectual. These three patterns unfold as sine waves starting from the date of birth, with periods of 23 days for the physical cycle, 28 days for the emotional cycle, and 33 days for the intellectual cycle. The biorhythmic cycles are defined based upon these numbers.

The *biopage.cgi* script (Example 4-1) builds the HTML page, including the form used to enter the data for the script. It then passes the data to the *biorhythm.cgi* script (Example 4-2), which uses the GD::Graph module to create a biorhythm chart from the data and sends it to the browser as a PNG image data stream. The *biopage.cgi* script is accessed for the first time without any data fields with the URL *http://www.yoururl.com/cgi-bin/biopage.cgi*.

Example 4-1. Generating the HTML for biorhythm graphing example

```perl
#!/usr/local/bin/perl
#
# Example 4-1. biopage.cgi
#
use GD;
use CGI;

# First get the parameters passed into the script
# Use the CGI module to parse the CGI form submission.

my $q = new CGI;
my $dob = $q->param('dob');
my $start = $q->param('start');
my $end = $q->param('end');

# Use the CGI module to create the HTML for the page
# Print the header and opening tags

print $q->header(-type => 'text/html');
print $q->start_html(-title => "Biorhythm!");
```

Example 4-1. Generating the HTML for biorhythm graphing example (continued)

```
if ($dob && $start && $end) {

    # Output the html for the image tag. This passes the data
    # on to the bio.cgi script to generate the image data.

    print $q->h1("Your biorhythm from $start to $end");
    print $q->img({ src => "biorhythm.cgi?".
                           "dob=$dob&start=$start&end=$end",
                  width => 500, height => 300 });
    print $q->br;

} else {

    # In this case, no data has been passed to the script; this
    # may be because this is the first invocation of the script or
    # blank fields were submitted. We can just print an
    # appropriate headline...

    print $q->h1('Get your biorhythms here!');
}

# Print the form used to enter the dates

print $q->start_form({ method => 'post',
                       action => 'biopage.cgi' }),

    "Date of Birth:",

    $q->input({ type => 'text',
                name => 'dob',
                size => 10,
                value => $dob }),

    "Calculate biorhythms from  ",

    $q->input({ type => 'text',
                name => 'start',
                size => 10,
                value => $start }),
    " to ",

    $q->input({ type => 'text',
                name => 'end',
                size => 10,
                value => $end }),
    $q->input({ type => 'submit',
                value => 'Give me my biorhythm!' }),
    $q->end_form(),
    $q->end_html();
```

The HTML page that is output from this script is shown in Figure 4-4.

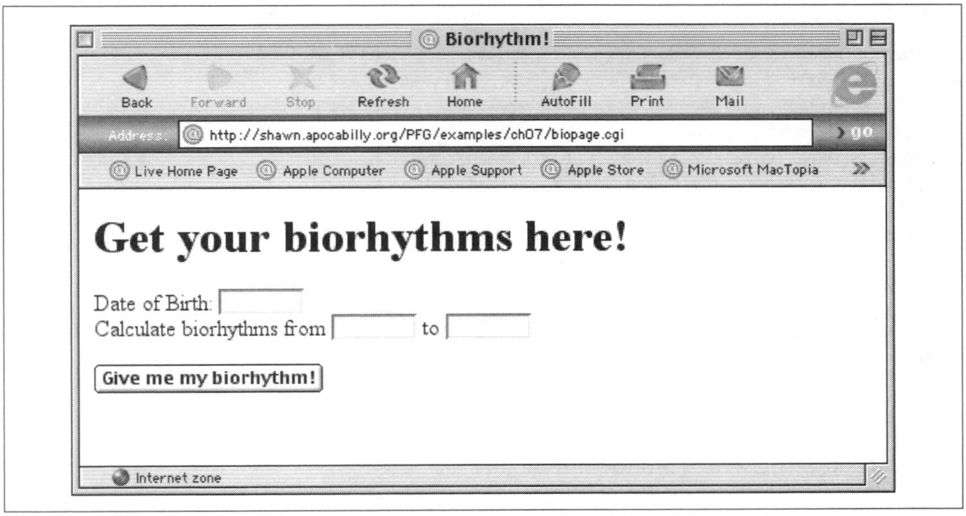

Figure 4-4. Accessing biopage.cgi for the first time

When a user enters data into the form fields and hits the Submit button, the *biopage. cgi* script is called again with the new data. Assuming the user has entered valid data, it creates a new HTML page with an embedded IMG tag that calls the *biorhythm.cgi* script to generate the graph.

The *biorhythm.cgi* script (Example 4-2) is the one that actually does the graphical grunt work. It uses the GD::Graph::bars module to plot the bar graph, and the Date:: Calc module to perform the required date calculations. Date::Calc must be installed on the system running the script.

The script first uses the CGI module to get the date of birth, start date, and end date parameters that were passed from the form. It then calculates the number of days between the start and end dates and the number of days between the date of birth and the start date.

Example 4-2. Dynamically generating a biorhythm bar graph from form data

```perl
#!/usr/local/bin/perl -w
#
# Example 4-2. biorhythm.cgi

use GD::Graph::bars;
use Date::Calc;
use CGI;

# We'll need a good value for Pi later

my $pi = 4 * atan2(1,1);

my $query = new CGI;
```

Example 4-2. Dynamically generating a biorhythm bar graph from form data (continued)

```
my @dob = Date::Calc::Decode_Date_US($query->param('dob'));
my @start = Date::Calc::Decode_Date_US($query->param('start'));
my @end = Date::Calc::Decode_Date_US($query->param('end'));

my $days = Date::Calc::Delta_Days(@start, @end);
my $dobdiff = Date::Calc::Delta_Days(@dob, @start);

my @xvalues;

foreach my $day (0..$days) {
    # Add_Delta_days returns a date offset from the start date.
    # It returns a list in the form (yyyy, mm, dd)

    push @xvalues, (Date::Calc::Add_Delta_Days(@start,$day))[2];
}
```

The output of this script is shown in Figure 4-5.

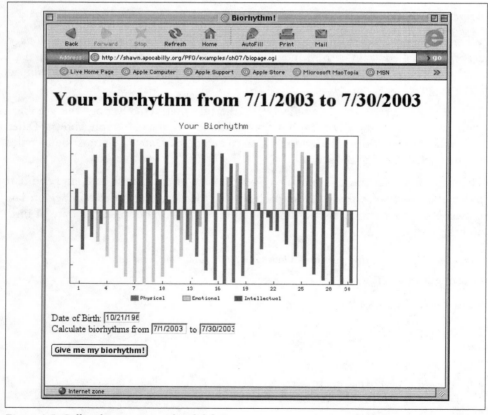

Figure 4-5. Calling biopage.cgi with valid data

The algorithm for creating the data set is relatively simple. Because the sine function starts at y=0 for the user's date of birth and continues oscillating through its cycle as time advances, the function has a certain starting value at the starting date of the range. The offset value is the number of days that the function has progressed into its cycle at the date indicated by $start. It can be calculated by finding the difference between the start date and the date of birth, dividing by the period, and taking the remainder.

The period of the sine wave for the p, e, and i sets are 23 days, 28 days, and 33 days, respectively. To compute the value at a particular day, we must first "shift" the sine wave to get the correct starting value, instead of computing every value from the person's birth date to the present. This shift is accomplished by adding the remainder of $dobdiff divided by the period of the wave as an offset. Note that the sin( ) function expects a value expressed in radians:

```perl
my (@pvalues, @evalues, @ivalues);

foreach my $count (0..$days) {
    push @pvalues, sin((($count+($dobdiff % 23))/23) * 2 * $pi);
    push @evalues, sin((($count+($dobdiff % 28))/28) * 2 * $pi);
    push @ivalues, sin((($count+($dobdiff % 33))/33) * 2 * $pi);
}

# Create a new bar graph

my $graph = new GD::Graph::bars(500,300);
```

Next, set the attributes. The y values represent nonquantitative "good" and "bad" values, so we won't plot numerical values on the y axis. Since we are using a bar graph, we want the x-axis labels along the bottom edge of the graph so it doesn't get messy (zero_axis_only).

```perl
# Set the attributes for the graph

$graph->set(
    x_label          => '',            # No labels
    y_label          => '',
    title            => 'Your Biorhythm',
    y_plot_values    => 0,
    y_max_value      => 1,             # sine range is -1 to 1
    y_min_value      => -1,
    y_tick_number    => 8,
    long_ticks       => 0,             # use short ticks on axes
    x_label_skip     => 3,             # print every third x label
    zero_axis        => 0,
    zero_axis_only   => 0,
);

# Add the legend to the graph

$graph->set_legend('Physical', 'Emotional', 'Intellectual');
```

```
# Plot the graph and write it to STDOUT

print STDOUT $query->header(-type => 'image/png');
binmode STDOUT;                          # switch to binary mode
my $gd = $graph->plot( [ \@xvalues,
                         \@pvalues,
                         \@evalues,
                         \@ivalues ] );
print STDOUT $gd->png;
```

You should now have a workable biorhythm server at this point—something every web site should have!

GD::Graph Methods

The following methods are applicable to any of the eight types of graphs.

gd( )

`$gd_obj = $graph->gd( )`

GD::Graph uses the GD module for its image generation capability. To gain access to the underlying GD::Image object, use the gd( ) method. This can be useful for compositing graphs with other images using GD, or using GD's drawing primitives directly on the graph.

new( )

```
$graph = new GD::Graph::area([width, height])
$graph = new GD::Graph::bars([width, height])
$graph = new GD::Graph::hbars([width, height])
$graph = new GD::Graph::lines([width, height])
$graph = new GD::Graph::linespoints([width, height])
$graph = new GD::Graph::points([width, height])
$graph = new GD::Graph::mixed([width, height])
$graph = new GD::Graph::pie([width, height])
```

The new( ) method creates a new graph object. The *width* and *height* parameters are optional; if they are not set, the graph is created with a default width of 400 pixels and height of 300 pixels. GD::Graph implements eight different kinds of graphs:

GD::Graph::area
   A graph with lines connecting the data points and the area under the line filled with a color.

GD::Graph::bars
   A graph where the data is represented as vertical bars.

GD::Graph::hbars
   A graph where the data is represented as horizontal bars.

GD::Graph::lines
   A graph with lines connecting the data points. Use a linespoints graph (described next) to plot the data points as well as the lines.

GD::Graph::linespoints
> A graph with lines connecting visible data points.

GD::Graph::points
> A graph with only the data points plotted.

GD::Graph::mixed
> A composite graph where each data set may be plotted using a different graph type (area, bars, lines, or linespoints).

GD::Graph::pie
> A graph where points in the data set are represented as slices of a pie.

plot( )

GD::Graph::plot(\@*data*)

The plot( ) method takes a data set, plots it according to the type of the graph object and the values of the attributes that have been set, and returns a GD::Image object containing the image. This object can then be output using any of the GD writing methods (see Chapter 2). Note that the data set is passed as a reference to an array. That array contains array references; the innermost array represents the values for the x axis, and each array after that represents a different set of y values to be plotted.

For example, the following data generates a graph with the month names on the x axis and two sets of numbers plotted against the y axis:

```
@data = (
    [ qw(JAN FEB MAR APR MAY JUN JUL AUG SEP OCT NOV DEC) ],
    [ 5,   8,   24,   32,   12,   18,   11,   21,   22,  9,   29,  16 ],
    [ 6.5,  12.8,  31.7,  3,   9,   15,   14.8,  21.2,  7,
       9.9, 10,   7.2 ]
);
print $graph->plot(\@data)->png( );
```

If the arrays are not set up correctly (for example, if they are not all the same length), Perl returns a fatal "length misfit" error. The data sets may be padded with undef values if the values are not to be plotted.

can_do_ttf( )

GD::Graph::can_do_ttf( );

This method returns true if the local version of GD has been installed with TrueType support. If so, you can use TrueType fonts in GD::Graph; otherwise, you are limited to GD's built-in bitmapped fonts.

get( )

@attributes = GD::Graph::get(*attribute1, attribute2* ...)

This method returns a list of the current values for all specified attributes. These attributes are explained in detail in the next section, "Attributes of GD::Graph Objects."

get_hotspot( )

`@hotspots = GD::Graph::get_hotspot([$dataset_index], [$point_index])`

The GD::Graph::Map module allows you to define "hotspots" so that the graph can be used as an HTML image map. The result is a list that can be used to construct an image map description file. If you specify both the data set index and a point within that data set, you are given a list like the following:

```
('rect', x, y, w, h )
```

If you provide only a data set index, you get a list of references to lists, one for each point in the data set:

```
( ['rect', x1, y1, w1, h1 ], ['rect', x2, y2, w2, h2 ], ... )
```

Similarly, if you fail to specify a data set or a point, you are returned a description for every point in every data set:

```
( [ ['rect', x11, y11, w11, h11 ],
    ['rect', x12, y12, w12, h12 ], ... ],
  [ ['rect', x21, y21, w21, h21 ],
    ['rect', x22, y22, w22, h22 ], ...], ... )
```

For each data point in a bar graph, a rectangular region description is returned. For a line graph, a line description is returned. For points graphs, a rectangular or circular region is returned. For area or pie graphs, a polygonal region is returned.

set( )

`GD::Graph::set(attribute1 => value1, attribute2 => value2 ...)`

The set method allows you to change the values of one or more attributes of a graph object. The attribute definitions should be passed as key/value pairs. For example, to change the point size of the line width of a graph with lines, use:

```
$linegraph->set( line_width => 4 );
```

Many of the attributes are applicable only to certain types of graphs; a pie chart has different attributes than a chart with axes, for example. These attributes are explained in detail in the "Attributes of GD::Graph Objects" section.

set_label_font( ), set_value_font( )

```
GD::Graph::set_label_font(fontname)
GD::Graph::set_value_font(fontname)
```

These methods may be applied only to pie charts. They allow you to set the font used to label the slices of a pie graph. Valid *fontname* values are gdSmallFont, gdLargeFont, gdMediumBoldFont, gdTinyFont, and gdGiantFont. If you wish to use a TrueType font, the *fontname* argument should be the pathname to a TrueType font file. If this is a relative path, it is relative to the path of the script.

```
$graph->set_label_font(gdLargeFont);
```

set_legend( )

GD::Graph::set_legend(@legend_keys)

A legend is a key that appears along the bottom or right side of a graph and gives a label for the color of each data set. If the set_legend( ) method is used to assign a list of legend strings to a graph, they appear centered under the x axis. The elements of the *@legend_keys* list correspond to the individual data sets described in the list sent to the plot( ) routine. Undefined or empty legend keys are skipped. See the stock graph example at the beginning of this chapter for an example of the use of set_legend( ).

```
$graph->set_legend('High', undef, 'Volume');
$graph->set_legend_font(gdLargeFont);
$graph->set(legend_placement => 'BR');
```

set_legend_font( )

GD::Graph::set_legend_font(*fontname*)

This method sets the font for the legend text. The *fontname* parameter can be any valid GD font name; the default is gdTinyFont. You must import the GD module first. If you wish to use a TrueType font, the *fontname* argument should be the pathname to a TrueType font file.

set_text_clr( )

GD::Graph::set_text_clr(*colorname*)

This method sets the color to be used for all of the text within a graph. The *colorname* must be a valid GD::Graph color name (see "Colors and Fonts in GD::Graph" later in this chapter). You can also set the colors of individual elements of a graph separately with the set( ) method and the attributes textclr, labelclr, and axislabelclr.

For example:

```
# dgreen is the same as #007F00
$somegraph->set_text_clr( 'dgreen' );
```

set_title_font( )

GD::Graph::set_title_font(*fontname*)

This method sets the font to be used for the title of the graph. The *fontname* parameter should be one of gdSmallFont, gdLargeFont, gdMediumBoldFont, gdTinyFont, or gdGiantFont. The default is gdLargeFont. Note that in order to use these fonts, you must first import the GD module with the command use GD. If you wish to use a TrueType font, the *fontname* argument should be the pathname to a TrueType font file.

set_x_label_font( ), set_y_label_font( ), set_x_axis_font( ), set_y_axis_font( )

```
GD::Graph::set_x_label_font(fontname)
GD::Graph::set_y_label_font(fontname)
GD::Graph::set_x_axis_font(fontname)
GD::Graph::set_y_axis_font(fontname)
```

These methods may be used only on graphs with axes (i.e., any graph but a pie chart). They allow you to set the font used to label the x and y axes, and the font used to label the individual values on each axis. Valid *fontname* values are gdSmallFont, gdLargeFont, gdMediumBoldFont, gdTinyFont, and gdGiantFont. The default font for the labels is gdSmallFont, and the default font for the axis values is gdTinyFont. Note that in order to use these fonts, you must first import the GD module with the command use GD. If you wish to use a TrueType font, the *fontname* argument should be the pathname to a TrueType font file.

Attributes of GD::Graph Objects

GD::Graph has several attributes that you can set to control the layout, color, and labels on your graph. Some of these attributes are applicable only to certain types of graphs; for example, the pie_height attribute should be set only for graphs of type GD::Graph::pie. These attributes are relegated to their own sections later in this chapter. The following section describes the attributes shared by all graphs.

Attributes of All Graphs

b_margin=>*integer*
t_margin=>*integer*
l_margin=>*integer*
r_margin=>*integer*

> These attributes allow you to set the bottom, top, left, and right margins, respectively. The margin is defined as the blank space between the bounding box of the graph and the edge of the PNG graphic. The default margins are 0 pixels.

width=>*integer*
height=>*integer*

> The dimensions of the final image, including margins.

transparent=>*boolean*

> If the transparent attribute is set to true, the background color (set with the bgclr attribute) is marked as transparent. The default value is true.

interlaced=>*boolean*

> The interlaced attribute allows you to indicate whether the graph is stored as an interlaced PNG. The default value is true.

```
bgclr=>colorname
fgclr=>colorname
boxcolor=>colorname
textclr=>colorname
labelclr=>colorname
axislabelclr=>colorname
legendclr=>colorname
valuesclr=>colorname
accentclr=>colorname
shadowclr=>colorname
```
These attributes set the colors of the various aspects of the graph: the background, foreground, graph box, text, label, axis label, legend, value label, accent, and shadow colors, respectively. The colorname should be a valid GD::Graph color name (see the upcoming section "Colors and Fonts in GD::Graph").

dclrs=>\@colornames

The dclrs (data colors) attribute controls the colors for the bars, lines, markers, or pie slices. The attribute should be given a reference to an array containing the desired set of color names. The first line/point/bar/slice is the color of the first element in the array, the second is the color of the second element, and so on. For example, if you set dclrs to the following array of color names:

```
$graph->set(dclrs => ['green', 'red', 'blue')]);
```

the first data set is green, the second is red, the third is blue, the fourth is green, the fifth red, and so on. That is, if you have more data sets than colors, colors are reused in order.

The default value is:

```
'lred', 'lgreen', 'lblue', 'lyellow', 'lpurple', 'cyan', 'lorange'
```

show_values=>boolean | array_ref

Set this attribute to a true value to draw the data value above each plotted data point. For greater control of the individual labels, you can assign this a reference to a data set, which is used for the corresponding value labels. Note that you may need to manually adjust the dimensions of the image to accommodate all data value labels. For example, set this attribute with some of the data at the beginning of this chapter:

```
$graph->set(show_values => 1 );
```

to produce the graph in Figure 4-6.

values_vertical=>boolean

If the show_values attribute is true, this attribute indicates whether the labels should be drawn vertically rather than horizontally. The default is 0 (horizontal).

values_space=>integer

If the show_values attribute is true, this attribute specifies the amount of vertical space between the data point and the value label. The default value is 4 pixels.

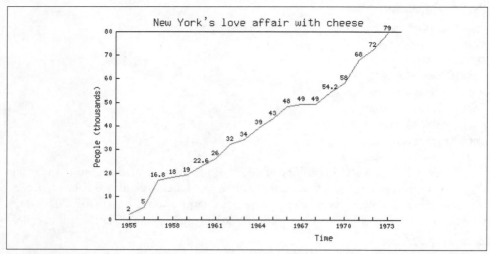

Figure 4-6. The show_values attribute forces each data point to be labeled

values_format=> *string | func_ref*

> If the show_values attribute is true, this attribute specifies a formatting template that should be used when drawing the value label. The template can be defined as a sprintf-style template string, or as a reference to a function that returns a properly formatted string given a data value.

Attributes of Graphs with Axes

box_axis=>*boolean*

> If this attribute is true, the axes are drawn as a box rather than as two lines. The default is true.

two_axes=>*boolean*

> If you have two data sets that you wish to plot against two axes on the same graph, you can set the two_axes attribute to a true value—the first data set is plotted against an axis to the left and the second set is plotted against the axis to the right. The default value is 0.

zero_axis=>*boolean*
zero_axis_only=>*boolean*

> If zero_axis is set to true, an axis is always drawn at the y=0 line. If zero_axis_only is true, the zero axis is the only axis that is drawn, and all x-axis values are plotted on this axis. If both attributes are 0, all x values are plotted along the bottom border of the graph. The default value for both attributes is true.

x_plot_values=>*boolean*
y_plot_values=>*boolean*

> If either of these attributes is set to 0, the values on the given axis are not printed. The tick marks are still plotted. The default value is true.

y_max_value=>*float,* y1_max_value=>*float,* y2_max_value=>*float*
y_min_value=>*float,* y1_min_value=>*float,* y2_min_value=>*float*

> These values control the maximum and minimum values to be plotted on the y axis of a graph. Setting a value of y_min_value that is greater than the smallest value in the data set, or a value of y_max_value that is less than the greatest value within the data set, results in an error. For bar and area graphs, the range of points defined by these attributes must include 0. If it does not, the values are extended to include 0.
>
> When plotting two data sets on two separate axes, use y1_min_value and y1_max_ value to define the range of the left axis, and y2_min_value and y2_max_value to define the range of the right axis.
>
> The default values are the minimum and maximum values of the data sets.

x_tick_number=>*integer*

> This attribute controls the number of ticks displayed on the x axis. By default, GD::Graph attempts to guess the optimal number of ticks based on the data. If undef, one tick is displayed for each data point.

x_min_value=>*float*
x_max_value=>*float*

> Normally, the maximum values of the x axis are calculated from the data. This attribute allows you to set arbitrary maximum and minimum values.

y_number_format=>*string*

> This attribute specifies a formatting template that should be used when drawing the labels on the respective axis. The template can be defined as a sprintf-style template string, or as a reference to a function that returns a properly formatted string given a data value.

x_label_skip=>*integer*
y_label_skip=>*integer*
x_tick_offset=>*integer*
x_all_ticks=>*boolean*

> If x_label_skip is set to an integer greater than 1, then only those ticks numbered as multiples of x_label_skip are labeled on the graph. (A tick is the position where a value is labeled on an axis.) For example, a value of 2 causes every second tick to be labeled, 5 means every fifth should be labeled, etc. The same holds true for y_label_skip. The default value for both attributes is 1. Use the x_ tick_offset attribute to specify the first x value that should be displayed. If x_ all_ticks is true, a tick is drawn for every x value, regardless of whether the label is drawn.

x_label_position=>*float*

> This attribute controls how the individual labels are aligned to the tick on the x axis. The value is a fraction that indicates the point on the width of the label that should be aligned with the tick. If x_label_position is 0, the left margin of the

label is aligned at the tick; a value of .5 means that the label is centered, and 1 means that it is right-aligned. The default value is .75.

y_label_position=>*float*

This attribute controls how the individual labels are aligned to the tick on the y axis. The behavior is similar to that of x_label_position, except that if the value is 0 the label is bottom-aligned, and if it is 1 the label is top-aligned. The default value is .5.

x_labels_vertical=>*boolean*

If true, the labels on the x axis are drawn vertically. The default is 0.

long_ticks=>*boolean*
tick_length=>*integer*

If the long_ticks attribute is true, the graph's ticks are all the same length as the axes, creating a grid across the graph. If long_ticks is 0, the ticks are as many pixels long as the value of the ticks_length attribute. The default value of long_ticks is 0, and of tick_length is 4.

x_ticks=>*boolean*

If x_ticks is set to 0, the ticks on the x axis will not be drawn. The default value is true.

y_tick_number=>*integer*

This attribute controls the number of ticks to be plotted on the y axis. Thus, the increment between ticks is (y_max_value − y_min_value) / y_ticks_number. The default value is 5.

axis_space=>*integer*

This attribute controls the amount of space (in pixels) to be left between each axis and its corresponding text. The default value is 4 pixels.

text_space=>*integer*

This attribute indicates the amount of space that should be left between the axis and any textual labels related to that axis. The default value is 8 pixels.

Attributes of Bar Graphs

correct_width=>*boolean*

If this attribute is true, the width of the graph is adjusted so that each data point is drawn using an integral number of pixels. This is set to true by default.

overwrite=>*{0..2}*

The overwrite attribute controls the appearance of bar graphs with multiple data sets. The attribute may be set to one of the following values:

0   Bars of different data sets are drawn next to each other. (This is the default.)

1   Bars of different data sets are drawn in front of each other.

2   Bars of different data sets are drawn on top of each other (to show a cumulative effect). See Figure 4-7, left.

`bar_width=>`*`integer`*

> By default, the `bar_spacing` attribute and the dimensions of the graph are used to determine the width of each bar. If you want to specify a fixed size for the bars, use this attribute.

`bar_spacing=>`*`integer`*

> This attribute sets the amount of space between bars. The default value is 0. Note that this attribute is ignored if the `bar_width` attribute is defined.

`shadow_depth=>`*`integer`*

> Use this attribute to specify the direction and size of the shadow cast by each bar. Positive values indicate shadows to the right and down; negative values produce a shadow to the left and up. The default value is 0 (no shadow). See Figure 4-7, right.

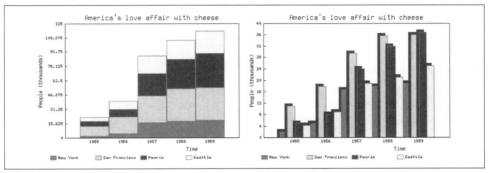

Figure 4-7. A bar graph with overwrite set to 2 (left) and with a shadow depth of −5 (right)

`borderclrs=>`*`integer`*

> This is a reference to a list of colors (like `dclrs`) that should be used to draw the "stroke" of the bar. One color should be specified for each data set.

`cycle_clrs=>`*`boolean`*

> Normally, all the bars of a given data set are drawn in the same color, which is determined by the list of colors in the `dclrs` list. If the `cycle_clrs` attribute is true, the bar for each data *point* (rather than for each data set) is drawn in the next color in the `dclrs` list.

`cumulate=>`*`boolean`*

> If this attribute is true, bars of different data sets are drawn stacked on top of each other vertically (see also the `overwrite` attribute). This attribute also applies to area graphs.

Attributes of Graphs with Lines

`line_types=>\@`*`typelist`*

> This attribute lets you specify the styles of lines with which each data set should be plotted on the graph. The list of line types is a reference to an array of integers.

The default value is [1], which means that all data sets are plotted as solid lines. You can choose from the following types:

1   Solid line

2   Dashed line

3   Dotted line

4   Dot-dashed line

To indicate that the first data set should be plotted as a dashed line, the second as a solid line, and the third as a dot-dashed line, set line_types with:

```
$graph->set(line_types => [2, 1, 4]);
```

line_type_scale=>*integer*

This attribute controls the length of the dashes in the dashed line types. The default value is 6 pixels.

line_width=>*integer*

This attribute controls the width of the lines in the graph. The default value is 1 pixel.

skip_undef=>*boolean*

In graphs with lines, undefined points are not plotted. However, by default a line is still drawn between the two points surrounding the undefined value, thus "implying" a value at that point. If skip_undef is true, this line is not drawn and a gap is left between the two points surrounding the undefined point.

Attributes of Graphs with Points

markers=>\@*markerlist*

The markers attribute controls the order and styling of the point markers used to plot points in graphs of type points or linespoints. The attribute is set with a reference to an array of integers that correspond to the following marker types:

1   Filled square

2   Open square

3   Horizontal cross

4   Diagonal cross

5   Filled diamond

6   Open diamond

7   Filled circle

8   Open circle

The default value is [1,2,3,4,5,6,7,8], which means that the first set of data points is plotted with filled squares, the second with open squares, and so on.

marker_size=>*integer*

This attribute controls the size of the point markers. The default is 4 pixels.

Attributes of Mixed Graphs

types=>\@*types*

This attribute is a reference to a list of strings that describe the types of graphs that should be drawn for each data set. Acceptable values are area, bars, lines, linespoints, and points. Data sets that do not have a corresponding value in this list or that have an undefined value are plotted using the default type as defined by the default_type attribute.

default_type=>*string*

The default graph type for data sets whose types are not specified by the types attribute. The default type is area.

Attributes of Pie Graphs

3d=>*boolean*

If the 3d attribute of a pie graph is set to true, it is drawn with a 3D look. The "thickness" of the pie chart is taken from the pie_height attribute. The default value of 3d is true.

pie_height=>*float*

This attribute sets the height of the graph if it is a 3D pie graph (i.e., if 3d is true). The default value for pie_height is 10% of the height of the total image.

start_angle=>*degrees*

This attribute gives the angle at which the first slice of a pie chart is plotted. The default starting angle is 0 degrees, which corresponds to 6 o'clock.

suppress_angle=>*degrees*

If a true value, pie slices with an angle less than this value are not labeled. The default value is 0, which means that labels are drawn.

Logos and Legends

logo=>*filename*
logo_position=>*position_code*
logo_resize=>*scalefactor*

You may associate a logo (a separate PNG file) for inclusion in the corner of a graph. This logo can be positioned and resized within the graph by setting the logo_position and logo_resize attributes. The value of position_code indicates one of the four corners of the graph with LL, LR, UL, or UR corresponding to the lower/upper left/right corners. The default position is LR (lower right corner). The logo_resize attribute should be expressed in multiples of the original logo size (i.e., 2 for 200%, .5 for 50%). For example, the following lines take the file *mylogo.png*, shrink it by 50%, and include it in the upper right corner of a previously defined graph named $graph:

```
$graph->set(logo           => 'mylogo.png',
            logo_resize    => .5,
            logo_position => 'UR',
            legend_placement=>'BL' );
```

`legend_placement=>{ 'BL', 'BC', 'BR', 'RT', 'RC', or 'RB'}`

This attribute controls placement of the legend within the graph image. The value is supplied as a two-letter string, where the first letter is placement (a B or an R for bottom or right, respectively) and the second is alignment (L, R, C, T, or B for left, right, center, top, or bottom, respectively). The default value is BC for center-aligned on the bottom of the graph. The legend is automatically wrapped, depending on its placement.

`legend_spacing=>integer`

This attribute specifies the number of pixels in the blank margin around the legend. The default value is 4 pixels.

`legend_marker_width=>integer`
`legend_marker_height=>integer`

These attributes control the height and width of a legend marker in pixels. The default values are width=12 and height=8.

`lg_cols=>integer`

This attribute allows you to force a legend at the bottom of a graph into a specified number of columns. The default value is intelligently computed when the legend is plotted.

Colors and Fonts in GD::Graph

All GD::Graph color routines that take *colorname* as a parameter expect a string with the name of a valid color. GD::Graph comes bundled with the GD::Graph::colour[*] package, which provides some methods for organizing and manipulating color name strings. GD::Graph has 29 predefined color name strings (see Table 4-1). The module is normally used simply to provide access to the standard color names, but it also provides methods for converting between color representations. You can define additional strings in an external file by using the read_rgb( ) method.

Table 4-1. The 29 predefined GD::Graph color names and their hex representations

Color name string	Red	Green	Blue	Hex representation
white	255	255	255	#FFFFFF
lyellow	255	255	0	#FFFF00
gold	255	215	0	#FFD700

[*] GD::Graph's author, Martien Verbruggen, lives in Australia, hence the Australian spelling of "colour." Note that the GD::Graph methods that deal with colors (set_text_clr( ), for example) have abbreviated the word to alleviate the need for multiple method names.

Color name string	Red	Green	Blue	Hex representation
cyan	0	255	255	#00FFFF
pink	255	183	193	#FFB7C1
lgray	191	191	191	#BFBFBF
lorange	255	183	0	#FFB700
lbrown	210	180	140	#D2B48C
lgreen	0	255	0	#00FF00
yellow	191	191	0	#BFBF00
orange	255	127	0	#FF7F00
dpink	255	105	180	#FF69B4
green	0	191	0	#00BF00
marine	127	127	255	#7F7FFF
gray	127	127	127	#7F7F7F
dyellow	127	127	0	#7F7F00
dgreen	0	127	0	#007F00
lpurple	255	0	255	#FF00FF
dbrown	165	42	42	#A52A2A
dgray	63	63	63	#3F3F3F
purple	191	0	191	#BF00BF
lred	255	0	0	#FF0000
red	191	0	0	#BF0000
dpurple	127	0	127	#7F007F
dred	127	0	0	#7F0000
lblue	0	0	255	#0000FF
blue	0	0	191	#0000BF
dblue	0	0	127	#00007F
black	0	0	0	#000000

Call the use method with the :colours tag to import the functions _rgb( ), _hue( ), and _luminance( ). The :lists tag imports only colour_list( ) and sorted_colour_ list( ), and the :files tag imports the read_rgb( ) function.

The various methods are as follows.

colour_list

GD::Graph::colour::colour_list([*number*])

The colour_list method returns a list of strings of valid color names known to GD::Graph. The number of strings returned is specified with the optional *number* parameter; if no number is specified, all the defined names are returned. The default list contains all 29 colors listed in Table 4-1.

hex2rgb

`GD::Graph::colour::hex2rgb(hex_string)`

This method takes a string in the hexadecimal color format and returns a list of integers representing the red, green, and blue values.

```
use GD::Graph::colour qw(:colours);
print join ',', hex2rgb("#FF69B4");     # prints 255,105,180
```

rgb2hex

`GD::Graph::colour::rgb2hex(R, G, B)`

This method takes red, green, and blue integer values and returns a hexadecimal color string for the color.

read_rgb

`GD::Graph::colour::read_rgb(filename)`

This method allows you to use color names other than those predefined for GD::Graph. You must first specify the new colors in a text file in the same format as the *rgb.txt* file used to define colors in the X Window system. Each color is represented as a line in the file, with the red, green, and blue values followed by the color name string. Fields are separated by whitespace. For example, a file named *newcolors.txt* that defines the three colors "Slate-Blue", "SeaGreen", and "PeachPuff" would look like:

```
106 90 205 SlateBlue
46 139 87 SeaGreen
255 218 185 PeachPuff
```

and could be used in a GD::Graph script with the addition of the following lines:

```
use GD::Graph::colour qw(:files);
read_rgb('newcolors.txt');
```

sorted_colour_list

`GD::Graph::colour::sorted_colour_list(number)`

The `sorted_colour_list()` method returns a list of strings of valid color names known to GD::Graph, sorted in order of decreasing luminance. The number of strings returned is specified with the optional *number* parameter; if no number is specified, all the defined names are returned. The default return value is the list of the 29 colors listed in Table 4-1, sorted by luminance.

## CHAPTER 5

Scripting the Gimp with Perl

The GNU Image Manipulation Program (Gimp) has been around since 1995. The story of the Gimp began with two Berkeley students named Spencer Kimball and Peter Mattis, who started writing a "Photoshop-like" program for an undergraduate class in computer science. Over the course of the next year they crafted the program into a smart, expandable image manipulation system. The first public release was Version 0.54, at which point they invited others to help contribute. A couple of years and several thousand lines of code later, Gimp 1.0 was released. This was a remarkably slick and stable platform for creating computer graphics, particularly graphics intended for use on the Web. The version documented in this chapter, Gimp 1.2, is a significant improvement on Version 1.0. Version 2.0 will likely be a complete rewrite of the Gimp base code, along with a plug-in architecture that may be different the one described here.

This chapter is not intended as a manual for the Gimp—there are already several fine ones available. Instead, this chapter is geared toward those who don't necessarily start by reading the manual, and who want to immediately begin using the Gimp for making web graphics and creating plug-ins with Perl for advanced web graphics applications. The chapter starts with a quick tour of the Gimp by stepping through the process of creating an animated "electronic marble," then describes the Perl-Gimp interface that allows you to write powerful image manipulation scripts with Perl.

You may also find some of the Gimp information in the appendixes helpful. Appendix B is an overview of the interface of Gimp Version 1.2. Many of the examples in this chapter presuppose a familiarity with this interface.

Getting and Installing the Gimp

The Gimp is free software, covered by the GNU Public License. You can download the program and libraries and use them for free, but you should read and understand the license if you plan on redistributing the Gimp or reusing any of the code covered by the GPL.

There are a number of ways of getting the Gimp. The main FTP site is *ftp://ftp.gimp.org*, which also lists 20 or so mirror sites around the world. The Gimp home page is at *http://www.gimp.org*. A wide array of online information and resources is available, some of which is listed on the Gimp home page.

The Gimp installs easily on most Unix systems. There is a port available for Mac OS X, OS/2, and Win32 systems. The Win32 port is not supported directly by the core Gimp development team, and it requires an X Server and a number of supporting DLLs to operate.

You can also grab a binary image from the *binaries* subdirectory of the main FTP site. These are available as Debian packages, RPM packages, and a dynamically linked, precompiled binary for Solaris. Binaries are also available for other platforms. However, you still need the source code in order to compile the Gimp-Perl modules.

Installing the Gimp

Before you can build and install the Gimp, you'll need to assemble the following:

The GTK libraries
> GTK is the stylish widget set that the Gimp uses for its GUI. You must install GTK before you install the Gimp. The latest stable version of the GTK toolkit should be available at *ftp://ftp.gimp.org/pub/gtk*, or you can go directly to the GTK home page at *http://www.gtk.org*.

Supporting libraries
> You may need supporting libraries for specific file formats such as JPEG, TIFF, or PNG.

Optional extras
> There are two optional collections of add-ons available with the standard distribution: *Gimp-data-extras* and *Gimp-plugins-unstable*. The first contains a number of gradients, patterns, and brushes that may be used with the Gimp. The second consists of a number of plug-ins from the registry that are either in development or are not-quite-ready-for-prime-time. They may not all work perfectly, but there's some nice work in there. Most of these plug-ins can be retrieved individually from *http://registry.gimp.org* as well.

Scripting language requirements
> There are additional requirements for using Perl, Python, or Java as your scripting language of choice. The requirements for the Perl scripting interface are described in the next section.

To install the Gimp from source, take the following steps:

1. Install GTK
2. Install support libraries (JPEG, PNG, TIFF, etc.) if needed

3. Enter the Gimp source directory and run the configure shell script by typing `./configure`

4. Type `make`

5. Type `make install`

6. Install the Gimp-data-extras, if desired

That's all there is to it! If you have problems, someone else has probably already encountered it and reported it to the mailing list; check there first. Most installation problems occur when upgrading the Gimp without cleanly uninstalling the previous version. By following the instructions explicitly, you should have no problem installing the program.

Installing the Perl Scripting Extension

Gimp-Perl comes with the standard Gimp distribution and is considered an officially supported scripting extension. The relevant source code is located in the *plugins/ common/perl/* subdirectory of the Gimp source tree. In addition to GTK and the Gimp, the following pieces of software are required to get the extension off the ground:

The Perl interpreter
You should have at least Version 5.005; older versions may not work.

The Perl Gtk module
This module is the interface between Perl and GTK. It is used to create all of the user interface components of plug-in scripts written in Perl.

The PDL (Perl Data Language) module
The PDL module allows you to easily manipulate large amounts of raw pixel data, and is used by certain Gimp-Perl methods for manipulating raw image tiles and pixel regions. PDL may be retrieved from CPAN. Version 1.99906 or greater is required.

All of these may be retrieved from the Comprehensive Perl Archive Network (*http:// www.cpan.org*). The PDL and Gtk modules are installed the way most Perl modules are installed:

1. Run the script *Makefile.PL* to configure the module and create an appropriate Makefile for your system by typing `perl Makefile.PL`

2. Run `make`

3. Run `make install`

Gimp-Perl is installed with the standard distribution by default, along with two other scripting interfaces: Script-Fu and Gimp-Python. This behavior can be changed with the `--disable-perl` option when configuring the Gimp source. If, for some reason, your Perl distribution is in an odd location, use the configure option `--enable-perl=prefix` to let it know where Perl resides.

Writing Gimp Plug-ins in Perl

A Gimp plug-in* is a small program that adds functionality to the Gimp. The plug-ins reside in one of two directories, the global plug-in directory or a user's own plug-in directory. Each plug-in is queried when the Gimp starts up to determine the parameters that the plug-in takes and the types of values it returns. The plug-in is then installed in the Gimp's Procedural Database (PDB), which is a big list containing information about all of the functions available to the Gimp through the core Gimp API and other installed plug-ins and scripts.

The Gimp-Perl scripting interface, designed chiefly by Gimp developer Marc Lehmann (*http://www.goof.com/pcg/marc/gimp.html*), provides the ability to use the image manipulation engine and the graphic user interface from standalone Perl scripts or from scripts integrated into the Gimp itself. Gimp-Perl scripting conveniences make writing plug-ins simpler in Perl than in C. And, with Perl's integrated PDL (Perl Data Language) module, you can perform complex operations on raw pixel data almost as fast as you could in pure C.

The Gimp and Gimp::Fu Modules

The Gimp-Perl interface is composed of a suite of modules, only two of which really concern the beginning plug-in author. The Gimp module provides the basic interface to the Gimp and the PDB. The Gimp::Fu module provides a framework to simplify the process of writing basic plug-ins.

The Gimp module provides the following capabilities:

- Allows you to write a script in Perl using the same plug-in structure that you would use to write a plug-in in C.

- Provides access to the functions in the core Gimp API and the PDB, which may be imported into your script's namespace.

- Provides a number of constants that can be imported into your namespace.

- Reimplements a number of functions (such as progress_init) and defines some new helper functions (such as xfld_size, which parses XLFD font descriptors, and bounds, which returns the offsets and dimensions of a drawable).

Gimp::Fu allows you to condense the activity of the plug-in to a call to the Gimp::Fu::register function and a call to the Gimp::main function. Gimp::Fu handles most aspects of the user interface by default. For simple scripts that just need the user to provide a few starting values, the default behavior of Gimp::Fu should be sufficient.

The entire suite of modules is shown in Table 5-1.

---

* Note that the terms "script" and "plug-in" are used interchangeably throughout this chapter. The term "script" should be taken to mean a plug-in that executes using the Gimp-Perl scripting extension.

Table 5-1. *The modules that make up the Gimp-Perl extension*

Module name	Description
Gimp	This is the main module of the Gimp-Perl interface. This is really all you need to write a Gimp plug-in in Perl, but you probably want to use the Gimp::Fu interface also.
Gimp::Fu	The Fu.pm module provides a simplified framework for Gimp-Perl scripts, similar to (but more robust than) the Script-Fu interface.
Gimp::Data	This module allows you to save and retrieve global data within the Gimp. This is used by Gimp::Fu to save the parameter settings between invocations of a plug-in, for example.
Gimp::Feature	This module provides functions that allow you to test for the presence of a particular feature or software version in the user's environment.
Gimp::PDL	This module allows you to treat large arrays of pixel data as Perl Data Language objects (see the section "Filters and Effects" in Chapter 3 for more on using PDL).
Gimp::Pod	This module lets you write the documentation for a plug-in using Perl's Plain Old Documentation (POD) format.
Gimp::Util	This module is a repository for convenience functions, some of which may be rolled into future versions of the core Gimp module.
Gimp::Compat	This module smooths over some of the compatibility problems between different versions of the Gimp.

Typically, you want the functionality of both the Gimp and Gimp::Fu modules. Specifying the :auto tag imports all of the Gimp API and PDB functions into your namespace, along with the constants from the Gimp source code file *gimpenums.h*:

```
use Gimp qw(:auto);    # The Gimp module
use Gimp::Fu;          # The Gimp::Fu framework
```

Types of Plug-ins

Most scripts end up in one of three categories:

Automation scripts
> This type of script automates a sequence of actions, not necessarily operating on raw image data. It acts as a kind of macro or shortcut for a particular effect that may be achieved manually via a sequence of commands from the user interface. Sometimes automation scripts are more than mere macros; they can perform actions to a precision that is unattainable from the user interface. Examples of automation Perl scripts are the Webify and Perl-o-tine scripts that are bundled with the Gimp-Perl distribution, and the Apply Tint script outlined later in this chapter.

Filtering or special-effect scripts
> This type of script accesses and manipulates raw image data. Often it is better to write this type of script in a compiled systems language such as C, but the PDL module also allows you a very efficient means of implementing filters and special effects scripts in Perl. Examples are the colour_to_alpha script distributed with the Gimp, and the Colorize script provided later in the chapter.

Standalone scripts

This type of script can have a wide range of functionality, but it is meant to be called from the command line or hooked into a web server using the Common Gateway Interface (CGI). An example of a standalone script is the Query PDB example later in the chapter.

Of course, other application areas exist. You could, for instance, easily write a file save/load handler using Perl. However, this is (arguably) the kind of plug-in that should not be written in a scripting language. Access to file formats is an integral feature that should probably be written in C so that it can be integrated into the Gimp core.

The remainder of this chapter provides examples of Gimp plug-ins and serves as a crash course on the syntax and vagaries of the Gimp-Perl interface.

Your First Gimp Script

When a plug-in is selected from one of the Gimp's menus, it looks at the Procedural Database to determine which function should be called. For a plug-in written in Perl, this means that it calls whatever subroutine you have registered. The Gimp collects parameter data from the user via a dialog box (see also the "Standalone Scripts" section at the end of this chapter), and then passes it off to the Perl script.

Every script written using Gimp::Fu starts with a call to the `register` method, which adds the script to the PDB. The `register` method performs the following functions:

- Defines the plug-in documentation
- Defines the plug-in's place in the menu hierarchy
- Defines the types of images accepted by the plug-in
- Defines the arguments expected by the plug-in
- Defines the values returned by the plug-in
- Installs the plug-in in the Procedural Database
- Performs additional error checking and feature checking

See Appendix B for a reference table that covers all of the parameters and types expected by `register`.

The introductory script in Example 5-1 illustrates the use of the text tool and the proper way of handling font information. The example takes a string and breaks it up into a grid of characters, as shown in Figure 5-1.

First we import the Gimp and Gimp::Fu modules. The Gimp uses a program called *gettext* to handle the translation of strings into different languages; the imported `N_` function is used to mark the menu path string so that *gettext* may translate it. This is included here as an example of good form; internationalization is a major topic that

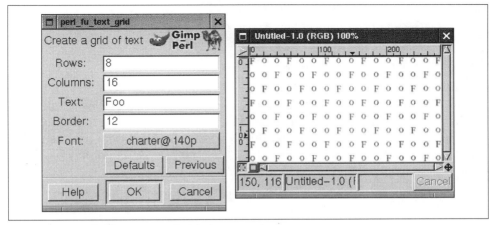

Figure 5-1. A grid of letters created with the text tool

is beyond the scope of this book. The parameter type constants (e.g., PF_INT32) are documented in detail in Appendix B.

Example 5-1. Creating a grid of letters with the text tool

```perl
#!/usr/bin/perl -w
#
# Example 5-1. Text Grid
# A plug-in for the GIMP, written in Perl.

use strict;
use Gimp qw(:auto __ N_);
use Gimp::Fu;

# Fonts must be specified in XLFD format

my $default_font =
    "-*-charter-medium-r-normal-*-*-140-*-*-p-*-iso8859-1";

register(
        "perl_fu_text_grid",                    # Name
        "Create a grid of text",                # Blurb
        "=pod(HELP)",                           # Help
        "=pod(AUTHOR)",                         # Author
        "=pod(COPYRIGHT)",                      # Copyright
        "=pod(DATE)",                           # Date
        N_"<Toolbox>/Xtns/ORA Examples/Text Grid",  # Menu path
        "",                                     # Images
        # The parameters
        [
          [ PF_INT32,  "rows", "Number of rows", 8 ],
          [ PF_INT32,  "columns", "Number of columns", 8 ],
          [ PF_STRING, "text", "Text", "Foo" ],
          [ PF_INT32, "border", "Border, in pixels", 12 ],
```

Example 5-1. Creating a grid of letters with the text tool (continued)

```
            [ PF_FONT, "font", "The font to use", $default_font ],
        ],
        [],              # return values
        \&text_grid      # the plug-in subroutine
);
```

The final argument to `Gimp::Fu::register` is a reference to a subroutine (or an anonymous block of code) that does the work of the plug-in. The `text_grid` routine starts by retrieving the five parameters passed to it when it is called from the Gimp. The parameters are retrieved via the `@_` array, just like they would be for any other Perl subroutine.

Next the convenience function `xfld_size` is called to parse the font for two bits of information: the font size, and whether the size is represented in points or pixels. This information is used to size each grid unit so that it is large enough to hold the largest letter in the string. Since all letters have the same height (based on the font size), we just need to find the letter with the maximum width. Make sure the string is long enough to fill the whole grid; if not, repeat the string an appropriate number of times.

```
    sub text_grid {
        # The plug-in subroutine.

        my ($rows, $columns, $text, $border, $font) = @_;

        my @font_size = Gimp::xlfd_size($font);
        my ($cell_w, $cell_h, $max_w, $size_in_pixels) = (0,0,0,0);
        foreach my $letter (split("", $text)) {
            my ($tmp_w, $tmp_h, $tmp_a, $tmp_d) =
                Gimp->text_get_extents_fontname($letter,
                                                @font_size,
                                                $font);
            if ($tmp_w > $max_w) {
                $max_w = $tmp_w;
                $cell_h = $tmp_h - $tmp_d;    # subtract the descender
                $size_in_pixels = $tmp_h;
            }
        }

        if (length($text) < ($rows * $columns)) {
            $text = $text x (int(($rows * $columns)/length($text))+1);
        }
```

Now that all the dimensions are calculated, we create the new image by calling the `gimp_image_layer_new` method (see the next section for the exact calling syntax).

Add a new layer to the image, which becomes our *drawable*. A drawable is, simply, something on which you can draw.

```
        my $w = $columns * $cell_w + ($columns+1) * $border;
        my $h = $rows * $cell_h + ($rows+1) * $border;
```

```
my $img = new Gimp::Image($w, $h, RGB);

my $drawable = $img->layer_new($w, $h, RGBA_IMAGE,
                               "Background",
                               100, NORMAL_MODE);

$img->add_layer($drawable, -1);      # Place at top of stack
$drawable->gimp_edit_fill(1);        # Fill with background
```

Drawables can be layers, individual color channels of an image, or even a selection mask. The new layer automatically becomes the currently selected layer, which gets filled with the current background color. The new layer is created as an RGB image with an alpha channel (or *alpha mask*). The Gimp deals with transparency by allowing a fourth channel to be included with each layer of an image. The alpha channel is an 8-bit mask (i.e., each pixel can be one of 256 values) that indicates the translucency of the pixels on the underlying image layer. This example does not really utilize transparency; see the Colorize example later in the chapter.

Next, iterate over the list of characters and draw each in a separate grid cell with the text tool. First initialize the progress bar, which appears along the bottom of the image window and gives the user an indication of how much processing the plug-in has done. The progress bar is incremented as each row is drawn.

```
Gimp->progress_init ("Generating text grid...");

my @chars = split("", $text);
my ($x, $y, $char);
my ($x_extent, $y_extent, $ascent, $descent);
my $progress = 0;

for (my $i = 0; $i < $rows; $i++) {
    for (my $j = 0; $j < $columns; $j++) {

        $char = shift(@chars);
        ($x_extent, $y_extent, $ascent, $descent) =
            Gimp->text_get_extents_fontname($char,
                                            @font_size,
                                            $font);
        $y_extent -= $descent;        # Subtract descender

        $x = $border + $j * ($cell_w + $border) +
                        ($cell_w - $x_extent)/2;
        $y = $border + $i * ($cell_h + $border);

        # Use the text tool to draw the text at the coordinate

        $drawable->text_fontname($x, $y, $char,
            0, 1, $size_in_pixels, 0, $font);
    }
    $progress += 1/$rows;
    Gimp->progress_update ($progress);
}
```

The text_get_extents( ) method returns metrics information about a specific string. Here it is used to calculate the upper left corner of the text block, which is needed by the text tool. The character is centered within the grid cell.

At the end of the loop, the progress bar is updated as each row is completed. Note that this results in a less responsive progress bar for images that are more horizontal than vertical.

After the text has been added, the last bit of text added still resides in a floating selection, just as if you had added it manually with the text tool. Before returning the image, we'll merge it with the drawable layer using the gimp_floating_sel_anchor( ) method.

The return value must be specified explicitly with the return statement, or by leaving the return value as the last line of the subroutine.

```
    $img->floating_selection->floating_sel_anchor;
    return ($img);
}
```

At the end of each plug-in, you should return control to the Gimp with:

```
exit main;
```

Documentation of the plug-in is formatted as POD text. In the register functions, strings in the format =pod( ) refer to sections of the POD documentation.

```
# Embedded POD documentation follows

=head1 NAME
Text Grid

=head1 HELP
This script takes a string and places each character in a separate
cell of a rows x columns grid, with each cell padded by the number
of pixels indicated by border. Characters are rendered in the
foreground color, with the given font. If there are not enough
characters to fill the grid, they are repeated.

=head1 AUTHOR
Shawn Wallace

=head1 COPYRIGHT
(c) 2003 The Institute for Folk Computing

=head1 DATE
2003-03-12
```

To install the script, it must be placed in either the global plug-in directory or your own plug-in directory. The Gimp assumes that each file in these directories is a plug-in that is meant to be loaded at runtime. If the plug-in is written in C, it must be built and installed with the *gimptool* utility so that a binary object file sits in the plug-in directory.

The *gimptool* utility is a little tool that comes with the Gimp distribution and helps you build plug-ins from source and install plug-ins and scripts. It is a shell script and resides in the same directory as the Gimp executable. If the plug-in is written in Perl, you can either copy the script itself manually into the plug-in directory, or you can use the *gimptool*, which automatically sets the proper permissions. The following command installs the Perl script in the user's personal plug-in directory:

```
gimptool --install-bin text_grid.pl
```

When the Gimp launches, it first makes sure that the script is parseable and has all of the information that it expects, and then it executes the `Gimp::Fu::register` method. The `main` function call then returns control to the Gimp, which finishes its startup sequence. If there is a problem along the way and your script crashes, you get an error message on the command-line console saying:

```
wire_read: unexpected EOF (plug-in crashed?)
```

If this happens while the Gimp is starting up, it may give you a helpful error message on the console. If the error happens during runtime, it is a problem with the logic of your script. It is a good idea to test the syntax of your script before you install the plug-in with perl's -c switch.

After the plug-in is installed, launch the Gimp. If everything is installed properly, you will see a splash screen and a progress bar listing the various steps of the startup process. Startup is usually very quick, but it can get bogged down if you have many brushes or patterns installed. The Toolbox appears (as well as a helpful tip of the day from Wilbur the Gimp) when the program is loaded. The new plug-in should appear in the Toolbox menu under the ORA Examples subheading.

This is a good time to make a note about menu structure in the Gimp. There are two menus attached to the Toolbox: File and Xtns. The items in the File menu are for creating new files, opening existing files, editing preferences, etc. The Xtns menu contains extensions such as the Procedural Database Browser and scripts that generate new images. Once an image window is open, you can access a menu associated with the image by holding down the right mouse button. This menu provides options that apply only to the image contained in that window. In this example, menu items refer to the image menu (and not the Toolbox menu) unless specifically stated otherwise. On the Gimp mailing lists and text-based documentation, menu items are generally referred to in the form MenuName → Item → SubItem, which indicates the menu option SubItem that is the hierarchical child of Item in the MenuName menu. We use this convention in this chapter also.

Object-Oriented Versus Procedural Scripting

If you are familiar with the structure of Gimp plug-ins written in C, you will immediately notice a few details of the previous example that differ between Perl and C. Because Gimp-Perl is a scripting extension that acts as a high-level interface to libgimp (the Gimp API), you do not necessarily have to use the clumsy PDB-style calling syntax that you must use in C.

All libgimp functions and additional plug-ins are registered in the Procedural Database. The entries in the PDB serve to document the Gimp API; you can use the PDB Browser (found under the Xtns menu) to search the API. As shown in Figure 5-2, the browser displays the function interfaces using C syntax. For example, if you want to copy a layer using the function `gimp_layer_copy( )`, you would look up the function in the browser and write the function call (in C) as:

```
ret_vals = gimp_run_procedure("gimp_layer_copy",
                              &nret_vals,
                              PARAM_LAYER, layerID,
                              PARAM_INT32, TRUE,
                              PARAM_END);
```

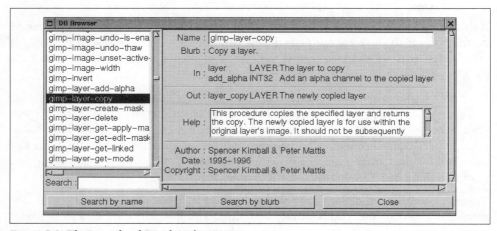

Figure 5-2. The Procedural Database browser

In Perl you can call the function more simply:

```
$new_layer = gimp_layer_copy($layer, 1);
```

Note that the style shown above can be used only if you have imported the Gimp API function names with the `:auto` tag. Otherwise, you would have to specify the package name:

```
$new_layer = Gimp::gimp_layer_copy($layer, 1);
```

You can get away with sticking to the simple procedural-style calling syntax, or you can use the object-oriented style provided by Gimp-Perl. To copy a layer, use:

```
$new_layer = $layer->copy(1);
```

The first thing you should notice about this function call is that the PDB interface definition for `gimp_layer_copy` calls for two parameters: the layer, and a Boolean flag indicating whether an alpha channel should be added to the copied layer. Here, we only have one parameter: the Boolean flag. This can occur partly because of some help by the Gimp module, and partly because of the "more than one way to do it" nature of Perl's object-oriented architecture. The rules of thumb are:

- If you are calling another plug-in, you can optionally leave off the `run_mode` parameter. The run mode simply tells the Gimp whether the plug-in was executed via the UI or from the command line, which the Gimp module can figure out for you. The `run_mode` with which the Perl script was called is available in the `Gimp::$run_mode` package variable.

- If the function expects both an image and a drawable as parameters (as most plug-ins do), the object-oriented syntax allows you to leave these out.

- All of the objects defined in Gimp are listed in Table 5-2. Each object may be used to call different classes of libgimp functions. Because Perl always passes the object as the first parameter when using the "method style" object-oriented syntax, you should expect this behavior. The following examples illustrate this:

```perl
$i = new Gimp::Image;
$d = new Gimp::Drawable;
$c = new Gimp::Channel;

$h = $i->height();        # Calls gimp_image_height()
@list = $i->list();       # WRONG: gimp_image_list() does not take
                          # an image as its first argument

$d->fill(FG_IMAGE_FILL);  # Calls gimp_drawable_fill()

$d->blur();               # Calls plug_in_blur(), which takes
                          # 3 arguments: run_mode, an image and a
                          # drawable, all of which are optional
                          # when called in this manner.

$o = Drawable->get_opacity($img->get_active_layer);
                          # This actually calls the function
                          # gimp_layer_get_opacity. It is unclear
                          # why you would want to use this type
                          # of syntax; in fact, you probably
                          # shouldn't, even though it works.
```

In some cases you may not want to use the object-oriented syntax. The Apply Tint script shown a bit later uses the procedural-style syntax:

```perl
gimp_undo_push_group_start($img);
```

instead of the object-oriented:

```perl
$img->undo_push_group_start()
```

because the latter implies that an action is being performed on the image, when in fact we are performing an action on the image's undo stack. In the end, of course, this is simply a matter of personal style and preference.

Table 5-2 lists the objects defined by the Gimp module and the classes of libgimp functions that they may be used to call.

Table 5-2. Gimp objects and the classes of libgimp functions they can call

Object	Range of libgimp functions
Brushes	gimp_brushes_
Channel	gimp_ gimp_channel_ gimp_drawable_ gimp_selection_ gimp_image_ gimp_layer_ perl_fu_ plug_in_
Display	gimp_display_
Drawable	gimp_ gimp_drawable_ gimp_floating_sel_ gimp_image_ gimp_layer_ perl_fu_ plug_in_
Edit	gimp_edit_
GDrawable	gimp_gdrawable_
Gimp	gimp_
Gradients	gimp_gradients_
Image	gimp_image_ perl_fu_ plug_in
Palette	gimp_ gimp_palette_
Patterns	gimp_patterns_
PixelRgn	gimp_pixel_rgn_
Plugin	plug_in_
Progress	gimp_progress_
Tile	gimp_tile_

Adding New Features to the Gimp

As we will see in the last section of this chapter, it is possible to write standalone scripts that communicate with the Gimp as a separate process. First, however, we will concentrate on Gimp-Perl plug-ins that create new filters, special effects, or shortcuts for manipulating images with the Gimp's user interface. We'll cover selection areas, layers, undo and redo, pixel regions, and creating alternative user interfaces.

Handling Selections and Layers

The example in this section operates on a region of pixels selected by the user and illustrates the handling of layers and floating layers. It is also a Perl script that acts as a kind of macro for a sequence of actions, with a bit of extra capability such as allowing the option of working on a copy of the image.

The Apply Tint plug-in overlays a colored tone on an image, resulting in a simulated duotone or sepia-tone effect. It is most dramatic on grayscale images, but it also works on RGB images. The final effect may be duplicated manually using the Gimp's toolbox by following these nine steps:

1. Convert the image to RGB mode with <Image> → Image → Mode → RGB.

2. Using one of the selection tools, select the area to be tinted.

3. Select <Image> → Edit → Copy.

4. Paste the selection into a new floating selection layer with <Image> → Edit → Paste.

5. Apply <Image> → Filters → Blur → Gaussian Blur (IIR) with a radius of 5.

6. Invert the floating layer with <Image> → Image → Colors → Invert.

7. Use the <Image> → Filters → Colors → Colorify plug-in to colorize the light areas of the selection.

8. Change the floating layer's composition mode to Overlay in the Layers and Channels dialog.

9. Anchor the floating selection by selecting the anchor in the Layers and Channels dialog.

The script in Example 5-2 consists of two function calls: one to `Gimp::Fu::register` and one to `Gimp::main`. Other plug-ins may call this one through the PDB using the name `perl_fu_apply_tint`. It has become common practice to place all Gimp-Perl scripts in the `perl_fu_` namespace so that they may be easily cataloged in documentation generators such as the DB Browser. Note that this naming scheme should not be extended to the placement of the script in the menu hierarchy; that should be determined by the plug-in's application.

Example 5-2. The Apply Tint script

```perl
#!/usr/bin/perl -w
#
# Example 5-2. Apply Tint
# A plug-in for the GIMP, written in Perl.

use strict;
use Gimp qw(:auto);
use Gimp::Fu;

Gimp::set_trace(TRACE_ALL);              # Set to full trace mode
```

Example 5-2. The Apply Tint script (continued)

```
register(
        "perl_fu_apply_tint",                   # Name
        "Apply a tint to an image.",            # Blurb
        "=pod(HELP)",                           # Help
        "=pod(AUTHOR)",                         # Author
        "=pod(COPYRIGHT)",                      # Copyright
        "=pod(DATE)",                           # Date
        N_ "<Image>/ORA Examples/Apply Tint",   # Menu path
        "RGB*, GRAY*",                          # Images accepted
        # The parameters
        [
          [ PF_COLOR,  "tint_color",
                       "The color to apply", [255, 0, 0]],
          [ PF_TOGGLE, "work_on_copy",
                       "Work on a copy?", 0],
        ],
        [],                     # return values
        \&apply_tint            # A reference to the plug-in code
);

exit main;
```

The algorithm is implemented in the apply_tint( ) subroutine. At the beginning of the routine, we start an undo group. The Gimp has multiple levels of undo (and redo); you can find these commands under the Edit menu if you make a mistake somewhere along the line. All of the commands executed between the start and end of the undo group can be undone with a single call to Undo.

```
sub apply_tint {
    # The plug-in subroutine.
    # First get the parameters passed to the procedure...

    my ($img, $drawable, $tint_color, $work_on_copy) = @_;
    my $return_val = undef;

    gimp_undo_push_group_start($img);
```

Next, create a new copy of the image if work_on_copy is a true value; otherwise, use the current layer as the drawable. If the image is a grayscale, convert it to RGB mode first.

```
    if ($work_on_copy) {
        $img = channel_ops_duplicate($img);
        $return_val = $img;

        # Set the drawable to the new active layer.
        $drawable = $img->get_active_layer;
    }
    unless ($drawable->is_rgb()) {
        $img->convert_rgb();
    }
```

Since the plug-in operates on a selection area, select the whole image if nothing is already selected and copy the selection into the paste buffer. Paste the contents of the paste buffer and deselect the current selection. The drawable is now a new, temporary "floating selection" layer.

```
unless ($drawable->mask_bounds) {
    $img->selection_all;
}
gimp_edit_copy($drawable);
my $floating_layer = gimp_edit_paste($drawable, 0);
```

The next steps are to apply a Gaussian blur filter and invert the floating layer. We need to invert the selection because the plug_in_colorify plug-in colors the white parts of a drawable, and we want to color the black parts. Apply the Colorify filter to the floating layer:

```
plug_in_gauss_iir($img, $floating_layer, 5, 1, 1);
$floating_layer->invert();
plug_in_colorify($img, $floating_layer, $tint_color);
```

When layers are composed to make an image, various layer modes control how the compositing is handled. Next, we set the layer mode to "overlay" before merging the floating layer back onto the drawable with gimp_floating_sel_anchor. To get an idea of the layer composing modes, experiment with the settings in the Layers and Channels dialog box.

```
$floating_layer->set_mode(OVERLAY_MODE);
$floating_layer->anchor;
```

Finally, update the drawable with the changes by calling its update( ) method. Gimp:: Fu expects the procedure to return an image only if a new image is created by the script (or to return an array if more than one image is created). If the script operates only on an existing image, it should return undef.

```
$drawable->update(0, 0, $drawable->width, $drawable->height);
gimp_undo_push_group_end($img);    # End the undo group
return ($return_val);
}
```

The documentation is appended to the bottom of the script, marked up in Perl's POD format:

```
# Embedded POD documentation follows

=head1 NAME
Apply Tint

=head1 HELP
Applies a colored tint to an image (works best on grayscale
images). The end result is kind of a sepia-tone or duotone effect.

=head1 AUTHOR
Shawn P. Wallace
```

```
=head1 COPYRIGHT
(c) 2002 The Institute for Folk Computing

=head1 DATE
2003-03-12
```

Manipulating Raw Data with Pixel Regions

A Pixel Region is an abstraction representing a matrix of image pixels that can be used to manipulate the raw channel data of an image. You might think that it wouldn't be a good idea to handle enormous amounts of image data with Perl, a mere "scripting" language that is slower than C for pure number crunching. However, the scientific community has provided us with a solution to this problem called PDL, or Perl Data Language (*http://pdl.perl.org/*). The PDL package, much of which is written in C, provides a framework for quickly manipulating large multidimensional matrices.

The PixelRgn object

Any plug-in that operates on the raw pixels of an image should access the image data through a Pixel Region structure, represented in Gimp-Perl by a Gimp::PixelRgn object. The abstraction of the PixelRgn object affords you the following conveniences:

- Drawing operations follow the boundaries of selection areas.
- A progress bar can be updated as pieces of the Pixel Region are manipulated.
- The undoing of raw-pixel changes is handled correctly.

To get a new Pixel Region for a particular drawable, you must first get the drawable's GDrawable structure (represented as a Gimp::GDrawable object). A GDrawable is simply an abstraction of a drawable that contains more information about the drawable, such as its boundaries. The GDrawable is retrieved by calling gimp_drawable_get( ). You can then create a PixelRgn object from the GDrawable:

```
my $gdrawable = $drawable->get;
# Calls gimp_pixel_rgn_init( ) and returns a Gimp::PixelRgn object

my $pr = $gdrawable->pixel_rgn(
    0, 0, 256, 256,            # bounding box
    1,                         # Is this a dirty region?
    1                          # Use a shadow tile buffer
);
```

Alternately, you can create a PixelRgn object by calling its new method:

```
my $pr = new PixelRgn($gdrawable, 0, 0, 256, 256, 1, 1);
```

Once you have a pixel region, you can use any of the pixel region functions to retrieve rectangular sections of the region:

```
# All of the pixel data for the region
$pixel_data = $pr->data;

# A 50x50 rectangle starting at the origin
$pixel_data = $pr->get_rect(0, 0, 50, 50);

# The same as $pr->data
$pixel_data = $pr->get_rect(0, 0, $pr->w, $pr->h);

# 100 pixels from the 50th row, starting at 50, 50
$pixel_data = $pr->get_row(50, 50, 100);

# A single pixel at 50,50
$pixel = $pr->get_pixel(50, 50);
```

Each of these functions returns a packed byte structure that is blessed as a PDL object and referred to as a "piddle." A piddle is simply a multidimensional matrix of bytes that contains (*channels* × *width* × *height*) elements.

PDL objects

You can perform operations on the entire matrix of pixel data using the PDL functions. PDL overloads several of Perl's built-in operators so that they iterate over each element of the matrix (see Table 5-3). For example:

```
$piddle += 2;                                    # Add 2 to each element
                                                 # in the matrix
$piddle++;                                       # Add 1 to each element
$piddle = 255-$piddle;                           # Invert each element
$dot_product = sum($piddle1*$piddle2)            # Dot product of $piddle1
                                                 # and $piddle2
$piddle = $piddle1 x $piddle2                    # x is overloaded as matrix
                                                 # multiplication operator
```

Table 5-3 shows the Perl operators overloaded by PDL to operate on matrices, and whether the operation is performed in place.

Table 5-3. Perl built-in operators overloaded by PDL

Type	Operator	Perform operation in place?
Arithmetic operators	+ - * / ** % ^ exp x	No
Autoincrement/autodecrement	++ --	Yes
Bitwise operators	<< >> & | ~	Yes
Comparison operators	<= >= == != <=>	N/A
Trigonometric functions	sin log abs atan2 sqrt cos	No

You have to consider memory usage when using PDL, particularly if the image you are manipulating is a large one. When certain operations are performed, a temporary copy of the matrix may be created, doubling the amount of memory used.

Take the following operation:

```
$piddle = $piddle + 1;
```

This creates a temporary copy of $piddle, which, if $piddle is a 5 MB image, would consume 10 MB of memory. Some operations, however, are performed "in place," which means that the operation is performed directly on the data without the temporary copy being made. The increment operation shown above can be performed in-place with the autoincrement operator:

```
$piddle++;
```

or:

```
$piddle += 1;
```

The third column of Table 5-3 indicates whether the set of operations is performed in-place or not. You can force an in-place execution with the inplace( ) function:

```
$piddle = inplace($piddle)+1;
```

The PDL slice( ) and index( ) functions allow you to quickly refer to subsets of the matrix. These functions return a reference to the original object, so if you modify the data in the slice, you are modifying the contents of the object to which it is referring. To create a reference to red, green, and blue channels of an RGB image, for example, you can use the index function:

```
$pixel_data = $pixel_region->data;
$red = $pixel_data->index(0);
$green = $pixel_data->index(1);
$blue = $pixel_data->index(2);
```

All PDL indices are based on a (0,0) origin. When assigning to an indexed subset of a piddle, you must use Perl's string assignment operator .=, which has been overloaded for this purpose. Continuing the above example, if you wish to remove the red channel from the image, you would use the .= operator to assign 0 to each element of the red slice of data:

```
$red .= 0;        # Set the red channel to 0
```

The slice( ) function can be used to reference more specific regions. The following command creates a reference to the green and blue channels of the 20×50 rectangle starting at (10,30):

```
$piddle = $pixel_data->slice("1:2,10:19,30:79");
```

The argument to slice indicates which indices in a particular dimension should be included in the sliced set. The argument is a comma-delimited string specifies one of the following formats:

"" *or* ":"

> Include the whole dimension. If slice is called with an empty string, therefore, it returns the entire matrix. Likewise, if dimensions are not specified, the entire dimension is included.

"n"

Include only the value with the index *n* of the given dimension.

"a:b"

Include the range of values with the indices a through b of the given dimension.

"a:b:c"

Include the range a to b with a step of c. Thus, "0:10:2" includes the even indices between 0 and 10.

 When manipulating raw image data, you are generally iterating over multiple *tiles* within a pixel region. Tiles currently have a maximum size of 64×64, but some tiles in the region may be smaller than this (unless the width and height of the region are exactly divisible by 64). Using the slice function to extract specific areas of a tile should be done with care.

A filter plug-in using pixel regions

The Colorize example is an implementation of a plug-in that colorizes an image. This differs from the Colorify plug-in that comes with the Gimp distribution in that Colorify operates on the lighter portions of the image, while Colorize operates on the darker portions. The first part of the script should be familiar by now.

```perl
#!/usr/bin/perl -w
#
# Colorize. A plug-in for the Gimp, written in Perl.

use strict;
use Gimp qw(:auto N_);
use Gimp::Fu;
use PDL;
use Gimp::Util;

register(
        "perl_fu_colorize_with_progress",      # Name
        "Colorify the dark parts of an image.", # Blurb
        "=pod(HELP)",                          # Help
        "=pod(AUTHOR)",                        # Author
        "=pod(COPYRIGHT)",                     # Copyright
        "=pod(DATE)",                          # Date
        N_ "<Image>/ORA Examples/Colorize",
                                               # Menu path
        "RGB*, GRAY*",                         # Images accepted
        # The parameters
        [
          [ PF_COLOR,  "color", "The color to use", [255, 0, 0]],
        ],
        # return values
        [],
        \&colorize
);
```

The beginning of the colorize routine is also similar to the Apply Tint example:

```perl
sub colorize {
    # First get the parameters passed to the procedure...

    my ($img, $drawable, $color) = @_;
    Gimp->progress_init("Colorizing...");
    unless ($drawable->is_rgb()) {
        $img->convert_rgb();
    }
    unless ($drawable->mask_bounds) {
        $img->selection_all;
    }
```

To create a PixelRgn object, we must first retrieve the dimensions and a GDrawable structure for the drawable. Here we actually create two pixel regions, one to read from and one to write to. An object known as a PixelRegionIterator (returned by gimp_pixel_rgns_register) is then used to iterate over each of the tiles within the region. This allows us to update the progress bar as each tile is operated on.

The pixel_rgn method takes two arguments in addition to the drawable bounds. The first is a "dirty" flag, which should be set to 1 if the pixel region is going to be changed (or "dirtied"). The last argument is the "shadow tile buffer" flag, which is set for the destination pixel buffer. The shadow buffer allows the current selection to mask any changes to the region.

```perl
my @bounds = $drawable->bounds;         # Provided by Gimp::Util
my $gdrawable = $drawable->get;
my $src_region = $gdrawable->pixel_rgn(@bounds, 0, 0);
my $dest_region = $gdrawable->pixel_rgn(@bounds, 1, 1);

# pixel_rgns_register returns a PixelRegionIterator

my $iterator = Gimp->pixel_rgns_register($src_region,
                                         $dest_region);
my ($pixel_data, $channel);
my $area = $bounds[2]*$bounds[3];
my $progress = 0;
```

Next, we get the pixel data for the region and modify each channel individually using the overloaded PDL operators. Note that the pixel data is modified in-place. Update the region with the data and update the progress bar. The gimp_pixel_rgns_process() function returns true as long as there are more tiles to process in the region.

```perl
do {
    $pixel_data = $src_region->data;
    foreach (0..2) {
        # Get the pixel data for a single channel
        $channel = index($pixel_data, $_);
        $channel .= 255-(255-$channel)*(255-$color->[$_])/255;
    }
    $dest_region->data($pixel_data);
```

```
    $progress += ($src_region->w * $src_region->h)/$area;
    Gimp->progress_update($progress);

} while (Gimp->pixel_rgns_process($iterator));
```

The shadow tile buffer must be merged into the drawable with the `merge_shadow` method. Then update the drawable. Because the plug-in operates on the current image, return `undef`.

```
    $drawable->merge_shadow(1);
    $drawable->update(@bounds);
    return ( );
}

exit main;

# Embedded POD documentation follows

=head1 NAME
Colorize with progress bar

=head1 HELP
Colorize a region. Update the progress bar to let the user
know how things are going.

=head1 AUTHOR
Shawn Wallace

=head1 COPYRIGHT
(c) 2003 The Institute for Folk Computing

=head1 DATE
2003-03-12
```

So far, all of the plug-ins have used the Gimp::Fu module to provide a standard user interface for entering plug-in parameters. It is also possible to create more elaborate interfaces, as shown in the next section.

Alternative User Interfaces

If you need to create a more complex user interface than that offered by Gimp::Fu (or if you just want to create a custom interface), you can bypass the conveniences of Gimp::Fu and just use the Gimp module. In this case, you need to follow the same steps as that for a plug-in written in C. You need at least a query( ) and a run( ) function, which are registered with the Gimp using the Gimp::on_query( ) and Gimp::on_run( ) functions. If you want a user interface, you have to roll your own using the Perl Gtk module.

The query function of each plug-in is invoked when the Gimp is first started. This function simply defines information about the interface, just like Gimp::Fu:: register( ).

The run function is executed when the plug-in is selected from a menu or called from another function in the Gimp.

The following plug-in adjusts the alpha channel of a layer by manipulating the spline control points of a curve. Its behavior emulates that of the <Image> → Colors → Curves menu item, but the changes are applied to the alpha channel rather than to the individual color components. The input dialog uses the Gtk::Curve widget to get a vector of data from the user, which the plug-in uses to modify the specified channel.

```perl
#!/usr/bin/perl -w
#
# Adjust Alpha
# A plug-in for the GIMP, written in Perl.
#
use strict;
use Gimp qw(:auto N_);

Gimp::on_query(\&query);
Gimp::on_run(\&run);

sub query {
    gimp_install_procedure(
        "perl_fu_adjust_alpha",                 # Name
        "Adjust the curves of a channel.",      # Blurb
      "Similar to <image>->Colors->Curves, for alpha channel.",
                                                # Help
        "Shawn Wallace",                        # Author
        "(c) 2003 IFC",                         # Copyright
        "2003-3-12",                            # Date
        N_ "<Image>/ORA Examples/Adjust Alpha", # Menu path
        "RGBA, GRAYA",                          # Images accepted
        Gimp::PROC_PLUG_IN,
        [
         [PARAM_INT32, "run_mode",
                         "Interactive, [non-interactive]"],
         [PARAM_IMAGE, "image", "The image"],
         [PARAM_DRAWABLE, "drawable", "The drawable"],
      ],
      []
      );
}
```

The gimp_install_procedure( ) function is used to install the plug-in code in the PDB. The main difference between this function and the register function is that here we must provide a procedure type (PROC_PLUG_IN) that tells the Gimp whether the procedure is a plug-in, an extension, or an internal function.

Note that the plug-in will accept only images with an alpha channel. If the image does not have an alpha channel, the Apply Alpha menu item will be grayed out.

The run routine handles some things that a Gimp::Fu script does not, such as setting the run mode and returning appropriate success or error values. If the plug-in has been invoked in the interactive run mode (i.e., it was selected from a menu in the user interface rather than from a standalone script), the adjust_alpha_dialog routine is called, which draws a dialog box for getting the plug-in arguments.

```
sub run {
    # First get the parameters passed to the procedure...

    my ($run_mode, $img, $drawable) = @_;
    if ($run_mode == Gimp::RUN_INTERACTIVE) {
        my $vector = adjust_alpha_dialog();
```

If the dialog box successfully returns a set of data (it should be a list of 256 data points), the curves_explicit function is called with the data. The first argument to curves_explicit is the channel (the alpha channel is the 4th channel), the second is the number of data points, and the last is a reference to the list of data points.

After the drawable is updated, you must flush all updates to the user interface with the displays_flush method. This is another detail that was previously handled by the Gimp::Fu module.

```
    if ($vector) {
        gimp_undo_push_group_start($img);
            Gimp->progress_init("Adjusting alpha...");
            $drawable->curves_explicit(4, 256, $vector);
            $drawable->update(0, 0,
                            $drawable->width, $drawable->height);
            gimp_undo_push_group_end($img);
            Gimp->displays_flush();
        }
    return STATUS_SUCCESS;

    } else {
        return STATUS_CALLING_ERROR;
    }

}
```

Finally, we write the code to draw the dialog box. The dialog is constructed with Gtk widgets, including the special Curves widget for getting a set of data from a graph that the user can manipulate. The dialog box is a simple Gtk interface; it consists of a window that contains the curve widget and an OK button (Figure 5-3).

The "close window" and the OK button both have actions associated with them by the signal_connect method calls. See the documentation for the Gtk module for a more complete discussion of creating Gtk interfaces.

```
sub adjust_alpha_dialog {
    my $return_val;
```

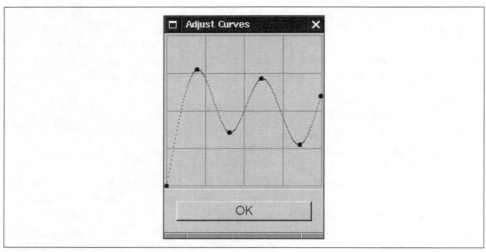

Figure 5-3. The input dialog for the Adjust Alpha plug-in.

```
Gimp::gtk_init( );
my $window = new Gtk::Dialog;
$window->set_title("Adjust Curves");
$window->signal_connect(destroy => sub { $return_val = 0;
                                          Gtk->main_quit });
my $curve = new Gtk::Curve( );
$curve->set_range(0, 255, 0, 255); # x-min, x-max, y-min, y-max
$curve->set_curve_type('spline');
$window->vbox->add($curve);

my $button = new Gtk::Button("OK");
$button->can_default(1);
$button->grab_default;
$button->signal_connect(clicked => sub { $return_val = 1;
                                         Gtk->main_quit });
$window->action_area->add($button);

$window->show_all;
main Gtk;
```

The get_vector( ) method of the Curve widget returns 256 values taken from the
current setting of the Curve widget:

```
if ($return_val) {
    return ([$curve->get_vector(256)]);
} else {
    return undef;
}
}

exit main;
```

Standalone Scripts

It is possible to write Gimp-Perl scripts that can be executed directly from the command line rather than from within the Gimp's user interface. The Gimp::Fu module will even start up the Gimp if it is not already running. Because of the length of time it takes for the Gimp to load, however, you probably want to execute standalone scripts that communicate with an instance of the Gimp that is already running. This communication is handled on the script's side by the Gimp::Net module, and on the Gimp's side by the Perl Server extension.

To launch the Perl Server, select the <Toolbox> → Xtns → Perl → Server menu option. You'll see a message on the command line stating that the Perl Server is now accepting connections.

 If you do not explicitly launch the Perl Server from the Xtns menu, a separate instance of the Gimp is launched each time the script is run. This adds many seconds to the runtime of your script.

Launching the Perl Server extension creates a socket through which local scripts may communicate with the Gimp. You can also tell the Perl Server to listen on a TCP port (10009 is the default) by setting the GIMP_HOST environment variable before starting the Gimp. See the Gimp::Net manpages for a complete discussion of this behavior.

When writing a standalone Gimp-Perl script, you should not register the script with the Gimp's PDB. All you need to do is define a net( ) subroutine and register it with the Gimp::on_net( ) function. Example 5-3 is a standalone script that queries the Gimp's procedural database and prints out the name, author, and help blurb from each function in the Procedural Database.

Example 5-3. A standalone script that extracts information from the Gimp's PDB

```perl
#!/usr/bin/perl -w

# This is a standalone script, so it needs to
# define a net( ) callback

use Gimp;

Gimp::on_net(\&net);

sub net {
    # The net( ) procedure is called when the script is started
    # by the Perl network server extension, rather than
    # being started directly by the Gimp.

    my ($blurb, $help, $author, $copyright, $date,
        $type, $args, $rvals);
```

Example 5-3. A standalone script that extracts information from the Gimp's PDB (continued)

```
    # Get the names of all the procedures from the PDB

    my @procnames = Gimp->procedural_db_query(qw(.* .* .* .*
                                                 .* .* .*));
    shift @procnames;        # discard the number returned

    # Now iterate through the names, get the 8 info fields
    # for each and print out the name, author, and help fields

    foreach my $name (@procnames) {
        ($blurb, $help, $author,
         $copyright, $date, $type,
         $args, $rvals) = Gimp->procedural_db_proc_info($name);
        print "$name\n";
        print '-' x length($name);
        print "\nAuthor: $author\nWhat it does: $help\n\n";
    }
}

exit main;
```

If you are creating a standalone script that has to manage multiple Perl Server connections, you can use the get_connection( ) function to get a unique ID for the current connection, and the set_connection( ) function to change to a different connection.

## PART II

Vector Images and Animations

## CHAPTER 6

SVG: The Scalable Vector Graphics Format

SVG is a file format for storing vector graphics, particularly graphics designed for use on the Web. SVG's strength is that it was developed as an open standards–based grammar for graphics that plays nicely with all of the other standard formats in the World Wide Web Consortium (W3C) family. An SVG document is written in XML, which means that its components can be easily integrated into larger documents with other types of XML.

The Document Object Model (DOM) provides a convenient interface for manipulating the structure of SVG documents, and stylesheets can be used to create a concise, consistent look and feel. Because SVG is XML, the XSLT language can be used to transform data stored in other XML formats into SVG documents. You can take advantage of the growing library of XML software tools to write SVG files. (See Chapter 1 for a summary of modules.)

SVG's drawbacks are the same as XML's. The code for representing simple documents can be overly verbose (although you can compress SVG files with *gzip*). Also, the computation involved in parsing and rendering an XML tree can require a lot of resources; it has taken some time for SVG viewers to catch up to the speed of SWF-based user agents. These drawbacks are more than made up for by the advantages offered by an XML-based design. The most compelling feature of SVG is the tight integration of the representation of images with the representation of other document elements within a browser.

Because the structure of an SVG image is so exposed, it is necessary to have a firm grounding in the basic tags and the way that an SVG document is structured. The first part of this chapter talks about how SVG documents are presented in HTML documents and how the document tree is rendered. The second part describes the set of basic structural, drawing, text, and linking tags. Chapter 7 goes on to present a number of recipes for creating SVG images using Perl, and touches on advanced topics such as SVG animation.

SVG Document Structure

SVG is an XML grammar for describing image documents. An image can be a vector graphic, a raster image, a collection of textual glyphs, or any combination of the three within a frame. Most elements appearing in an SVG document can have hyperlinks associated with them or can activate scripts by responding to user input events. Animation tags provide most of the functionality found in the Macromedia Flash format.

SVG takes advantage of other standard XML technologies such as:

XSL
> The Extensible Stylesheet Language standard is an evolution of the Cascading Style Sheets (CSS) language for describing stylesheets. All aspects of an SVG document are styleable, using the same standard as HTML/XHTML.

XSLT
> XSL Transformations is an XML-based scripting language for converting one form of XML into another. Using XSLT, you can write a series of rules that would convert, say, a database result set into SVG. A transformation script is run through an XSLT interpreter such as the Apache project's Xalan processor (which, incidentally, has a Perl interface) to produce the output XML.

XLink
> The XLink standard describes a way to implement linking between documents. XLink is used by SVG for specifying hyperlinks.

RDF
> SVG adheres to the Resource Description Framework standard, which means that metadata stored in image files can be added to the pool of metadata available to RDF-aware applications.

DOM
> The Document Object Model describes a standard way of representing and accessing the various components of a document tree. Elements in an SVG image can be manipulated using scripting languages that implement the DOM interface.

XHTML
> The eventual goal of the W3C is for SVG images to be seamlessly incorporated into HTML/XHTML documents.

Mobile SVG
> The SVG Tiny and SVG Basic standards describe a subset of the SVG standard that is appropriate for use with mobile devices.

Viewing SVG Documents

An SVG-capable user agent must pass the W3C's SVG Test Suite (*http://www.w3. org/Graphics/SVG/Test/*), ensuring that it implements the entire specification. A user

More About XML

An XML document is a series of elements (or tags), optionally with attributes. Elements can contain data (usually text) or other elements. These *container tags* or grouping tags are delimited by a start tag (bound by < and > angle brackets) and an end tag (also bound by angle brackets, with the tag name preceded by a forward slash):

```
<container attribute="foo">
  <tag>Some content</tag>
  More content
  <tag>Son of content</tag>
</container>
```

Sometimes a tag does not have any content. These tags are sometimes referred to as *empty tags*, and they are terminated with the token />.

```
<tag attribute="foo" attribute2="gum"/>
```

A comment in an SVG file is enclosed in <!-- and -->. Comments do not nest.

```
<!-- Here's where things get interesting -->
```

In XML, all tag and attribute names are case sensitive, so the tags <element> and <Element> are different. Even though this gives XML authors a larger playing field when defining a new XML language, it does not address the issue of tag names overlapping between formats. The whole idea of XML is that a wide variety of data types can be comingled in the same document and sensibly accessed through the same tree. Each element type may be handled by separate software modules.

To this end, each XML format should declare a *namespace* in which its particular entities reside. The simplest way of declaring a namespace is by adding a namespace prefix to the local tag name. A simple SVG document declared with absolute namespace references would look something like this:

```
<svg:svg width="3in" height="3in"
         xmlns:svg="http://www.w3.org/2000/svg">
  <svg:desc>A blue square</svg:desc>
  <svg:rect width="1.5in" height="1.5in" fill="#0000FF"/>
</svg:svg>
```

Here, the namespace is defined by a unique URL that points to the *w3.org* web site. The 2000 in the URL, incidentally, stands for the year that the specification was accepted as a final draft, not for the current version of the specification. Namespaces can be imported into your XML. The use of hyperlinking, for example, requires us to import the XLink namespace, as illustrated in the later "Linking in SVG" section.

---

agent can be a standalone viewer, such as the Apache project's Batik viewer (written in Java; *http://xml.apache.org/batik/*), or it can be a web browser plug-in, such as Adobe's SVG viewer. SVG viewers should accept data with the MIME type image/svg+xml. SVG documents may be encountered in one of three flavors: standalone, embedded links, or embedded images.

Standalone SVG documents

An SVG document can actually implement almost all the same functionality as an HTML document can. The example developed in Chapter 7 illustrates a standalone SVG application for creating slide presentations. Many illustration programs (such as Adobe's Illustrator or the free Sketch program) use SVG as a native storage format.

To view a standalone SVG document, you can use either an SVG-capable viewer or a web browser. With web browsers, however, you should make sure that the browser gets the correct MIME type. If you are serving SVG files from a web server, check your MIME type configuration. For the Apache web server, the MIME content types are usually stored in the configuration file *conf/mime.types*. This file is a hash of content types and the file extensions that should be associated with that type. You can also use Apache's AddType directive:

```
AddType image/svg+xml .svg
```

A standalone SVG document can also be linked from a web page (for example, `<a href="shemscape.svg">`).

Embedding SVG as an image reference

In an HTML document, you can use the IMG tag to include an SVG document within a page:

```
<IMG src="http://shawn.apocabilly.org/images/shempscape.svg"
     alt="The Shempscape Now! logo">
```

The OBJECT tag can be used for the same purpose, but is not as widely supported as the IMG tag:

```
<OBJECT data="http://shawn.apocabilly.org/images/shempscape.svg"
        type="image/svg+xml">
  The Shempscape Now! logo
</OBJECT>
```

To view, you must have an SVG-capable browser or a plug-in for rendering SVG content.

Embedding SVG as an inline image

The XHTML specification proposes that SVG graphics can be included directly in the body of an HTML document:

```
<html xmlns="http://www.w3.org/1999/xhtml">
  <head>
    <title>Inline SVG in a nutshell</title>
  </head>
  <body>
    <p>An inline SVG image:</p>
    <svg:svg width="3in" height="3in"
             xmlns:svg="http://www.w3.org/2000/svg">
      <svg:desc>A blue square</svg:desc>
```

```
        <svg:rect width="1.5in" height="1.5in" fill="#0000FF"/>
    </svg:svg>
  </body>
</html>
```

Unfortunately, at the time of this writing most browsers don't support inline SVGs.

Serving Compressed SVGs

SVG files can be compressed using *gzip* compression (see *http://www.gzip.org*). SVG viewers should know to decompress gzipped files on the fly (Adobe's viewer and Batik both do this). The file extension *.svgz* is typically used to mark compressed SVGs. Use *gzip*'s -S switch to append a *z* to the compressed filename. For example:

```
gzip -S z shemp.svg
```

produces the file *shemp.svgz*, which can be unzipped with:

```
gunzip -S z shemp.svgz
```

If you are serving compressed SVG files from a web server, be sure to associate the correct MIME type with the *.svgz* extension. On an Apache web server, you can add the following directive to your *httpd.conf* file:

```
AddType  image/svg+xml  svgz
```

Rendering an SVG Document Tree

Each element coordinate space can be thought of as a canvas to which paint is applied. Since SVG supports alpha blending, successive elements are composited with underlying elements using whatever alpha masks are associated with the current element or group.

Elements are rendered in the order in which they appear in the document. If elements are grouped together within a <g> tag, they are first rendered as a separate group canvas, then composited on the main canvas using whatever filters or alpha masks are associated with the group.

The user agent parses the XML tokens and generates an internal DOM tree. If the SVG is embedded in another SVG document, an XHTML document, or some other XML file, the image's tree is merged with the parent document's tree. The elements of the image are rendered subject to manipulation by any scripting actions (which may be defined elsewhere in the parent document) or animation tags that may be in effect.

Views and Coordinate Systems

An SVG graphic (i.e., everything enclosed between <svg> start and end tags) can be thought of as a viewport or frame around an image. That viewport has its own internal coordinate system called the *user coordinate system*. The origin is in the upper left corner of the coordinate grid, and units are defined in terms of an ideal "user unit" denoted by the abbreviation px. Each user unit translates to a device pixel, more or less. Alternately, in most SVG elements you can use any of the units in Table 6-1, which are automatically translated into user units.

Table 6-1. Standard SVG units

Units	Abbreviation	Equivalent in user coordinate units
Points	1 pt	1.25 px
Picas	1 pc	15 px
Millimeters	1 mm	3.543307px
Centimeters	1 cm	35.43307px
Inches	1 in	90 px

All coordinate values in an element are expressed in terms of the element's coordinate space, which initially corresponds to the user coordinate space. However, elements can be scaled, rotated, moved, or skewed, resulting in a similar transformation of the element's coordinate system relative to the user coordinate system. Similarly, an <svg> element may be embedded within another XML element and transformed within the coordinate system of the top-level element. The examples later in this chapter should illustrate the distinction between element and user coordinate spaces.

The Basic SVG Tags

This section provides a basic overview of a subset of the SVG specification. Because it is next to impossible to condense a 600-page technical specification (*http://www. w3.org/2000/svg*) into 10 pages, this section describes a set of core concepts around the following types of SVG elements:

- Structural elements
- Basic shape and path elements
- Textual elements
- Linking elements

Several more-complex or less frequently used topics are not covered here, such as:

- Gradients and filters
- Embedded font glyph data
- Clipping and masking
- Color management

All of the elements have a set of common attributes that are not necessarily listed in the attribute charts. For example, any element can be given a unique identifier (so that it can be referenced by scripts or hyperlinks). This identifier is assigned with the id attribute:

```
<!-- Define an arced path -->
<path id="path1"
      d="M50,200 A150,150 0 1,0 350,200"
      fill="none" stroke="black" />

<!-- Reference a previously defined path -->
<textPath xlink:href="#path1">Some text on a path</textPath>
```

Most elements have additional attributes that describe optional language space and style attributes. These attributes are indexed in the SVG specification. For a more complete introduction to SVG, read *SVG Essentials* by J. David Eisenberg (O'Reilly).

Structural Tags

The structural tags define the basic building blocks of an SVG document: the top-level viewport, groups, definition blocks, and tags for labeling sections of code.

Example 6-1 draws four brightly colored squares and rotates them 45 degrees as a group. The result is scaled to fit the bounds of the graphic (see Figure 6-1).

Example 6-1. A simple SVG graphic

```
<svg width="3in"
     height="3in"
     xmlns="http://www.w3.org/2000/svg">
  <g transform="translate(144,0) rotate(45) scale(.70)">
    <desc>A blue square</desc>
    <rect width="1.5in" height="1.5in" fill="#0000FF"/>
    <desc>A red square</desc>
    <rect x="0in" y="1.5in"
          width="1.5in" height="1.5in" fill="#FF0000"/>
    <desc>A yellow square</desc>
    <rect x="1.5in" y="0in"
          width="1.5in" height="1.5in" fill="#FFFF00"/>
    <desc>A green square</desc>
    <rect x="1.5in" y="1.5in"
          width="1.5in" height="1.5in" fill="#00FF00"/>
  </g>
</svg>
```

The top-level `<svg>` container declares a graphic that is 3×3 inches (288×288 px units) in size. The `xmlns` attribute indicates that the SVG namespace is the default namespace for all elements contained within (and we don't have to preface every-thing with annoying svg: prefixes).

The next element defines a group. All four rectangles within the group are subject to the three transformations listed in the group's `transform` attribute (see Table 6-4). Each rectangle is drawn on the canvas for the group. When the `</g>` tag is encoun-

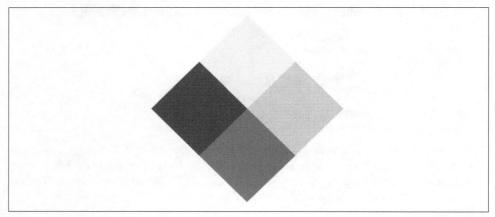

Figure 6-1. Four rectangles transformed as a group

tered, the group is drawn to the main canvas, at which point it is moved to the coordinate (144,0) in the user coordinate space, rotated 45 degrees, and scaled by 70%.

The <desc> tags within the group are used to provide alternative nonvisual indications of the contents of the document. The <desc> tags are not rendered unless the user agent is in a nonvisual mode.

The <defs> tag in Example 6-2 creates a definition block in which you can define elements that are not explicitly displayed but can be referenced by other elements in the document. This is useful for creating paths that can be used by the <textPath> tag, for example (see the later "Text Elements" section). Or, you can define elements once within a <defs> block and then reuse them throughout the document with the <use> tag. Example 6-2 generates the same four rotated squares as in the previous example using the <defs> tag.

Example 6-2. An alternative way of drawing the same simple SVG graphic

```
<svg width="3in"
     height="3in"
     xmlns="http://www.w3.org/2000/svg">
     xmlns:xlink="http://www.w3.org/1999/xlink">
  <defs>
    <rect id="square" width="1.5in" height="1.5in"
          transform="translate(144,0) rotate(45) scale(.70)"/>
  </defs>
  <desc>A blue square</desc>
  <use xlink:href="#square" fill="#0000FF"/>
  <desc>A red square</desc>
  <use xlink:href="#square"
       x="-.75in" y=".75in" fill="#FF0000"/>
  <desc>A yellow square</desc>
  <use xlink:href="#square"
       x=".75in" y=".75in" fill="#FFFF00"/>
  <desc>A green square</desc>
```

```
<use xlink:href="#square"
     y="1.5in" fill="#00FF00"/>
</svg>
```

The basic structural tags and their attributes are listed in Table 6-2.

Table 6-2. The basic structural tags

Tag	Basic attributes	Description
`<svg>`	**xmlns** The XML namespace. This attribute points to the specification that describes the SVG format: "http://www.w3.org/2000/svg". **version** The version of the SVG specification to which this document complies. As of this writing, the only acceptable value is "1.0". **x, y** The coordinate of the upper left corner of the SVG graphic (if it is embedded within another graphic). These attributes have no relevance for the outermost `<svg>` element. **width, height** The dimensions of the graphic.	The `<svg>` element is the top-level description of the SVG document. These elements can be embedded in other SVG documents. Most presentation attributes can be included in a `<svg>` element and are inherited by members of the group.
`<g>`	**transform** A list of transformations, as in Table 6-4.	A container element that is used to collect a group of objects with similar attributes. Most presentation attributes can be included in a `<g>` element and are inherited by members of the group. See the SVG specification for more details.
`<desc>`, `<title>`	None.	Both of these elements can provide a textual description of the parent element. Like the HTML ALT attribute, this text is not displayed by visual browsers, but can help describe the structure of the document.
`<defs>`	None.	A definition block. Elements enclosed in a `<defs>` block are defined but not drawn to the canvas. They can, however, be referenced by other elements.
`<use>`	**xlink:href** A link to the previously defined element. Additionally, any other attributes that are valid for the linked element may be listed, which supersedes the previously defined values.	A `<use>` tag references a previously defined reusable element and applies additional attributes to it.

Shapes, Paths, and Images

Several built-in shape functions are provided for drawing rectangles, circles, ellipses, and lines. The `<rect>` tags in the example earlier in this section illustrated the use of these tags. Additionally, there are elements to represent polygons and arbitrary paths of straight and curved line segments. External raster images in the JPEG or PNG format can also be included in an SVG document.

A <path> element represents a series of brush strokes on the canvas; the brush can move in straight lines or curves, or it can lift off the canvas, move to a new location, and begin drawing again. All of the strokes drawn within a path have the same attributes. Example 6-3 draws a complex symbol with a single path and two circles, as shown in Figure 6-2.

Example 6-3. Using the <path> tag

```
<svg width="280"
     height="220"
     xmlns="http://www.w3.org/2000/svg">
  <desc>Hobo symbol: Fresh water and campsite</desc>
  <g stroke="#000000"
     fill="none"
     stroke-width="4">
    <path d="M20,40
             Q40,10 60,40
               80,70 100,40
               120,10 140,40
               160,70 180,40
               200,10 220,40
               240,70 260,40
             M20,80 L260,200
             M260,80 L20,200" />
    <circle cx="70" cy="140" r="10"/>
    <circle cx="210" cy="140" r="10"/>
  </g>
</svg>
```

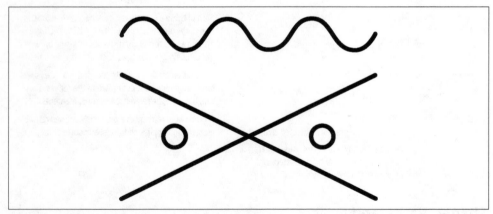

Figure 6-2. A path is an arbitrary collection of pen strokes

Because the path and the circles are in the same group, they are drawn with a 4px black stroke and no fill. The <path> element consists entirely of a path data string. This string represents a series of drawing commands that are pulled from the simple grammar described in Table 6-3. Individual drawing commands in the path data string are separated by whitespace.

For the above example, the commands translate to the following pseudocode:

1. Move to the absolute coordinate (20,40)
2. Draw a quadratic curve to the point (60,40), using (40,10) as a control point
3. Continue the curve, adding five more curve segments with the given control and end points
4. Move to the coordinate (20,80)
5. Draw a straight line from (20,80) to (260,200)
6. Move to the coordinate (60,80)
7. Draw a straight line from (20,80) to (20,200)

The two circles are added to the group at the specified center points.

Table 6-3 shows the path data commands. Capital letters indicate that the parameters are in the absolute coordinate space; lowercase letters indicate relative positioning.

Table 6-3. The path data commands

Operand	Parameter	Description
M, m	x,y	Move to a point.
L, l	x,y	Draw a line to a point.
H, h	x,y	Draw a horizontal line to a point.
V, v	x,y	Draw a vertical line to a point.
C, c	x1,y1 x2,y2 x,y	Draw a cubic Bezier curve to a point. (x1, y1) and (x2, y2) are control points.
S, s	x1,y1 x,y	A simplified version of the cubic Bezier curve, where the second control point is a reflection of (x1, y1).
Q, q	x1,y1 x,y	Draw a quadratic Bezier curve to a point, using (x1, y1) as a control point.
T, t	x,y	A simplified version of the quadratic Bezier curve where the control point is a reflection of either the previous control point or the current point (if there was not a previous control point).
A, a	rx,ry x-axis-rotation large-arc-flag, sweep-flag x,y	Draw an elliptical arc with the given x and y axis radii to a point (x, y). The x-axis-rotation parameter is the angle to which the horizontal axis may be rotated. The large-arc-flag is used only by authoring tools. The sweep-flag indicates whether the arc should be drawn clockwise (1) or counterclockwise (0). Spaces and commas must be retained in the parameter list.
Z	-	Close the path.

A polygon element represents a closed path of straight lines that is defined by a space-delimited list of coordinates. The <polyline> element can be used to draw a polygon that is not closed (i.e., the beginning and end points are not connected). Example 6-4 illustrates the use of the <polygon> and <polyline> elements.

Example 6-4. Using polygons and polylines

```
<svg width="280"
     height="220"
     xmlns="http://www.w3.org/2000/svg">
  <desc>Hobo symbol: Man with gun lives here</desc>
  <g stroke="black"
     fill="none"
     stroke-width="4">
    <polyline points="140,140 220,60 220,10 270,60 220,60"/>
    <polyline points="140,140 60,60 60,10 10,60 60,60"/>
    <polygon points="140,40 260,200 20,200"
             fill="white" />
  </g>
</svg>
```

The output is shown in Figure 6-3.

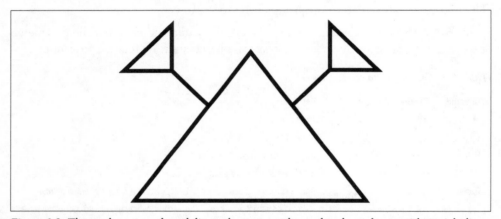

Figure 6-3. The <polygon> and <polyline> elements can be used to draw shapes with straight lines

Rather than attempt to figure out the coordinates at which the lines intersect the triangle, the lines are simply drawn from the center of the graphic. The polygon is drawn in white so that it obscures the overlapping lines.

All shapes (and other elements such as groups or text) may be subject to transformations defined by the transform attribute. This attribute takes a string that is a space-separated list of any of the transformation commands listed in Table 6-4. The transformations are executed in the order in which they appear in the string.

Table 6-4. Transform list commands

Transform type	Parameters	Description
translate()	x [, y]	Move the element to the absolute coordinate in user space units.
scale()	x_scale [, y_scale]	Scale the element by the specified amount in the given dimension. If y_scale is not provided, the element is scaled proportionately.

Table 6-4. Transform list commands (continued)

Transform type	Parameters	Description
rotate( )	rotate_angle [, cx, cy]	Rotate the element by the given amount, expressed in degrees. If cx, cy is provided, the element is rotated around that point.
skewX( ), skewY( )	skew_angle	Skew the element along the specified axis.

The basic shape elements are listed in Table 6-5. There are a few additional elements (such as `<marker>`) that are beyond the scope of our limited introduction. See the SVG specification for a complete accounting of elements.

Table 6-5. The basic shape and path tags

Tag	Attributes	Description
`<circle>`	cx, cy The center coordinate. r The radius. transform A list of transformations, as in Table 6-4.	A circle of a given radius and center point.
`<ellipse>`	cx, cy The center coordinate. rx, ry The radii of the x and y axes. transform A list of transformations, as in Table 6-4.	An ellipse defined by a center point and two radii.
`<image>`	x, y The coordinate of the upper left corner of the image. width, height The width and height of the image (both attributes are required). transform A list of transformations, as in Table 6-4.	An externally referenced SVG, PNG, or JPEG image.
`<line>`	x1, y1 The start coordinate. x2, y2 The end coordinate.	A line segment between the points (x1, y1) and (x2, y2).
`<path>`	d A string representing the path data. This string is constructed using the path commands described in Table 6-3. pathLength The calculated length of the path. This attribute should be set by authoring tools as a way to speed up the rendering of the path. transform A list of transformations, as in Table 6-4.	A path is a collection of line segments and curves of arbitrary length. The path is described by a sequence of drawing commands for positioning and moving a pen.

Table 6-5. The basic shape and path tags (continued)

Tag	Attributes	Description

`<polygon>`	`points`
	A string listing the points in the polygon, delimited by spaces (required).
	
	`transform`
	A list of transformations, as in Table 6-4
		A polygon is a closed shape consisting of line segments. It is defined by a list of points; e.g., setting the points attribute to the string "0,0, 100,100 100,0" would result in a triangle.

`<polyline>`	`points`
	A string listing the points in the polyline, delimited by spaces (required).
	
	`transform`
	A list of transformations, as in Table 6-4.
		A polyline is an open shape consisting of line segments. Setting the points attribute to the string "0,0, 100,100 100,0 0,0" would result in the same triangle as described for `<polygon>`.

`<rect>`	`x, y`
	The coordinate of the upper left corner of the rectangle.
	
	`width, height`
	The dimensions of the rectangle.
	
	`rx, ry`
	If these values are provided, the rectangle will have rounded edges with the given radii.
	
	`transform`
	A list of transformations, as in Table 6-4.
		This is a rectangular shape with straight or rounded corners.

The shape elements can also have any of the attributes listed in Table 6-6. These attributes can be shared by a group of elements by assigning them to a `<g>` or `<svg>` element.

Table 6-6. Fill and stroke attributes

Attribute	Values	Description
`fill`	Paint colors may be specified using the hexadecimal format #RRGGBB (e.g., "#FF0000" for red) or a color keyword (e.g., "lightsalmon"). The value can also be a URL to a pattern, gradient, or ICC profile defined elsewhere in the document (see the SVG specification for information on these topics).	The fill color.
`fill-opacity`	A percentage value, where 0 is completely transparent and 1 is opaque.	The opacity of the fill affects how it is composited with other elements and the background.
`stroke`	See `fill`.	The color of the stroke.
`stroke-dasharray`	A comma-separated list of lengths representing the dashes and the space between dashes. For example, "5,5,10,5" means "a 5-unit dash followed by 5 units of space, followed by a 10-unit dash followed by 5 units of space."	Use this to create dashed lines.

Table 6-6. Fill and stroke attributes (continued)

Attribute	Values	Description
stroke-dashoffset	A length.	This indicates the point on the line at which the dashes should begin.
stroke-linecap	butt | round | square	The style used to render the ends of lines.
stroke-linejoin	miter | round | bevel	The style used to render line edges.
stroke-miterlimit	A percentage value.	A "mitered" edge is elongated so that the outer edges of the two strokes meet. This attribute limits this behavior.
stroke-opacity	A percentage value, where 0 is completely transparent and 1 is opaque.	A value representing the alpha channel of the stroke.
stroke-width	A width, in any units.	The width of the stroke.
visibility	visible | hidden	Indicates whether or not the element should be rendered.

Text Elements

Text elements are used to draw strings on a canvas. All the fill, stroke, and transformation operations that may be performed on shape elements can also apply to text elements.

The baseline of a text element is positioned at the starting coordinate given by its x and y (or transform) attributes. This point becomes the current text point. As each glyph of the string is drawn, the current text point is moved in the direction of the text by the width of the glyph. The orientation of the text can be adjusted using the direction, glyph-orientation-horizontal, and glyph-orientation-vertical attributes. The current text point is reset to the origin (or to the origin of any enclosing <g> elements) when the </text> tag is encountered.

To change the attributes of the text in the middle of a single text element, use the <tspan> tag. This tag can also be used to render multiple lines of text in a single <text> element, as shown in Example 6-5.

Example 6-5. Rendering text in an image

```
<svg width="400"
     height="200"
     xmlns="http://www.w3.org/2000/svg">
  <desc>Hobo poetry</desc>
  <text x="200" y="50"
        font-family="Times"
        font-size="24"
        text-anchor="middle"
        fill="black">
  I'm heading for a land that&#x2019;s far away,
  <tspan x="200" dy="36">
    Beside the crystal fountain
  </tspan>
```

Example 6-5. Rendering text in an image (continued)

```
  <tspan x="200" dy="36">
    So, come with me; we&#x2019;ll go and see
  </tspan>
  <tspan x="200" dy="36">
    The <tspan font-style="italic">Big Rock Candy Mountain</tspan>
  </tspan>
  </text>
</svg>
```

This example draws four lines of centered text with a single <text> tag. The dy attribute of the <tspan> tag indicates that the text point should be moved relative to the current text point. Each of these tags has the effect of adding 36px of leading between each line. Each line returns to the center axis (x=200) of the graphic; since the text-anchor attribute is set to "middle", each line of text is centered around this axis. The result is shown in Figure 6-4.

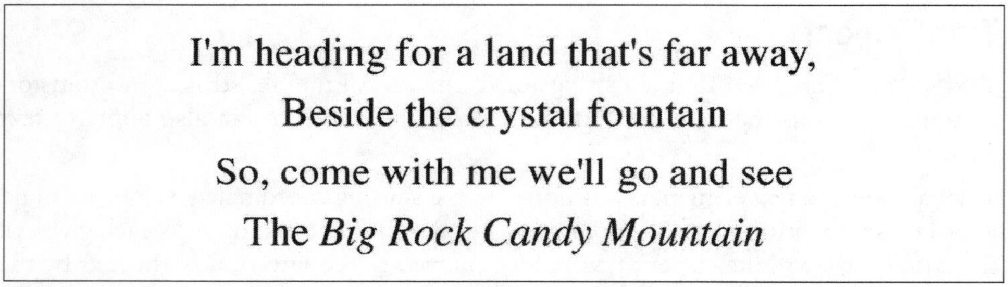

I'm heading for a land that's far away,

Beside the crystal fountain

So, come with me we'll go and see

The *Big Rock Candy Mountain*

Figure 6-4. The <text> and <tspan> elements are used to render strings of text

Unicode characters can be included in a <text> element by specifying the glyph's Unicode entity number. For example:

```
&#x222B;   An integral sign
&#xFD16;   A glyph in the Arabic character space
&#x8FB2;   An ideograph in the CJK unified character space
```

See the charts provided by the Unicode Consortium (*http://www.unicode.org/charts*) for a reference to Unicode characters.

Text can be made to follow a path with the <textPath> tag, as shown in Example 6-6.

Example 6-6. Rendering text on a path

```
<svg width="400"
     height="220"
     xmlns="http://www.w3.org/2000/svg"
     xmlns:xlink="http://www.w3.org/1999/xlink">
  <desc>Text on a path</desc>
  <path id="path1"
        d="M50,200 A150,150 0 1,1 350,200"
        fill="none" stroke="black"/>
  <path id="path2"
```

Example 6-6. Rendering text on a path (continued)

```
        d="M100,200 A100,100 0 1,1 300,200"
        fill="none" stroke="black"/>
  <text font-family="Helvetica"
        font-size="36"
        fill="black"
        text-anchor="middle">
    <textPath xlink:href="#path1"
            startOffset="50%">
      <tspan dy="-10">Lasciate ogne speranza</tspan>
    </textPath>
    <textPath xlink:href="#path2"
            startOffset="50%">
      <tspan dy="-10">voi ch'intrate</tspan>
    </textPath>
  </text>
</svg>
```

Figure 6-5 illustrates this example, where two lines of text are drawn along two different curves. The additional `xmlns` namespace attribute is necessary to let the user agent know that we are using a tag (`xlink:href`) that is defined outside of the SVG namespace by the XLink specification. The two paths are drawn using the elliptical arc tool to draw a 180 degree semicircle in the clockwise direction. The `startOffset` attribute indicates that the text should start at the midway point on the displayed arc; because `text-anchor` is set to "middle", the text is centered around this point. The `<tspan>` element is used to specify an additional vertical displacement (relative to the curve) for the text.

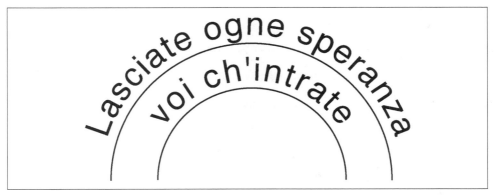

Figure 6-5. A <textPath> element is used to draw a string of text along a previously defined path

If you don't want the curved paths to be drawn, you can wrap the two `<path>` tags in a `<defs>` block.

The basic text elements are listed in Table 6-7. Several text-related tags are not covered here; these are described in the SVG specification. The most notable omission is the `<font>` element, which can be used to encode glyph outlines so that complete fonts may be embedded in an SVG document.

Table 6-7. The basic text elements

Tag	Attributes	Description
`<text>` `<tspan>`	**font-family** The name of the font family (e.g., "Times", "Helvetica") **font-size** The size of the font used to render the text. Not necessarily in points; any unit can be used (px is the default). **font-stretch** One of the following values: normal semi-condensed wider semi-expanded narrower expanded condensed extra-expanded extra-condensed ultra-expanded ultra-condensed **font-style** One of the following values: normal italic oblique **font-variant** One of the following values: normal small-caps **font-weight** One of the following values: normal, bold, bolder, lighter, 100, 200, 300, 400, 500, 600, 700, 800, 900 **direction** The direction in which the text is written. ltr (left-to-right) rtl (right-to-left) inherit **glyph-orientation-horizontal** Include this attribute to draw glyphs horizontally. **glyph-orientation-vertical** Include this attribute to draw glyphs vertically. **letter-spacing** Set the amount of space between glyphs. **text-anchor** Determines the alignment of the text: start middle end **word-spacing** Set the amount of space between words. **x, y** The starting coordinate for the baseline of the string. Text is drawn from this point according to the text-anchor attribute. **dx, dy** For `<tspan>` elements, you can move the text insertion point relative to the current point. **transform** A list of transformations, as in Table 6-4. *fill/stroke attributes* Any of the fill/stroke attributes in Table 6-6.	The `<text>` element is used to draw a string of text on the canvas. The font and style of the text are consistent throughout the element. `<tspan>` can be used to change text attributes within a `<text>` element. The attributes defined by the tag are used to draw the text contained in the text span element.

Table 6-7. The basic text elements (continued)

Tag	Attributes	Description

`<textPath>`	All of the above (except x,y and dx,dy), plus:
	
	`startOffset`
	A percentage value representing the position along the path at which the text should begin.
	
	`method`
	If set to `stretch`, the glyphs are warped to match the curve. If set to `align` (the default), the glyphs are rotated to be parallel to the tangent of the curvature of the path.
	
	`spacing`
	If `auto` (the default), the user agent should make adjustments to the text spacing to correct for the curvature of the path. If `exact`, the text is drawn using its normal letter spacing.
		Text can be constrained to follow a predefined path with this element. The position of the element on the page is determined by the position of the path.

Linking in SVG

SVG provides a mechanism for simple HTML-like linking with the `<a>` tag. Each item contained in the `<a>` element becomes a separate link to the specified URL. As in the previous `<textPath>` example, Example 6-7 imports the XLink namespace into your SVG document before using the `xlink:href` attribute of the `<a>` tag.

Example 6-7. Links within an image

```
<svg width="400"
    height="300"
    xmlns="http://www.w3.org/2000/svg"
    xmlns:xlink="http://www.w3.org/1999/xlink">
  <desc>A table of contents</desc>
  <g font-family="Avant-Garde"
     font-size="14"
     fill="black">
    <text x="20" y="40"
          font-size="36"
font-weight="bold">
      Perl for Graphics
    </text>
    <a xlink:href="http://shawn.apocabilly.org/PFG/ch01/">
      <text x="20" y="60">
        1. Raster Graphics File Formats
      </text>
    </a>
    <a xlink:href="http://shawn.apocabilly.org/PFG/ch02/">
      <text x="20" y="80">
        2. SWF File Format
      </text>
    </a>
    <a xlink:href="http://shawn.apocabilly.org/PFG/ch03/">
      <text x="20" y="100">
        3. The SVG Format
      </text>
    </a>
```

Example 6-7. Links within an image (continued)

```
    <desc>...Contents truncated for brevity...</desc>
  </g>
</svg>
```

Note that you can't enclose <tspan> elements in an anchor, which would have made this particular example easier. Most other tags can be links, however.

Table 6-8 describes the attributes of the link element.

Table 6-8. The link element

Tag	Attributes	Description
<a>	xlink:href A URL. xlink:show If new, the linked resource is loaded in a new window. The default value is replace, where the linked content replaces the contents of the current window. target If the parent of the SVG document is an HTML document with multiple frames, the target attribute can be used to direct the linked resource to a particular frame.	The <a> element allows you to create hyperlinks, just like in HTML. All elements enclosed between the <a> and </a> tags will be linked to the given resource.

The next chapter details how to use Perl to generate SVG images and covers advanced SVG topics such as animation, scripting, and XSLT transformations.

## CHAPTER 7

Creating SVG with Perl

The SVG specification describes several more elements than those described in Chapter 6. In particular, the animation tags allow you to animate SVG elements, and the `<script>` element can be used to attach JavaScript code to an SVG document. This chapter starts with a sample SVG application that generates slide presentations from custom XML templates, and then develops two animation examples: a simple bouncing ball using the animation tags, and an animation graphic using JavaScript to dynamically reposition objects within the image. The remainder of the chapter presents tips for inserting Unicode strings in SVGs and a tutorial on using the XSLT transformation language to convert arbitrary XML formats into SVG.

A Slide-Show Presentation

Many programs let you build presentations, the biggest and best-known of which is Microsoft's Powerpoint. In this section we develop a program that transforms an XML file describing a slide-show presentation (slides, bullet items, etc.) into an SVG file that is the presentation.

The input file consists of a collection of any of the following six tags:

`<slideshow>`
> The top-level tag

`<slide>`
> A new slide in the sequence

`<block>`
> A block can be either a line of text or a bullet list

`<bulletlist>`
> A group of `<bullet>` elements

`<bullet>`
> An indented line of text with a bullet prepended

`<image>`
> An image to place in the upper left corner of the slide

A complete slide show file written in this format looks like Example 7-1.

Example 7-1. Sample slideshow file

```
<slideshow subdir="./slideshow1/">
  <slide title="Perl for Graphics">
    <image>http://shawn.apocabilly.org/PFG/examples/shawn.png
    </image>
    <block type="textline">Section I: File Formats</block>
    <block type="bulletlist">
      <bullet>1. Raster Graphics Formats</bullet>
      <bullet>2. Efficient Multimedia with SWF</bullet>
      <bullet>3. The SVG format</bullet>
      <bullet>4. Printing with PostScript and PDF</bullet>
    </block>
    <block type="textline">Section II: Tools</block>
              ...
  </slide>
  <slide title="Chapter 1">
    <image>http://shawn.apocabilly.org/PFG/examples/shawn.png
    </image>
    <block type="textline">Web Graphics Basics</block>
    <block type="bulletlist">
      <bullet>Fields and Streams</bullet>
      <bullet>Color tables</bullet>
      <bullet>Transparency and alpha</bullet>
      <bullet>Compression</bullet>
      <bullet>Interlacing</bullet>
      <bullet>Which to use when?</bullet>
    </block>
              ...
  </slide>
</slideshow>
```

When given the file in Example 7-1, the output of our program is the presentation shown in Figure 7-1.

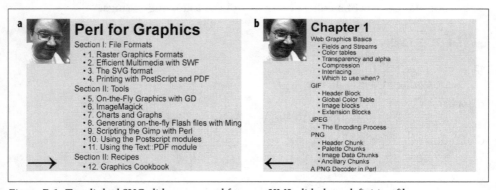

Figure 7-1. Two linked SVG slides generated from an XML slideshow definition file

There are several ways of transforming XML files from one format to another. An XML purist would try to use the XSLT transformation language to write a set of rules for rearranging the input XML tree into an output tree. In this chapter, we'll try a different method: translating the input file into an intermediate data structure (in this case, a big hash).

This simple example uses the XML::Simple module for the parsing of the file. This module provides all of two functions for reading and writing XML (XMLin and XMLout). A more robust application may want to use one of the other fine modules available on CPAN for XML parsing.

XML::Simple reads the previously described XML document into a hash where each of the keys is a tag name. If an element has a child, that child is represented as an anonymous hash. If there are several children, they are grouped together as an anonymous array of hashes.

Our script iterates through the elements of the hash and, with the help of the XML::Writer module (a basic XML library for writing simple tags), generates one SVG file for each <slide> element.

Each slide actually consists of two <svg> elements, one top-level graphic and one that encapsulates the textual area. This structure allows the text to be drawn in one pass and scaled to fit the dimensions of the top-level graphic.

The code for the slide generator is shown in the following example. First it creates a new simple XML parser. XML::Simple only implements two functions: XMLin and XMLout. Calling XMLin creates a hash representing the XML tree.

If an element has more than one child of the same type, they are stored in an anonymous array. If there's only one child of a particular type, it appears as a hash reference. For this reason, we use a subroutine called dereference( ) that sorts out the data type of the child and always returns a dereferenced array.

```perl
#!/usr/bin/perl -w

# SVG presentations

use strict;
use XML::Simple;    # Used to parse the XML input
use XML::Writer;    # Used to write the SVG output
use IO::Scalar;     # Allows you to easily redirect
                    # output from a filehandle to a scalar
my $height = 400;
my $width = 600;
my $titlesize = 36;

my $parser = new XML::Simple( );
my $slideshow = $parser->XMLin($ARGV[0]);
my @slides = dereference($slideshow->{'slide'});
```

Next, iterate through the slide elements. Normally the XML::Writer module writes to an IO::Handle filehandle. The IO::Scalar module subclasses IO::Handle and ties the filehandle output to a scalar. This provides an easy means of buffering the XML output so that we can embed one <svg> element within another.

```
my $dir = $slideshow->{'subdir'};

my $n = 0;                   # the current slide
my $max = $#slides+1;        # the total number of slides

foreach my $s (@slides) {
    my $y = 0;
    $n++;
    my $textblock = new IO::Scalar;
    my $writer = XML::Writer->new(OUTPUT=>$textblock);
```

The setDataMode( ) and setDataIndent( ) methods control the formatting of the output XML; here we enter newlines around elements and indent them:

```
$writer->setDataMode(1);
$writer->setDataIndent(2);
```

Use XML::Writer's startTag( ) method to start a tag and the endTag( ) method for the closing tag. Attributes are added for each additional named parameter. The characters( ) method writes strings to the XML output, escaping all special characters:

```
$writer->startTag('svg',         # Start an SVG element
                width=>"2000",
                height=> "2000");
$writer->startTag('text',
                transform => "translate(0, $titlesize)",
                style => "font-size:$titlesize;".
                "font-weight:bold;fill:#000000");
$writer->characters($s->{'title'});
$writer->endTag('text');          # Close the text element
$y += $titlesize + 10;            # track the current y position
```

Next, iterate through all the blocks in the slide, adding a new line of SVG text for each textline element in the original template.

```
my @blocks = dereference($s->{'block'});
foreach my $b (@blocks) {
    if ($b->{'type'} eq 'textline') {
        $y +=18;
        $writer->startTag('text',
                transform => "translate(0, $y)",
                style => 'font-size:18;fill:#000000');
        $writer->characters($b->{'content'});
        $writer->endTag('text');
    }
```

A bulletlist contains a sequence of bullet items, each of which is indented and starts with a Unicode bullet character. Unfortunately, the characters( ) method escapes the Unicode bullet character, so we'll bypass it by printing directly to the text block.

```
if ($b->{'type'} eq 'bulletlist') {
    $y += 4;             # give it a little space
    my @bullets = dereference($b->{'bullet'});
    foreach my $bulleted_text (@bullets) {
        $y += 18;
        $writer->startTag('text',
                    transform => "translate(20, $y)",
                    style => 'font-size:18;fill:#000000');

        print $textblock "&#x2022; ";   # A Unicode bullet
        $writer->characters($bulleted_text);
        $writer->endTag('text');
    }
    $y += 4;             # Add more space after the list
  }
}
$writer->endTag('svg');      # Close the 'text block' SVG graphic
$writer->end();
```

Compute an appropriate scaling factor. If the text block already fits, leave it as is; otherwise, shrink it.

```
my $scale =1;
    if ($y > ($height-40)) {
        $scale = ($height-40)/$y;
    }
```

Now create the final, top-level SVG graphic. Add an image (if specified in the original template) to the upper left corner.

```
my $toplevel = new IO::Scalar;
$writer = XML::Writer->new(OUTPUT=>$toplevel);
$writer->setDataMode(1);
$writer->setDataIndent(2);
$writer->startTag('svg',
            height => $height,
            width  => $width,
            'xmlns:xlink'=>"http://www.w3.org/1999/xlink");

$writer->emptyTag('rect',              # Draw a colored background
            height => $height,
            width  => $width,
            fill   => '#EEEEEE');
if (defined($s->{'image'})) {              # Add the image
    $writer->startTag('image',
            x => 20,
            y => 20,
            width => 100,
            height => 100,
```

```
                            'xlink:href' => $s->{'image'});
            $writer->endTag('image');
    }
```

Add a scaled group that contains the text block SVG. We have the complete SVG code sitting in the $textblock scalar; add it to the top-level SVG. We have to print it directly because the characters() method escapes all of the special characters.

```
        $writer->startTag('g',
                        id => 'SlideBody',
                        transform => "translate(130, 20) scale($scale)");

        print $toplevel $textblock;
        $writer->endTag('g');              # End the group
```

Add the Next and Previous navigation buttons:

```
        my $prev = $n-1;
        my $next = $n+1;
        unless ($prev < 1) {        # Previous button
            $writer->startTag('a',
                            'xlink:href' => "slide$prev.svg"
                            );
            $writer->startTag('text',
                            transform => "translate(20, 380)",
                            style => 'font-size:72;fill:#000000');
            print $toplevel "&#x2190;";    # A Unicode left arrow
            $writer->endTag('text');
            $writer->endTag('a');
        }
        unless ($next > $max) {     # Next button
            $writer->startTag('a',
                            'xlink:href' => "slide$next.svg"
                            );
            $writer->startTag('text',
                            transform => "translate(20, 360)",
                            style => 'font-size:72;fill:#000000');
            print $toplevel "&#x2192;";    # A Unicode right arrow
            $writer->endTag('text');
            $writer->endTag('a');
        }
        $writer->endTag('svg');
        $writer->end();
```

Finally, create the slide SVG in the specified subdirectory:

```
        open(OUT, ">$dir/slide$n.svg") or
            die "Couldn't open $dir/slide$n.svg!";
        print OUT $toplevel;
        close OUT;
    }
```

The dereference() subroutine is needed because of the slightly inconsistent manner in which XML::Simple represents the XML tree. If the parameter is an array reference, dereference and return it. Otherwise, return the parameter unchanged.

```
sub dereference {
    my $ref = shift;
    if (ref($ref) eq 'ARRAY') {
        return (@$ref);
    } else {
        return ($ref);
    }
}
```

The next section deals with the specifics of the animation tags.

SVG Animation

Up until now, we have seen only static, single-frame SVG documents. However, SVG can also be used for animation, just like Flash. Rather than describing the specific state of each element in each frame of the animation, SVG wraps up a sequence of high-level animation transformations in one of four animation tags. An *animation tag* tells how an object should be moved between two points and the time it should take to get there, or it describes a color transformation that should be applied at a particular moment in time.

SVG animation is an evolution of the World Wide Web Consortium's convoluted SMIL (Synchronized Multimedia Interchange Language) standard. Luckily, the four animation tags provided are relatively easy to understand:

`<animate>`
> This tag is used to modify a particular attribute of an element over a period of time.

`<animateMotion>`
> This tag is used to move an element along a predefined path over a period of time.

`<animateColor>`
> This tag is used to apply a color transform to the specified element.

`<animateTransform>`
> This tag can be used to perform a number of transformations on an element.

The following `<animate>` element, for example, causes the circle to expand to 5 times its original size over the course of 10 seconds, after which it stops.

```
<circle id="ball" r="10" fill="#FF0000">
  <animate attributeName="r" from="10" to="50" dur="10s"/>
</circle>
```

The remainder of this section details the use of the `<animateMotion>` tag to create the effect of a bouncing ball. An `<animateMotion>` tag can be associated with most elements, including: `<g>`, `<text>`, `<image>`, `<line>`, `<path>`, `<rect>`, `<circle>`, `<ellipse>`, `<polyline>`, and `<polygon>`.

The `<animateMotion>` element takes several attributes:

dur

> The duration of the animation. This can be expressed in time units ranging from a millisecond to an hour (ms, s, min, and h).

path

> A list of path data describing the path to be followed.

calcMode

> This attribute defines how the object should be moved from point to point on the path. If `discrete`, the object is moved from one point to another with no interpolation. If `linear`, intermediate frames are added where the object moves at an even pace between each pair of points. In our bouncing ball example, we need to use `spline` interpolation so that the ball moves faster on the longer segments of the curved path and slower on the shorter segments.

repeatCount

> This attribute indicates the number of times (if any) the animation should repeat. A value of `indeterminate` means that the animation loops indefinitely.

values

> An alternative to the `path` attribute, `values` allows you to specify a list of key frames that corresponds to the keytimes attribute list. The object is moved to each point in this list when the associated keytime is reached.

keytimes

> A list of moments in time that corresponds to the `values` keyframe entries.

Other attributes are available for different applications; see the SVG specification for more details.

Creating a Bouncing Ball

The example in this section creates a simple bouncing ball. We use the XML::Writer module to create the SVG output. The make_bounce_path( ) function returns a properly formatted path data string. The $ground variable indicates the y coordinate of the "ground line" off which the ball bounces. The bounce path follows the positive part of a sine wave.

Here's the first part of the code:

```
#!/usr/bin/perl -w
# The bouncing ball.

use strict;
use XML::Writer;     # Used to write the SVG output

my ($width, $height) = (300, 300);

my $writer = XML::Writer->new( );
```

```
$writer->setDataMode(1);      # Auto insert newlines
$writer->setDataIndent(2);    # Auto indent
$writer->startTag('svg',
                   height => $height,
                   width  => $width,
                   'xmlns:xlink' => 'http://www.w3.org/1999/Xlink');
```

The circle is in the <circle></circle> format (rather than as an empty tag). It contains two animation tags. The <animateMotion> tag causes the circle to move along a path. The <animate> tag causes the radius of the ball to be increased over the course of the animation.

```
$writer->startTag('circle',
                   id => 'ball',
                   r => 10,
                   fill   => '#FF0000');
$writer->emptyTag('animateMotion',
                   calcMode=> 'spline',
  dur => "10s",
  path => make_bounce_path(300, 200, 4),
  repeatCount => "indefinite");
$writer->emptyTag('animate',
                   attributeName => "r",
                   from => 10,
                   to => 50,
                   dur  => "10s",
                   repeatCount => "indefinite"
                   );
$writer->endTag('circle');
$writer->endTag('svg');
```

The make_bounce_path( ) function returns a properly formatted SVG path data string. The parameters are the x axis for the sine wave (the "ground" off which the ball bounces), the height of the bounce, and the number of bounces. The sin( ) function returns a value in radians; multiply by 2p to convert to a number in the range –1 to 1. With each bounce, the ground is moved up to take into account the changing radius of the ball, which varies from 10 to 50 pixels over the course of the animation.

```
sub make_bounce_path {
    my ($ground, $bounce_height, $bounces) = @_;
    my $pi = atan2(1,1) * 4;
    my $points = "M0,$height ";
    my $y;

    for (my $x=1; $x < $width; $x+=5) {
        $y = int($ground - abs(($bounce_height *
              sin(($x/($width*2/$bounces)) * 2 * $pi))));
        $points .= "L$x,$y ";
        $ground -= 40/($width/5);
        $height -= 40/($width/5);
    }
    return $points;
}
```

Figure 7-2 shows the bouncing ball with the animation path highlighted.

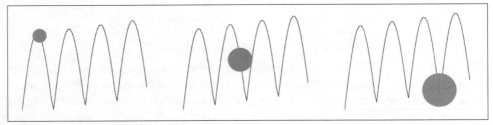

Figure 7-2. A bouncing ball, the canonical animation example

SVG Scripting with JavaScript

SVG elements can be manipulated using ECMAscript (better known as JavaScript). JavaScript scripts are attached to SVG objects as callbacks associated with a particular event. A script can be called when an element is first loaded, when the mouse passes over it, or when the mouse button is clicked on the element. Some of the element events are:

```
onfocusin
onfocusout
onactivate
onclick
onmousedown
onmouseup
onmouseover
onmousemove
onmouseout
onload
```

Scripts can also be called for certain document events:

```
onunload
onabort
onerror
onresize
onscroll
onzoom
```

Or they can be triggered at three points in the execution of an animation:

```
onbegin
onend
onrepeat
```

XML specifies a special tag for character data such as scripts that may have embedded XML tags. The script should be wrapped up in a character data (CDATA) tag:

```
<![CDATA[ ...character data goes here... ]]>
```

With JavaScript, you can access and manipulate most attributes of an element using the DOM interface. JavaScript can be used as an alternative to the animation tags for creating animations. For a complete reference to JavaScript, see *JavaScript: The Definitive Guide* by David Flanagan (O'Reilly).

The next example uses XML::Writer to create an SVG file that is very similar to the SWF::DisplayItem example in Chapter 9. The result is two SVG images: a top-level image that consists of a pink background, and the block of animated squares. Each of the squares in the grid has a `mouseover` event associated with it that turns the square red when the mouse is positioned over it. The user can also click on a point on the pink background to reposition the center of the animated object.

```perl
#!/usr/bin/perl -w
#
# Twirling squares.

use strict;
use XML::Writer;     # Used to write the SVG output
use IO::Scalar;

my ($width, $height) = (200,200);
my $sprite = new IO::Scalar;
my $writer = XML::Writer->new(OUTPUT => $sprite);
$writer->setDataMode(1);
$writer->setDataIndent(2);

$writer->startTag('svg',
                  id => 'sprite',
                  height => $height,
                  width  => $width,
                  onload => "StartAnimation(evt)",
                  'xmlns:xlink' => 'http://www.w3.org/1999/Xlink');
```

Add the CDATA element containing the script:

```perl
$writer->startTag('script',
                  type => "text/ecmascript");
print $sprite <<ENDSCRIPT;
<![CDATA[
    var delay = 1;
    var angle=0;
    var cx = 100;
    var cy = 100;
    var frames = 30;
    var direction = -1;
    var count = 0;
    var element = new Array();
    var xIncrement = new Array();
    var yIncrement = new Array();
    var parent;
    var i,x,y;
```

The grid of animated squares defines three JavaScript functions. The first is StartAnimation( ), which initializes the variable used to calculate the center of the block and the table used to keep track of the position and direction of each square. A reference to each element is also stored in the elements[ ] table for convenience. This function is called when the SVG image is first loaded.

```
function StartAnimation(evt) {
    parent =evt.target.ownerDocument;
    for (i=0; i<25; i++) {
        element[i] = parent.getElementById("box"+i);
        x = element[i].getAttribute("x");
        y = element[i].getAttribute("y");
        xIncrement[i] = (cx-element[i].getAttribute("x"))/frames;
        yIncrement[i] = (cy-element[i].getAttribute("y"))/frames;
    }
    MoveElements( );
}
```

The MoveElements( ) function is called after the environment is initialized and after the center point is moved by the user. This function is a loop that moves each of the squares in the grid toward (or away from) the center and rotates each square.

```
function MoveElements( ) {
    angle = angle+360/frames;
    count = count+1;
    if (count==frames) {
      direction=direction*-1;
      count =0;
    }
    for (i=0; i<25; i++) {
        x = element[i].getAttribute("x");
        y = element[i].getAttribute("y");
        element[i].setAttribute("transform",
            "rotate("+angle+","+x+","+y+")");
        element[i].setAttribute("x",
            x - direction * xIncrement[i]);
        element[i].setAttribute("y",
            y - direction * yIncrement[i]);

    }
    setTimeout("MoveElements( )", delay)
}
```

The ChangeColor( ) function is called whenever a mouseover event occurs for any of the 25 squares. It changes the fill attribute of the square to red. When the mouse is no longer over a square, ChangeColorBack( ) changes its fill back to transparent.

```
function ChangeColor(evt) {
    evt.target.setAttribute("fill", "#FF0000");
}

function ChangeColorBack(evt) {
    evt.target.setAttribute("fill", "none");
```

```
        }
    ]]>
    ENDSCRIPT
    $writer->endTag('script');
```

Next, add 25 squares in a grid:

```
    foreach my $row (1..5) {
        foreach my $col (1..5) {
            $writer->emptyTag('rect',
                        id => "box".(($row-1)*5+$col-1),
                        onmouseover => "ChangeColor(evt)",
                        onmouseout => "ChangeColorBack(evt)",
                        width => 20, height => 20,
                        'stroke-width' => 1,
                        stroke => '#000000',
                        fill  => 'none',
                        x => 30*$col, y => 30*$row);
        }
    }
    $writer->endTag('svg');
```

Now create the top-level wrapper SVG:

```
    my $toplevel = new IO::Scalar;
    $writer = XML::Writer->new(OUTPUT => $toplevel);
    $writer->setDataMode(1);
    $writer->setDataIndent(2);
    $writer->startTag('svg',
                    height => $height,
                    width  => $width,
                    'xmlns:xlink' => 'http://www.w3.org/1999/Xlink');
    $writer->startTag('script',
                    type => "text/ecmascript");
```

The top-level SVG image defines one JavaScript function, MoveCenter(), which
moves the center of the animated block of squares to the point that the user clicked.

```
    print $toplevel <<ENDSCRIPT;
    <![CDATA[
        function MoveCenter(evt) {
            var sprite = evt.target.ownerDocument.getElementById("sprite");
            sprite.setAttribute("x", evt.clientX-$width/2);
            sprite.setAttribute("y", evt.clientY-$height/2);
        }
    ]]>
    ENDSCRIPT
    $writer->endTag('script');
```

Finally, add a pink background that doubles as a button:

```
    $writer->emptyTag('rect',
                    id => "background",
                    onmousedown => "MoveCenter(evt)",
                    width => 400, height => 400,
                    fill  => 'pink');
```

```
print $toplevel $sprite;
$writer->endTag('svg');

print $toplevel;
```

Using Unicode Text in SVG Images

In 1998, RFC 2277 declared that the Internet was an international phenomenon, and that all new Internet standard protocols, languages, and formats should use Unicode (also referred to as ISO 10646) character set encodings. Sounds great; how do we do that in an SVG image?

Unicode is a standard set of character codes for representing multilingual text. In the early days of computing, vendors invented their own character encodings; it wasn't until 1968 that the ANSI standards group proposed the US-ASCII specification, which put forth an encoding table that represented all of the Latin alphanumeric characters in a standard 7-bit mapping. In the '80s, an attempt was made to create an internationalized character set with the ISO-8859-1 standard that provided a table for Latin, Cyrillic, Arabic, Greek, and Hebrew characters. Unicode is the modern synthesis of the standard encodings that came before it, with the goal of adding support for all the world's languages.

The early versions of Unicode proposed to represent a set of about 65,000 glyphs using 16 bits. The scope of the current version of Unicode has been expanded to potentially encode over a million different character glyphs, including glyphs from historic or ancient languages. More information on Unicode is available at the Unicode Consortium's web site, *http://www.unicode.org/*.

The Unicode standard provides three different methods for implementing the encoding:

UTF-8

In UTF-8, character glyphs are represented as variable-length byte sequences. Standard Latin alphanumeric characters that correspond to the ASCII set are encoded in 8 bits, so if you are using only these characters, UTF-8 looks just like ASCII. UTF-8 is used by web browsers and is useful for keeping Unicode applications compatible with older software.

UTF-16

In UTF-16, characters are encoded in 16 bits. This gives you access to just about every character you would ever use; some less frequently used characters are encoded using two 16-bit words.

UTF-32

In UTF-32, each character is encoded using 32 bits. This encoding scheme is not popular, but may become more popular as massive computing resources become prevalent.

The Adobe SVG viewer supports both UTF-8 and UTF-16 character encodings. In Perl (Version 5.005_50 or later), strings are stored in the UTF-8 encoding, so we don't really have to worry about the low-level details of the encoding.

If your text input device supports the input of UTF-8 characters, you should be able to include the Unicode characters directly in your Perl code. If not, you can use NCR (Numeric Character References) notation. An NCR can be expressed as a hex value:

```
&#x05D0;          # The Hebrew aleph
```

or as a decimal value:

```
&#1488;
```

If you need to look up a particular character, the Unicode Consortium provides charts that give the hex values for each set of characters.

All that remains is to make sure you have a font that has glyphs for the character range you wish to display (not all fonts include all glyphs). Again, the Unicode Consortium maintains a list of resources for finding fonts for particular platforms that can render certain character ranges.

Example 7-2 displays some Katakana characters (in the range 0x30A0 to 0x30FF) underneath the Latin characters "O'Reilly". (Katakana characters are Japanese glyphs for representing foreign words phonetically.) To display the Katakana characters, you need a font like MSGothic (Windows), AppleGothic (Mac), or Caslon (Unix). A collection of Unicode-enabled fonts is available at Alan Wood's Unicode Resources page *http://www.hclrss.demon.co.uk/unicode*.

Example 7-2. Using Unicode characters in SVG

```perl
#!/usr/bin/perl -w
#
# Example 7-2. Unicode in SVG

use strict;
use XML::Writer;    # Used to write the SVG output
use IO::Scalar;     # Used to buffer the XML::Writer output

my $output = new IO::Scalar;
my $writer = XML::Writer->new(OUTPUT => $output);
$writer->setDataIndent(2);

$writer->xmlDecl("UTF-8");

$writer->startTag('svg',
                  width => 200,
                  height => 100,
                  'xmlns:xlink' => 'http://www.w3.org/1999/Xlink');
$writer->startTag('text',
                  x => 100,
                  y => 50,
                  'font-family' => 'Arial',
```

Example 7-2. Using Unicode characters in SVG (continued)

```
                    'font-size' => 40,
                    'text-anchor' => 'middle',
                    fill    => '#000000');
$writer->characters("O'Reilly");
$writer->startTag('tspan',
                    'font-family' => 'Gothic MS',
                    'font-size' => 24,
                    x => 100, dy => 24);

# Add Katakana glyphs

print $output "&#x30AA;&#x30E9;&#x30A4;&#x30EA;&#x30FC;";
$writer->endTag('tspan');
$writer->endTag('text');
$writer->endTag('svg');

print $output;
```

Technically, we should always provide the XML header specifying the charset used in this document (in this case, UTF-8). The xmlDecl( ) function adds a header that looks like this:

```
<?xml version="1.0" encoding="UTF-8"?>
```

Figure 7-3 illustrates the output. For more on Perl and Unicode see the Perl/Unicode FAQ at *http://rf.net/~james/perli18n.html*.

Figure 7-3. Text in Katakana and Latin characters

Transformation with XSLT and Perl

The XML Stylesheet Language Transformations (XSLT) specification describes an XML-based scripting language that can be used to create rules for transforming one XML format into another. In some cases you may wish to use XSLT instead of a Perl-based solution. You can still use Perl to interpret the XSLT rules, however. The XSLT specification is available online at *http://www.w3.org/TR/xslt*.

Example 7-3 reimplements part of the slide-show generator script introduced in Chapter 6, this time using XSLT. The example uses a slightly different version of the slide XML description language discussed there.

Example 7-3. A slightly different XML slide presentation format

```
<slide title="Perl for Graphics">
    <image>http://shawn.apocabilly.org/PFG/examples/shawn.png
    </image>
    <textline>Section I: Raster Graphics</textline>
    <bulletlist>
        <bullet>1. PNG, GIF, and JPEG</bullet>
        <bullet>2. Using GD</bullet>
        <bullet>3. Using Image::Magick</bullet>
        <bullet>4. Using GD::Chart</bullet>
        <bullet>5. Scripting Gimp plug-ins</bullet>
    </bulletlist>
    <textline>Section II: Vector graphics</textline>
    <bulletlist>
      <bullet>6. The SVG format</bullet>
      <bullet>7. SVG Recipes</bullet>
      <bullet>8. The SWF format</bullet>
      <bullet>9. Generating SWF files with Ming </bullet>
    </bulletlist>
    <textline>Section III: Printing formats</textline>
    <bulletlist>
      <bullet>10. PostScript and PDF</bullet>
      <bullet>11. Using the Postscript modules </bullet>
      <bullet>12. Using the Text::PDF module </bullet>
    </bulletlist>
  </slide>
```

That is our input XML; the output is an SVG image for the slide.

XSLT is an evolutionary child of Cascading Style Sheets (CSS) and the Extensible Stylesheet Language (XSL). XSLT defines a collection of XML elements (in the xsl namespace) that forms almost a kind of internal XML scripting language. An XSLT document is applied to a source XML document, and provides a series of rules or "templates" that match elements in the source document. Each template can add new XML elements or rearrange the source XML tree. Templates are applied to the entire source document; if a template matches an element, the rule is applied. If it doesn't match any text in the source document, the source text is passed on unmodified to the output tree.

Our example uses only three XSLT elements to transform the slide description format into SVG:

`<template>`

A template element is a block of XML that is passed on to the output tree when a piece of input text is matched. The match attribute allows you to match a tag name; every tag of the matched type has this template applied to it. For example, the following template:

```
<xsl:template match="slide">
    <foo>Bar</foo>
</xsl:template>
```

indiscriminately replaces each <slide> element (and anything contained within it) with the given <foo> tag.

<apply-templates>

This element allows you to recursively apply the same set of XSLT templates to elements or content wrapped up in other elements.

<value-of>

This element retrieves the value of an element or attribute, whose value replaces the <value-of> tag. To retrieve an attribute from the tag that has been matched with the <template> tag, use the syntax:

```
<xsl:template match="tag">
    <xsl:value-of select="@attribute"/>
</xsl:template>
```

Additionally, you can retrieve the content of any element with the tag {*element*}, where *element* is the first tag that matches that name. This is used to extract the image URL in the following example.

The XSLT script in Example 7-4 uses these basic XSLT commands to convert the source XML into a valid SVG document.

Example 7-4. An XSLT transform

```
<xsl:stylesheet version="1.0"
     xmlns:xsl="http://www.w3.org/1999/XSL/Transform">
<xsl:template match="slide">
  <svg width="600" height="400"
       xmlns="http://www.w3.org/2000/svg"
       xmlns:xlink="http://www.w3.org/1999/xlink">
   <text x="130" y="48" style="font-size:24;fill:#000000">
   <xsl:value-of select="@title"/>
   </text>
   <image x="20" y="20" width="100" height="100"
              xlink:href="{image}"/>
   <text x="150" y="60" style="font-size:14;fill:#000000">
    <xsl:apply-templates/>
   </text>
  </svg>
</xsl:template>

<xsl:template match="textline">
   <tspan x="130" dy="20" font-size="16">
       <xsl:apply-templates/>
   </tspan>
</xsl:template>

<xsl:template match="bulletlist">
   <xsl:apply-templates/>
</xsl:template>

<xsl:template match="bullet">
   <tspan x="150" dy="16">
```

Example 7-4. An XSLT transform (continued)

```
        &#x2022; <xsl:apply-templates/>
    </tspan>
</xsl:template>

<xsl:template match="image">
</xsl:template>

</xsl:stylesheet>
```

Example 7-4 defines five templates, one for matching each of the XML element types in the input document. When a `<slide>` element is encountered, the first template is matched, and the following actions occur:

- An SVG header is added to the output XML.
- A `<text>` element for the title is added. The `@title` variable matches the title attribute of the `<slide>` element.
- The image is added to the upper left corner. The image URL is extracted from the `<image>` element with the `{image}` string.
- The `<apply-templates>` tag causes the remainder of the input document to be parsed, and the result is inserted here.

The remaining four templates perform the following actions:

- The template matching a `<textline>` creates a new `<tspan>` element and applies the templates to its content. If the content does not match any of the templates, the text is passed directly to the output file.
- Nothing is done for the template matching a `<bulletlist>`, except that the templates are applied to each child of the `<bulletlist>`.
- The template matching a `<bullet>` creates a new `<tspan>` element and inserts a Unicode bullet before its text content.
- Any image elements that appear in the document are discarded. The first template (matching the `<slide>` element) has already extracted the image URL by this point.

Once we have created an XSLT script, we need to apply it to the input XML. For this you can use one of several freely available XSLT processors, many of which have Perl interfaces. Example 7-5 uses the Sablotron module, available on CPAN. Sablotron (see *http://www.gingerall.com/* for more information) builds on the free Expat XML parser.

The Sablotron processor object maintains a set of internal "named buffers" that hold the result of a processed file. Example 7-5 is a simple wrapper that passes an XML file and template (XSLT) file to the Sablotron processor and prints the result in the internal `arg:/result` buffer.

Example 7-5. A simple XSLT processor

```perl
#!/usr/bin/perl
#
# Example 7-5. Using XSLT.

use strict;
use XML::Sablotron;

unless (defined($ARGV[0]) && defined $ARGV[1]) {
    die "Usage: xsltprocessor.pl xml_input.xml xslt_input.xslt\n";
}

my $processor = new XML::Sablotron();
$processor->runProcessor($ARGV[1],
                         $ARGV[0],
                         'arg:/result',
                         undef, undef);

print $processor->getResultArg("arg:/result");
```

The output is shown in Figure 7-4.

Perl for Graphics

Section I: File Formats
- 1. Raster Graphics Formats
- 2. Efficient Multimedia with SWF
- 3. The SVG format
- 4. Printing with PostScript and PDF

Section II: Tools
- 5. On-the-Fly Graphics with GD
- 6. ImageMagick
- 7. Charts and Graphs
- 8. Generating on-the-fly Flash files with Ming
- 9. Scripting the Gimp with Perl
- 10. Using the Postscript modules
- 11. Using the Text::PDF module

Section III: Recipes
- 12. Graphics Cookbook

Figure 7-4. An SVG image generated from an XSLT transformation

## CHAPTER 8

SWF: The Flash File Format

The SWF file format is a highly optimized specification for creating scriptable multimedia files to be distributed over a network and viewed on a screen. An SWF file, typically called a *movie*, allows for the representation of an animation by defining objects (such as vector-based shapes, bitmaps, or buttons) that are placed into frames and encoding a kind of script that sets the order and rate at which the frames are displayed. Nearly every aspect of a movie is scriptable using ActionScript, an integrated scripting environment very similar to ECMAscript (JavaScript). A movie can be a traditional, sequential animated narrative, or it can be used to implement a complete user interface or application. We don't cover ActionScript in this book; if you want to learn more, see Colin Moock's *ActionScript: The Definitive Guide* (O'Reilly).

The Ming module described in Chapter 9 provides an object-oriented API for creating SWF files. Each of the objects described in the next chapter corresponds to an element of an SWF file described in the section "The Format and Function of SWF Files." The sections "Anatomy of a Tag" and "Parsing an SWF File with Perl" go into the low-level details of the SWF file format. These sections are useful if you really want to know what's going on under the hood, but most readers can safely read the first section and move on to Chapter 9.

The History of Flash and SWF

The SWF format began in early 1996 as the file format used by a program called FutureSplash Animator. By the end of 1996, Macromedia (*http://www.macromedia. com/*) had purchased FutureSplash as a complement to its Shockwave multimedia platform (the acronym SWF expands to ShockWave/Flash*), and FutureSplash

---

* The MIME type for an SWF file is application/x-shockwave-flash.

became Flash 1.0. For more on the history of Flash, see *Untold History: The History of Flash* at *http://untoldhistory.weblogs.com/stories/storyReader$4/*.

In 1998, Macromedia released the SWF file format specification to the public as an open standard. In practice, however, the public release of the specification has always lagged behind the latest version of Flash, and has been riddled with errors. The OpenSWF group (*http://www.openswf.org*) has been good about correcting and reposting the specifications.

To play back an SWF movie, you need an SWF player. Macromedia makes a freely downloadable player and browser plug-in that is available for all popular desktop platforms (including Linux). Several third-party SWF players are also available. Two benefits of the Macromedia plug-in are that it is relatively innocuous at just under 200K, and it is synchronized with the latest release of Flash. As of this writing, 90% of the clients on the Web are equipped with the Flash plug-in.

It is important to note the distinction between the Macromedia Flash platform and the SWF file format. "Flash" was originally just the name of Macromedia's tool for creating and editing SWF files. Now that Macromedia has several Flash tools, it is probably more accurate to refer to those as the "Flash platform." Flash is a registered trademark of Macromedia; you need a license from them if you want to describe your software as "Flash-enabled." You will actually run into at least two other file formats that belong to the Flash platform:

.fla
> A proprietary file format generated by the Flash editing tool. Not directly playable by Flash players, it is intended as a working file format that saves metadata and structures that make the job of the editing tool easier.

.swt
> A template file for Macromedia's server-side Generator tool.

We'll be dealing only with SWF files in this book.

The Format and Function of SWF Files

Like PNG or MNG, SWF is a binary tagged file format. Each movie begins with a *header* that encodes most of the global information that a player needs to play back the file, such as the frame rate, the dimensions of the movie, etc. The header is followed by one or more tags, and finally by a single end tag. Tags are one of two types: *definition* tags or *control* tags.

As the player software (typically a browser plug-in) reads the definition tags, the objects that they describe are placed in a structure called the Dictionary. Control tags add and remove the objects from a structure called the display list, which represents the layers of the movie.

Definition Tags

A definition tag describes a reusable object that is to appear in the movie. Each of these objects has a unique ID associated with it that identifies it as a *character* in the movie. Control tags (or other definition tags) that appear after a character has been defined can refer to that character by its ID. The defined object can be a shape, a sound, a button, or any of the other types of objects listed below. Almost all of the elements of an SWF file have a full alpha channel, allowing you to control the transparency of any objects placed in the movie.

Shapes

A shape is defined by one of three tags: DefineShape, DefineShape2, or DefineShape3. The latter two tags are variations of the DefineShape tag that were introduced in successive revisions of the SWF specification (several tags have multiple version numbers). DefineShape2 allows the shape to have more styles, and DefineShape3 allows you to use RGBA colors for all line and fill styles. Later in this chapter, we dissect a DefineShape3 tag bit by bit.

A shape is defined as a collection of fill and line styles, followed by a list of instructions for setting the active styles, moving the pen, and drawing straight or curved edges. A sample shape is pictured in Figure 8-1. Although it looks as if several "shapes" appear in this frame, they are all defined by a single DefineShape3 tag.

Figure 8-1. A complex SWF shape

Text and fonts

Rendering text from portable documents is always troublesome. Different systems may have different fonts, and different platforms can render fonts differently, yielding an inconsistent look from one system to another. To avoid these issues, any fonts used in an SWF file can be encoded as glyph shapes and sent along with the file.

Fonts are described by DefineFont tags, which encode each of the individual glyphs of a font. The font is stored as an object in the dictionary and may be used by any Text objects in the file (which are defined with DefineText tags). Because each glyph is stored as an SWF shape, text may be easily rotated, scaled, or morphed, just like other shapes.

Bitmaps

Although SWF is primarily known as a vector image file format, bitmaps can also appear as characters in a movie. The DefineBits tag (along with the DefineBitsJPEG2 and DefineBitsJPEG3 tags) allows you to define a bitmap object from JPEG-formatted data. As with all JPEG image data, these tags are primarily used for photo-like images. For line drawings or images with large areas of solid color, the DefineBitsLossless and DefineBitsLossless2 tags should be used. These tags store data using zlib compression (just like PNG files).

Buttons

Buttons are objects that can react to the user's actions. ActionScript scripts may be associated with a button so that code is executed in response to mouse movements or clicks. The DefineButton and DefineButton2 tags are used to create buttons.

Sounds

Sounds can also be stored as objects within an SWF file. These sounds can be played back in response to certain events (using the Sound tag) or they can run continuously in the background (using the SoundStreamHead, SoundStreamHead2, and SoundStreamBlock tags). Sounds can be sampled at 5.5 kHz, 11 kHz, 22 kHz and 44 kHz and can have mono or stereo channels. MP3s can also be attached to a movie.

Morph shapes

An SWF morph shape is a special type of shape; it is actually defined in two parts, a start shape and an end shape. As the movie is played back, the shape "morphs" from the start shape into the end shape, at a rate defined when the shape is created with the DefineMorphShape tag.

Sprites

Complete SWF movies (and QuickTime movies) can be encapsulated and included in other movies. These encapsulated movies are called Sprites. Sprites have their own set of objects and can be controlled independently of the parent movie. Sprites are created with the DefineSprite tag.

Control Tags

The definition tags describe the characters in the movie, and the control tags define the script. A control tag indicates when a character is to be added to or removed from a frame, when a sound is to be played, or when a piece of ActionScript code is to be executed. Control tags can also affect global properties of the movie (such as the background color) and can control the sequence in which frames are displayed.

The most significant control tags are:

PlaceObject
> This tag adds an object to the current frame. A reference to the object is added to the display list.

RemoveObject
> This tag removes an object from the current frame. The reference at the given depth is removed from the display list.

ShowFrame
> This tag indicates that the current frame is complete and ready to be rendered to the screen.

DoAction
> This tag indicates that an ActionScript script should be executed when the frame is complete.

End
> This tag is always the last tag in a file. It marks the end of the tag list.

SetBackgroundColor
> This tag changes the background color.

Protect
> This tag indicates that the SWF file is locked or password-protected; SWF file editors should allow only authenticated users to edit the file.

The Dictionary and Display List

Objects that are defined and waiting to be placed on-screen reside in the dictionary. Once an object is placed on-screen (on-stage), a reference to that object is placed in the display list. To better understand how an SWF file is played back, let's look at a sample file and trace the dictionary and display list as the file is parsed. Figure 8-2 shows the process; to the left is the sequence of tags from the SWF document, in the center are the dictionary and display list, and to the right is the stage.

In Figure 8-2, the definition and control tags are identified first. Objects are placed in the dictionary as they are defined in the sequence of tags. Objects are added to the display list as soon as a PlaceObject control tag is identified. A ShowFrame control tag causes the completed frame to be rendered to the screen.

Elements in the display list are displayed according to their *depth*. Each element can be thought of as existing in its own unique layer. Objects with lower depth values are obscured by objects with higher values. The PlaceObject2 control tag also allows you to use a character as a *clipping layer* that masks objects beneath it to the clipping layer's boundaries.

As of Version 5 of the SWF specification and the introduction of the Sprite object, the display list can actually be considered a hierarchical tree rather than a simple array. Sprites encapsulate their own dictionaries and display lists that may be manipulated and controlled independent of the parent movie.

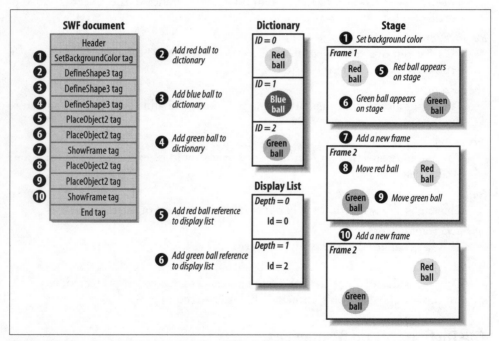

Figure 8-2. Tracing the interpretation of an SWF document

SWF Data Types

The SWF specification takes advantage of a number of techniques to achieve as small a file as possible. Because one of the overriding design principles was to have a format that could be decoded and played as a stream, compression techniques that require all of the file to be available in memory before it could be decoded were not an option. Instead, SWF "compression" is achieved by packing information into the smallest structures possible. The following techniques are used in SWF files:

- Variable-length data fields. Data is stored in the smallest number of bits necessary.
- Sensible default values. Some less commonly used features may be omitted and default values used instead.
- Only changes between frames are described in the file. Objects that are placed on the screen remain there until they move or are removed.
- Characters are defined only once and reused throughout the movie. Characters may be scaled and transformed without defining new characters.

Some of these strategies will become apparent as we go bit by bit through a sample tag definition later in this chapter. A few of the data types we will deal with are highlighted below.

Integer fields

Integers in SWF files may be represented in 8, 16, or 32 bits. They can be either signed or unsigned integers. The SWF specification uses the notation in Table 8-1.

Table 8-1. The integer data types

Type	Description
UI8	8-bit unsigned integer
UI16	16-bit unsigned integer
UI32	32-bit unsigned integer
UI8[n]	An array (of length n) of 8-bit unsigned integers
UI16[n]	An array (of length n) of 16-bit unsigned integers
UI32[n]	An array (of length n) of 32-bit unsigned integers
SI8	8-bit signed integer
SI16	16-bit signed integer
SI32	32-bit signed integer
SI8[n]	An array (of length n) of 8-bit signed integers
SI16[n]	An array (of length n) of 16-bit signed integers

All integer values stored in SWF tags are represented in little-endian byte order. This means that, for integers that are 16 bits or 32 bits long, the byte order is *reversed,* with the lowest-order byte stored in the highest-order byte. For example, the 16-bit little-endian integer:

```
0x0a00
```

should be read as:

```
0x000a = 10
```

and the 32-bit little-endian value:

```
0x0a0b0c0d
```

should be read as:

```
0x0d0c0b0a = 218,893,066
```

In Perl, you can convert a little-endian binary value into an integer with the unpack function using the v or V code:

```
unpack ("v", $16_bit_structure);    # a short unsigned integer
unpack ("V", $32_bit_structure);    # a long unsigned integer
```

Converting a little-endian value to a signed integer is a little more complicated:

```
# Unpack a 16-bit little-endian value as a signed short integer
unpack('s', pack('s', unpack('v', $16_bit_structure));

# Unpack a 32-bit little-endian value as a signed long integer
unpack('l', pack('l', unpack('V', $32_bit_structure));
```

Bit fields

Many of the structures in SWF files are stored in packed bit fields to save space. Table 8-2 lists the different types of bit fields that may appear.

Table 8-2. The bit field data types

Type	Description
UB[nBits]	An unsigned integer value represented in nBits bits
SB[nBits]	A signed integer value represented in nBits bits
FB[nBits]	A signed fixed-point number represented in nBits bits

Packed bit fields take up only the space allocated to them; they are not padded out to match byte boundaries. Other data types are aligned on byte boundaries, however, so if a bit field is followed by a non-bit field, the bit field is padded out with 0's so that the next field starts with the next byte.

Unlike the integer data types, bit values are not stored in little-endian order. Unsigned integers should be converted from bit values by padding out the high-order bits with 0's. Signed integers are represented using *two's complement* notation. For a 16-bit signed integer, the values in the range 2^{15} to $2^{16} - 1$ represent the negative values in the range −32767 to −1. Signed integers are converted from bit values using a technique called *sign extension*, where the high-order bits are padded out with the same value as the high-order bit of the bit field.

To manipulate packed bit fields in Perl, you can use the unpack( ) function with the B code to convert a binary structure to a string of 1's and 0's:

```
my $n = 42;

# Unpack treats its second argument as a string: in this case, the
# two characters '42'.

my $bit_string = unpack('B16', $n);
```

After the string is unpacked, $bit_string has a value of 0011010000110010. This is because chr(52) = '4' = 00110100 and chr(50) = '2' = 00110010.

To convert the low-order six bits back into an unsigned integer (let's say a long integer), you could use the following unpack statement, which uses substr( ) to access the individual bits and pads the string out with enough 0's to give us 32 ones and zeros. Because the bytes are already in high to low order (big-endian) we use the N code:

```
# Print the last 5 bits padded out to an unsigned long integer.
# The result is the integer 25.

print unpack("N", pack("B32", '0'x27 . substr($bit_string, 10, 5)));
```

The coordinate system

The SWF coordinate system is a grid with the origin in the upper left hand corner. For the sake of efficiency, some coordinates are expressed relative to the global coordinate system, and some are expressed relative to the current pen position or to the origin of an object. All coordinates are represented in units called *twips*. One twip is equal to 1/20 of a logical pixel (i.e., an actual screen pixel, the size of which may vary between different monitors). You can think of each logical pixel as being made up of 400 twips[2]. The use of twips makes it easy to create objects that can be scaled or viewed at different sizes.

By default, SWF players render edges that fall in between pixel boundaries using antialiasing. For example, a 30-twip-wide line (1.5 logical pixels) are drawn with antialiased edges no matter where you put it on the grid.

Anatomy of a Tag

We don't have enough space to get into the details of all the tags defined in the SWF specification. However, it is worthwhile to step through one tag as an example of how the fields of a definition tag are structured. This section presents the DefineShape3 tag, which is used to describe arbitrary shapes. The shape we're describing is pictured in Figure 8-3.

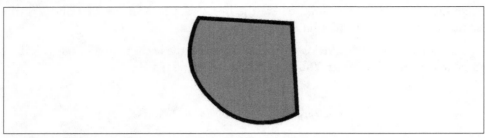

Figure 8-3. A simple shape: two straight edges and a curved one, filled with red

This shape is represented in a mere 44 bytes; if you tack on an SWF header, a Place-Object, and an end tag to make a complete SWF file, the total is 81 bytes. A similar shape in SVG would take up almost five times as many bytes.

The raw binary data (44 bytes) that makes up the tag for the shape in Figure 8-3 looks like this:

```
0x2a 0x08 0x01 0x00   0x70 0x14 0x0c 0x30   0x01 0x40 0x91 0x00
0x01 0x00 0xff 0x00   0x00 0xff 0x01 0x50   0x00 0x7f 0x00 0x00
0xff 0x11 0x35 0x2c   0x86 0x47 0xe0 0xbb   0x87 0x8a 0x26 0x16
0x51 0x20 0x00 0x00   0x00 0x17 0x68 0x00
```

A DefineShape3 tag is composed of seven pieces (also shown in Table 8-3 and described in detail in the following sections).

- A *tag header* that contains a code indicating the type of the tag and the length of the body of the tag (in bytes).

- A *character id* that uniquely identifies this shape in the dictionary.

- The *bounding box*, a data structure containing the coordinates of the rectangle that encloses the shape.

- The *fill style array*, a list of all the fill styles used in this shape. After this array is defined, all references to fill styles need only provide an index to this list.

- The *line style array*, which defines all the line styles available in this shape.

- The *number of bits* used to represent the number of elements in the fill style array and the line style array, respectively. The minimum number of bits are used to store the array indices; if there's only one element in the fill or line style array, only 1 bit is used for the index. If there are, say, 200 different fill styles, each index is stored in 7 bits.

- A list of *shape records*, each of which is a structure that describes the way edges should be drawn, changes in fill or line styles between edges, or movements of the pen position.

Table 8-3. The DefineShape3 tag

Field	Data type	Description
Header	SHORTHEADER or LONGHEADER	The tag ID (in this case, 32) followed by the length. The number of bytes in the header depends on whether this is a "short" or a "long" tag (see Tables 8-4 and 8-5).
ShapeId	UI16	The character ID, a unique number used to refer to this character in the dictionary.
ShapeBounds	RECT	A structure that defines the rectangle that bounds the shape.
FillStyleArray	FILLSTYLEARRAY	A list of fill styles.
LineStyleArray	LINESTYLEARRAY	A list of line styles.
NumFillBits	UB[4]	The number of bits used when representing indices in the fill style array.
NumLineBits	UB[4]	The number of bits used when representing indices in the line style array.
ShapeRecord	SHAPERECORDS	A list of shape records.

Let's look at the tag byte by byte.

The Header Record

Every tag starts with a header record, which encodes an ID field that identifies the type of tag and the length of the tag body (in bytes). Because many tags are relatively small, the SWF specification defines two types of headers: a "short" tag header used for tags 62 bytes or smaller, and a "long" tag header used for tags 63 to $2^{32} - 1$ bytes long. The two types of headers are described in Tables 8-4 and 8-5.

Table 8-4. SHORTHEADER, the header record for a short tag

Field	Data type	Description
Code	UI16	The tag ID is encoded in the high-order 10 bits; the length is encoded in the low-order 6 bits.

Table 8-5. LONGHEADER, the header record for a long tag

Field	Data type	Description
Code	UI16	The tag ID is encoded in the high-order 10 bits; the length is encoded in the low-order 6 bits, which are all 1's.
Length	UI32	The length of the tag body in bytes.

In this analysis, we will be doing some hexadecimal to binary conversions and some binary to decimal conversions. For those of you who might be a little rusty in this area, I've provided a little Perl tool (see the sidebar "Binary and Hex Conversions with Perl") to help with the conversions.

The first 16 bits of our shape tag are:

```
0x2a 0x08
```

which in binary is:

```
00101010  00001000
```

This number is stored in little-endian order (because it is defined as a UI16 data type), so we must swap the high- and low-order bits to get:

```
00001000  00101010
```

Since the 6 low-order bits are not all 1's, this is a short tag. The tag type (the 10 high-order bits) is 32 and the length of the tag is 42 bytes.

Character ID

The character ID is a number assigned to a tag by the program that created the file; the ID is contained in the next two bytes:

```
0x01  0x00
```

When read as a little-endian unsigned integer, this is equal to 1.

Bounding Box

The bounding box is encoded in a RECT structure, which is a list of variable-length bit fields. Like many SWF files, the RECT structure has been defined in such a way that a minimal number of bits are used while still allowing a wide range of allowable rectangular sizes to be reproduced. A RECT structure is made up of the fields listed in Table 8-6.

Table 8-6. The RECT structure

Field	Data type	Description
Nbits	UB[5]	The number of bits used to represent each of the following fields
Xmin	SB[Nbits]	The x coordinate of the left side of the bounding box (in twips)
Xmax	SB[Nbits]	The y coordinate of the top of the bounding box (in twips)
Ymin	SB[Nbits]	The x coordinate of the right side of the bounding box (in twips)
Ymax	SB[Nbits]	The y coordinate of the bottom of the bounding box (in twips)

Note that all of these fields are packed into a single structure that spans several bytes. For our shape, the bounding box is contained in the next 8 bytes:

```
0x70 0x14 0x0c 0x30 0x01 0x40 0x91 0x00
```

which is, in binary:

```
01110 00000010100000  01100001100000  00000010100000
01001000100000  000
```

The field values are:

    Nbits = 01110 = 14 bits per field
    Xmin = 00000010100000 = 160 twips

Xmax = 01100001100000 = 6240 twips
Ymin = 00000010100000 = 160 twips
Ymax = 01001000100000 = 4640 twips

The remaining 3 bits are padded out with 0's because the next structure must be aligned to a byte boundary.

The Fill Style Array

The fill style array is a list of all the fill styles used in this shape. The structure of the array is shown in Table 8-7.

Table 8-7. The fill style array

Field	Data type	Description
FillStyleCount	UI8	The number of items in the array.
FillStyleCountExtended	UI16	This field appears only if FillStyleCount is equal to 0xFF. It allows you to represent the count in 16 bits.
FillStyleList	FILLSTYLE (x FillStyleCount)	A list of fill styles.

Table 8-8 shows the fields of the FILLSTYLE element.

Table 8-8. A FILLSTYLE element

Field	Data type	Description
FillStyleType	UI8	One of the following values:
		• 0x00, a solid color
		• 0x10, a linear gradient
		• 0x12, a radial gradient
		• 0x40, a tiled bitmap
		• 0x41, a clipped bitmap
Color	4 bytes, one each for R, G, B, A	This field is present only if FillStyleType = 0x00
GradientMatrix	MATRIX	This field is present only if FillStyleType = 0x10 or 0x12
Gradient	GRADIENT	This field is present only if FillStyleType = 0x10 or 0x12
Bitmap	BITMAP	This field is present only if FillStyleType = 0x40 or 0x41
BitmapMatrix	MATRIX	This field is present only if FillStyleType = 0x40 or 0x41

Our shape is filled with solid red, so we need only one element in the fill style array. The array is contained in the next 6 bytes:

```
0x01 0x00 0xff 0x00 0x00 0xff
```

where the individual fields are:

FillStyleCount = 0x01 = 1 element in the array
No FillStyleCountExtended field

FillStyleType = 0x00 = a solid color fill
Color = 0xff 0x00 0x00 0xff = red with a nontransparent alpha channel

The Gradient and Bitmap-related fields are not included because they are not necessary. They are documented fully in the SWF specification.

The Line Style Array

The line style array defines a set of color and line width styles that are used in the shape. It is similar in structure to the fill style array, as shown in Table 8-9.

Table 8-9. The line style array

Field	Data type	Description
LineStyleCount	UI_8	The number of items in the array.
LineStyleCount-Extended	UI_16	This field appears only if LineStyleCount is equal to 0xFF. It allows you to represent the count in 16 bits.
LineStyleList	LINESTYLE (x LineStyleCount)	A list of line styles.

Table 8-10 shows the fields of the LINESTYLE element.

Table 8-10. A LINESTYLE element

Field	Data type	Description
Width	UI16	The width (in twips) of the line.
Color	4 bytes, one each for R, G, B, A	The color of the line, with alpha.

The line style array is contained in the next 7 bytes:

    0x01 0x50 0x00 0x7f 0x00 0x00 0xff

where the individual fields are:

LineStyleCount = 0x01 = 1 element in the array
No LineStyleCountExtended field
Width = 0x50 0x00 = 80 twips = 4 logical pixels
Color = 0x7f 0x00 0x00 0xff = a darker red with a nontransparent alpha channel

NumFillBits and NumLineBits

Before we move on to the shape records, we need to know how many bits are used to store the indices to the fill and line style arrays. These two values, NumFillBits and NumLineBits, are encoded in the high-order 4 bits and the low-order 4 bits, respectively, of the next byte. Since the line and fill arrays have only one entry apiece, the next byte is:

    0x11

So NumFillBits and NumLineBits are each 1.

Binary and Hex Conversions with Perl

Here are two little utility scripts for converting between hex and binary strings. The first, *hexconvert*, takes a list of hexadecimal strings (*not* using the 0x00 notation), concatenates them, and prints the value out as a binary string. The input string can be of any length; if it is less than 32 bits, the script outputs the value as a decimal value. If it is 16 or 32 bits long, it interprets the value in little-endian format and outputs the value in its bit-swapped form.

```perl
#!/usr/bin/perl -w
#
# hexconvert.pl

my $hex = join '',@ARGV;
print "Hex: $hex\n";
print "Binary: ", unpack ('B'.(length($hex)*4),
                          pack('H'.(length($hex)*2),$hex)), "\n";
if (length($hex) <= 8) {
    print "Decimal: ",unpack ('N', pack('H32','0'x(8-length($hex)).$hex)), "\
n";
}

if (length($hex) == 4) {
    print "UI_16 (little-endian): ",unpack ("v", pack("H4",$hex)), "\n";
}

if (length($hex) == 8) {
    print "UI_32 (little-endian): ",unpack ("V", pack("H8",$hex)), "\n";
}
```

The *binaryconvert* script does the same thing as *hexconvert*, but takes a string of 1's and 0's and outputs the hex, decimal, UI16, and UI32 values, if the input string is of the appropriate length.

```perl
#!/usr/bin/perl -w
#
# binaryconvert.pl

my $bin = join '',@ARGV;
print "Binary: $bin\n";
my $paddedbin = $bin;
if (length($bin) % 4) {
    $paddedbin = '0' x (4-(length($bin) % 4)) . $bin;
}
print "Hex: ", unpack ("H".(length($paddedbin)/4),
                       pack('B'.length($paddedbin),$paddedbin)), "\n";
if (length($bin) <= 32) {
    print "Decimal: ",
          unpack ('N', pack('B32','0'x(32-length($bin)).$bin)), "\n";
}
```

—continued—

```
    if (length($bin) == 16) {
        print "UI_16 (little-endian): ",
              unpack ("v", pack("B16",$bin)), "\n";
    }
    if (length($bin) == 32) {
        print "UI_32 (little-endian): ",
              unpack ("V", pack("B32",$bin)), "\n";
    }
```

The ShapeRecord List

The shape itself is defined by a collection of shape records that can be thought of as a script of drawing commands that produce the shape when executed. Each of the shape records is one of four types, as determined by the first few bits of the record. These types are:

- Straight edge records
- Curved edge records
- Style change records
- End records

Any arbitrary shape can be constructed with enough of these records. Our shape is defined by five shape records, in the following order:

- A style change record
- A straight edge record
- A straight edge record
- A curved edge record
- An end record

These records are contained in the remaining 18 bytes of the tag:

```
0x35 0x2c 0x86 0x47   0xe0 0xbb 0x87 0x8a      0x26 0x16 0x51 0x20
0x00 0x00 0x00 0x17   0x68 0x00
```

Each shape record is a collection of packed bit structures that span several bytes. To determine the type of the record, look at the first bit. If the first bit is a 0, the record is a change or end record; otherwise, it's a straight or curved edge record. Since I've already revealed that the first record is a style change record, let's start there. A StyleChangeRecord signals a change in line or fill style, a change in the current pen position, or any combination of the three.

Table 8-11 describes the fields of a state change record.

Table 8-11. A state change record

Field	Data type	Description
TypeFlag	UB[1]	Always 0, indicating that this is a non-edge record
StateNewStyles	UB[1]	If this flag is 1, a new collection of fill and line styles is appended to the end of this record
StateLineStyle	UB[1]	If this flag is 1, the line style changes
StateFillStyle1	UB[1]	If this flag is 1, fill style 1 changes
StateFillStyle0	UB[1]	If this flag is 1, fill style 0 changes
StateMoveTo	UB[1]	If this flag is 1, the current location of the pen moves
MoveBits	UB[5]	If StateMoveTo=1, these bits provide the move bit count, as used below
MoveX	SB[MoveBits]	If StateMoveTo=1, these bits are the amount to move on the x axis, relative to the shape origin
MoveY	SB[MoveBits]	If StateMoveTo=1, these bits are the amount to move on the y axis, relative to the shape origin
Fill0Style	UB[nFillBits]	If StateFillStyle0=1, this is the index of the new Fill 0 Style
Fill1Style	UB[nFillBits]	If StateFillStyle1=1, this is the index of the new Fill 1 Style
LineStyle	UB[nLineBits]	If StateLineStyle=1, this is the index of the new line style
FillStyles	FILLSTYLEARRAY	If StateNewStyles=1, an array of new fill styles is appended here
LineStyles	LINESTYLEARRAY	If StateNewStyles=1, an array of new line styles is appended here
NumFillBits	UB[4]	If StateNewStyles=1, this is the number of fill index bits for new styles
NumLineBits	UB[4]	If StateNewStyles=1, this is the number of line index bits for new styles

The record is made up of 31 bits:

```
0 0 1 1 0 1 01001 011001000 011001000 1 1
```

which, when parsed according to the field layout in Table 8-11, give us:

```
Type = 0
StateNewStyles = 0
StateLineStyle = 1
StateFillStyle1= 1
StateFillStyle0 = 0
StateMoveTo = 1
MoveBits = 01001 = 9 bits
MoveDeltaX (9 bits) = 011001000 = 200 twips
MoveDeltaY (9 bits) = 011001000 = 200 twips
FillStyle1 = 1
LineStyle = 1
```

You will notice that the change record refers to two different fills. Every edge has two fill styles associated with it: FillStyle0 and FillStyle1. FillStyle0 affects how the area to the left of the edge is filled, and FillStyle1 affects how the area to the right of the edge is filled. The left and right sides of an edge are relative to the direction in which the edge is drawn.

The next two records, 22 bits each, are straight edge records (see Table 8-12). This type of record indicates that a horizontal or vertical line should be drawn.

Table 8-12. A straight edge record

Field	Data type	Description
TypeFlag	UB[1]	Always 1, indicating that this is an edge record
EdgeFlag	UB[1]	Straight edge; always 1
NumBits	UB[4] + 2	Number of bits per value
GeneralLineFlag	UB[1]	General line equals 1
DeltaX	SB[NumBits]	If lineFlag = 1 X delta
DeltaY	SB[NumBits]	If lineFlag = 1 Y delta
VertLineFlag	UB[1]	If lineFlag = 0 Vertical Line equals 1
DeltaX	SB[NumBits]	If vertFlag = 0 X delta
DeltaY	SB[NumBits]	If vertFlag = 1 Y delta

The first record represents the horizontal line at the top of the shape:

```
11 1100 0 0 01011101110000
```

which translates into the fields:

Type = 1
StraightFlag = 1
NumBits = (next 4 bits +2) = 14 bits
GeneralLineFlag = 0 = Vert/Horiz line
VertLineFlag = 0 Horizontal Line
DeltaX (14 bits) = 01011101110000 = 6000 twips

The next shape record represents the vertical line at the right of the shape:

```
11 1100 0 1 01000100110000
```

which parses into the fields:

Type = 1
StraightFlag = 1
NumBits = (next 4 bits +2) = 14
GeneralLineFlag = 0 = Vert/Horiz line
VertLineFlag =1 Vertical Line
DeltaX (14 bits) = 010111011 = 4400 twips

The next record is a curved edge record, indicating that a curve should be drawn. In SWF files, curves are represented as quadratic Bezier curves, which require two anchor points and one control point that determines how the curve is to be drawn. The fields of a curve record are listed in Table 8-13.

Table 8-13. A curved edge record

Field	Data type	Description
TypeFlag	UB[1]	Always 1, indicating that this is an edge record
EdgeFlag	UB[1]	Curved edge; always 0
NumBits	UB[4] + 2	Number of bits per value
ControlDeltaX	SB[NumBits]	X control point change
ControlDeltaY	SB[NumBits]	Y control point change
AnchorDeltaX	SB[NumBits]	X anchor point change
AnchorDeltaY	SB[NumBits]	Y anchor point change

The next 24 bits are the curved edge record:

    10 1100 10100010010000 00000000000000 00000000000000 10111011010000

which correspond to the fields:

    Type = 1
    StraightFlag = 0
    nBits = 14
    ControlDeltaX = 10384
    ControlDeltaY = 0
    AnchorDeltaX = 0
    AnchorDeltaY = 11984

The last record in a shape record list is always an end record. The end record is defined in Table 8-14.

Table 8-14. The end shape record

Field	Data type	Description
TypeFlag	UB[1]	Always 0, indicating a non-edge record
EndOfShape	UB[5]	All 5 bits are 0

Thus, the last six bits of the structure are all zeros, with an additional zero added to the end to pad it out to the next byte boundary.

As you can see, the space-saving techniques used by the SWF specification do indeed result in a compact representation of an image. It is not easily readable, though!

Parsing an SWF File with Perl

The example in this section reads in the binary data from a provided filename, identifies the header fields, and lists each of the tags in the file. Although the script as shown ignores the body of each of the individual tags, it could easily be extended into a tool for querying a file for specific information or for manipulating an SWF file on a tag-by-tag basis. It would be a simple exercise, for example, to modify the script so that it removes any Protect control tags (tag id=24) that are sometimes used to lock or password-protect a file to prevent it from being edited.

The *AnalyzeSWF.pl* script prints a report to STDOUT. For example, running the script on a simple one-frame file (the file containing the example shape discussed in the previous section, in fact) yields the following output:

```
Header Information
Signature/Version: FWS5
File length: 81 bytes
Min X: 0 twips
Max X: 6400 twips
Min Y: 0 twips
Max Y: 4800 twips
Frame rate: 12
Frame count: 1

Tag type: SetBackgroundColor (3 bytes)
Tag type: DefineShape3 (42 bytes)
Tag type: PlaceObject2 (6 bytes)
Tag type: ShowFrame (0 bytes)
Tag type: End (0 bytes)
```

The script takes the name of an SWF file as an argument. All of the data is read into a buffer before it is analyzed. This may be inefficient memory-wise and time-wise, but it simplifies the example by allowing us to ignore buffer management issues. This could take up a lot of resources if the file in question contains embedded MP3 samples, for example. The example starts by defining a lookup hash of all the SWF tag codes.

```perl
#!/usr/bin/perl -w
#
# SWFAnalyze

use strict;

my %tags = (
    0 => 'End',
    1 => 'ShowFrame',
    2 => 'DefineShape',
    3 => 'FreeCharacter',
    4 => 'PlaceObject',
    5 => 'RemoveObject',
    6 => 'DefineBits',
    7 => 'DefineButton',
    8 => 'JPEGTables',
    9 => 'SetBackgroundColor',
    10 => 'DefineFont',
    11 => 'DefineText',
    12 => 'DoAction',
    13 => 'DefineFontInfo',
    14 => 'DefineSound',
```

```
    15 => 'StartSound',
    17 => 'DefineButtonSound',
    18 => 'SoundStreamHead',
    19 => 'SoundStreamBlock',
    20 => 'DefineBitsLossless',
    21 => 'DefineBitsJPEG2',
    22 => 'DefineShape2',
    23 => 'DefineButtonCxform',
    24 => 'Protect',
    26 => 'PlaceObject2',
    28 => 'RemoveObject2',
    32 => 'DefineShape3',
    33 => 'DefineText2',
    34 => 'DefineButton2',
    35 => 'DefineBitsJPEG3',
    36 => 'DefineBitsLossless2',
    37 => 'DefineEditText',
    39 => 'DefineSprite',
    40 => 'NameCharacter',
    43 => 'FrameLabel',
    45 => 'SoundStreamHead2',
    46 => 'DefineMorphShape',
);

my $filename = shift;
unless (defined($filename)) {
    die "Please provide a file name.\n";
}
open(SWF, $filename) or die "Couldn't open $filename: $!\n";
binmode(SWF);
$/ = undef;
my $buffer = <SWF>;
```

Unpack the binary data into the buffer. Two global variables are used to track the current position in the buffer and the number of frames read so far.

```
$buffer = unpack("B".(length($buffer)*8), $buffer);
my $pos = 0;
my $frames = 0;
```

Start by parsing the header:

```
my $signature = chr(read_ui8()).
                chr(read_ui8()).
                chr(read_ui8());
my $version = read_ui8();
my $file_length = read_ui32();
my @frame_size = read_rect();
```

For some reason that is not made clear in the SWF spec, an SWF reader should read the frame rate as a 16-bit integer, but ignore the low-order byte.

```
my $frame_rate = read_ui16() >> 8;
my $frame_count = read_ui16();
```

Print out the header information.

```
print "Header Information\n";
print "Signature/Version: $signature$version\n";
print "File length: $file_length bytes\n";
print "Min X: $frame_size[0] twips\n";
print "Max X: $frame_size[1] twips\n";
print "Min Y: $frame_size[2] twips\n";
print "Max Y: $frame_size[3] twips\n";
print "Frame rate: $frame_rate\n";
print "Frame count: $frame_count\n";
print "\n";
```

Parse each tag in the remaining data. Just print out the tag type and the length of the tag. Tags are either short or long, as described earlier. If the tag is a ShowFrame tag, increment our frame count. Skip the remainder of the tag.

```
while ($pos < length($buffer)) {
    my $code = read_ui16();          # Read the tag code
    my $id = $code >> 6;         # Extract the tag id
    my $length = $code & 0x3f;   # and the length
    if ($length == 63) {
        $length = read_ui32();     # A Long tag; the length is in the next 32 bits
    }

    if (defined($tags{$id})) {
        print "Tag type: $tags{$id} ($length bytes)\n";
    } else {
        print "Unidentified tag: $id ($length bytes)\n";
    }

    if ($id == 1) {
        $frames++;
    }
    $pos += $length*8;           # Skip remainder
}

print "Number of frames: $frames\n";

exit;
```

The get_bits() function retrieves a number of bits from the buffer:

```
sub get_bits {
    my $nbits = shift;
    my $bits = substr($buffer, $pos, $nbits)
        or  die "Premature end of file!\n";
    $pos += $nbits;
    return $bits;
}
```

The move_to_byte_start() function moves the pointer to the next byte boundary in the buffer for handling byte-aligned types. If we're already at the start of a byte, ($pos % 8) is 0.

```
sub move_to_byte_start {
    if ($pos % 8) {
        $pos += 8-($pos % 8);
    }
}
```

The next three functions read 8-bit, 16-bit, and 32-bit unsigned integers from the buffer, respectively.

```
sub read_ui8 {
    move_to_byte_start();     # This type is byte-aligned
    my $ui8 = ord(pack("B8", get_bits(8)));
    return $ui8;
}

sub read_ui16 {
    move_to_byte_start();     # This type is byte-aligned
    my $ui16 = unpack("v", pack("B16", get_bits(16)));   # Short, little-endian
    return $ui16;
}

sub read_ui32 {
    move_to_byte_start();      # This type is byte-aligned
    my $ui32 = unpack("V", pack("B32", get_bits(32)));   # Long, little-endian
    return $ui32;
}
```

The read_rect() function reads a RECT structure from the buffer. The first line determines the length (in bytes) of the rect field:

```
sub read_rect {
    my $nbits = ord(pack("B8", "000".get_bits(5)));

    my $pad = '0'x(32-$nbits);         # Pad each of the values out to 32 bits
    my @rect = ();

    for (my $i=0; $i<4; $i++) {
        push @rect, unpack("N",pack("B32",            # big-endian byte order
                        $pad.get_bits($nbits)));
    }
    return (@rect);
}
```

CHAPTER 9
Using Ming

Ming is a library written in C that provides a simple API for creating SWF files (described in Chapter 8). In addition to the Perl wrapper described in this chapter, Ming comes with interfaces to PHP, Python, Ruby, Java, and C++. The Ming library was created by Dave Hayden of Opaque Industries and is released under the LGPL (Lesser GNU Public License).

Most web-graphics designers create SWF files with Macromedia's Flash software, which provides a GUI and tools for drawing and manually piecing together the timeline of a movie. With Ming, you can create an assembly line of scripts that automatically update the SWF content of your web site. You can also use Ming with CGI scripts to dynamically generate SWF documents from various data sources. In some cases, it may even make sense to use Ming instead of the Flash tool, or to supplement Flash with Ming at various places in the workflow.

This chapter is divided into three sections. The first introduces a comprehensive Flash application (a game called Astral Trespassers) that touches on all of the basic Ming objects. Next is a reference guide to Ming's Perl interface. The last section of the chapter provides solutions to some problems you may encounter when using Ming. By the end of the chapter you will be able to draw circles using cubic Bezier curves, attach a preloader to your movie, and communicate between an SWF client and a Perl backend using sockets.

Installation

To install Ming, download the source distribution from *http://www.opaque.net/ming*. Ming was designed to not rely on any external libraries, which complicates some aspects of using the library. For example, fonts and images must be converted into special Ming-readable exchange formats instead of being read directly (using a library such as *libpng* or Freetype). The lack of dependencies makes for a simple installation, though; everything is set up from a preconfigured Makefile. The library should work on most platforms, including Windows.

The Perl wrapper, an XS interface to the C library written by Soheil Seyfaie, can be installed after the library is installed. The Perl interface comes with the standard Ming distribution, and has been successfully tested on Unix and MacOS-based systems.

Overview of the Perl Interface

The Perl interface consists of 14 modules in the SWF namespace:

SWF::Movie
> This module implements a top-level timeline as a Movie object.

SWF::Sprite
> Also called a MovieClip, a Sprite object is an encapsulated movie that can be combined with other Sprites on a Movie timeline.

SWF::DisplayItem
> Once an object has been placed on the Stage of a Movie, the instance of that object can be manipulated as a DisplayItem.

SWF::Shape
> This is a reusable vector shape object.

SWF::Button
> A button is an object that defines shapes within a frame that can respond to mouse and keyboard events.

SWF::Bitmap
> An image can be read from a file and placed as a Bitmap object within the Movie.

SWF::Text
> The Text object allows you to draw strings on a frame.

SWF::TextField
> A TextField can be used for interactive forms or for boxes of text that need to be dynamically updated.

SWF::Font
> A Font object describes the glyph shapes used to draw Text and TextField objects.

SWF::Fill
> This is a description of one of a variety of fills that can be associated with a Shape.

SWF::Gradient
> This is a description of a gradient that can be used to create a Fill object.

SWF::Morph
> A Morph object represents the gradual transition between two shapes.

SWF::Sound
> An MP3 can be read from a file and placed on the timeline as a Sound object.

SWF::Action

This is an object containing a block of ActionScript that can be associated with a timeline or another object.

The following example features most of Ming's object types. The example is followed by a function reference for each of the Perl modules.

The Astral Trespassers Game

Astral Trespassers is a simple shoot-em-up space game. When executed, it generates a self-contained SWF file that implements the game shown in Figure 9-1. The player uses the mouse to control a gun positioned at the bottom of the screen—if the mouse button is clicked within the frame, a photon bullet is fired. The player is responsible for destroying a phalanx of aliens (represented by primitive blue SWF:: Shape objects) that advance down the screen. This example will illustrate the use of the Ming API to create simple shapes, attach ActionScript to buttons and frames, and manipulate multiple Sprites. It also provides a rough template for your own interactive applications.

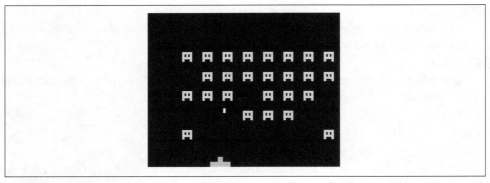

Figure 9-1. Astral Trespassers, a sample application created using the Ming SWF library

The document is created in five stages:

1. Create the SWF::Shape objects that are used to build the Sprites for the gun, aliens, and photon bullet.

2. Assemble the Shapes into Sprites.

3. Assemble the Sprites on the main timeline of the SWF::Movie object.

4. Attach ActionScript to individual Sprites and the main timeline. The Action-Script is interpreted by the Flash player and controls the movement of sprites on the Stage and user interaction when the movie is played back.

5. Write the Movie to a file (or STDOUT) formatted as SWF data.

The SWF document (we'll call it *astral_trespassers.swf*) is about 2k in size. The following code loads the modules and sets the default scale:

```perl
#!/usr/bin/perl -w
#
# Astral Trespassers

use strict;
use SWF qw(:ALL);              # Import all of the Ming modules

SWF::useSWFVersion(5);         # This script uses some Flash 5 ActionScript

# Set the scale. 20 is the default, which means that
# all scalar values representing coordinates or dimensions
# are indicated in twips (1/20th of a pixel).

SWF::setScale(20);
```

Now we must create the shapes that make up the Sprites. The player's gun consists of two red rectangles, where the origin of the gun is centered on the barrel. The drawRect( ) function is defined at the end of this script and adds a rectangular path to the shape. The arguments are a Shape object, *width*, *height*, *dx*, and *dy*. The upper left corner of the rectangle is drawn shifted by *dx,dy* from the origin of the shape.

```perl
my $s = new SWF::Shape( );
$s->setLeftFill($s->addFill(255, 0, 0));
drawRect($s, 10, 10, -5, 0);
drawRect($s, 40, 10, -20, 10);
```

Now we'll create an alien, with the origin of each centered between its legs. Each alien will be a Sprite object consisting of two frames to simulate the movement of its legs. Let's define the two shapes here.

```perl
my $s2 = new SWF::Shape( );
$s2->setLeftFill($s2->addFill(0, 0, 255));
drawRect($s2, 20, 15, -10, -15);    # The body
drawRect($s2, 5, 5, -10, 0);        # Left leg
drawRect($s2, 5, 5, 5, 0);          # Right leg
drawRect($s2, 3, 5, -5, -10);       # Left eye
drawRect($s2, 3, 5, 2, -10);        # Right eye

my $s3 = new SWF::Shape( );
$s3->setLeftFill($s3->addFill(0, 0, 255));   # Blue
drawRect($s3, 20, 15, -10, -15);    # Body
drawRect($s3, 5, 5, -7, 0);         # Left leg
drawRect($s3, 5, 5, 2, 0);          # Right leg
drawRect($s3, 3, 5, -5, -10);       # Left eye
drawRect($s3, 3, 5, 2, -10);        # Right eye
```

The photon bullet is a simple white rectangle:

```perl
my $s4 = new SWF::Shape( );
$s4->setLeftFill($s4->addFill(255, 255, 255));
drawRect($s4, 5, 10, -3, -10);
```

Finally, we need to define a shape for the button that collects the player's mouse clicks. The button has the same dimensions as the movie:

```
my $s5 = new SWF::Shape( );
$s5->setRightFill($s5->addFill(0, 0, 0));
drawRect($s5, 400, 400, 0, 0);
```

Movies can be nested within each other. The SWF::Sprite module represents a movie clip that has its own timeline and can be manipulated as a discrete object on the root movie timeline. The next step is to create all of the sprites needed in the movie. Start with the player's gun, which is one frame long:

```
my $gun = new SWF::Sprite( );
$gun->add($s);
$gun->nextFrame( );
```

Next, create the alien sprite, which is four frames long: two with shape $s2 and two with shape $s3. The $item object is of type SWF::DisplayItem, returned when the sprite is added to the movie clip's timeline.

```
my $alien = new SWF::Sprite( );
my $item = $alien->add($s2);
$alien->nextFrame( );
$alien->nextFrame( );
$alien->remove($item);
$alien->add($s3);
$alien->nextFrame( );
$alien->nextFrame( );
```

The photon bullet is another single-frame sprite:

```
my $bullet = new SWF::Sprite( );
$bullet->add($s4);
$bullet->nextFrame( );
```

Next, create a TextField object for the "Game Over" message. Note that the font definition file (see the "The SWF::Font Module" section later in this chapter) called *serif.fdb* must be in the same directory as this script.

```
my $f = new SWF::Font("serif.fdb");
my $tf = new SWF::TextField( );
$tf->setFont($f);
$tf->setColor(255,255,255);
$tf->setName("message");
$tf->setHeight(50);
$tf->setBounds(300,50);
```

Next we will assemble these pieces on the main timeline. The final movie timeline consists of four frames:

Frame 1
   Contains ActionScript that initializes variables used to move aliens and bullets.

Frame 2
   Contains the "hit region" button, the gun sprite, 40 alien sprites, and an off-screen bullet sprite.

Frame 3

Contains ActionScript that moves the gun, the aliens, and the bullet, and checks to see if a bullet has collided with an alien. If an alien reaches the bottom of the screen, the movie stops.

Frame 4

Creates an event loop by returning to the previous frame.

Some objects have ActionScript code attached to them. ActionScript is a JavaScript-like interpreted language that is parsed and executed by the SWF player. In our example, ActionScript is attached to the first, third, and fourth frames of the movie, and also to a screen-sized button that is used to gather the user's mouse clicks. Figure 9-2 shows the various objects on the main timeline and the ActionScript (if any) that is attached to each object.

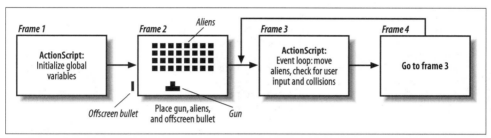

Figure 9-2. The main timeline of the Astral Trespassers example

Now, we'll create a new Movie object:

```
my $m = new SWF::Movie;
$m->setDimension(400, 400);
$m->setBackground(0, 0, 0);
$m->setRate(16);                # Frames per second.
```

The first frame is a keyframe that initializes two variables. The `direction` array keeps track of whether each alien is moving left (–1), right (1), or not moving (0, after it has been shot). `onScreenBullet` is a Boolean indicating whether the bullet is on the screen.

```
$m->add(new SWF::Action(<<ENDSCRIPT
    direction = new Array();
    for (i=0; i<40; i++) {
        direction[i] = 1;
    }
    onScreenBullet = 0;
ENDSCRIPT
));
$m->nextFrame();
```

In the second frame we add the sprites to the Stage. First we add the button that acts as a "hot spot" for collecting mouse clicks. The user must click in the area defined by the shape $s5. Note that the first click gets the button's focus, and subsequent clicks fire bullets.

```
my $b = new SWF::Button( );
$b->addShape($s5, SWF::Button::SWFBUTTON_HIT);

# Add Actionscript that is activated when the button is pressed.

$b->addAction(new SWF::Action(<<ENDSCRIPT
if (onScreenBullet == 0) {
    onScreenBullet = 1;
    _root["bullet"]._x = _root["gun"]._x;
    _root["bullet"]._y = _root["gun"]._y;
}
ENDSCRIPT
), SWF::Button::SWFBUTTON_MOUSEDOWN);

$item = $m->add($b);          # Add the button to the Stage
$item = $m->add($tf);         # Add the "Game Over" text field
                              # Initially it is empty
$item->moveTo(75, 100);
$item = $m->add($gun);        # Add the gun to the Stage
$item->setName("gun");        # Label the gun for use in later
                              # Actionscripts
$item->moveTo(200, 380);      # Position the gun at the bottom
                              # of the screen
foreach my $row (1..5) {      # Add a phalanx of 40 aliens
    foreach my $col (1..8) {
        $item = $m->add($alien);            # Add alien
        $item->moveTo(40*$col, 40*$row);    # Position alien
        $item->setName("alien".             # Label alien
                     (($row-1)*8+$col-1));  # (e.g. 'alien1')
    }
}

$item = $m->add($bullet);     # Add bullet to stage
$item->moveTo(-10, -10);      # Position it off screen
$item->setName("bullet");     # Label it
$m->nextFrame( );
```

Add ActionScript to the third frame for the event loop. If you've never used Action-Script before, Appendix D is an ActionScript reference geared toward Ming developers.

The movement of the gun, aliens, and bullet are all controlled by the following bit of ActionScript that is executed every time Frame 3 is executed. The script moves the player's gun, moves each of the aliens, checks for a collision with the bullet, the edge of the screen, or the bottom of the screen, and moves the bullet:

```
$m->add(new SWF::Action(<<ENDSCRIPT
    /* Move the gun to follow the mouse. Note that the
       gun moves faster the farther it is from the mouse */
    dx = int(_xmouse - _root["gun"]._x)/10;
```

```
        xPos = _root["gun"]._x + dx;
        if ((xPos > 0) && (xPos < 400)) {
            _root["gun"]._x += dx;
        }

        /* Move each of the aliens */
        for (i=0; i<40; i++) {
            /* If an alien reaches the bottom, end the game */
        if (_root["alien"+i]._y > 380) {
                message = "Game Over";
                stop();
        }

        /* If an alien hits one of the margins, reverse direction */
        if (_root["alien"+i]._x > 380) {
                direction[i] = -1;
                _root["alien"+i]._y += 20;
                }
            if (_root["alien"+i]._x < 20) {
                direction[i] = 1;
                _root["alien"+i]._y += 20;
            }

            /* Move the alien */
            _root["alien"+i]._x += direction[i] * 5;

            /* Check to see if the bullet has collided with the alien
               If so, move the bullet and alien off screen */
            if (onScreenBullet & _root["bullet"].hitTest(_root["alien"+i])) {
                _root["bullet"]._y = -10;
                _root["alien"+i]._y = -10;
                onScreenBullet = 0;
                direction[i] = 0;
            }
        }

        /* If the bullet is on the screen, move it upward. */
        if (onScreenBullet) {
            _root["bullet"]._y -= 10;
            if (_root["bullet"]._y < 0) {
                onScreenBullet = 0;
            }
        }
    }
ENDSCRIPT
));
```

The fourth frame closes the event loop by returning to Frame 3:

```
$m->nextFrame();
$m->add(new SWF::Action(<<<ENDSCRIPT
    prevFrame();
    play();
ENDSCRIPT
));
$m->nextFrame();
```

Write the result to a file with the save( ) method:

```
$m->save("astral_trespassers.swf");\
exit( );
```

drawRect( ) is a helper procedure used to draw rectangles within a shape:

```
sub drawRect {
    my $shape = shift;
    my ($w, $h, $dx, $dy) = @_;
    $shape->movePenTo($dx, $dy);
    $shape->drawLine($w, 0);
    $shape->drawLine(0, $h);
    $shape->drawLine(-$w, 0);
    $shape->drawLine(0, -$h);
}
```

This script could easily be converted to a CGI script by outputting the appropriate HTTP header and using the output( ) method instead of the save( ) method.

The SWF Module

The top-level SWF module implements only two functions; the rest are defined by the other modules described below. By default, the SWF module does not import any of the other modules. You can import all of them with the directive:

```
use SWF qw(:ALL);
```

or you can import just the modules you intend to use by supplying a list of module names:

```
use SWF qw(Movie Text Font);
```

The following two functions affect global properties of the generated SWF movie.

setScale( )

SWF::setScale(*scale*)

By default, all coordinates and dimensions supplied to any of the functions described in this chapter are expressed in twips, or 1/20 of a pixel (see Chapter 8 for more on the SWF coordinate system). The setScale( ) function lets you write scripts using different scales. For example:

```
SWF::setScale(1);
```

indicates that all of the scalar coordinates and dimensions specified in the script represent actual pixels in the resulting movie.

Note that the scale defined by this function does not apply to coordinates in ActionScript strings. ActionScript code should always represent coordinates using twips.

setVersion( )

`SWF::setVersion(version)`

This command indicates the latest version of the SWF specification to which the file conforms. In other words, if the file contains ActionScript syntax that was defined in Version 5.0 of the SWF specification, you should indicate that with the command:

`SWF::setVersion(5);`

If you specify Version 4 (4 and 5 are the only options), all of your ActionScript is parsed by a Version 4.0 interpreter, and you get an error if non-4.0 code is encountered.

The SWF::Movie Module

The Movie object defines the top-level timeline of an SWF document. To create a movie clip that can be included as an object on a timeline with other movie clips, use the SWF::Sprite module. Many of the movie methods apply to sprites also.

add( )

`$displayItem = $movie->add(object);`

The add( ) method places an object on the movie's Stage (the current frame). The object can be an SWF::Sprite, SWF::Shape, SWF::Button, SWF::Bitmap, SWF::Text, SWF::Text-Field, SWF::Morph, or SWF::Sound. A new DisplayItem object is returned, which may be used to position or manipulate the object within the frame, as described later in the "The SWF::DisplayItem Module" section. The same object can be added multiple times to the same movie, where a new DisplayItem is created for each addition.

addAction( )

`$movie->addAction(action)`

This method adds ActionScript code to the current frame of the movie. The `action` parameter is an SWF::Action object. The script is executed when the frame is encountered in the timeline.

labelFrame( )

`$movie->labelFrame(label)`

This method associates a name with the current frame. The label can be used to identify this frame in an SWF::Action script (see the later section "The SWF::Action Module").

new( )

```
$movie = new SWF::Movie( );
```

This method creates a new Movie object.

nextFrame( )

```
$movie->nextFrame( )
```

When you are finished constructing a frame of a movie, use the nextFrame( ) method to move on to the next frame. A new frame is added to the movie. Note that all of the objects present in the previous frame remain on the Stage in the next frame, and DisplayItems may still be used to access items within the frame.

output( )

```
$movie->output( )
```

This method prints the movie to STDOUT as a formatted SWF file. Remember to use binmode( ) on systems where that is necessary.

If you are sending the output directly to a web browser as part of a CGI script, print the HTTP header for an SWF file first:

```
print "Content-type: application/x-shockwave-flash\n\n";
$movie->output( );
```

remove( )

```
$movie->remove(displayItem)
```

This method removes a particular item from the display list. The item no longer appears in the current frame.

save( )

```
$movie->save(filename)
```

This method attempts to open the file with the given name (using fopen( )) and writes the SWF document to the file.

setBackground( )

```
$movie->setBackground(red, green, blue);
```

This function sets the background color of the movie. Specify the RGB components of the color as numbers between 0 and 255.

setDimension( )

`$movie->setDimension(width, height)`

This method sets the width and height (expressed in twips) of the movie. The rendered dimensions of the movie are subject to the scaling proportion set with `SWF::SetScale( )`.

setFrames( )

`$movie->setFrames(frames)`

This method sets the total number of frames in the movie.

setRate( )

`$movie->setRate(frameRate);`

The playback rate for the movie can be controlled with this method. The given frame rate (expressed in frames per second) is the maximum frame rate; the SWF player may slow the movie down or skip frames if it can't render the frames fast enough.

setSoundStream( )

`$movie->setSoundStream(sound)`

This method adds an MP3 sound to the SWF file at the current frame. The *sound* parameter should be an SWF::Sound object, which represents an MP3 file to be embedded in the SWF document. See the later section "The SWF::Sound Module" for more on sounds.

The SWF::Sprite (or SWF::MovieClip) Module

The SWF specification defines an object called a Sprite, an encapsulated movie with its own timeline that can be added to another movie's timeline. The sprite plays concurrently with any other objects or MovieClips on the main timeline. Flash users may be more familiar with the term MovieClip; you can use the alias SWF::MovieClip for a sprite if you want to.

The behavior of SWF::Sprite methods is identical to that of the methods described for the SWF::Movie object. The following methods may be called on a sprite:

```
new( )
add( )
remove( )
nextFrame( )
setFrames( )
labelFrame( )
```

Remember that the add() method returns a DisplayItem that refers to the object on the sprite's timeline, not on the parent movie's timeline. See the Astral Trespassers script at the beginning of this chapter for an example of an application using multiple sprites.

Several ActionScript commands operate on sprites, but ActionScript uses the term MovieClip instead of sprite. For example, the duplicateMovieClip() ActionScript method can be applied to a sprite to create a new copy of itself. See Appendix D for a complete ActionScript command reference.

The SWF::DisplayItem Module

Each object that is on-screen at any particular time has an entry in a data structure in the SWF player called the *display list*. The display list keeps track of the position of the object, the depth of the object, and a transformation matrix that affects how the object is drawn on the screen. The SWF::DisplayItem object defines methods for moving, transforming, and arranging objects in the display list. The following attributes are contained in a DisplayItem:

Name
> A label used to refer to the item in ActionScript scripts

Position
> The x, y coordinate of the item within a frame

Scale
> A horizontal and vertical scale multiplier

Rotation
> An angular offset

Skew
> A horizontal and vertical skew offset

Depth
> The position of the item in the display list

Ratio
> If the displayed item is a Morph object, the ratio attribute determines which frame of the morph transition is displayed

Color transform
> The object's red, green, blue, and alpha components may have a color offset applied to them

DisplayItems do not have their own constructors. New DisplayItems are created when a displayable object is added to a movie or a sprite; the add() method of these objects returns an SWF::DisplayItem object.

In the example at the beginning of this chapter, we moved the various items around the Stage using an ActionScript event loop. Example 9-1 creates a 60-frame animation where each shape is manually placed within the frame by maintaining a list of DisplayItems for each object on the Stage.

Example 9-1. Using SWF::DisplayItem to position each element of each frame

```perl
#!/usr/bin/perl -w
#
# Example 9-1. A grid of red squares collapses in on itself,
# then expands to its original state.

use strict;
use SWF qw(Movie Shape DisplayItem);

SWF::setScale(1.0);

# Define a grid

my $grid = 8;
my ($w, $h) = ($grid*100, $grid*100);

# Create a square

my $s = new SWF::Shape();
$s->setLineStyle(1, 255, 0, 0);
$s->movePenTo(0,0);
$s->drawLineTo(0, 50);
$s->drawLineTo(50, 50);
$s->drawLineTo(50, 0);
$s->drawLineTo(0, 0);

# The displayList array holds the DisplayList objects as they are placed onstage

my @displayList = ();
my $m = new SWF::Movie();
$m->setDimension($w, $h);

# Place a grid of squares on the stage and store the reference to each DisplayItem

foreach my $i (0..$grid-1) {
    foreach my $j (0..$grid-1) {
        my $item = $m->add($s);
        $item->moveTo($i*100, $j*100);
        push @displayList, $item;
    }
}

# Now create 30 frames; in each frame, move each square
# 1/30th of the way toward the center of the grid, and rotate
# the square 360/30 degrees. Then repeat the same thing in the
# opposite direction, ending up where we started.
```

```
my $frames = 30;
my ($cx, $cy) = ($w/2, $h/2);
foreach my $direction (1, -1) {          # 1 =in, -1 = out
    foreach my $f (1..$frames) {
        foreach my $i (0..$grid-1) {
            foreach my $j (0..$grid-1) {
                $displayList[$i*$grid+$j]->move(
                    $direction*(int($cx-$i*100)/$frames),
                    $direction*(int($cy-$j*100)/$frames));
                $displayList[$i*$grid+$j]->rotate(360/$frames);
            }
        }
    }
    $m->nextFrame();
}

# Create the SWF file

$m->save("example9-1.swf");
```

Note that the resulting file is quite large for a Flash movie (around 68k). In this particular example, you would be better off moving each square using ActionScript rather than creating static frames for each step of the animation.

move( )

```
$displayItem->move(dx, dy)
```

This function moves the origin of the specified item to a new coordinate that is offset from its current position by (*dx*, *dy*).

moveTo( )

```
$displayItem->moveTo(x, y)
```

This function moves the origin of the specified item to the given (*x*, *y*) global coordinate. The item remains at the same depth within the display list.

remove( )

```
$displayItem->remove( )
```

This method removes the specified item from the display list with which it is associated. Same as SWF::Movie::remove( ).

rotate( )

$displayItem->rotate(*degrees*)

This method adds the specified number of degrees to the DisplayItem's current rotation value.

rotateTo( )

$displayItem->rotateTo(*degrees*)

This method sets the rotation attribute of the DisplayItem (initially 0), expressed in degrees. When drawn on the frame, the object is rotated around its origin by the given amount.

scale( )

$displayItem->scale(*x_scale, y_scale*)

This method scales the object like scaleTo( ), but multiplies the current scale by the given values.

scaleTo( )

$displayItem->scaleTo(*x_scale, y_scale*)

Each DisplayItem has a scaling attribute that is initially set to 1, indicating that the object should be drawn on the frame using the dimensions with which it was originally defined. The scaleTo( ) function sets the horizontal and vertical scale to the specified values, replacing the current scale value. Scaling an object affects the object's local coordinate space, so line widths are scaled along with any objects positioned inside the scaled object (if it is a sprite). If scaleTo( ) is called with only one value, the object is scaled proportionately.

setColorAdd( )

$displayItem->addColor(*red, green, blue* [,*alpha*])

This method adds the given values to the color components of the item. If the item is a sprite, all of the objects within the sprite have the color transform applied to them also.

setColorMult( )

$displayItem->multColor(*red, green, blue* [,*alpha*])

This method multiplies each of the color components of the item by the given values. Component values greater than 255 are taken to be 255.

setDepth( )

`$displayItem->setDepth(depth)`

This method sets the depth of the item in the display list. Each item displayed in a frame has its own unique depth value that determines the order in which it is drawn on the screen.

setName( )

`$displayItem->setName(name)`

This method labels the item in the display list with the given name. This name can be used to identify the item in ActionScript code.

setRatio( )

`$displayItem->setRatio(ratio)`

The *ratio* attribute applies only to SWF::Morph items. The ratio is a real number between 0 and 1.0 that represents a point in the transformation between the two extremes of the morph. Setting the ratio to .5, for example, causes the shape that is halfway between the morph's extremes to be displayed. See the example code under "The SWF::Morph Module" for an example of this.

skewX( ), skewY( )

`$displayItem->skewX(x)`
`$displayItem->skewY(y)`

These methods add the given value to the current horizontal or vertical skew. See skewXTo( ) and skewYTo( ).

skewXTo( ), skewYTo( )

`$displayItem->skewXTo(x)`
`$displayItem->skewYTo(y)`

These functions set the horizontal and vertical skew attributes for the item. The skew value is expressed as a real number where 0 indicates no skew and 1.0 is a 45 degree skew. Positive numbers indicate a counterclockwise skew anchored at the origin.

The SWF::Shape Module

The SWF::Shape object holds a data structure that represents a shape as described in Chapter 8. A shape consists of a series of points, a fill style, and a line style.

Example 9-2 uses the methods of the Shape object to draw a logarithmic spiral using the Golden Mean (see *http://mathworld.wolfram.com/GoldenRatio.html*).

The spiral starts at the origin and the pen moves in a counterclockwise direction. The direction of the curve is determined by cycling through the @dx and @dy arrays; the first segment should be drawn in the positive x and y directions, the second in the positive x, negative y directions, etc. The control points are always on the outside edges of the curve. The result is pictured in Figure 9-3.

Figure 9-3. A logarithmic spiral shape

Example 9-2. A program for drawing a logarithmic spiral shape

```perl
#!/usr/bin/perl -w
#
# Example 9-2. An example using SWF::Shape()

use strict;
use SWF::Shape;

SWF::setScale(1.0);
my $s = new SWF::Shape();          # Create a new Shape object
$s->setLineStyle(1, 255, 0, 0);

my @dx = (1, 1, -1, -1);
my @dy = (1, -1, -1, 1);
my ($x, $y) = (0, 0);
my ($x1, $y1) = (0, 0);
my $w = 100;
my ($cx, $cy);

$s->movePenTo($x, $y);

for(my $i=0; $i <= 10; $i++) {

    $x1 = $x1 + $dx[$i%4] * $w;
    $y1 = $y1 + $dy[$i%4] * $w;

    if ($i % 2) {                  # An odd turn
        ($cx, $cy) = ($x1, $y);
```

Example 9-2. A program for drawing a logarithmic spiral shape (continued)

```
    } else {                        # An even turn
        ($cx, $cy) = ($x, $y1);
    }

    $s->drawCurveTo($cx, $cy, $x1, $y1);  # Add a curve segment to the Shape
    $x = $x1;                              # Set the current point.
    $y = $y1;
    $w = $w * .618034;     # The width of the bounding box for the next curve segment
                           # is determined by the Golden Mean
}

# Create a Movie to hold the Shape

my $m = new SWF::Movie( );
$m->setDimension(300,300);
$m->add($s)->moveTo(0,10);
$m->nextFrame( );


$m->save("example9-2.swf");
```

You may notice that the curves in this shape seem a little flattened; this is because Ming (and the SWF specification) uses quadratic Bezier curves (with one control point) rather than the more flexible cubic Bezier curves (with two control points).

addFill( )

```
$fill = $shape->addFill(r, g, b [, a])
$fill = $shape->addFill(bitmap [, flags])
$fill = $shape->addFill(gradient [, flags])
```

Each shape contains a list of fill styles, any or all of which may be used to draw the shape. This method creates a new SWF::Fill object that can be used with setLeftFill( ) or setRightFill( ). The method can be called in one of three ways:

1. If called with RGBA components, a solid fill is added to the shape's fill style list.
2. If called with an SWF::Bitmap object, a bitmap fill is added to the shape's fill style list. The *flags* argument can be:

   ```
   SWF::Fill::SWFFILL_TILED_BITMAP (the default)
   SWF::Fill::SWFFILL_CLIPPED_BITMAP
   ```

3. If an SWF::Gradient object is the first argument, a gradient fill is added to the shape's list of fill styles. The *flags* argument can be:

   ```
   SWF::Fill::SWFFILL_LINEAR_GRADIENT (the default)
   SWF::Fill::SWFFILL_RADIAL_GRADIENT
   ```

Note that the fill must be created with the addFill( ) method, and each fill object is associated with a particular Shape object. In the case of a gradient fill, the gradient must be defined *before* the shape is created. Fill objects cannot be used interchangeably between shape objects. Figure 9-4 shows illustrations of the bitmap and gradient fill styles.

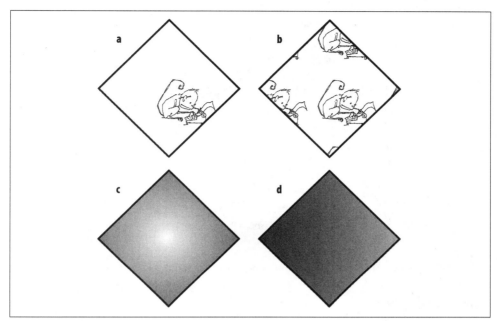

Figure 9-4. Bitmap and gradient fill flags: a) SWFFILL_CLIPPED_BITMAP, b) SWFFILL_TILED_BITMAP, c) SWFFILL_RADIAL_GRADIENT, and d) SWFFILL_LINEAR_GRADIENT

drawCurveTo( )

`$shape->drawCurveTo(controlX, controlY, x, y)`

This method draws a curved line from the current point to (*x*, *y*) using (*controlX*, *controlY*) as a control point. After this operation, the current point is (*x*, *y*). Figure 9-5 illustrates a quadratic Bezier curve, where the curvature between two points is defined by a single control point. (Compare to the cubic Bezier curves used by PostScript in Chapter 10.)

drawCurve( )

`$shape->drawCurve(controlDx, controlDy, dx, dy)`

This method draws a curved line from the current point (*x*, *y*) to the point (*x+dx*, *y+dy*) using (*x+controlDx*, *y+controlDy*) as a control point. After this operation, the current point is (*x+dx*, *y+dy*).

drawCircle( )

`$shape->drawCircle(r)`

This method draws a circle with radius *r* centered at the current point. This operation does not affect the current point.

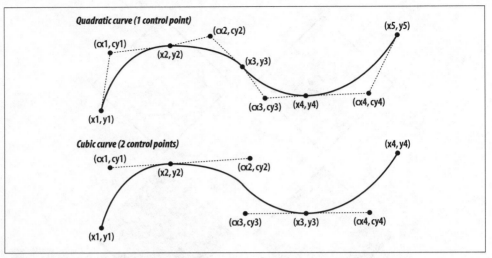

Figure 9-5. SWF uses quadratic curves (top) as opposed to cubic curves (bottom)

drawFontGlyph( )

`$shape->drawFontGlyph(font, char)`

This method draws a single character at the current point in the specified font, which must be an SWF::Font object. The origin of the baseline of the glyph is anchored at the current point.

drawLine( )

`$shape->drawLine(dx, dy)`

This method draws a straight line from the current point (*x*, *y*) to (*x+dx*, *y+dy*) using the current line style. After this operation, the current point is (*x+dx*, *y+dy*).

drawLineTo( )

`$shape->drawLineTo(x, y)`

This method draws a straight line from the current point to (*x*, *y*) using the current line style (which is set using `setLineStyle( )`). After this operation, the current point is (*x*, *y*).

movePenTo( )

`$shape->movePenTo(x, y);`

When drawing a shape, all coordinates are expressed in relation to the origin of the shape itself, not to the frame containing the shape. This method moves the current point of the pen to (*x*, *y*) in the shape's coordinate space.

movePen( )

`$shape->movePen(dx, dy)`

With the current point at (*x*, *y*), this method moves the pen to the point (*x+dx*, *y+dx*) without creating a path between the two points.

new( )

`$shape = new SWF::Shape( )`

This method returns a new Shape object.

setLeftFill( ), setRightFill( )

`$shape->setLeftFill(fill)`
`$shape->setLeftFill(red, green, blue, [alpha])`
`$shape->setRightFill(fill)`
`$shape->setRightFill(red, green, blue, [alpha])`

The SWF specification does not provide a way of defining shapes such that they have an "inside" area that can be filled with a particular fill style. Instead, each line in a shape has one fill style to its left and one fill style to its right. These fills can be set using the forms given above. In the first instance, *fill* must be an SWF::Fill object, which is created by the `SWF::Shape::addFill( )` method. For a simple colored fill, you can use the second form.

setLineStyle( )

`$shape->setLineStyle(width, red, green, blue [, alpha])`

This method sets the properties of the line used to stroke the shape. You provide the stroke width (in twips, subject to the scale defined by `setScale( )`) and color (with an optional alpha channel).

The SWF::Button Module

A Button is an object that can be used to track user input such as mouse movements, mouse clicks, or keyboard events. When defining a button, you must supply at least a hit area, which is a Shape object that describes the area of the button that is receptive to user input.

You may also supply Shape objects that are displayed when the button is in one of its three states:

Up
> Displayed when the button has not received an event.

Down
> Displayed when the mouse has been clicked on the hit area.

Over

Displayed when the mouse cursor is moved over the button's hit area.

The SWF::Button module defines three methods and four alias methods.

addShape( )

`$button->addShape(`*shape, state_flag*`)`

This method adds a shape to one of the button's four states, indicated by the value of *state_flag*:

`SWF::Button::SWFBUTTON_HIT`

The shape defines the hit area of the button. The shape is not displayed on the screen.

`SWF::Button::SWFBUTTON_UP`

Displayed when the button has not yet been pressed.

`SWF::Button::SWFBUTTON_DOWN`

Displayed when the button is pressed down on the hit area.

`SWF::Button::SWFBUTTON_OVER`

Displayed when the mouse cursor is over the hit area of the button.

If a shape is not filled, only the path will act as a button, not the area bounded by the path. The next four methods can be used as aliases for setting the shape of each of the four states.

new( )

`new SWF::Button( )`

This method creates a new Button object.

setAction( )

`$button->setAction(`*action, event_flag*`)`

This adds an SWF::Action object to the button. The script is activated when the button receives one of the following events, as indicated by the *event_flag* parameter:

`SWF::Button::SWFBUTTON_MOUSEUP`

Execute the script when the mouse button is pushed down over the button's hit area, then released. This is the default value for $event_flag.

`SWF::Button::SWFBUTTON_MOUSEOVER`

Execute the script when the mouse cursor enters the button's hit area.

`SWF::Button::SWFBUTTON_MOUSEOUT`

Execute the script when the mouse cursor leaves the button's hit area.

`SWF::Button::SWFBUTTON_MOUSEDOWN`

Execute the script when the mouse button is pressed within the button's hit area.

`SWF::Button::SWFBUTTON_DRAGOVER`

Execute the script when the mouse enters the button's hit area with the button pressed down.

```
SWF::Button::SWFBUTTON_DRAGOUT
```
Execute the script when the mouse leaves the button's hit area with the button pressed down.

Consider the following snippet of code, where $shape is a previously defined SWF::Shape object, and $movie is a previously defined SWF::Movie:

```
my $b = new SWF::Button( );
$b->addShape($shape, SWF::Button::SWFBUTTON_HIT);
$b->addShape($shape, SWF::Button::SWFBUTTON_UP);
my $item = $movie->add($b);
$item->setName("button1");
$b->setAction(new SWF::Action("_root.button1._xscale++;"),
              SWF::Button::SWFBUTTON_MOUSEDOWN);
```

Every time the button is clicked, the button's horizontal scale is incremented.

setHit( )

```
$button->setHit(shape)
```

This method sets the shape that defines the hit area of the button. Same as:

```
$button->addShape($shape, SWF::Button::SWFBUTTON_HIT);
```

setDown( )

```
$button->setDown(shape)
```

This method sets the shape that is displayed when the mouse button is held while over the hit area. Same as:

```
$button->addShape($shape, SWF::Button::SWFBUTTON_DOWN);
```

setOver( )

```
$button->setOver(shape)
```

This method sets the shape that is displayed when the mouse cursor is over the hit area. Same as:

```
$button->addShape($shape, SWF::Button::SWFBUTTON_OVER);
```

setUp( )

```
$button->setUp(shape)
```

This method sets the shape that is displayed when the button is at rest (i.e., hasn't been hit). Same as:

```
$button->addShape($shape, SWF::Button::SWFBUTTON_UP);
```

The SWF::Bitmap Module

The SWF::Bitmap object can be used to add bitmap images read from external files. The image must be in JPEG or DBL format.

One of the design goals of Ming was that it not require any external libraries. As a result, you cannot directly read a PNG image into a Bitmap object; first you must convert it into the DBL format using the *png2dbl* tool provided in the *utils* directory of the Ming distribution. DBL is a Ming-specific format (okay, that's a euphemism for "hack") that stores an image file as a DefineBitsLossless block that can be easily incorporated into an SWF file. In the future it may be possible to read PNG files directly, so check the documentation for additional functionality in the latest version.

Example 9-3 shows how to incorporate a bitmap image into a movie by assigning it as a fill to a Shape object. The shape is used as a kind of clipping path for the bitmap, and can be used anywhere a shape can be used, for instance, as a button.

Example 9-3. Reading in a bitmap image

```perl
#!/usr/bin/perl -w
#
# Example 9-3. Reading in a bitmap image
#

use strict;
use SWF qw(Movie Shape Bitmap);

# Fill a Shape with a Bitmap. The .dbl file has been
# previously created from a PNG file using the png2dbl tool.

my $b = new SWF::Bitmap("bitmap.dbl");

# Fill must be created before the Shape is drawn

my $s = new SWF::Shape();
my $f = $s->addFill($b);
$s->setRightFill($f);

# Get the dimensions of the bitmap and draw the Shape for the bounding box.
# A smaller bounding shape would act as a clipping path.

my $w = $b->getWidth();
my $h = $b->getHeight();
$s->drawLine($w, 0);
$s->drawLine(0, $h);
$s->drawLine(-$w, 0);
$s->drawLine(0, -$h);

my $m = new SWF::Movie();
$m->setDimension($w, $h);
$m->add($s);

$m->save("example9-3.swf");
```

getHeight( )

`$bitmap->getHeight( )`

This method returns the height (in pixels, not twips) of the bitmap.

getWidth( )

`$bitmap->getWidth( )`

This method returns the width (in pixels, not twips) of the bitmap.

new( )

`new SWF::Bitmap(file)`

This method creates a new Bitmap object of the given filename. The file must be a JPEG or a DBL file, as described above.

The SWF::Text Module

The SWF::Text object can be used to draw simple blocks of colored text. The following code excerpt creates a two-line text block:

```
my $f = new SWF::Font("./Arial.fdb");
my $t = new SWF::Text( );
$t->setFont($f);
$t->setHeight(1200);
$t->moveTo(200,1200);
$t->setColor(255, 0, 0);
$t->addString("Foo ");
$t->moveTo(200, 2400);
$t->addString("Bar.");
```

Use the SWF::Shape::drawGlyph( ) method if you want to draw characters with special fills or morph into other characters. If you need to create a block of text that can be updated dynamically, use the SWF::TextField object.

addString( )

`$text->addString(string)`

This method adds a string to the Text object at the current text cursor position.

getStringWidth( )

`$width = $text->getStringWidth(string)`

This method returns the width (in twips) of the given string as it is rendered using the Text object's current font and size settings. Note that the returned width takes into account the scale of the Text object.

moveTo( )

`$text->moveTo($x, $y)`

This method moves the position of the text cursor (i.e., the point at which text is added) to the specified point within the coordinate system of the Text object. The baseline of the text is drawn at the current text cursor point.

new( )

`$text = new SWF::Text( )`

This method creates a new Text object.

setColor( )

`$text->setColor(red, green, blue [, alpha])`

This method sets the text color; specify a red, green, blue, and optional alpha component.

setFont( )

`$text->setFont(font)`

This method sets the current font for the text object, where *font* is an SWF::Font object.

setHeight( )

`$text->setHeight(height)`

This method sets the font size, in twips (subject to any scaling in effect). The default height is 240.

setSpacing( )

`$text->setSpacing(spacing)`

This method defines the amount of space (in twips) between each character.

The SWF::TextField Module

Like the SWF::Text object, a TextField represents a block of text. However, Text-Fields cannot be transformed or skewed when displayed. The contents of a Text-Field can be changed over the course of a movie. (The Astral Trespassers example at the beginning of this chapter uses a TextField for the "Game Over" message.) Text-Fields are represented on the screen as user-editable text by default; this can be adjusted by creating the TextField with the appropriate flags.

addString( )

`$textField->addString(string)`

This method adds a string of text to the TextField, which is appended to the existing text.

align( )

`$textField->align(alignment)`

Unlike with SWF::Text objects, you can use a TextField to draw centered, justified, or left- or right-aligned text. Specify one of the following constants for the *alignment* parameter:

```
SWF::TextField::SWFTEXTFIELD_ALIGN_LEFT
SWF::TextField::SWFTEXTFIELD_ALIGN_RIGHT
SWF::TextField::SWFTEXTFIELD_ALIGN_CENTER
SWF::TextField::SWFTEXTFIELD_ALIGN_JUSTIFY
```

new( )

`$textField = new SWF::TextField([flags])`

This method creates a new TextField object whose behavior is determined by zero or more flags:

SWF::TextField::SWFTEXTFIELD_NOEDIT
: The TextField is non-editable.

SWF::TextField::SWFTEXTFIELD_PASSWORD
: User input is obscured by asterisks.

SWF::TextField::SWFTEXTFIELD_DRAWBOX
: A box is drawn bordering the TextField.

SWF::TextField::SWFTEXTFIELD_MULTILINE
: The TextField can accommodate multiple lines.

SWF::TextField::SWFTEXTFIELD_WORDWRAP
: On a multiline TextField, a string is wrapped to the next line once it reaches the margin of the field.

SWF::TextField::SWFTEXTFIELD_NOSELECT
: When the user clicks on the TextField, it is not selected.

More than one flag can be used by OR-ing them together:

```
use SWF::TextField qw(:TextField);
$textField = new SWF::TextField(SWFTEXTFIELD_MULTILINE |
                                SWFTEXTFIELD_WORDWRAP);
```

setBounds( )

`$textField->setBounds(width, height)`

This method sets the width and height (in twips, subject to scaling) of the bounding box of the TextField. Text in the field is cropped to this box. Note that you still have to set the font height with the setHeight( ) method.

setColor( )

`$textField->setColor(red, green, blue [, alpha])`

This method sets the color of the text. The default is black.

setFont( )

`$textField->setFont($font)`

This method indicates the font that should be used to draw the text in the TextField. The parameter must be an SWF::Font object.

setHeight( )

`$textField->setHeight(height)`

This method sets the font size. The default value is 240 twips (subject to scaling), or 12 pixels.

setIndentation( )

`$textField->setIndentation(width)`

This method sets the indentation of the first line of the TextField.

setLineSpacing( )

`$textField->setLineSpacing(height)`

This method sets the amount of space between the bottom of the descender in one line and the top of the ascender in the next line. If you are familiar with typography, note that this is different from "leading." The default value is 40 twips, or 2 pixels.

setMargin( ), setLeftMargin( ), setRightMargin( )

```
$textField->setMargins(left, right)
$textField->setRightMargin(width)
$textField->setLeftMargin(width)
```

These methods allow you to set the margins of the text block (in twips, subject to scaling).

setName( )

```
$textField->setName(name)
```

This method assigns a label to the TextField, which can later be referenced with Action-Script to add or change the text in the TextField.

The SWF::Font Module

The Font object represents a set of glyphs that can be used to draw text. At this time, Ming does not directly support PostScript or TrueType fonts. The only type of font supported is a specially created FDB file.

An FDB file is a document containing a font encoded as an SWF Font Definition Block. To create an FDB file you must use the *makefdb* tool contained in the *util* directory of the Ming distribution. The *makefdb* program takes an SWT Generator template file and extracts the font information from it. To convert a particular font for use with Ming, follow these steps:

1. If you have Macromedia's Flash tool (Version 4 or 5), download the Generator Authoring Extensions, a set of free Flash plug-ins that can be used to make SWT files.

2. Add some text to a movie using the font that you wish to translate. Save this movie as an SWT file.

3. Run the *makefdb* program to extract the Font Definition Block from the SWT file.

As of this writing, there are no other solutions for generating FDB files without the Flash tool. You have to rely on the kindness of strangers, who have translated several popular fonts already (see *http://shawn.apocabilly.org/PFG/fonts*). The Generator Authoring Extensions used for creating SWT files are available as a Flash plug-in from *http://www.macromedia.com/software/flash/*.

new( )

```
$font = new SWF::Font($filename)
```

This method creates a new instance of a font from the given FDB filename.

The SWF::Fill Module

Each Fill object must be associated with a particular Shape object and cannot be used interchangeably with other Shapes. Because of this, there is no explicit constructor for a Fill. A new Fill object is returned by the SWF::Shape::addFill() method. Fills can be one of three types: solid color (with or without an alpha channel), gradient, or bitmap. A gradient fill can be either linear or radial, and a bitmap fill can be tiled to fill the region, or clipped to fit the region.

The following constants are defined by this module:

```
SWFFILL_SOLID
SWFFILL_GRADIENT
SWFFILL_LINEAR_GRADIENT
SWFFILL_RADIAL_GRADIENT
SWFFILL_BITMAP
SWFFILL_TILED_BITMAP
SWFFILL_CLIPPED_BITMAP
```

The SWF::Fill module defines five methods that may be used to move the origin of the fill or to transform the fill. None of these methods affect solid fills.

moveTo( )

$fill->moveTo(*x, y*)

The origin of the fill is moved to the coordinate (*x, y*) in the coordinate space of the shape.

rotateTo( )

$fill->rotateTo(*degrees*)

This method rotates the fill from its original orientation.

scaleTo( )

$fill->scaleTo(*x_scale, y_scale*)

Each Fill object has a scaling attribute that is initially set to 1. The scaleTo( ) function sets the horizontal and vertical scales to the specified values, replacing the current scale values.

skewXTo( ), skewYTo( )

$fill->skewXTo(*x*)
$fill->skewYTo(*y*)

These functions set the horizontal and vertical skew attributes for the Fill object. The skew values are expressed as real numbers where 0 indicates no skew, and 1.0 is a 45 degree skew. Positive numbers indicate a counterclockwise skew anchored at the origin of the fill.

The SWF::Gradient Module

A gradient consists of a list of color values, each value with a set position. The gradient can be scaled to fill a given region and can appear as a linear gradient or a radial gradient (illustrated back in Figure 9-4). The color of the points between the two defined end points gradually transforms from the color of the first point to the color of the second.

A gradient is constructed by adding color entries at particular positions:

```
my $gradient = new SWF::Gradient( );
$gradient->addEntry(0.0, 255, 0, 0);
$gradient->addEntry(1.0, 255,255,255);
my $fill = $s->addFill($gradient);
$fill->scaleTo(.1);              # A method of the SWF::Fill object
```

See "The SWF::Fill Module" for additional methods for controlling gradient fills.

addEntry( )

$g->addEntry(*ratio, red, green, blue* [, *alpha*])

This method is used to add color entries to a gradient object. The ratio is a number between 0 and 1 that represents the position of the color in the gradient. Calls to addEntry( ) should be made in order of increasing ratios, or an error will occur.

new( )

$g = new SWF::Gradient( )

The new( ) method creates a new, empty gradient object.

The SWF::Morph Module

A Morph is an object that encapsulates all the different transition states that represent the transformation of one shape into another. To use a Morph, you set an initial state and a final state (both SWF::Shape objects). As the first shape is transformed into the second, all of the original shape's attributes (color, rotation, etc.) are gradually adjusted to match those of the final state. Once the Morph is placed within a frame, you can set the state of the Morph to any of the infinite number of transitional states between the two extreme shapes using the setRatio( ) method. A value of .5 displays an item that is halfway morphed between the starting and ending state. In the following example, the Morph changes from a square to a star in 10 frames, then changes back to a square in another 10 frames.

Both the initial and final shapes must contain an equal number of points. If the two states are defined by shapes with different numbers of points, you'll get inconsistent results in the final movie (typically random lines and noise).

In Example 9-4, a red square morphs into a blue eight-pointed star over the course of 10 frames, then morphs back into a square. Figure 9-6 shows a few of the stages.

Figure 9-6. In a morph, the starting and ending shapes must have the same number of points

Example 9-4. Morphing between two shapes

```perl
#!/usr/bin/perl -w
#
# Example 9-4. Morphing between a square and a star.
#
use strict;
use SWF::Movie;
use SWF::Morph;
use SWF::Shape;
use SWF::DisplayItem;

SWF::setScale(1.0);

my $morph = new SWF::Morph();
my $s = $morph->getShape1();        # The initial state of the morph; a red square
$s->setLine(0,0,0,0);
$s->setLeftFill($s->addFill(255, 0, 0));
$s->movePenTo(0, 0);
$s->drawLine(500,0);    $s->drawLine(500,0);              # Top
$s->drawLine(500,0);    $s->drawLine(500,0);
$s->drawLine(0, 500);   $s->drawLine(0, 500);            # Right
$s->drawLine(0, 500);   $s->drawLine(0, 500);
$s->drawLine(-500,0);   $s->drawLine(-500,0);            # Bottom
$s->drawLine(-500,0);   $s->drawLine(-500,0);
$s->drawLine(0, -500);  $s->drawLine(0, -500);           # Left
$s->drawLine(0, -500);  $s->drawLine(0, -500);

my $s2 = $morph->getShape2();  # The final state: a blue star with a thicker stroke
$s2->setLine(200,0,0,0);
$s2->setLeftFill($s2->addFill(0, 0, 255));
$s2->movePenTo(-500,-500);
$s2->drawLine(1000, 500);       $s2->drawLine(500, -500);   # Top
$s2->drawLine(500, 500);        $s2->drawLine(1000, -500);
```

Example 9-4. Morphing between two shapes (continued)

```
$s2->drawLine(-500, 1000);   $s2->drawLine(500, 500);      # Right
$s2->drawLine(-500, 500);    $s2->drawLine(500, 1000);
$s2->drawLine(-1000, -500);  $s2->drawLine(-500, 500);     # Bottom
$s2->drawLine(-500, -500);   $s2->drawLine(-1000, 500);
$s2->drawLine(500, -1000);   $s2->drawLine(-500, -500);    # Left
$s2->drawLine(500, -500);    $s2->drawLine(-500, -1000);

my $m = new SWF::Movie( );
$m->setDimension(4000,4000);
$m->setBackground(0xff, 0xff, 0xff);

# Add the Morph object to the Movie

my $i = $m->add($morph);
$i->moveTo(750, 750);

for (my $r=0; $r<=20; ++$r)
{
    $i->setRatio(abs((10-$r)/10));
    $m->nextFrame( );
}

$m->save("example9-4.swf");
```

The SWF::Morph module defines three methods. The setRatio( ) method belongs to the SWF::DisplayItem object; it can be used only after a Morph has been placed within a frame with the add( ) method.

getShape1( )

$shape = $morph->getShape1( )

When the Morph is created, it creates two new SWF::Shape objects, one for the initial and one for the final state of the morph transition. This method returns a reference to the initial state Shape object, which should be used to draw the initial shape using any of the SWF:: Shape functions (see also getShape2( )).

getShape2( )

$shape = $morph->getShape2( )

This method returns a reference to the final state Shape object of the Morph (see getShape1( )).

new( )

$morph = new SWF::Morph( )

This method creates a new Morph object.

The SWF::Sound Module

The SWF::Sound object allows you to read in an MP3 file that can be played in the background of a movie. Add the sound to a particular frame of the movie with the SWF::Movie::setSoundStream( ) method, as in the following example:

```
my movie = new SWF::Movie;
my $sound = new SWF::Sound("goldenhair.mp3");    # A 30-second MP3
$movie->setRate(24);

# Make sure we have enough frames to accommodate the sound clip
# 30 seconds * 24 fps = 720 frames

$movie->setFrames(720);
$movie->setSoundStream($sound);
```

If the movie is shorter than the length of the sound clip, the sound is truncated, so we add enough frames to the movie to accommodate the entire 30 seconds.

new( )

`$sound = new SWF::Sound(filename)`

This creates a new Sound object. The `filename` should be the path to an MP3 file.

The SWF::Action Module

The SWF::Action object encapsulates a segment of ActionScript code that can be associated with a particular frame of a movie, a button event, or a particular Display-Item (anything with an `AddAction( )` method). You write the ActionScript code and pass it to the ActionScript object as a string. When the SWF file is created, the JavaScript-like ActionScript is parsed and translated into ActionScript bytecode, which is embedded in the file. Ming uses different bytecode interpreters for Version 4- and Version 5-compatible code (as specified with the `SWF::setVersion( )` function).

new( )

`$a = new SWF::Action($script)`

The new( ) constructor creates an Action object from a given string. The string should be a syntactically correct piece of ActionScript code. See Appendix D for a complete Action-Script reference.

SWF Recipes

As soon as you start using the Ming library to dynamically generate SWF files with Perl, you start to run into some issues that may make you think of turning to a tool like Flash. The simple act of drawing a circle, for example, is not as simple as you would think, as SWF only allows the use of cubic Bezier curves.

This section anticipates a few of these issues, and provides solutions to the following:

- Drawing a circle with cubic Bezier curves
- Creating a preloader with Ming
- Using a custom XML file format that can be used to assemble composite documents from previously created movie clips
- Using the XMLSocket ActionScript object to create a chat client that communicates with a Perl-based chat server

Drawing a Circle

The SWF specification allows you to represent curved lines using cubic Bezier curves. With only one control point, it is impossible to draw a perfect circle using only cubic Bezier curves. However, by applying a little math, we can get a pretty good approximation.

SWF generation tools such as Flash provide their own circle objects that construct a group of cubic Bezier curves to accurately represent a circle. Since we are creating an SWF file at a relatively low level (with the Ming library), we have to do some of the math ourselves. There's an upside to the hands-on approach, however—our circle generation script is able to draw a circle using any number of arc segments. This is useful for morphing with circles, where the starting shape must have the same number of points as the end shape.

Three points define a cubic Bezier curve: a start point, an end point, and a control point. The start and end points are easy to calculate. If we are drawing a circle of radius R made up of four quarter-circle segments, the starting and ending points would be (clockwise, starting at the origin in the SWF coordinate space):

Start angle	Start point	End angle	End point
0	(R, 0)	90	(0, R)
90	(0, R)	180	(-R, 0)
180	(-R, 0)	270	(0, -R)
270	(0, -R)	0	(R, 0)

Since we want to be able to divide the circle into any arbitrary number of curve segments (not just four), we can generalize this using the parametric equation for representing a circle:

```
x = R cos(θ)
y = R sin(θ)
```

where θ is the angle of the line (relative to the positive x axis) drawn from the origin to that point on the circle. The trigonometric functions in Perl use radians to represent angles instead of degrees, so we would actually use the values 0, $\pi/2$, π, and $3\pi/2$ for the angles.

Now that we know how to find the starting and ending points of each arc, we need to calculate the placement of the control point. We want the control point to be positioned such that the resulting curve follows the curvature of an ideal circle (as represented by our parametric equation above) as closely as possible. A cubic Bezier curve is represented by the following parametric equation:

```
x(t) = (1-t)² xₛ + 2t(1-t)xc + t²xₑ
y(t) = (1-t)² yₛ + 2t(1-t)yc + t²yₑ
```

where t is a number between 0 and 1. At the start of the curve, the x coordinate would be:

```
x(0) = xₛ + 2*0(1-0)xc + 0²xₑ = xₛ
```

At the endpoint, it would be:

```
x(1) = (0)² xₛ + 2(1-1)xc + 1²xₑ = xₑ
```

and at the midpoint:

```
x(.5) = (1-.5)² xₛ + (1-.5)xc + .5²xₑ
      = .25xₛ + .5xc + .25xₛ
```

Since we want the Bezier curve to mirror the circle, we can say that the parametric equations for the circle and the cubic Bezier curve should be equal at the midpoint:

```
R cos(θ) = .25xₛ + .5xc + .25xₛ
R sin(θ) = .25yₛ + .5yc + .25yₛ
```

where θ is the angle of the midpoint of the curve. This is presented graphically in Figure 9-7, in which one segment, (a), is defined by the starting point (x1, y1), the ending point (x2, y2), and the control point (cx, cy). The angles θ1 and θ2 correspond to the starting and ending angles in Example 9-5, respectively.

With this bit of math figured out, we can write a routine `draw_arc( )` that draws a circular arc segment. To draw a circle with an arbitrary number of curve segments, we simply need to iteratively call `draw_arc( )` with the appropriate starting point, ending point, and midpoint angle, as in Example 9-5.

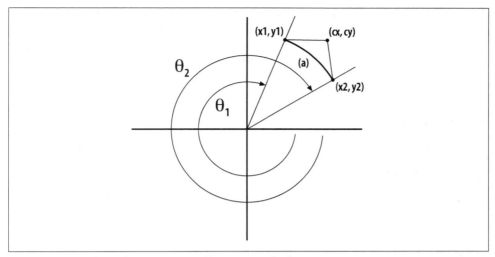

Figure 9-7. A circle can be approximated by a group of cubic Bezier curve segments

Example 9-5. Drawing a circle using an arbitrary number of cubic Bezier segments

```perl
#!/usr/bin/perl -w
#
# Example 9-5. Drawing a circle with cubic Bezier curves

use strict;
use SWF::Shape;

SWF::setScale(1.0);

my $PI = 3.1415926535;      # pi
my $r = 50;                 # the radius
my $start = 0;              # start angle
my $end = 0;                # end angle
my $segments = 6;           # number of segments

# Create a new Shape object

my $s = new SWF::Shape();
$s->setLineStyle(1, 255, 0, 0);
$s->movePenTo($r,0);

for (my $end=360/$segments; $end<=360; $end+=360/$segments) {

    # Calculate the midpoint angle. The control point
    # lies on this line

    my $midpoint = $start+($end-$start)/2;

    # draw_arc() draws a circular arc between 2 points
```

Example 9-5. Drawing a circle using an arbitrary number of cubic Bezier segments (continued)

```
    draw_arc($s,
        $r*cos(radians($start)),$r*sin(radians($start)),
        $r*cos(radians($end)), $r*sin(radians($end)),
        radians($midpoint));
    $start=$end;
}

# Create a Movie to hold the Shape

my $m = new SWF::Movie( );
$m->setDimension(300, 300);
my $item = $m->add($s);
$item->moveTo(100,100);
$m->nextFrame( );

$m->save('circle.swf');

exit;

sub draw_arc {

    # Take a shape, a start coordinate, end coordinate and
    # pre-computed mid-point angle as arguments

    my ($s, $x1, $y1, $x2, $y2, $angle) = @_;
    my $cx = 2*($r*cos($angle)-.25*$x1-.25*$x2);
    my $cy = 2*($r*sin($angle)-.25*$y1-.25*$y2);

    # Draw the curve on the Shape

    $s->drawCurveTo($cx, $cy, $x2, $y2);
}

sub radians {
    return ($_[0]/180)*$PI;        # Convert to radians
}
```

The result is pictured in Figure 9-8. If you want to create a circle that morphs into a star with 15 points, simply set the $segments variable to 15. A circle made of 8 segments (i.e., eight 45 degree arcs) is the best-looking circle with the minimum number of points.

Creating a Preloader with Ming

Large SWF documents (say, over 100k) should display some sort of message telling the user to be patient while the document loads. The preloader has become an idiom of the Flash world (if not an art form); there's no good reason why you can't use one with Ming as well.

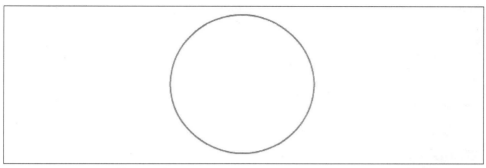

Figure 9-8. A near "perlfect" circle

The Flash plug-in starts playing your document as soon as it receives a complete frame. The function of a preloader is twofold: to give the user feedback, and to control the playback so that frames are not displayed before the whole movie is ready to be played.

A preloader is simply a couple of frames at the beginning of your document containing a couple of snippets of ActionScript. Sometimes people create preloaders that are complicated, artsy eye candy. This is fine, as long as it doesn't get so complicated that it requires its own preloader!

The preloader in this example is plain and functional: a simple red progress bar that displays the number of kilobytes loaded above it in a text field. The progress bar is a one-frame sprite that has ActionScript attached to it. The progress bar's script scales the sprite horizontally each time it loops, using the getBytesLoaded( ) and getBytesTotal( ) methods to calculate how much of the document has loaded so far.

The result of Example 9-6 is shown in Figure 9-9. When running this example, make sure that the bitmap is big enough that it takes some time to load; that is the whole point of a preloader, after all.

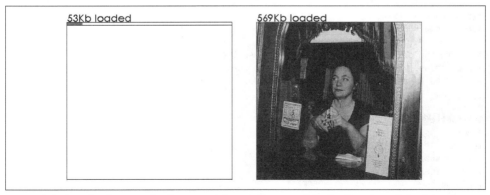

Figure 9-9. A preloader provides the user with an indication of the loading time of the document

Example 9-6. Creating an SWF file with a preloader

```perl
#!/usr/bin/perl -w
#
# Example 9-6.

use strict;

use SWF qw(:ALL);

SWF::useSWFVersion(5);

my $bitmap = new SWF::Bitmap("bitmap.dbl");
my $w = $bitmap->getWidth();
my $h = $bitmap->getHeight();

# Create a new Movie

my $m = new SWF::Movie;
$m->setDimension($w, $h+15);

# Create the feedback TextBlock. This displays a message: "X Kb loaded"

my $font = new SWF::Font("serif.fdb");
my $tf = new SWF::TextField();
$tf->setFont($font);
$tf->setColor(0,0,0);
$tf->setName("feedback");
$tf->setHeight(10);
$tf->setBounds(300,50);
my $item = $m->add($tf);
$item->moveTo(0,2);

# Outline the bounding box of the bitmap

my $s = new SWF::Shape();
$s->setLineStyle(1, 0, 0, 0);    # Black stroke
drawRect($s,$w,10,0,0);
$item = $m->add($s);
$item->moveTo(0,15);

# Create the preloader bar. It is a Sprite so that it can
# encapsulate its own ActionScript code for changing the
# scale based on the number of bytes loaded

my $s2 = new SWF::Shape();
$s2->setLeftFill($s2->addFill(255, 0, 0));
drawRect($s2,$w,10,0,0);
my $bar = new SWF::Sprite();
$item = $bar->add($s2);
$bar->nextFrame();
$bar->add(new SWF::Action(<<ENDSCRIPT
    this._xscale = (_root.getBytesLoaded() / _root.getBytesTotal()) * 100;
    _root.feedback = int(_root.getBytesLoaded()/1024) + "Kb loaded";
```

Example 9-6. Creating an SWF file with a preloader (continued)

```
ENDSCRIPT
));
$bar->nextFrame();
$item = $m->add($bar);
$item->moveTo(0,15);

my $s3 = new SWF::Shape();          # Outline the bar in black
$s3->setLineStyle(1, 0, 0, 0);      # Black stroke
drawRect($s3, $w, $h, 0, 0);
$item = $m->add($s3);
$item->moveTo(0,15);
$m->nextFrame();

# Create a loop with ActionScript. Jump out when the whole document is loaded.

$m->add(new SWF::Action(<<ENDSCRIPT
if (_root.getBytesLoaded() < _root.getBytesTotal()){
   prevFrame();
   play();
} else {
   nextFrame();
}
ENDSCRIPT
));
$m->nextFrame();

# Add the bitmap

my $s4 = new SWF::Shape();
my $f = $s4->addFill($bitmap);
$s4->setRightFill($f);
drawRect($s4, $w, $h, 0, 0);
$item = $m->add($s4);
$item->moveTo(0,15);
$m->nextFrame();

$m->save("preloader.swf");

exit();

# drawRect() is a helper procedure used to draw rectangles

sub drawRect {
   my $shape = shift;
   my ($w, $h, $dx, $dy) = @_;
   $shape->movePenTo($dx, $dy);
   $shape->drawLine($w, 0);
   $shape->drawLine(0, $h);
   $shape->drawLine(-$w, 0);
   $shape->drawLine(0, -$h);
}
```

Assembling Sprite-Based Documents with XML

One of the reasons to use a web application environment like ColdFusion is that it allows you to dynamically piece together documents that are composites of modular Flash files. Using Ming, it is relatively easy to roll your own XML format for describing a top-level document that is a collection of modular SWF files. This format could be used for integrating advertising with content dynamically, or for creating modular graphical user interfaces from pre-created components.

Let's say that you want to generate an SWF document that is built dynamically using a library of individual SWF movies. You could just piece these together in an HTML file using Cascading Style Sheets to position the movies on the page, but then the movies couldn't reference each other's Document Object Model, nor could you apply transformations. Another option is to create a simple XML format for representing a composite movie and writing an interpreter that translates the XML into a top-level SWF file.

We'll call the XML description format SWFscript. A sample SWFscript document would look like this:

```
<movie filename="index.swf" width="400" height="400">
    <sprite url="sprite2.swf">
        <scaleTo x="2" y="8"/>
        <moveTo x="100" y="100"/>
    </sprite>
    <sprite url="sprite2.swf">
        <scaleTo x="5" y="5"/>
        <moveTo x="200" y="200"/>
    </sprite>
    <sprite url="sprite2.swf">
        <moveTo x="300" y="300"/>
        <rotateTo degrees="45"/>
    </sprite>
    <nextFrame/>
</movie>
```

This document indicates that a top-level movie with the filename *index.swf* is created. The three modular SWF movies are read into the top-level movie as sprites and transformed according to the provided transformation tags.

The interpreter reads in the XML file and parses it using the XML::Parser module. Each time a start tag is encountered, the start_tag( ) handler is called, and each time an end tag is encountered, the end_tag( ) handler is called. The SWF file that is created is kind of a skeletal framework; each sprite is an empty SWF::Sprite that has a movie loader script attached to it. When the movie is loaded, each empty sprite uses the loadMovie( ) method to replace itself (at its current position, subject to transformation) with the specified SWF file. The movie URLs are relative to the top-level document, so if you move the top-level movie, be sure to bundle the component files with it.

```perl
#!/usr/bin/perl -w
#
# Assemble a skeletal framework of Sprites

use strict;
use SWF qw(:ALL);
use XML::Parser;       # Used to parse the XML input file

my $filename = '';     # The output filename
my $sprites = 0;       # The number of <sprite> tags so far
my $m = undef;         # The top-level Movie
my $item = undef;      # The current DisplayItem

SWF::useSWFVersion(5);

my $parser = new XML::Parser(Handlers => { Start => \&start_tag,
                                           End   => \&end_tag,
                                         });
if (defined $ARGV[0]) {
    $parser->parsefile($ARGV[0]);  # Parse the input XML
} else {
    die "Please provide the name of an XML file.\n";
}
```

The start_tag( ) function is called whenever the parser encounters a start tag (<tag>):

```perl
sub start_tag {
    my $expat = shift;     # This is an Expat XML parser object
                           # that we don't use here.
    my $tag = shift;       # The tag name
    my %a = @_;            # The tag's attributes

    # Check the tag type

    if ($tag eq 'movie') {
        $m = new SWF::Movie;                # Create a new Movie
        if ($a{'width'} && $a{'height'}) {
            $m->setDimension($a{'width'}, $a{'height'});
        }
    } elsif ($tag eq 'sprite') {
        if ($m) {
            $item = new_sprite($a{'url'});   # Create a new (empty) Sprite that
                                             # loads the external movie clip
        }
    } elsif ($tag eq 'moveTo') {
        if ($item) {
            $item->moveTo($a{'x'}, $a{'y'}); # Move the current item
        }
    } elsif ($tag eq 'scaleTo') {
        if ($item) {
        $item->scaleTo($a{'x'}, $a{'y'});    # Scale the current item
        }
    } elsif ($tag eq 'rotateTo') {
        if ($item) {
```

```
                    $item->rotateTo($a{'degrees'});    # Rotate the current item
            }
        } elsif ($tag eq 'remove') {
            if ($item) {
                $item->remove();                        # Remove the current item
                $item = undef;
            }
        } elsif ($tag eq 'nextFrame') {
            if ($m) {
                $m->nextFrame();                        # Go to the next frame
            }
        }
    }
```

The end_tag( ) function is called when an end tag (</tag> or />) is encountered. It takes two parameters: the XML::Parser object and the tag name. If the parser is at the end of a movie tag, output the SWF movie. Otherwise, discard the current sprite object.

```
sub end_tag {
    my ($expat, $tag) = @_;      # The Expat object and the tag name
    if ($tag eq 'movie') {
        $m->output();
    } elsif ($tag eq 'sprite') {
        $item = undef;          # The sprite is no longer the current item
    }
}
```

The new_sprite( ) function takes the URL of the external movie clip to be loaded and returns a new sprite with the ActionScript to load the movie clip at runtime.

```
sub new_sprite {
    my $url = shift;      # The URL of the external movie clip to load
    $sprites++;          # Increment number of sprites

    my $sprite = new SWF::Sprite();
    $sprite->nextFrame();
    my $i = $m->add($sprite);
    $i->setName("sprite$sprites");
    $m->add(new SWF::Action("loadMovie('$url','sprite$sprites');"));
    return $i;
}
```

Figure 9-10 shows a composite document created from three transformed copies of a component.

Communicating Between an SWF Client and a Perl Backend

SWF documents can easily communicate with other processes running on the Internet. Web and XML content may be loaded into an SWF file using ActionScript. In this section, we use ActionScript to create a simple chat client that can communicate with copies of itself via a central chat server written in Perl.

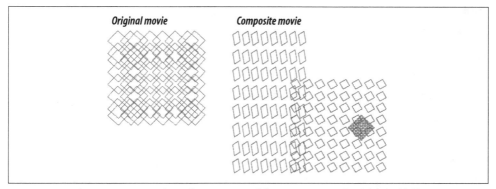

Figure 9-10. The composite on the right was created from an intermediate XML file format

First we'll write the simple chat server. It uses the IO::Select and IO::Socket modules (part of the standard Perl distribution) to open and manage the sockets for communicating to a number of clients. This server is a non-forking server; one instance of the server handles queued requests from many clients.

The IO::Socket::INET module (a subclass of IO::Socket) creates a new socket object that listens on a particular port (in this case, port 9999). The Listen attribute indicates how many connection requests are queued before new requests are refused (in this case, 10).

The IO::Select module provides a high-level interface to the system select( ) call. It provides the can_read( ) and can_write( ) methods that return a list of all the open sockets that have data waiting to be read from or written to.

The simple chat server looks something like Example 9-7. The client is shown in Example 9-8.

Example 9-7. A chat server that communicates with an SWF client

```perl
#!/usr/bin/perl -w
#
# Example 9-7. The server.

use IO::Socket;    # Part of the base Perl distribution,
use IO::Select;    # these are used for implementing socket
                   # communication

my $server = new IO::Socket::INET( LocalPort => 9999,
                                   Listen => 10);

my $select = IO::Select->new($server);
my @messages;      # The outgoing message buffer
$/="\0";           # Set the line input separator
print STDERR "Server started...\n";
```

Example 9-7. A chat server that communicates with an SWF client (continued)

```
# Loop in 'daemon mode' until killed

while (1) {
    @messages = ( );

    # Loop through the open handles that are ready with data

    foreach my $client ($select->can_read(1)) {
        if ($client==$server) {

            # In this case, we have a new connection request
            $client = $server->accept( );
            $select->add($client);
        } else {

            # Read the data from the client and push it on
            # the buffer, if the client is still there

            my $data = <$client>;
            if (defined($data)) {
                push @messages, $data;
            } else {
                $select->remove($client);
                $client->close;
            }
        }
    }

    # Loop through the handles waiting for input
    # and send them the buffered messages

    foreach my $client ($select->can_write(1)) {
        foreach my $m (@messages) {
            print $client "$m";
        }
    }
}
```

All this server does is:

1. Open a new connection for each connection request
2. Loop though the IO::Handle objects that have data waiting to be read
3. If it has received a connection request, open a new handle
4. Otherwise, read in the waiting data and push it into a buffer
5. Loop through all of the connections that are waiting to be written to and send them a copy of the data buffer

Up until now, we haven't been interested in the form of the input data because the server is simply forwarding the input data to the connected clients. Each client sends chat message data to the server formatted as a single XML tag. Each tag is delimited by a null character (as required by the SWF specification), which explains why we set the data input delimiter to "\0" in the server.

ActionScript provides an easy way to send XML between applications with the XML-Socket object. This ActionScript object opens up a socket to a particular port on a given host computer and calls one of several callbacks when something interesting happens with the socket:

- XMLSocket.onXML is called when XML data is received.
- XMLSocket.onConnect is called when a connection is attempted.
- XMLSocket.onClose is called when a connection is closed.

These callbacks initially do not have any code associated with them. You must provide your own code for these hooks.

Our chat client, shown in Example 9-8, consists of three TextField objects and a submission button. The TextFields are for displaying messages, holding the user's name or "handle," and entering new messages, respectively. The first frame of the movie is a keyframe holding the ActionScript that sets up the environment and opens the socket to the chat server.

Example 9-8. An SWF chat client

```perl
#!/usr/bin/perl
#
# Example 9-8. The client.

use SWF qw(:ALL);
use SWF::TextField qw(:Text);

SWF::useSWFVersion(5);

# Create a new Movie

my $m = new SWF::Movie;
$m->setDimension(400,400);

# ActionScript for intializing the XMLSocket object that
# handles all of our communication and XML parsing needs

$m->add(new SWF::Action(<<ENDSCRIPT
    socket = new XMLSocket();
    socket.connect('localhost', 9999);
    socket.onXML = dataReceived;
    socket.onConnect = welcome;
    socket.onClose = goodbye;

    function welcome (success) {
            if (success) {
                _root["chatwindow"] = "Welcome!\n";
```

Example 9-8. An SWF chat client (continued)

```
            } else {
                _root["chatwindow"] = "Couldn't connect!\n";
            }
        }

    function goodbye () {
            _root["chatwindow"] = "Goodbye!";
        }

    function dataReceived (input) {
        var e = input.firstChild;
        _root["chatwindow"] = e.attributes.handle + ": " +
            e.attributes.text+"\n"+_root["chatwindow"];
        }
ENDSCRIPT
));
$m->nextFrame();

# Create a TextField for displaying messages

my $font = new SWF::Font("serif.fdb");
my $tf = new SWF::TextField(SWFTEXTFIELD_DRAWBOX|
                            SWFTEXTFIELD_MULTILINE|
                            SWFTEXTFIELD_WORDWRAP);
$tf->setFont($font);
$tf->setColor(0,0,0);
$tf->setName("chatwindow");
$tf->setHeight(10);
$tf->setBounds(300,260);
my $item = $m->add($tf);
$item->moveTo(0,10);


# Create a TextField for holding the chatter's handle

my $tf2 = new SWF::TextField(SWFTEXTFIELD_DRAWBOX);
$tf2->setFont($font);
$tf2->setColor(0,0,0);
$tf2->setHeight(10);
$tf2->setName("handle");
$tf2->addString("Mr. Foo");
$tf2->setBounds(50,10);
$item = $m->add($tf2);
$item->moveTo(0,280);


# A TextField for entering new messages

my $tf3 = new SWF::TextField(SWFTEXTFIELD_DRAWBOX);
$tf3->setFont($font);
$tf3->setColor(0,0,0);
$tf3->setHeight(10);
$tf3->setName("message");
$tf3->setBounds(200,10);
```

Example 9-8. An SWF chat client (continued)

```
$item = $m->add($tf3);
$item->moveTo(50,280);

# Create a 'submit' button

my $s = new SWF::Shape();
$s->setLineStyle(1, 0, 0, 0);    # Black stroke
$s->setLeftFill($s->addFill(255, 255, 255));
$s->drawLine(35, 0);
$s->drawLine(0, 10);
$s->drawLine(-35, 0);
$s->drawLine(0, -10);
my $t = new SWF::Text();
$t->setFont($font);
$t->setColor(0, 0, 0);
$t->setHeight(10);
$t->addString("SUBMIT");
$item = $m->add($t);
$item->moveTo(260,290);

# Add the action script that sends the message and handle as
# XML to the chat server

my $b = new SWF::Button();
$b->addShape($s, SWF::Button::SWFBUTTON_HIT);
$item = $m->add($b);
$item->setName("button1");
$b->setAction(new SWF::Action(<<ENDSCRIPT
    var xmlObj = new XML();
    var m = xmlObj.createElement("message");
    m.attributes.handle = _root["handle"];
    m.attributes.text = _root["message"];
    xmlObj.appendChild(m);
    socket.send(xmlObj);
ENDSCRIPT
), SWF::Button::SWFBUTTON_MOUSEDOWN);
$item->moveTo(260,280);
$m->nextFrame();

# Loop

$m->add(new SWF::Action(<<ENDSCRIPT
    prevFrame();
    play();
ENDSCRIPT
));
$m->nextFrame();

$m->save('chatclient.swf');

exit();
```

Figure 9-11 shows a sample session between two chatters.

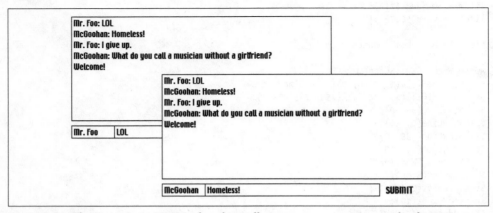

Figure 9-11. The ActionScript XMLSocket object allows you to communicate with other processes

## PART III

Documents and Printing

## CHAPTER 10

Printing with Postscript and PDF

People like paper. Despite years of talk about the future "paperless" electronic office and the environmental impact of using as much paper as we do, people still like paper. In this chapter we look at PostScript, a programming language for representing printed pages. We also look at the Portable Document Format (PDF), an extension of Post-Script that represents a good attempt at transcending today's paper-bound office. This chapter presents the language features and some of the drawing primitives that will be needed to understand the higher-level Perl APIs presented in Chapters 11 and 12.

PostScript in a Nutshell

PostScript is a *page description language*. A PostScript file is simply a text file that contains the PostScript code to draw one or more page. This file is sent to a *Post-Script interpreter*, which executes the program and draws the pages. In most applications, the PostScript interpreter is embedded in the output device; a laser printer, for example, has a built-in PostScript interpreter that renders the final pages.

For PostScript development work there is also the *Ghostscript* package, available for most operating systems, which consists of a number of PostScript rendering tools, including an interpreter and a PostScript viewer. Ghostscript is used by many of the software packages in this book (such as the Gimp and ImageMagick) for parsing and generating PostScript, EPS, and PDF files. It also comes as a standard part of most Linux distributions (see the sidebar "Getting Ghostscript").

Several aspects of the PostScript imaging model are worthy of note, starting with the way that PostScript defines a page.

The Page

A PostScript page is defined in terms of an ideal coordinate system, with the point (0,0) in the lower left-hand corner, and x and y values increasing up and to the right (Figure 10-1). This coordinate system is called the *default user space*, and its definitions may be changed within a PostScript program using a number of transformation

Getting Ghostscript

Ghostscript is a free PostScript interpreter. There are actually two different versions of Ghostscript: the Aladdin Systems distribution and the GNU distribution. The distinction is in the licensing; the Aladdin Free Public License allows the free use and redistribution of the Ghostscript source code, but does not allow the free commercial distribution of the code. The GNU distribution is covered by the GNU General Public License, which allows commercial distribution as part of an open source package. The GNU distribution generally lags behind the Aladdin distribution by a version number or so (as of this writing, the current version of Aladdin Ghostscript is 5.10, whereas GNU Ghostscript is at 4.03). Both versions are available at the Ghostscript home page, *http://www.cs.wisc.edu/~ghost/*.

Ghostscript runs on virtually any platform. To view the PostScript examples in this chapter, you must send the code to the Ghostscript interpreter (or to a PostScript printer, generating even more wasted paper!), which then renders the page. In a command-line environment, this can be done by typing at the shell prompt:

```
gs filename.ps
```

where *filename.ps* is the name of the PostScript file generated by the example. There is also a PostScript viewer with a GUI called GSView, which is also available from the main Ghostscript site.

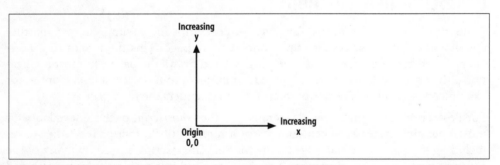

Figure 10-1. The PostScript page is defined in terms of an ideal coordinate system with its origin anchored in the lower left corner

operators such as scale, rotate, and translate. The default grid unit size is 1/72 of an inch (a *point*); this convention is inherited from the print industry, where the *printer's point* is defined as 1/72.27 inch. A point on the grid of the page may be represented using any arbitrary number. For example:

```
40.345 60.234 moveto
```

is a valid PostScript statement, and it is rendered to the resolution of the final output device. The device may not be able to make the distinction between 40.3 and 40.345, so it renders it according to its own internal *device space* (which we, as PostScript programmers, do not have to worry about). The transformation operators imbue

PostScript with a great deal of power for rendering complex page descriptions, but they are beyond the scope of this introduction, and are documented in many of the fine books on PostScript listed at the end of this chapter.

PostScript can handle any arbitrary page size, but the sizes of interest are those corresponding to the standard paper sizes listed in Table 10-1. The numbers of the "A" and "B" paper series are defined by rotating the previous numbered paper type from "portrait" to "landscape" (that is, such that the width is greater than the height) and splitting the paper in two vertically. Thus, an A0 sheet has the same area as two A1 sheets, four A2 sheets, sixteen A3 sheets, etc. This is useful when the final output is intended for a commercial printer who prints many pages on a single larger sheet that will later be folded or cropped to the desired final page size.

Table 10-1. Standard paper sizes, in points

Paper type	Dimension in points (width x height)	Paper type	Dimension in points (width x height)
Letter (8.5" x 11")	612 x 792	B0	2920 x 4127
Legal (8.5" x 14")	612 x 1008	B1	2064 x 2920
Ledger (17" x 11")	1224 x 792	B2	1460 x 2064
Tabloid (11 x 17")	792 x 1224	B3	1032 x 1460
A0	2384 x 3370	B4	729 x 1032
A1	1684 x 2384	B5	516 x 729
A2	1191 x 1684	B6	363 x 516
A3	842 x 1191	B7	258 x 363
A4	595 x 842	B8	181 x 258
A5	420 x 595	B9	127 x 181
A6	297 x 420	B10	91 x 127
A7	210 x 297	#10 Envelope	297 x 684
A8	148 x 210	C5 Envelope	461 x 648
A9	105 x 148	DL Envelope	312 x 624

A PostScript page consists of a series of drawing operations. When the page has been completely drawn, the showpage operator is called to render the page and clear the current page. The next drawing commands are executed on a blank page, and so on. The trivial program in Example 10-1 outputs two separate pages, as shown in Figure 10-2.

Example 10-1. Drawing two pages with text

```
/Times-Roman findfont 48 scalefont setfont
100 400 moveto
(This is Page 1) show
showpage
100 400 moveto
(This is Page 2) show
showpage
```

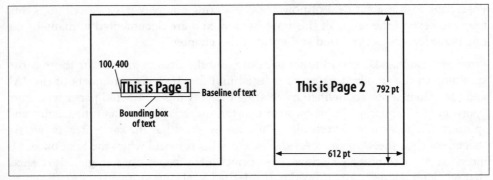

Figure 10-2. Output of a simple PostScript program that draws two pages (reduced)

Some PostScript Functions

Looking at the example above, note that the parameters associated with an operator are listed before the operator, rather than after the operator as in most procedural languages such as Perl.* This is because PostScript uses an *operand stack* to hold numbers, objects, and the results of executed commands. In the second line of the example, the integers 100 and 400 are placed on the operand stack. The moveto function then pops the two values from the top of the stack and uses them as its arguments. If the function returns a value, it is pushed to the top of the stack. In the following addition operation, the operand stack would be left with the value 4 on top:

```
2 2 add
```

PostScript is a full-blown programming language with many features and subtleties. In this chapter we use only a simple subset of the available collection of PostScript functions. Consider these to be the core set of procedures needed to do anything useful with PostScript. These functions can be strung together to create complex drawings. Example 10-2 produces the spiral in Figure 10-3.

Example 10-2. A spiral

```
100 50 moveto
100 100 lineto
50 100 50 0 180 arc
37.5 100 37.5 180 360 arc
50 100 25 0 180 arc
37.5 100 12.5 180 360 arc
.5 setgray
8 setlinewidth
stroke
showpage
```

* PostScript is actually very much like the FORTH programming language.

Figure 10-3. Complex paths may be created by stringing several drawing functions together

The moveto function sets the *current point* to a coordinate value without adding to the *current path*. You may think of the moveto function as lifting the pen off the paper and placing it at a new coordinate.

The arc function adds the path of a counterclockwise arc to the current path. This function takes five parameters: the x and y values of the coordinate at the center of the arc; the radius of the arc; and two angles that describe the sweep of the arc. For example, the path of a complete circle with radius 25 centered at (50,50) would be created with:

```
50 50 25 0 360 arc
```

Note that this statement just lays out the path of the arc. To actually draw the path, you must call the stroke function, which draws the line on the page in the current tint and with the current line width. The *tint* of the line, expressed as a percentage of black, can be set with the setgray function. The current line width can be set with the setlinewidth function, where the width is expressed in points.

The save and restore functions can be used to save a path for later use. If you wish to draw a box that is filled with a 20% gray screen and stroked with a 2 pt black line, you have to create two separate paths: one to tell the fill function which area to fill, and one to tell the stroke function how to draw the line. The path for the box may be created once for the fill, saved, and later restored for the stroke operation:

```
0 0 moveto
0 100 lineto 100 100 lineto
100 0 lineto 0 0 lineto      % Draw a box
gsave                        % Save the current path
.8 setgray fill              % Fill with a 20% screen
                             % (1 = white, 0 = black)
grestore                     % Restore the path before
                             % stroking the lines
0 setgray 2 setlinewidth     % Now draw the outline of the
                             % box with a 2 pt line
stroke
showpage
```

PostScript files describe a set of commands for drawing arbitrary shapes on a page. Text is drawn in the same way that a line or a circle would be drawn; it is treated as a collection of paths that make up the shapes of the letterforms. These letterform descriptions are stored in *fonts*. The current font may be specified within a Post-Script program with the setfont function, which expects a *font dictionary* on the operand stack. A font dictionary may be loaded with the findfont function. Once a font dictionary is loaded, it may be scaled to a particular size with the scalefont function. Typically, you would specify a font with the sequence:

```
/Times-Roman findfont    % Assuming you have the font
                         % Times-Roman on your system
12 scalefont             % Set the size of the font
setfont                  % Use 12 pt Times-Roman as
                         % the current font
```

The show function can then be used to draw a string on the page with the current font:

```
/Times-Roman findfont 12 scalefont setfont
(Yowza yowza yowza!) show
```

PostScript is generally used to create vector graphics, but it can also render raster graphics with the use of the image function. Image inclusion in PostScript documents is advanced programming territory and is beyond the scope of this introduction. However, the ImageMagick module described in Chapter 3 (which also depends on the Ghostscript interpreter) provides an easy way of reading in a raster image (such as a PNG) and generating the PostScript code necessary to render the image.

PostScript Document Structuring Conventions

Like most modern programming languages such as C or Perl, PostScript is loose in its definition of a "properly structured" program. As with other languages, poor program structure can make a PostScript program unreadable by programmers and, in certain cases, unprintable by certain rendering devices. Certain structuring conventions have been proposed by Adobe, and these should be followed by PostScript programs that define page descriptions. The purpose of these conventions is to:

- Ensure that each page of the document may be rendered independently of any other page
- Guarantee that the resources needed by the program are available
- Allow the program to be handled by printer utility programs such as print spoolers and log generators
- Allow the easy generation of cover pages or trailer pages
- Allow overlays such as "draft" markings or watermarks to be added to a document
- Allow the document to be easily included in other documents

- Provide the PostScript interpreter with sufficient information to render the document as efficiently as possible
- Allow better error reporting

Conformance to the Document Structuring Conventions (DSC) is achieved by adding comments that identify the various parts of the document. PostScript structural comments have a %% or %! at the beginning of a line, and end with a newline. Note that Version 3.0 of the Document Structuring Conventions is a document of over 100 pages describing these rules in depth. The following is an overview of the conventions applicable to this chapter.

A PostScript document is divided into two main sections: the *prolog* and the *body*.

The prolog

The prolog consists of a *header* and a section for defining procedures that are to be made available to every page of the document. The header contains information about the document as a whole, such as the number of pages, title, creator, colors used, etc. The header is terminated with the %%EndComments comment. The prolog itself is terminated with the %%EndProlog comment.

The %! "magic number" and version
> Every PostScript program must start with the string %!. This string is a two-byte "magic number" that designates the file as a PostScript file. The first line should also contain a string that describes the version of the Document Structuring Conventions being used. For our purposes, each PostScript file we generate will start with the line:
>
> ```
> %!PS-Adobe-3.0
> ```

Information for print spoolers
> Several structural comments have been defined specifically so that print spoolers can obtain information about a document to help identify it. Some of these are:
>
> ```
> %%Title:
> %%Creator:
> %%CreationDate:
> %%For:
> ```

Number of pages
> The document header should contain the comment %%Pages: followed by the number of pages in the document. If this is not known at the outset, the information can be filled in later or included at the end of the document by including the comment %%Pages:(atend) in the prolog, then specifying the page count in a comment at the end of the file.

Bounding box
> The bounding box of the document is represented as the lower left and upper right corners of the box that describes the maximum bounds of all drawing to be

done in the document. Typically, this corresponds to the page size in points (refer to Table 10-1). For example:

```
%%BoundingBox: 0 0 612 792
```

indicates a document to be rendered on a letter-sized page.

Procedural definitions

The procedural definitions section typically contains a number of custom generic procedures generated by a specific application for drawing text and images. PageMaker, for example, generates a standard prolog of proprietary functions and definitions that are used to render files formatted by PageMaker. These prologs tend to be copyrighted (and fairly obfuscated), so be careful about copying functions from other files' prologs!

The beginning of the procedures section is marked with a %%BeginProlog comment. Each procedure definition should be enclosed within a %%BeginResource: procset and a %%EndResource comment. An example of a properly commented procedure definition is the following:

```
%%BeginProlog
%%BeginResource:procset
%
% define a procedure to draw a scalable unit circle
%
/circle { 0 0 .5 0 360 } def
%%EndResource
...
%%EndProlog
```

The body

The Body of a properly structured document should consist of a succession of page descriptions, with each page starting with a %%Page: comment. It is important that each page be independent of any other page in the document. The code to generate the page cannot rely on the graphics state left by the previous page. Fonts loaded in the course of rendering previous pages should be reloaded, and procedures defined on other pages should be redefined or moved to the prolog section, where they are available document-wide.

The code for each page description should end with a showpage operand, which renders the page and clears the current page to white. With these conventions in mind, a typical PostScript program might look something like Example 10-3.

Example 10-3. A properly formatted PostScript document

```
%!PS-Adobe-3.0
%%Title: Felt for Farnsworth
%%Creator: ShempMaker 5.0
%%For: Tuti Cuandohead
%%Pages: (atend)
```

Example 10-3. A properly formatted PostScript document (continued)

```
%%BoundingBox: 0  0  612  1008
%%EndComments

%%BeginProlog
%%BeginResource:procset
% A procedure could go here
%%EndResource

% A list of procedures can follow

%%EndProlog

%%Page: 1
% Code to draw page 1
/Times-Roman findfont 48 scalefont setfont
100 400 moveto
(This is Page 1) show
showpage

%%Page: 2
% Code to draw page 2
/Times-Roman findfont 48 scalefont setfont
100 400 moveto
(This is Page 2) show
showpage

%%Page: 3
% Code to draw page 3
/Times-Roman findfont 48 scalefont setfont
100 400 moveto
(This is Page 3) show
showpage

%%Trailer
%%Pages: 3
%%EOF
```

Remember that the conventions described above are merely that subset of the Document Structuring Conventions used in this chapter. To do larger-scale development work with PostScript, you should retrieve the full DSC document from Adobe's web site.

Portable Document Format (PDF)

If any electronic document format were to herald the onset of the paperless world, PDF would be it. PDF is a file format for creating multi-page documents with graphics, images, and text that are intended to be viewed on a wide variety of platforms. PDFs are designed to be suitable for screen display or high resolution printing.

PDF is a kind of simplification and extension of PostScript. The problem with using PostScript as a portable interchange format is that it is a little too flexible and forgiving. The PDF specification adds a layer of structure that allows for applications that depend on more information than the raw graphical data needed to render a page.* Here's a rough outline of PDF's features and improvements on PostScript:

Font management

- Type 1 fonts and TrueType fonts can be embedded in a document, so you don't have to worry about whether the end user has the correct fonts.

- To save space, you can embed only the subset of glyphs actually used.

- Fourteen standard fonts are guaranteed to be available for use by any PDF viewer; these fonts can be used without being included in the document.

- External fonts may be used. A *font descriptor* is included for each font in the document, allowing the viewer to make an intelligent substitution if an external font is not available.

Efficient document storage

- JPEG compression is used for images. LZQ and Flate compression algorithms may be applied to textual and graphic objects in the document.

- The drawing instruction language defined in the PDF specification is implemented as sequences of short operators. PDF drawing instructions are much more succinct than those in the PostScript language, and are almost as flexible.

Interactivity

- The PDF format provides for dynamic form fields that may be filled in by the user.

- Navigation buttons and hyperlinks may be incorporated into page content.

- Documents may be annotated.

Collaborative editing and security

- PDF files may be encrypted.

- The way that objects are defined in a PDF file allows for incremental updates to the document while preserving the revision history.

PDF documents can be viewed on most platforms with Adobe's freely distributed Acrobat Reader, or with GhostView (distributed with Ghostscript). If you are using X Windows, you may want to try the *XPdf* viewer if GhostView doesn't suit your needs.

Chapter 12 describes how to generate PDF documents with Perl using the PDF::API2 module. The remainder of this chapter details the internals of the PDF file format.

---

* If you are familiar with the TEX and LATEX typesetting languages, note that the development of PDF atop PostScript is kind of an analog to the development of the LATEX macros for high-level page definition that extend the TEX typesetting language.

Structure of a PDF File

At its most basic level, a PDF file is a sequence of 8-bit bytes that are grouped into tokens separated by whitespace. PDF documents can be created using only characters in the readable ASCII set, or they can optionally contain unreadable binary data (e.g., image or compressed data). All of the keyword tokens appear in readable ASCII characters, however.

Unlike a PostScript file, you can't really create a PDF file by writing it with a text editor. A PDF file depends on a cross-reference table that is a byte-by-byte index to the file. You need to create or modify a PDF file with a tool that can keep track of the document structure and update the locations of objects within the document.

The structure of a simple document is illustrated in Figure 10-4. The rest of this section outlines a PDF file that describes a sample two-page document.

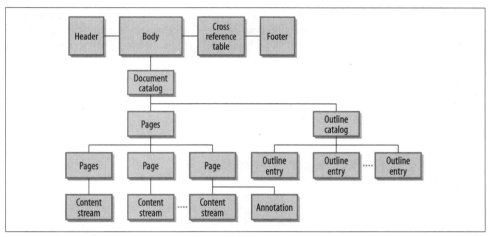

Figure 10-4. The structure of a PDF file

A file is composed of four sections:

- The header
- The body
- The cross-reference (XREF) table
- The trailer

The header and trailer contain information about the structure of the file. The body contains the sequence of objects that describe the pages of the document, and the cross-reference table acts as an index to all of the document's objects. All tokens in the document are delimited by arbitrary whitespace (i.e., one or more spaces, line feeds, tabs, or carriage returns).

The header

Every PDF file starts with a two-line header. The first line specifies the version of the PDF specification with which the document complies (as of this writing, the latest version is 1.3). If the file contains unreadable binary data, the PDF specification recommends that the second header line be a comment containing at least four characters in the range 0x80 to 0xFF. This way, certain programs (such as file viewers or file transfer programs) know to handle the file as a binary file.

```
%PDF-1.3
%<C7><EC><8F><A2>
```

The start of a PDF-style comment is indicated by a percent sign (%), and the comment extends to the end of the line, similar to Perl-style comments.

The body

The body consists of a sequence of objects that can represent pages, fonts, graphics, images, or other components of the document. Each object starts with an object number and a version number, followed by the obj token. Objects are defined by *dictionaries*, which are collections of key/value pairs enclosed in double angle brackets (<< and >>).

The first object in a document is generally a Catalog object, which acts as the root of our document's hierarchy:

```
1 0 obj
<<
  /Type   /Catalog
  /Pages  2 0 R
>>
endobj
```

Each attribute of the dictionary is represented as a token called a *name object*, a string that is preceded by a forward slash. Each dictionary must have a Type attribute that describes what kind of object it is. Each type of dictionary has its own required and optional attributes that are explained in detail in the PDF specification. In this minimal example, only the required attributes for each dictionary are included.

The types of dictionary objects that appear in our example document include:[*]

Catalog
> An object representing a page tree.

Pages
> An object representing a collection of pages, all of which have the same dimensions and access the same collection of resources.

---

[*] Other dictionary objects may be found in a more complicated PDF file. These objects include outlines, outline entries, article threads, interactive forms, and named destinations, all of which are described in detail in the PDF specification.

Page

An object representing a single page.

Stream

An object containing a sequence of drawing commands or image data.

Font

An object that encapsulates a table of glyph descriptions.

For a Catalog dictionary, the only required attribute is a Pages field, which provides a reference to the Pages object that is the root of the page tree. An object reference is represented as two numbers followed by an R; in the above example, the object reference is 2 0 R. The first number indicates the number of the object; the second number is a version count that is used only when updating existing PDF documents. Each time a change to an object is committed, the original is preserved and a new object is added with the same object number and a higher version number.

The pages of a document are represented as a hierarchy of objects, the root of which is a Pages object:

```
2 0 obj
<<
  /Type       /Pages
  /MediaBox   [ 0 0 612 792 ]
  /Count      2
  /Resources << /Font
               << /Times 5 0 R
                  /Helv  6 0 R >>
            >>
  /Kids       [ 3 0 R 4 0 R ]
>>
endobj
```

The Pages object requires three attributes: Type, Count, and Kids. This particular document also provides a MediaBox attribute that describes the bounding box of the pages in this collection. This is followed by a Resources attribute that lists the resources needed by this collection of pages (in this case, two fonts). Both of these attributes are inherited by each of the children in the collection of pages.

The Pages object is followed by the individual Page objects, one for each page in the collection.

```
3 0 obj
<<
  /Type       /Page
  /Parent     2 0 R
  /Contents   [ 7 0 R ]
>>
endobj
4 0 obj
<<
  /Type       /Page
  /Parent     2 0 R
```

```
    /Contents [ 8 0 R ]
  >>
  endobj
```

The Contents attribute of each page is a reference to a Stream object (defined below) that contains the graphics commands for drawing the text on each page.

The Page objects are followed by two Font objects that encapsulate a table of glyph descriptions for a particular font. Fourteen base fonts are guaranteed to be available in any PDF viewer (see Table 10-2).

Table 10-2. The 14 base fonts guaranteed to be available to any PDF viewer

Courier	Times-Roman	Helvetica	Symbol
Courier-Bold	Times-Bold	Helvetica-Bold	ZapfDingbats
Courier-Oblique	Times-Italic	Helvetica-Oblique	
Courier-BoldOblique	Times-BoldItalic	Helvetica-BoldOblique	

Since Times-Roman and Helvetica are two of the guaranteed fonts, their glyph data does not need to be included in this particular document.

```
  5 0 obj
  <<
    /Type      /Font
    /Subtype   /Type1
    /Name      /Times
    /BaseFont  /Times-Roman
  >>
  endobj
  6 0 obj
  <<
    /Type      /Font
    /Subtype   /Type1
    /Name      /Helv
    /BaseFont  /Helvetica
  >>
  endobj
```

The objects numbered 7 and 8 are Stream objects that contain a sequence of drawing commands or image data that make up the content of the page. Object number 7 draws a four-line text string on the first page, and number 8 draws a single line of text on the second page. The Length attribute contains the number of bytes in the stream.

```
  7 0 obj
  <<
    /Length 622
  >>
  stream
  BT                        % Begin text block
    /Times 72 Tf            % Use 72 pt Times-Roman
    150 500 Td              % Move to (150, 500)
    (The best) Tj           % Place a string
```

```
  1 Tr                       % Change the stroke mode
  0 -72 TD                   % Move to next line
  (sauce) Tj                 % Place a string
  0 Tr                       % Change stroke mode
  T*                         % Move to next line
  (is a good) Tj             % Place a string
  T*                         % Move to next line
  (applesauce)Tj             % Place a string
ET                           % End text block
endstream
endobj
8 0 obj
<<
  /Length 357
>>
stream
255 0 0 rg                   % Change fill color to red
BT                           % Begin text block
   175 450 Td                % Move to (175, 450)
   /Helv 12 Tf               % Use 32 pt Helvetica
   (Now is the winter) Tj    % Place a string
   ( of our discotheque) Tj  % Place a string
ET                           % End text block
endstream
endobj
```

The sequences of drawing commands are explained in detail in the section "PDF Operators for Drawing Graphics."

The cross-reference table

The cross-reference table affords a PDF viewer quick random access to any of the objects in the document, and contains a list of byte offsets for each object. The table starts with the token xref and is followed by one entry for each object in the file:

```
xref
0 9
0000000000 65535 f
0000000015 00000 n
0000000064 00000 n
0000000209 00000 n
0000000276 00000 n
0000000343 00000 n
0000000428 00000 n
0000000510 00000 n
0000001182 00000 n
```

The table can actually have multiple subsections as it is revised; the first line of the xref section indicates the subsection (version) number, followed by the number of items in the table. The first element in the table is a count of the total number of bytes in the document. This is followed by entries for objects 1 through 8. The n keyword indicates that the object is "in use," i.e., that it has not been deleted from the document.

The trailer

Most PDF viewing applications actually start reading a PDF file from the end. That's because the trailer of the file contains a pointer (i.e., a byte offset from the start of the document) to the beginning of the cross-reference table. It also contains information about the structure of the document, such as the number of objects that comprise it and a reference to the root object of the document's hierarchy. A simple trailer looks like this:

```
trailer
<<
   /Size 9
   /Root 1 0 R
>>
startxref
1589
%%EOF
```

If the PDF document is encrypted, an encryption dictionary that describes the type of encryption used is found within the trailer dictionary.

And that's all there is to the structure of a simple PDF document. In the next section we'll look a little closer at the drawing language used to create the graphics and text that make up a page in the document.

PDF Operators for Drawing Graphics

In a PDF file, any number of content stream objects can describe the appearance of a page. Each content stream consists of a sequence of device-independent drawing operators that can be thought of as a kind of shorthand for the PostScript code that they represent. It is worth going a little deeper into this command notation, as it will come in handy when we use the PDF::API2 module in Chapter 12.

Drawing graphics can be simplified to three steps: constructing paths, defining the graphics state, and stroking and filling the paths.

Constructing paths

Just like PostScript, the PDF drawing language uses stack-based *postfix* notation. Operands are pushed onto an operand stack until an operator is encountered, at which point the operators are popped off the stack and handed off to the operator as its parameters. PDF operators are simpler than their PostScript counterparts.

A path is constructed by adding segments (or *subpaths*) to the current path. Most operations are performed using the current point as a starting point; other information may be determined by the current graphics state. The current path is considered to be all the subpaths that were created until one of the stroking or filling operators is invoked, or until the n operator is used to end a path without stroking or filling it.

All of the basic path construction and drawing operators and their arguments are listed in Table 10-3.

Table 10-3. The basic set of PDF graphic drawing operators

Operator	Description	Arguments
B	Fill and stroke the current path.	None
B*	Fill and stroke the current path, using the even-odd rule to determine the fill region.	None
b	Close, fill, and stroke the current path.	None
b*	Close, fill, and stroke the current path, using the even-odd rule to determine the fill region.	None
c	Add a cubic Bezier curve to the current path. After this operation, the current point is (x3, y3). The v and y operators (described in the PDF specification) can alternately be used to draw Bezier curves using a different syntax.	*x1* The x coordinate of the first control point. *y1* The y coordinate of the first control point. *x2* The x coordinate of the second control point. *y2* The y coordinate of the second control point. *x3* The x coordinate of the end point. *y3* The y coordinate of the end point.
f	Fill the path.	None
f*	Fill the path, using the even-odd rule to determine the fill region.	None
h	Close the current path by adding a straight line between the current point and the starting point of the path.	None
l	Add a straight line to the current path. The line is traced from the current point to the point (x, y). After this operation, the current point is (x, y).	*x* The x coordinate of the end point of the line. *y* The y coordinate of the end point of the line.
m	Move to a new coordinate and start a new path segment that is considered part of the current path.	*x* The x coordinate to move to. *y* The y coordinate to move to.
n	End a path without stroking or filling it.	None
re	Add a rectangular subpath to the current path with the lower left-hand corner of the rectangle at (x, y).	*x* The x coordinate of the lower left-hand corner of the rectangle. *y* The y coordinate of the lower left-hand corner of the rectangle.
S	Stroke the current path.	None
s	Close and stroke the current path; equivalent to h S.	None

The PDF drawing code in Example 10-4 produces the spiral shown in Figure 10-5. (This is similar to the spiral shown in Figure 10-3.)

Example 10-4. A set of PDF graphic commands for drawing a spiral

```
% Construct the path
350 350 m                        % Move to (100, 50)
350 400 l                        % Draw a line
350 475 250 475 250 400 c        % Draw four cubic bezier curves
250 350 325 350 325 400 c
```

Example 10-4. A set of PDF graphic commands for drawing a spiral (continued)

```
325 437.5 275 437.5 275 400 c
275 382 300 382 300 400 c

% Set the graphics state
.5 G                           % Set the gray level to 50%
8 w                            % Set the width of the pen to 8 pts

% Stroke the path
S                              % Stroke the path without closing it
```

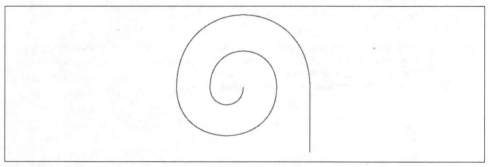

Figure 10-5. A spiral drawn with the PDF drawing commands

When we start with a blank piece of paper, the current point is the lower left-hand corner of the page (0,0). The first line of Example 10-4 moves the current point to (350, 350). The next line adds a line to the current path from the current point to (350, 400) and makes that the current point.

The next four lines of the code add four cubic Bezier curves to the current path. A cubic Bezier curve is defined using four points: a starting point, an ending point, and two control points. The c operator takes three coordinates as parameters: the first two are the control points, and the third is the end point (the starting point for the curve is the current point). After this operation, the current point is the end point of the curve.

Setting the graphics state

Before stroking or filling the curve, you can adjust the current graphics state so that the path is drawn with the desired color and thickness. Some of the graphics state controls available are listed in Table 10-4. The graphics state actually consists of several additional parameters, such as the current transformation matrix (which allows you to automatically transform any graphic into a warped coordinate space) or the clipping path (which allows you to create a path that specifies the drawing boundary of any graphic). These advanced parameters are beyond the scope of this introduction; refer to the PDF specification for an in-depth discussion of these features.

Table 10-4. The basic graphics state operators

Operator	Description	Arguments
d	Set the dash style to be used when stroking paths.	*dash_array* *dash_phase*
g	Set the non-stroke color (e.g., the color used for fills) to the specified level of gray in the grayscale colorspace.	*gray* The gray value, expressed as a number between 0.0 (black) and 1.0 (white)
G	Set the stroke color to the specified level of gray in the grayscale colorspace.	*gray* The gray value, expressed as a number between 0.0 (black) and 1.0 (white)
j	Set the line cap style.	*linecap* The style to use
J	Set the line join style.	*linejoin* The style to use
k	Set the non-stroke color to the specified value in the CMYK colorspace. All values are expressed as a number between 0.0 (none of this component) to 1.0 (maximum concentration of this component).	*C* The value of the cyan component *M* The value of the magenta component *Y* The value of the yellow component *K* The value of the black component
K	Set the stroke color to the specified value in the CMYK colorspace.	*C* The value of the cyan component *M* The value of the magenta component *Y* The value of the yellow component *K* The value of the black component
q	Save the current graphics state.	None
Q	Restore the graphics state.	None
rg	Set the non-stroke color to the specified value in the RGB colorspace.	*R* The value of the red component *G* The value of the green component *B* The value of the blue component
RG	Set the stroke color to the specified value in the RGB colorspace. Each value is expressed as a number between 0.0 (none of that component) to 1.0 (maximum intensity of that component).	*R* The value of the red component *G* The value of the green component *B* The value of the blue component
w	Set the line width.	*width* The width of the stroke, in points

Filling and stroking the path

In PostScript, you must create separate paths for the fill and the stroke. In the PDF drawing language, you have the option of filling and/or stroking a single path. The type and color of the fill and the width and color of the stroke are determined by the current values of the appropriate parameters in the graphics state. There are three ways of painting the path: filling only (the f operator), stroking only (the S operator), or filling and stroking (the B operator). When stroking, you also have the option of "closing" the path first by using the s or b operators. Closing a path adds a straight line connecting the starting and ending points. When filling, you must choose a fill method:

Non-zero winding rule method

　To determine whether a point should be considered part of the filled region, follow this algorithm for each point (see Figure 10-6 a):

　　a. Draw a line in any direction from the point to any arbitrary point outside of the region.

　　b. Starting at 0, count the number of times the path crosses the line. Add 1 each time the path crosses the line from left to right, and subtract 1 each time it crosses the line from right to left.

　　c. If the result is non-zero, the point is considered inside the fill region.

Even-odd method

　The even-odd method is described by the following algorithm (see Figure 10-6 b):

　　a. Draw a line from the point in any direction.

　　b. Count the number of times that the line crosses the path.

　　c. If the number is odd, the point is considered inside the fill region.

See Figure 10-6 for an illustration of all eight stroking and filling possibilities, as follows:

　a. B (fill and stroke, non-zero rule)

　b. B* (fill and stroke, even-odd method)

　c. b (close, fill and stroke, non-zero rule)

　d. b* (close, fill and stroke, even-odd method)

　e. f (fill only, non-zero rule)

　f. f* (fill only, even-odd method)

　g. s (close, stroke only)

　h. S (stroke only)

Just as in PostScript, textual glyphs are considered to be a collection of simpler paths. However, the PDF specification provides some commands that make it easier to position and draw text; these are discussed in the following section.

PDF Operators for Drawing Text

Text characters or strings can be drawn on a page by defining a *text block* within a command stream. Each text block has its own internal state information that does not persist between text blocks. Drawing a text block is generally done in five steps:

　1. Set the font used to draw the text.

　2. Position the current point on the page.

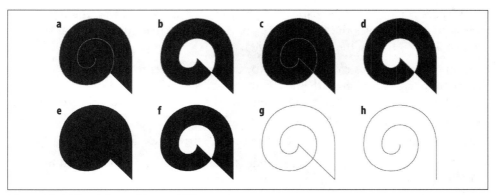

Figure 10-6. The eight stroking and filling operators

3. Change the text drawing mode for special fills or stroke effects.

4. Place a string on the page.

5. Repeat as necessary.

A string is drawn on the page as a series of glyphs, one for each character. Letter and word spacing can be controlled using the appropriate commands to modify the current text state. After a string is placed, the current point is positioned just after the last drawn character. The actual shapes of the character glyphs are described in a separate Font object, which also must be present in the PDF document.

The following block, extracted from the example earlier in this section, illustrates the sequence of commands for drawing a simple string on a page.

```
BT                      % Begin text block
   /Times 72 Tf         % Use 72 pt Times-Roman
   150 500 Td           % Move to (150, 500)
   (The best) Tj        % Place a string
   1 Tr                 % Change the stroke mode
   0 -72 TD             % Move to next line
   (sauce) Tj           % Place a string
   0 Tr                 % Change stroke mode
   T*                   % Move to next line
   (is a good) Tj       % Place a string
   T*                   % Move to next line
   (applesauce) Tj      % Place a string
ET                      % End text block
```

Each block of text is delimited by BT (begin text) and ET (end text) tokens. Strings within the text block are enclosed in parentheses. All parentheses and backslashes within a string must be escaped with a backslash.

The text state holds positioning information and other attributes needed to arrange glyphs into lines with uniform word, character, and line spacing. In text space, the "current point" should be thought of as the coordinate of the lower left-hand corner of the current line. Initially, this value is set to the origin (0,0); the current line point is independent of whatever paths were constructed before starting the text block. The Td operand moves the current line point to a particular coordinate on the page (which is (150, 150) in the above example).

The TD operator moves to the next line by adding an offset to the current line point. This command also changes the text state variables to reflect the offset. The left margin (if writing text horizontally) is moved, and the leading state variable is changed to the new y value. Initially, the leading state variable is 0.

The Tj operator places one or more strings at the current text point.

The Tr operator changes the stroke mode. Note that the stroke is affected by previous changes to the stroke attributes of the graphics state.

The T* operand moves to the next text line. The new current point is determined by the values of the state variables.

The next few lines place additional strings and change the stroke mode back to its original state.

Once a text block is closed with an ET token, the text state is reset, so the next text block has to reposition itself on the page.

The basic text drawing operators are shown in Table 10-5. These operators can appear only within text objects.

Table 10-5. The PDF text drawing operators

Operator	Description	Arguments
BT, ET	The delimiters for a text block. Every text block starts with a BT token and ends with an ET token. Text blocks may not be nested. The ET command effectively resets the text state information for the next text block.	None
T*	Move to the start of the next line using the leading state variable to determine the vertical offset between lines.	None
Tc	Set the character space state variable.	*char_space* The amount of space between characters
Td, TD	Move the pen to the next line, offset from the start of the current line by (x, y) units. If the TD operator is used, the current leading state variable is set to -y.	*x* The horizontal offset *y* The vertical offset
Tf	Set the font size state variable.	*font_size* The size of the font
Tj	Show a text string.	*string* The text string to draw
TJ	Show multiple text strings.	*string_array* An array of strings to draw
TL	Set the leading state variable.	*leading* The desired leading

Table 10-5. The PDF text drawing operators (continued)

Operator	Description	Arguments
Ts	Set the text rise state variable.	*leading* The desired leading
Tw	Set the word spacing state variable.	*word_space* The amount of space to add between words
Tz	Set the horizontal scaling state variable.	*hscale* A fractional amount or multiple of the default width

Drawing with the Text::PDF Module

Chapter 12 describes the PDF::API2 suite of modules, which provides a complete interface to a set of objects that automatically creates the correct syntax for a PDF file. That module is based on the lower-level Text::PDF module. Putting our knowledge of the PDF drawing command set to work with Text::PDF yields Example 10-5.

Example 10-5. Using Text::PDF to create a simple PDF document

```perl
#!/usr/bin/perl -w
#
# Example 10-5. Using Text::PDF

use Text::PDF::File;
use Text::PDF::Page;
use Text::PDF::SFont;

my $doc = Text::PDF::File->new;
my $page_root = new Text::PDF::Pages($doc);
my $page = new Text::PDF::Page($doc, $page_root);
my $page2 = new Text::PDF::Page($doc, $page_root);
my $font = new Text::PDF::SFont($doc, 'Times-Roman', 'Times');
my $font2 = new Text::PDF::SFont($doc, 'Helvetica', 'Helv');

$page_root->bbox(0, 0, 612, 792);
$page_root->add_font($font);
$page_root->add_font($font2);

my $stream1 = <<ENDSTREAM;
BT                        % Begin text block
  150 500 Td              % Move to (150, 500)
  /Times 72 Tf            % Use 72 pt Times-Roman
  (The best) Tj           % Place a string
  1 Tr                    % Change the stroke mode
  0 -72 TD                % Move to next line
  (sauce) Tj              % Place a string
  0 Tr                    % Change stroke mode
  T*                      % Move to next line
  (is a good) Tj          % Place a string
```

Example 10-5. Using Text::PDF to create a simple PDF document (continued)

```
  T*                    % Move to next line
  (applesauce)Tj        % Place a string
ET                      % End text block
ENDSTREAM

my $stream2 = <<ENDSTREAM;
255 0 0 rg              % Change fill color to red
BT                      % Begin text block
  175 450 Td            % Move to (175, 450)
  /Helv 12 Tf           % Use 32 pt Helvetica
  (Now is the winter) Tj % Place a string
  ( of our discotheque) Tj % Place a string
ET                      % End text block

ENDSTREAM

$page->add($stream1);
$page2->add($stream2);
$doc->out_file("example10-5.pdf");
```

The output of this program is the example PDF file described earlier in the chapter.

References

- *PostScript Language Tutorial and Cookbook,* Adobe Systems, Inc. Addison-Wesley, 1985. The "Blue Book" with many examples and recipes.
- *PostScript Language Reference Manual, Second Edition*, Adobe Systems, Inc. Addison-Wesley, 1990. The "Red Book," the official language reference.
- *PostScript by Example*, by Henry McGilton and Mary Campione. Addison-Wesley, 1992. A good introduction to PostScript, similar in purpose to the Blue Book.
- The Ghostscript Home Page: *http://www.cs.wisc.edu/~ghost*
- Adobe's Document Structuring Conventions: available via *http://partners.adobe.com/*
- The html2ps HTML to PostScript converter: *http://www.tdb.uu.se/~jan/html2ps.html*
- The PDF Specification: available via *http://partners.adobe.com/*
- John Warnock's original proposal for the Camelot project, which later became the PDF standard: *http://www.planetpdf.com/mainpage.asp?webpageid=1851*

## CHAPTER 11

Using the PostScript Modules

In this chapter, we develop a framework for easily generating PostScript code from Perl scripts. These modules are useful for creating printable reports from various data sources, and could even be used as the backend of a Perl-based page layout application. I've used this framework as part of a web-based scheduling database; the click of a hyperlink produced nicely formatted PostScript calendars and press releases. These reports could be previewed on a user's workstation using the GhostView PostScript viewer and then sent directly to the printer.

The PostScript package includes three main modules: PostScript::TextBlock, PostScript::Document, and PostScript::Elements.

This chapter starts by presenting the TextBlock module, which is a simple object for encapsulating a piece of text that can be composited into a square block on a page. The TextBlock object makes it easy to create tabular PostScript reports. The Document object builds on the TextBlock object, providing a "document" object that allows you to place text over multiple pages. A document can also have headers, footers, and page numbers. Finally, the Elements module provides methods for generating the PostScript code to draw primitive shapes such as lines, boxes, and circles. You can also place previously created EPS files with this module.

The metaphor followed by the TextBlock and Elements interfaces is similar to that of Adobe's PageMaker layout program. Starting with a blank page, blocks of text are placed at a given location within a particular bounding box; text that does not fit in the box is held back and is available for later placement. The PostScript for generating a TextBlock or Elements object is created with the Write( ) method. All your script has to do is create the objects, place them on a page by "writing" them, collect the resulting code, and assemble it into a PostScript document. The PostScript::Document module provides a higher level framework that can be used as an example of how to assemble a document.

The example at the beginning of this chapter illustrates one way of using these modules to automatically generate PostScript from a web interface. The remainder of the chapter is a reference for the three modules.

Creating PostScript from a Web Interface

One interesting use of the PostScript modules is as a means of creating printable documents from CGI scripts on the Web. As an example, we'll design a web page for an online record label, Apocabilly Records, that ships every purchase with a shipping invoice. Our web page processes the order and creates a PostScript shipping invoice all at once.

The web page takes information submitted from an HTML form and calls a script called *processorder.cgi*, which logs the order in some sort of database and creates the shipping invoice. The web page that the customer sees is shown in Figure 11-1. It is assumed that prior to this point, a shopping-cart script was used to catalog the user's selections as he navigated the site.

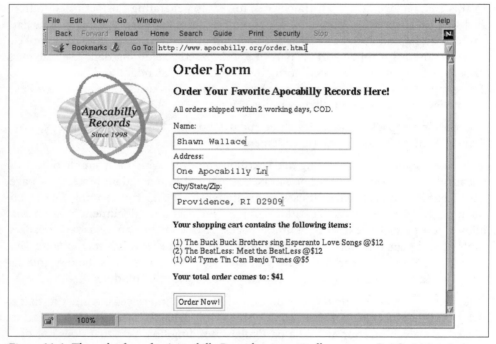

Figure 11-1. The order form for Apocabilly Records automatically creates a PostScript invoice

The HTML code for this web page would look something like Example 11-1. Notice the FORM element, with fields to retrieve the customer's name, address, and city/state/zip, and the hidden text fields containing the merchandise order and the total amount of the purchase. These fields were created by our hypothetical shopping-cart script and passed on to the *processorder.cgi* script upon submission of the form for inclusion in the final shipping invoice.

Example 11-1. The HTML document for the CGI example

```
<HTML>
<HEAD>
<META HTTP-EQUIV="Content-Type" CONTENT="text/html">
<TITLE>Apocabilly Records Order Form</TITLE>
</HEAD>
<BODY>

<TABLE CELLSPACING=0 BORDER=0>
<TR><TD VALIGN="TOP">
<P>
<IMG SRC="apocabilly2.gif" WIDTH=287 HEIGHT=96
        ALT="Apocabilly Records, Since 1998></P>
</TD>
<TD VALIGN="TOP">

<H1>Order Form</H1>
<H2>Order Your Favorite Apocabilly Records Here!</H2>
<P>All orders shipped within 2 working days, COD.</P>
<FORM ACTION="cgi-bin/processorder.cgi" METHOD="POST">

<P>Name:<BR>
<INPUT TYPE="text" MAXLENGTH="80" NAME="name">
<BR>

Address:<BR>
<INPUT TYPE="Address" MAXLENGTH="80" NAME="address">
<BR>
City/State/Zip:<BR>
<INPUT TYPE="text" MAXLENGTH="80" NAME="citystatezip">
</P><P>
<STRONG>Your shopping cart contains the following items:</STRONG>
</P><P>
(1) The Buck Buck Brothers sing Esperanto Love Songs @$12 <BR>
(2) The BeatLess: Meet the BeatLess @$12 <BR>
(1) Old Tyme Tin Can Banjo Tunes @$5
</P><P>

<INPUT TYPE="hidden" NAME="merchandise" VALUE="(1) The Buck Buck Brothers sing
Esperanto Love Songs @$12 \n(2) The BeatLess: Meet the BeatLess @$12 \n
(1) Old Tyme Tin Can Banjo Tunes @$5 \n">
</P><P>

<STRONG>Your total order comes to: $41</STRONG></P>
<P>
<INPUT TYPE="hidden" NAME="total" VALUE="$41">
<INPUT TYPE="submit"  VALUE="Order Now!" >
</P>
</FORM>
</TD></TR>
</TABLE>
</BODY>
</HTML>
```

When the form is submitted, the *processorder.cgi* script is called, which processes the order and creates a PostScript invoice on the server that can be later printed and mailed with the merchandise as a paper record of the transaction. Of course, if you were to implement a real online ordering system, you would have to deal with the various security issues involved with processing personal financial information online. Example 11-2 sidesteps that issue and merely prints the invoice.

Example 11-2. Drawing a PostScript invoice with TextBlocks and Elements

```perl
#!/usr/local/bin/perl -w
#
# Example 11-2. A CGI script that generates PostScript

use CGI;
use PostScript::TextBlock;
use PostScript::Elements;

# Get the parameters passed into the script

my $query = new CGI;
my $name = $query->param('name');
my $address = $query->param('address');
my $citystatezip = $query->param('citystatezip');
my $merchandise = $query->param('merchandise');
my $total = $query->param('total');

# Do whatever needs to be done to place an order here...
# If it is successful, continue...

print $query->header(-type => 'text/html');
print $query->start_html(-title => "Order completed!");
print "Your order has been placed. Thanks!";

# Generate a PostScript invoice

my $lines = new PostScript::Elements;

# First add a 2 pt line with a 36 pt margin around the page

$lines->addBox(points    => [36, 756, 540, 720],
               linewidth => 2);

# Now draw the line dividing the title and the address section

$lines->addLine(points => [46,650, 566,650]);

# Finally, draw the line separating the address and order sections

$lines->addLine(points => [46, 550, 566,550]);

# Altogether there are five discrete blocks of text, so we need
# five TextBlock objects...
```

Example 11-2. Drawing a PostScript invoice with TextBlocks and Elements (continued)

```
my $tb  = new PostScript::TextBlock;
my $tb2 = new PostScript::TextBlock;
my $tb3 = new PostScript::TextBlock;
my $tb4 = new PostScript::TextBlock;
my $tb5 = new PostScript::TextBlock;

my $date = "10/21/2002";

# Now add the text to the various text blocks

$tb->addText(text => "Apocabilly Records\n",
            size => 48, leading => 56);
$tb->addText(text => "Ordered on $date\n",
            size => 24, leading => 30);

$tb2->addText(text => "SHIP TO:\n $name\n $address\n".
                      "$citystatezip\n",
              size => 14,
              leading => 18 );

$tb3->addText(text => "FROM:\n Apocabilly Records\n".
                      "1249 Foo St.\n".
                      "   Hoosick Falls, NY 51209\n",
              size => 14,
              leading => 18 );

$tb4->addText(text => "YOUR ORDER:\n\n$merchandise",
            size => 16, leading => 30);

$tb5->addText(text => "TOTAL: $total",
            size => 16, leading => 30);

# Then generate the code by calling the Write( )
# method for each object

my $code = $lines->Write( );

# The Write( ) method for a TextBlock returns a list containing the
# code and the remainder that didn't fit in the specified region.
# In this example, we discard the remainder, only taking the code
# and appending it to the code generated thus far.

$code .= [$tb->Write(530, 100, 46, 756)]->[0];
$code .= [$tb2->Write(260, 130, 46, 640)]->[0];
$code .= [$tb3->Write(260, 130, 306, 640)]->[0];
$code .= [$tb4->Write(530, 480, 46, 560)]->[0];
$code .= [$tb5->Write(260, 30, 306, 76)]->[0];

# Write the PostScript code to the file called invoice.ps
# in a real system, this should be a unique filename
```

Example 11-2. Drawing a PostScript invoice with TextBlocks and Elements (continued)

```
open OUTFILE,">invoice.ps" or die "Couldn't open invoice.ps: $!";
print OUTFILE $code;
close OUTFILE;
```

The final output of this script is shown in Figure 11-2.

Figure 11-2. A shipping invoice generated via a CGI script using the PostScript package

The PostScript::TextBlock Module

The TextBlock module is an object that may be used to construct a block of text in PostScript. It is meant to be a simple, abstract interface for generating PostScript code from Perl scripts or CGI scripts, as in the example in the previous section. Example 11-3 introduces the TextBlock module.

Example 11-3. Using the TextBlock module

```
use PostScript::TextBlock;
my $tb = new PostScript::TextBlock;
$tb->addText( text => "Hullabalo in Hoosick Falls.\n",
              font => 'CenturySchL-Ital',
              size => 24,
              leading => 26
            );
$tb->addText( text => "by Charba Gaspee.\n",
              font => 'URWGothicL-Demi',
              size => 12,
```

Example 11-3. Using the TextBlock module (continued)

```
                leading => 14
        );
print 'There are '.$tb->numElements.' elements in this object.';
open OUT, '>psoutput.ps' or die "Couldn't open psoutput.ps: $!";
my ($code, $remainder) = $tb->Write(572, 752, 20, 772);
print OUT $code;
```

As you can see, the TextBlock module allows the web programmer to create printable documents without any knowledge of PostScript. The PostScript code generated by this script looks like this:

```
0 setgray 20 746 moveto
/CenturySchL-Ital findfont
24 scalefont setfont
(Hullabalo in Hoosick Falls.) show
0 setgray 20 732 moveto
/URWGothicL-Demi findfont
12 scalefont setfont
(by Charba Gaspee.) show
```

By itself, the TextBlock object can print only on a single page. In many cases, your project will require a multi-page PostScript document. The TextBlock::Write( ) method returns the code and a TextBlock representing the text that doesn't fit in the region passed to the Write( ) method. You can use this remainder to print a text block that spans multiple pages (if you have enough text, of course):

```
open OUT, '>psoutput.ps' or die "Couldn't open psoutput.ps: $!";
my $pages = 1;

# Create the first page

my ($code, $remainder) = $tb->Write(572, 752, 20, 772);
print OUT "%%Page:$pages\n";   # this is required by the Adobe
                               # Document Structuring Conventions
print OUT $code;
print OUT "showpage\n";

# Print the rest of the pages, if any

while ($remainder->numElements) {
    $pages++;
    print OUT "%%Page:$pages\n";
    ($code, $remainder) = $remainder->Write(572, 752, 20, 772);
    print OUT $code;
    print OUT "showpage\n";
}
```

Alternately, you could just use the PostScript::Document module described in the next section and not worry about it. The Document object handles everything for you.

The four methods implemented by PostScript::TextBlock are as follows.

new( )

```
$tb = new PostScript::TextBlock
```

This method instantiates a new object of class PostScript::TextBlock.

addText( )

```
$tb->addText( text   => text,
              font   => font,
              size   => size,
              leading=> leading )
```

The addText() method adds a new text element to the TextBlock object. A *text element* can be thought of as a section of text in which all the text has the same characteristics, i.e., where all the characters are the same font, size, and leading. This representation allows you to include text of different fonts and sizes within the same text block by including them as separate elements. Different alignment options have not been included in this version of the TextBlock module, but would be fairly easy to add. All text is left-aligned.

This method takes up to four attributes. If the font, size, or leading attributes are not provided, the default attributes for the TextBlock object are used. The attributes are:

text

> The text attribute is required, though nothing bad happens if you leave it out. This is simply the text to be rendered in the text block. Line breaks may be inserted by including a \n newline string.

font

> The font attribute is a string indicating the name of the font to be used to render this element. The PostScript package uses an internal description of the font metrics of various fonts, which is contained in the PostScript::Metrics module. The PostScript:: Metrics module supports the fonts listed in Table 11-1.

Table 11-1. The fonts encoded in the PostScript::Metrics module

AvantGarde-Book	Helvetica-Narrow-BoldOblique	Palatino-Roman
AvantGarde-BookOblique	Helvetica-Narrow-Oblique	StandardSymL
AvantGarde-Demi	Helvetica-Oblique	Symbol
AvantGarde-DemiOblique	NewCenturySchlbk-Bold	Times-Bold
Bookman-Demi	NewCenturySchlbk-BoldItalic	Times-BoldItalic
Bookman-DemiItalic	NewCenturySchlbk-Italic	Times-Italic
Bookman-Light	NewCenturySchlbk-Roman	Times-Roman
Bookman-LightItalic	NimbusMonL-Bold	URWBookmanL-DemiBold
CenturySchL-Bold	NimbusMonL-BoldObli	URWBookmanL-DemiBoldItal
CenturySchL-BoldItal	NimbusMonL-Regu	URWBookmanL-Ligh
CenturySchL-Ital	NimbusMonL-ReguObli	URWBookmanL-LighItal
CenturySchL-Roma	NimbusRomNo9L-Medi	URWChanceryL-MediItal

Table 11-1. The fonts encoded in the PostScript::Metrics module (continued)

CharterBT-Bold	NimbusRomNo9L-MediItal	URWGothicL-Book
CharterBT-BoldItalic	NimbusRomNo9L-Regu	URWGothicL-BookObli
CharterBT-Italic	NimbusRomNo9L-ReguItal	URWGothicL-Demi
CharterBT-Roman	NimbusSanL-Bold	URWGothicL-DemiObli
Courier	NimbusSanL-BoldCond	URWPalladioL-Bold
Courier-Bold	NimbusSanL-BoldCondItal	URWPalladioL-BoldItal
Courier-BoldOblique	NimbusSanL-BoldItal	URWPalladioL-Ital
Courier-Oblique	NimbusSanL-Regu	URWPalladioL-Roma
Dingbats	NimbusSanL-ReguCond	Utopia-Bold
Helvetica	NimbusSanL-ReguCondItal	Utopia-BoldItalic
Helvetica-Bold	NimbusSanL-ReguItal	Utopia-Italic
Helvetica-BoldOblique	Palatino-Bold	Utopia-Regular
Helvetica-Narrow	Palatino-BoldItalic	ZapfChancery-MediumItalic
Helvetica-Narrow-Bold	Palatino-Italic	ZapfDingbats

The font you use must be available to the PostScript interpreter that is used to render the page described by the program. If the interpreter cannot load the font, it usually attempts to substitute a similar font. If a font is substituted with a font that has different metrics, lines of text may overrun the right margin of the text block, as the length of a line is determined by the sum of the widths of the individual characters.

Consult the documentation of your printer or PostScript interpreter to determine how to find which fonts are available to you. You can get a list of the fonts currently supported by the PostScript::Metrics module with the following:

```
use PostScript::Metrics;
@okfonts = PostScript::Metrics->listFonts();
```

Note that just because the font is defined by PostScript::Metrics, it does not mean that it is installed on your system. You must make sure that it is installed and that your PostScript interpreter can access it.

size

The size of the font, in points.

leading

The amount of space left for the line, from baseline to baseline.

numElements( )

```
$tb->numElements()
```

This method returns the number of elements in the TextBlock object. An element is created each time the addText( ) method is called.

Accessing Font Information

Widths vary from font to font and character to character. The Write( ) method uses the PostScript::Metrics module to determine the width of each character. If you were writing a straight PostScript program, you would let the PostScript interpreter do this for you. The TextBlock module, however, needs to know the width of each character so that it knows where to break lines and pages. The PostScript::Metrics module contains the font metrics (i.e., a list containing the width of each character in the font) for the fonts listed under the description of the addText( ) method. This set of metrics starts with the descriptions for all of the default fonts with AFM files that came with Ghostscript. To add support for a new font, you must create an array with the metrics for that font and add it to the PostScript::Metrics module. This array looks like:

```
my %fonts = (
# 95 entries for each font, corresponding to ASCII 32-126
# Each character is based on a one point font size and is expressed
# in 1/1000ths of points

'NimbusSanL-Regu' => [
    278,278,355,556,556,889,667,221,333,333,389,584,278,584, 278, 278, 556,
556, 556, 556, 556, 556, 556, 556, 556, 556, 278, 278, 584, 584, 584, 556,
1015, 667, 667, 722, 722, 667, 611, 778, 722, 278, 500, 667, 556, 833, 722,
778, 667, 778, 722, 667, 611, 722, 667, 944, 667, 667, 611, 278, 278, 278, 469,
556, 222, 556, 556, 500, 556, 556, 278, 556, 556, 222, 222, 500, 222, 833, 556,
556, 556, 556, 333, 500, 278, 556, 500, 722, 500, 500, 500, 334, 260, 334, 584
],
# more font definitions here
);
```

For a font with an AFM file, the AFM file can be parsed to generate this table with Gisle Aas's Font::AFM module, available on CPAN. The table is used by the Metrics stringwidth method, which calculates the total width of a string at a given font size:

```
sub stringwidth {
    my ($string, $fontname, $fontsize) = @_;
    my $returnval = 0;

    foreach my $char (unpack("C*", $string)) {
        $returnval+=$fonts{$fontname}->[$char-32];
    }
    return ($returnval*$fontsize/1000);
}
```

Write( )

$tb->Write(*width, height, xoffset, yoffset*)

The Write( ) method generates the PostScript code that renders the text on a page when passed to a PostScript interpreter such as Ghostscript. The four parameters are expressed in points (1/72 inch) and indicate the width and height of the box within which the text should be printed, and the x and y offsets of the upper left corner of this box.

Unlike all of the other tools described in this book, which define the origin (0, 0) as the upper left-hand corner of the image, PostScript uses a Cartesian coordinate system. That is, the origin is at the lower left corner of the page.

Standard page sizes in points were listed in Table 10-1.

The Write( ) method returns two values: a string consisting of the PostScript code (suitable for printing to a file), and a TextBlock object containing the elements (and partial elements) that did not fit within the specified area, if any. If the entire text block fits with the area, the remainder is undef. The remainder can be used to lay out multiple pages and columns in a similar manner to most modern desktop publishing programs. In general, the Write( ) method should be called as in the following example, which writes the PostScript code to a file called *psoutput.ps*:

```perl
#!/usr/bin/perl -w

use PostScript::TextBlock;
my $tb = PostScript::TextBlock->new;

$tb->addText( text => "The next sentence is false. ");
$tb->addText( text => "The previous sentence is true. ");

# Open the file for output (always check return value...)

open OUT, '>psoutput.ps' or die "Couldn't open psoutput.ps: $!";

# Retrieve the code and write the portion that fits
# the proscribed area

my ($code, $remainder) = $tb->Write(572, 752, 20, 772);
print OUT $code;
```

It is very easy to create "style sheets" for a document:

```perl
# Define the styles

%body = ( font => 'URWGothicL-DemiObli',
          size => 12, leading => 16 );
%head1 = ( font => 'NimbusSanL-BoldCond',
          size => 24, leading => 36 );
%head2 = ( font => 'NimbusSanL-BoldCond',
          size => 18, leading => 30 );

# Use them where appropriate

$tb->addText(text => "Chapter 10\n", %head1);
$tb->addText(text => "Spokane Sam and His Spongepants\n", %head2);
$tb->addText(text => "It was a dark and stormy night and Spokane".
                     "Sam\'s Spongepants were thirsty...", %body);
```

The PostScript::Document Module

The PostScript::Document module comes with the PostScript package. It creates an abstract interface for creating generic multiple-page textual documents. You can think of a Document object as a big text block with additional attributes and methods that allow it to span multiple pages. You can also include page numbers, as well as textual headers and footers that appear on each page of the document.

You can use the Document object in a manner similar to the TextBlock object. First, instantiate a new Document using the new( ) method and a number of optional parameters defining the attributes of the page; add text elements to the document with the addText( ) method; create the PostScript as a string of code with the Write( ) method; then write the code to a file, pipe it to a process, or append it to other code. Example 11-4 is a sample script that reads a text file and appends a title, header, and footer to it.

Example 11-4. Using the Document object

```perl
#!/usr/bin/perl -w

use strict;
use PostScript::Document;
my $doc = new PostScript::Document;

$doc->addText( text => "Hullabalo in Hoosick Falls.\n",
               font => 'CenturySchL-Ital',
               size => 24,
               leading => 100
             );
$doc->addText( text => "by Charba Gaspee.\n",
               font => 'URWGothicL-Demi',
               size => 18,
               leading => 36
             );
$doc->addHeader(text => "Hullabaloo in Hoosick Falls",
                font => 'URWGothicL-Demi',
                size => 9,
                leading => 11
              );
$doc->addFooter(text => "Page ##Page",
                font => 'URWGothicL-Demi',
                size => 9,
                leading => 11
              );

# Now read in a big text file and add it

open I, "example.txt" or die "Couldn't open example.txt: $!";
undef $/;
my $text = <I>;
$doc->addText( text => $text,
```

Example 11-4. Using the Document object (continued)

```
                font => 'URWGothicL-Demi',
                size => 14,
                leading => 24
            );

open OUT, '>psoutput.ps' or die "Couldn't open psoutput.ps: $!";
my $code = $doc->Write();   # use defaults
print OUT $code;
```

The PostScript::Document module is installed when you install the PostScript package. The module implements the following five methods.

new( )

```
$doc = PostScript::Document->new( paper   => paper,
                                  width   => width,
                                  height  => height,
                                  rmargin => rmargin,
                                  lmargin => lmargin,
                                  tmargin => tmargin,
                                  bmargin => bmargin );
```

This method instantiates a new object of class PostScript::Document. There are seven attributes that may optionally be set when a new object is created: a paper attribute, which can be one of the valid paper size strings (e.g., 'Letter', 'Legal'); the width and height of the page (in points); and the four margins of the page (also in points). Note that if you specify the paper attribute, you do not have to include the width and height attributes, and vice versa. The default values are 'Letter' paper (612×792 points) and margins of .5 inches (36 points).

addText( )

```
$doc->addText( text=>text,
               font=>font,
               size=>size,
               leading=>leading )
```

The addText( ) method performs just like the PostScript::TextBlock::addText( ) method described in the previous section. In fact, the document simply calls the addText( ) method of its content TextBlock. If the font, size, or leading attributes are not provided, the default attributes for the TextBlock object are used.

addHeader( )

```
$doc->addHeader( text=>text,
                 font=>font,
                 size=>size,
                 leading=>leading   )
```

The addHeader( ) method allows you to specify a header that appears at the top of each page of the document. This header is drawn in the top margin of the page, with the same right and left margins as the page. Only that portion of the header that fits in the top margin is printed. If the font, size, or leading attributes are not provided, the default attributes for the TextBlock object are used.

The page numbers of individual pages may be included in the header by the use of the string ##Page within the header's text string. The ##Page string is replaced at runtime with the appropriate page number. For example, the following statement adds the appropriate page number in the upper left corner of each page in the default font, size, and leading:

```
$doc->addHeader( text => "Page ##Page" );
```

addFooter( )

```
$doc->addFooter( text=>text,
                 font=>font,
                 size=>size,
                 leading=>leading  )
```

The addFooter( ) method allows you to specify a footer that appears at the bottom of each page of the document. This footer is drawn in the bottom margin of the page, with the same right and left margins as the page. Only that portion of the footer that fits in the bottom margin is printed. If the font, size, or leading attributes are not provided, the default attributes for the TextBlock object are used.

The page numbers of individual pages may be included in the footer with the ##Page string, as described for the addHeader( ) method.

Write( )

```
$doc->Write( )
```

The Write( ) method generates the PostScript code for the document and returns it as a string. In general, you want to use the Write( ) method to write the code to a file that can be sent to a printer or other PostScript interpreter. The following writes the PostScript code to a file called *psoutput.ps*:

```
open OUT, '>psoutput.ps' or die "Couldn't open psoutput.ps: $!";
my $code = $doc->Write( );
print OUT $code;
```

The PostScript::Elements Module

The PostScript::Elements module incorporates support for drawing vector graphics in the form of lines, arc, and boxes (see Figure 11-3). It provides routines to draw these three shapes, and can be easily extended to encapsulate other shapes or more complex forms. The methods allow you to control the width of the line, the tint of the line (a percentage of gray), and the tint of the fill (a percentage of gray or transparent).

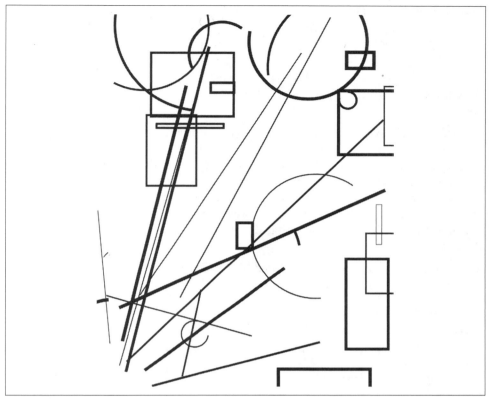

Figure 11-3. The PostScript::Elements module allows you to draw arcs, lines, and boxes

The Elements module can be used as in Example 11-5, which draws a random number of arbitrary lines, boxes, and arcs.

Example 11-5. Using the Elements module

```
#!/usr/bin/perl -w
# Example 11-5. Generate a random collection of lines, boxes, arcs

use strict;
use PostScript::Elements;

my $e = new PostScript::Elements;

my $r = rand(25);
for (my $i=0; $i<= $r; $i++) {
    $e->addArc(points  => [rand(612), rand(792),
                           rand(200), rand(360), rand(360)],
               linewidth => rand(8) );
    $e->addBox(points  => [rand(612), rand(792), rand(200), rand(200)],
               linewidth => rand(8) );
```

Example 11-5. Using the Elements module (continued)

```
    $e->addLine(points => [rand(612), rand(792), rand(200), rand(200)],
            linewidth => rand(8) );
}

open OUT, ">example.ps" or die "Couldn't open example.ps: $!";
print OUT $e->Write( );
close OUT;
```

For each form drawn, the points attribute passes on the description of the points in the line, box, or arc. It should be in the form of an anonymous list of points; the length of the list depends on which method is being called (arc takes five points, for example, and line takes four). The Elements module can be easily expanded to represent other shapes by adding an appropriate method name (e.g., addCube( )) that can call the addType( ) method with a descriptive type attribute (e.g., type="cube"). The Write( ) method must then be updated with the code to generate the appropriate PostScript.

The following methods are implemented by PostScript::Elements.

new( )

```
$e = new PostScript::Elements
```

This method instantiates a new object of class PostScript::Elements.

addArc( )

```
$e->addArc( points    => [ x, y, r, startangle, endangle],
            linewidth => linewidth,
            linetint  => linetint,
            filltint  => filltint )
```

The addArc( ) method adds an arc segment to the Elements object. It takes up to four parameters, of which only the points parameter is required:

points

> This parameter consists of a list specifying the center coordinate, the radius of the arc, and the starting angle and ending angle describing the sweep of the arc. For example:
>
> ```
> addArc(points=>[50,50,25,0,360])
> ```
>
> would add a complete circle centered at (50,50) with a radius of 25. Note that the list of points is in the same form as in the PostScript arc function.

linewidth

> The linewidth attribute can be used to specify the point size of the line with which the arc is to be stroked. If no value is given, the default line width is 1 point.

linetint

> The linetint attribute should be a number between 0 and 1 representing a shade of gray, with 1 as white and 0 as black. Therefore, .8 would be the equivalent of a 20% gray screen. If no value is given, the line is stroked in black (linetint=0).

filltint

> The filltint attribute should be either −1, or a number between 0 and 1 representing a percentage of gray, with 1 as white and 0 as black. If the value is −1, the shape is not filled in; it is transparent. Otherwise, the shape is opaque. The default value is −1.

addBox( )

```
$e->addBox( points    => [ x, y, width, height],
            linewidth => linewidth,
            linetint  => linetint,
            filltint  => filltint )
```

The addBox( ) method adds a square box to the Elements object. It takes up to four parameters, of which only the points parameter is required:

points

> The points attribute should be an anonymous list specifying the coordinate of the upper left corner of the box followed by the width and height of the box. Remember that PostScript's coordinate system uses the lower left corner of the page as its origin.

linewidth

> The linewidth attribute functions as described for addArc( ).

linetint

> The linetint attribute functions as described for addArc( ).

filltint

> The filltint attribute functions as described for addArc( ).

addEPS( )

```
$e->addEPS( points   => [ x, y ],
            filename => filename )
```

The addEPS( ) method adds a previously created Encapsulated PostScript (EPS) file to the Elements object. It takes two parameters:

points

> The points attribute should be an anonymous list of the coordinate at which the upper left corner of the image should be placed.

filename

> This is the name of the EPS file.

addLine( )

```
$e->addArc( points    => [ startx, starty, endx, endy],
            linewidth => linewidth,
            linetint  => linetint )
```

The addLine( ) method draws a line between two points. It takes up to three parameters (note that a filltint parameter is simply ignored):

points

> The points attribute should be given an anonymous array specifying the coordinate of the starting point (startx, starty) and the end point (endx, endy).

linewidth
> The `linewidth` attribute functions as described for `addArc( )`.

linetint
> The `linetint` attribute functions as described for `addArc( )`.

Write( )

`$tb->Write( )`

The `Write( )` method generates the PostScript code that renders any lines, boxes, or arcs that have been added to the Elements object. The `Write( )` method returns a string containing the PostScript code, which may be written to a file, piped to a process, or appended to other PostScript code.

Other PostScript Modules

There are several other modules dealing with PostScript that we don't cover in this book:

- The Font::AFM module, by Gisle Aas, provides the basic routines for parsing Adobe's Font Metrics file format.

    http://search.cpan.org/search?module=Font::AFM.

- The PostScript::FontMetrics module, by Johan Vromans, provides a robust interface for querying fonts for metric information.

    http://search.cpan.org/search?module=PostScript::FontMetrics

- The PostScript::PrinterFontMetrics module allows you to query Printer Font Metrics (PFM).

    http://search.cpan.org/search?module=PostScript::PrinterFontMetrics

- The PostScript::BasicTypesetter module, also by Johan Vromans, has similar functionality to the modules described in this chapter, but provides a more procedural interface.

    http://search.cpan.org/search?module=PostScript::BasicTypesetter

## CHAPTER 12

Creating PDF Documents with Perl

The PDF::API2 module can be used to dynamically create new PDF documents or manipulate existing PDF documents. The sample application in this chapter creates a tabular PDF report (address labels) from a collection of data. Later, we'll see how to add a "Confidential" stamp to each page of a document and how to add outlines or bookmarks to a PDF.

Like most of the other modules in this book, PDF::API2 is available on CPAN. Unlike most of the other modules, it does not work with the 5.005 series of Perl distributions; it requires Perl 5.6.x. It also requires the Compress::Zlib, Font::TTF, and Text::PDF modules to be preinstalled.

Introduction to PDF::API2

The top-level PDF::API2 object maintains an internal data structure that loosely resembles the PDF document structure. The top-level object knows how to construct the header, body, and cross-reference sections of the final PDF document. You then construct the document by creating objects and adding them to the top-level document. Three types of objects are defined: structural objects, content stream objects, and resource objects.

Structural objects are used to define the page, outline, and annotation trees of the document. A Page object describes a single page. The current version of PDF::API2 uses only a single-page hierarchy (see Chapter 10 for more about the page hierarchy). You can't create multiple page trees with shared resources. The Outlines object defines the root of a tree of outline entries. An Outline object is used to define a single outline entry. The Annotation object is used to add floating notes to a page.

To draw graphics or text on a page, use one of the content stream objects. Example 12-1 shows how to use the Text object to draw a simple "Hello World" string on a page. First, create a new page and set its dimensions. Add a Text object, which is a repositionable block of text. A Font object is assigned to the Text object;

in this case, the core Helvetica font is used. After that, the string is drawn, and the PDF is created with the stringify( ) method.

Example 12-1. Hello World with the Text object

```perl
#!/usr/bin/perl -w
#
# Example 12-1. Hello World

use strict;
use PDF::API2;

my $pdf=PDF::API2->new;
my $page=$pdf->page( );          # Add a new page
$page->mediabox(400, 200);       # Set the dimensions
my $text=$page->text( );         # Add the Text object
$text->translate(65, 75);        # Position the Text object
my $font = $pdf->corefont('Helvetica-Bold',1);
$text->font($font,48);           # Assign a font to the Text object
$text->text('Hello World');      # Draw the string

print $pdf->stringify( );        # Output the document as a PDF
$pdf->end;                       # Destroy the PDF object
exit;
```

The Gfx object is used to draw lines and shapes. A single Gfx object can be used to draw all of the graphics on a page. Example 12-2 adds a field of random-sized circles behind the text, as in the introductory examples in Chapters 2 and 3. The Gfx object is similar to the Text object; it is a movable block of lines and curves. The Gfx object is drawn to the screen with the stroke( ), fill( ), or fillstroke( ) methods.

Example 12-2. Hello World with graphics

```perl
#!/usr/bin/perl -w
# Example 12-2. Hello World with graphics

use strict;
use PDF::API2;

my $pdf=PDF::API2->new;
my $page=$pdf->page( );
$page->mediabox(400, 200);

my $g = $page->gfx( );               # Add a Gfx object
$g->strokecolor("#FF0000");          # Set the stroke color
$g->fillcolor("#FF0000");            # Set the fill color

for my $i (0..10) {
    for my $j (0..5) {
        # Draw a circle with random radius
        $g->circle($i*40, $j*40, rand(25)+1);
    }
}
```

Example 12-2. Hello World with graphics (continued)

```
$g->fillstroke( );                    # Fill and stroke

my $text=$page->text( );
$text->translate(65, 75);
$text->font($pdf->corefont('Helvetica-Bold',1),48);
$text->text('Hello World');

print $pdf->stringify( );
$pdf->end;
exit;
```

The result is shown in Figure 12-1.

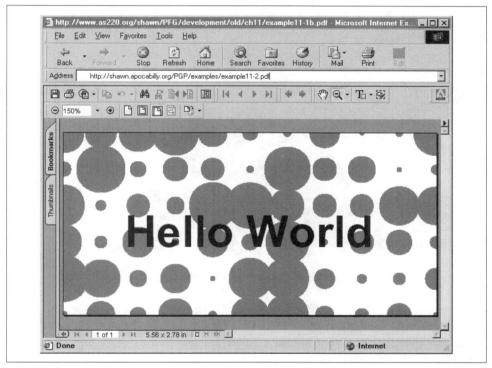

Figure 12-1. Hello World on a field of random circles

The Gfx object can also be used to draw images and clipping paths (a path that masks or clips another image or graphic). Example 12-3 first creates a circular clipping path, then adds a JPEG image that is read in from an external file.

Example 12-3. Inserting a JPEG image and clipping it

```
#!/usr/bin/perl -w
# Example 12-3. Images and clipping paths
```

Example 12-3. Inserting a JPEG image and clipping it (continued)

```
use strict;
use PDF::API2;

my $pdf=PDF::API2->new;
my $page=$pdf->page();
$page->mediabox(300, 300);

my $gfx = $page->gfx();
$gfx->circle(150, 150, 150);        # Draw a circular path
$gfx->clip();                       # Make this path the clipping path
$gfx->stroke();                     # Draw the path

my $img = $pdf->image('scotty.jpg'); # Read a JPEG image
$gfx->image($img, 0, 0);            # Add it to the page at the origin

print $pdf->stringify();
$pdf->end;
exit;
```

The result is shown in Figure 12-2.

Figure 12-2. Images and clipping paths

The application in the next section uses both Text and Gfx objects to create a tabular report from a collection of data.

Creating Address Labels

The following example takes an XML file representing a collection of mailing address labels and formats it as a multi-page PDF document with an arbitrary number of rows and columns. The space between columns and rows can be adjusted to accommodate different styles of label stock. This example uses the XML::Simple module to parse the input XML file. (See Chapter 7 for an example using the Sablotron XML parser.)

The example in this section writes the resulting PDF file to STDOUT. When the stringify( ) method is called, each object is translated into a string of PDF code along with the cross-reference table, headers, and trailers.

```perl
#!/usr/bin/perl -w
#
# Use the PDF::API2 module to generate columns of
# text for printing names and addresses on labels.

use strict;

use PDF::API2;        # Used to generate the PDF output
use XML::Simple;      # Used to parse the XML input

my %font = ( );       # A hash holding plain and bold font styles
my ($rows, $columns) = (11,3);     # Size of each label is calculated
my ($hspace, $vspace) = (6, 0);    # Space between columns and rows
my ($tmargin, $bmargin,            # The margins of the page
    $lmargin, $rmargin) = (36, 36, 36, 36);
my ($width, $height) = (612, 792); # Dimensions of page
my $print_grid_lines = 1;          # If true, print grid lines

# Calculate the width and height of each label

my $colwidth = ($width-$lmargin-$rmargin-
                ($columns-1)*$hspace)/$columns;
my $rowheight = ($height-$tmargin-$bmargin-
                ($rows-1)*$vspace)/$rows;
```

First create a new top-level PDF object. If you are creating a document from scratch, use the new( ) constructor. If you are modifying an existing file, use the open( ) method. Next, create a font element for each font used in the document and add these elements to the top-level PDF object. With the PDF::API2 module, you can use any of the 14 core fonts, TrueType fonts, or PostScript fonts. The second argument to the font constructor method should be true if you do *not* want the font to be embedded in the document. Since Helvetica is one of the 14 core fonts guaranteed to be available to any PDF viewer, we do not need to embed the font.

```perl
# Create a new top-level PDF document
# and initialize the font objects for later use

my $pdf=PDF::API2->new;
$font{'plain'} = $pdf->corefont('Helvetica',1);
$font{'bold'} = $pdf->corefont('Helvetica-Bold',1);
foreach (keys(%font)) {
    $font{$_}->encode('latin1');
}
```

```
# Create a new simple XML parser.
# XML::Simple only implements two functions: XMLin and XMLout.

my $parser = new XML::Simple();
my $data = $parser->XMLin($ARGV[0]);
my @labels = dereference($data->{'label'});
```

The first time through (and each time we hit the end of the last column on a page), a new page is created. Add pages to the document's page tree with the page( ) constructor method. Here, the dimensions of each individual page are set with the mediabox( ) method.

```
my ($page, $text, $label);

# Each element of @labels is a reference to a hash containing
# the parsed content of each name and address

PAGE: while (@labels) {
    $page=$pdf->page();                 # Add a new page
    $page->mediabox($width, $height); # Set the dimensions
```

A PDF::API2::Gfx object is created to draw grid lines on each page if the $print_grid_lines option is set to true. Note that each Gfx object is associated with a particular page when it is constructed with the page's gfx( ) method. When drawing graphics, first set the stroke and fill colors, then construct a path with the drawing commands. Here, the margins of the page are drawn in red using the rect( ) drawing command. When the path is complete, stroke it with the stroke( ) method. If you are finished with the path, destroy it (but not the Gfx object) with the endpath( ) method.

```
# Add a new graphic state element to be used if
# $draw_grid_lines is true.

my $g = $page->gfx();
$g->strokecolor("#FF0000");

if ($print_grid_lines) {

    # Draw the bounding box

    $g->rect($lmargin, $bmargin,
            $width-$lmargin-$rmargin,
            $height-$tmargin-$bmargin);
    $g->stroke();
    $g->endpath();
}
```

Each page also has a Text object associated with it, which is used to hold the content stream for the text.

```
# Add a text block that holds all of the text on the page

$text=$page->text();
```

For each column (except the first), draw two vertical grid lines that show the left margin of the column and the right margin of the previous column. Then, for each row, draw a horizontal grid line above and below the current cell (or label). The move( ) and line( ) methods are used to construct the path. Remember that the PDF coordinate system has its origin anchored in the lower left-hand corner!

```
# Loop through the columns

foreach my $c (0..$columns-1) {
    my $x = $lmargin + $c * ($colwidth + $hspace);

    if ($print_grid_lines && ($c>0)) {
        # Print a vertical grid line

        $g->move($x, 0);
        $g->line($x, $height);
        $g->move($x-$hspace, 0);
        $g->line($x-$hspace, $height);
        $g->stroke;
        $g->endpath( );
    }

    # Loop through the rows

    foreach my $r (0..$rows-1) {
        my $y = $height - $tmargin - $r * ($rowheight + $vspace);

        if ($print_grid_lines && ($r > 0)) {
            # Print two horizontal grid lines

            $g->move(0, $y);
            $g->line($width, $y);
            $g->move(0, $y+$vspace);
            $g->line($width, $y+$vspace);
            $g->stroke;
            $g->endpath( );
        }
```

Draw the name and address information as text within the current cell. The cr( ) method is used to move to the next line of text; each line is drawn in 10 point type with 16 point leading.

```
# Add three lines: fullname, address, and city/state/zip

$text->translate($x+6, $y-16);
my $label = shift(@labels);
$text->font($font{'bold'},10);
$text->text($label->{'fullname'});
$text->cr(-16);
$text->font($font{'plain'},10);
$text->text($label->{'address'});
$text->cr(-16);
$text->text("$label->{'city'} $label->{'state'} ".
            "$label->{'zip'}");
```

```
            unless (@labels) {
                last PAGE;        # Jump out if no more labels
            }
        }
    }
}
```

The PDF::API2 module offers three output methods—the result document can be written to a new external file, a file can be updated in-place, or the document can be written to a string. The stringify() method generates PDF code from a top-level PDF object and returns it as a string, suitable for printing as a CGI script. Here, we write the output document to STDOUT:

```
print $pdf->stringify();      # Print the object as a string
$pdf->end;
exit;
```

The dereference() function was called previously to simplify the parsing of the XML file:

```
sub dereference {

    # We need this function if the input XML has only one element.
    # If the parameter is an array reference, de-reference
    # and return it. Otherwise return the parameter unchanged

    my $ref = shift;
    if (ref($ref) eq 'ARRAY') {
        return (@$ref);
    } else {
        return ($ref);
    }
}
```

All that remains is to execute the script with an XML file in the appropriate format. The address label XML data should look something like this:

```
<labels>
  <label>
    <fullname>Buckminster Thomas</fullname>
    <address>942 Scrofulous Dr.</address>
    <city>Ashaway</city>
    <state>KY</state>
    <zip>28621</zip>
  </label>
  <label>
    <fullname>Elizabeth O'Neill</fullname>
    <address>426 Hollow Ct.</address>
    <city>West Warwick</city>
    <state>RI</state>
    <zip>13858</zip>
  </label>
  ...
</labels>
```

The XML::Simple module requires that the full path to the input XML file be specified, as in:

```
perl example11-1.pl ./labels.xml
```

The resulting PDF document is shown in Figure 12-3.

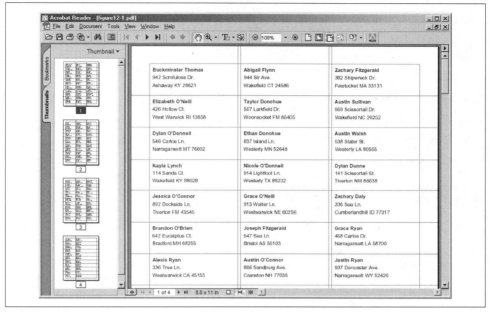

Figure 12-3. Multiple sheets of address labels as a PDF file

Adding to Existing PDF Files

Each PDF::API2 object represents a top-level PDF document. The document can be created from scratch by adding pages and drawing on them by adding Gfx or Text objects, or it can be read from an existing PDF file. To manipulate an existing file, use the open( ) method when creating the top-level PDF object.

Example 12-4 opens an existing PDF file (with the name provided when the script is invoked) and adds a rotated "Confidential" stamp to each page. Once the document is successfully opened, a new font resource is added first, in case the existing document does not use the Helvetica font. Then, each page is accessed in turn by calling the openpage( ) method, which returns a reference to the Page object for a particular existing page. Next, the stamp is added to the page with a Text object. The text is moved into place and rotated using the transform( ) method, as more than one transformation is being performed on the same object. The result is written back to the original document with the update( ) method.

Example 12-4. Modifying an existing PDF file

```perl
#!/usr/bin/perl -w
#
# Example 12-4. Add a stamp to an existing document.

use strict;

use PDF::API2;        # Used to generate the PDF output

unless (defined($ARGV[0])) {
    die "Please provide a filename.\n";
}

# Open the PDF file whose name was provided on the command line

my $pdf = PDF::API2->open($ARGV[0]) or
    die "Couldn't open $ARGV[0]!\n";

# Initialize the font used to create the stamp

my $font = $pdf->corefont('Helvetica');
my ($page, $text);

# Loop through the pages

for (my $n=1; $n <= $pdf->pages(); $n++) {
    $page = $pdf->openpage($n);

    # Create a new text block on the page, center and rotate it

    $text = $page->text();
    $text->transform( -translate => [198, 306],
                      -rotate => 45);

    # Set the font and fill color

    $text->font($font, 36);
    $text->fillcolor("#FF0000");

    # Add a string of text to the text block

    $text->text_center('C O N F I D E N T I A L');
}

# Update the original PDF file in-place

$pdf->update();

$pdf->end;
exit;
```

The result is pictured in Figure 12-4.

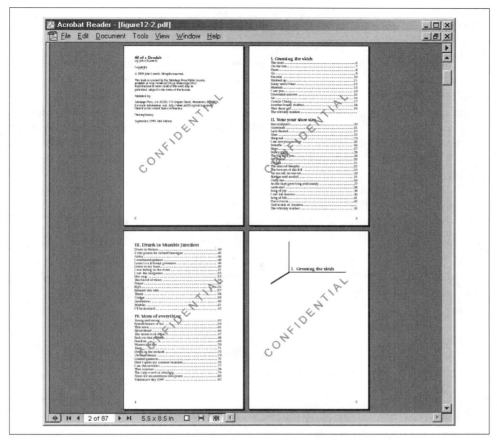

Figure 12-4. Stamping a string on the pages of an existing document

PDF::API2 Reference

The following methods and constructors are available to the top-level PDF object.

clonepage( )

`$page = $pdf->clonepage(`*`source, target`*`)`

This method creates a new page in the PDF document whose page number is `target` and whose content is a duplicate of the source page. A new Page object is returned. Use a target index of −1 to insert the duplicated page at the end of the document.

corefont( )

`$font = $pdf->corefont(`*`fontname`*` [, `*`noembed`*`])`

This method adds a font dictionary to the document, using one of the 14 "core" PDF fonts. A font dictionary (see Chapter 10) is a resource that can be referenced by any content stream in the document that draws text.

A font dictionary may contain only the name of the font (if you want the PDF viewer to figure out what font to use if an exact match is not available), or it may contain the glyph information for the entire font. If the noembed argument is false, the entire set of metrics for the font is embedded in the document.

The core fonts are shown in Table 12-1.

Table 12-1. The 14 core PDF fonts

Courier	Times-Roman	Helvetica	Symbol
Courier-Bold	Times-Bold	Helvetica-Bold	ZapfDingbats
Courier-Oblique	Times-Italic	Helvetica-Oblique	
Courier-BoldOblique	Times-BoldItalic	Helvetica-BoldOblique	

end( )

`$pdf->end( )`

This command actually destroys all data in the PDF object. It should be called only after you no longer need the document object.

image( )

`$image = $pdf->image(`*`filename`*`)`

This method creates a new Image object that is included in the PDF document as a content stream block. The image can be a JPEG, PNG, or PNM formatted file. The image can be placed on a page with the `PDF::API2::Gfx->image( )` function.

imagemask( )

`$pdf->imagemask(`*`image, file`*`)`

This method adds a mask to a previously created image object. The mask should be a grayscale JPG, PNG, or PNM file. The levels of gray correspond to the opacity of the mask at each pixel, with 0 being transparent and 255 being opaque. If the mask file is a PNG with an alpha channel, the alpha channel is used for the mask.

importpage( )

`$page = $pdf->importpage(pdfdoc, source, target)`

This method creates a new page in the PDF document whose page number is `$target` and whose content is a duplicate of the source page from `$pdfdoc`, a PDF::API2 object. Use a target index of −1 to insert the imported page at the end of the document.

info( )

`$pdf->info(%info_block)`

This method allows you to set the values in the PDF's Info block by providing a hash with the appropriate key/value pairs. The fields in the Info block are Title, Subject, Author, CreationDate, Creator, Producer, ModDate, and Keywords.

mediabox( )

`$pdf->mediabox(width, height)`
`$pdf->mediabox(x1, y1, x2, y2)`

This method sets the bounding box for the PDF document. The width and height are specified in points. Alternately, you can provide the coordinates of the lower left (*x1, y1*) and upper right (*x2, y2*) corners of the box.

new( )

`$pdf = PDF::API2->new( )`

The constructor method creates a new PDF::API2 object that represents a top-level PDF document.

open( )

`$pdf = PDF::API2->open(filename)`

This method opens an existing PDF file and reads it into a new PDF::API2 object.

openpage( )

`$page = $pdf->openpage(number)`

This method returns the Page object that represents the specified page of the PDF document.

outlines( )

```
$outlines = $page->outlines( )
```

This method returns a new top-level PDF::API2::Outlines object that can be used to hold an outline of the document. Outline entries are also referred to as bookmarks.

page( )

```
$page = $pdf->page( )
$page = $pdf->page(number)
```

This method creates a new PDF::API2::Page object and appends it to the end of the document or at the specified page. If *number* is –1 or undef, the page is inserted before the last page. If *number* is 1, the page is inserted at the beginning of the document.

pages( )

```
$n = $pdf->pages( )
```

This method returns the number of pages in the PDF document object.

pdfimage( )

```
$image = $pdf->pdfimage(file, page_number)
$image = $pdf->pdfimageobj(pdf_obj, page_number)
```

You can read in a page from another PDF file and include it as an image object. The pdfimageobj( ) function can be used to efficiently extract more than one page from a previously opened PDF document (where pdf_obj is a PDF::API2 object).

psfont( )

```
$font = $pdf->psfont(pfb_filename,afm_filename)
```

This method includes a font dictionary using a PostScript Type 1 font. The parameters are the file paths to the *.pfb* (Printer Font Binary) and *.afm* (Adobe Font Metric) files for the desired PostScript font. These files are parsed, and all of the glyph and metric data for the font is encapsulated into a font description dictionary embedded in the document.

saveas( )

```
$pdf->saveas(filename)
```

This method outputs the PDF document to the specified file.

stringify( )

`$string = $pdf->stringify( )`

This method outputs the PDF document to a string buffer. Use this method to write to STDOUT, for instance. If you are writing a CGI script that generates PDF output, use:

```
print "Content-type: application/pdf\n\n";
print $pdf->stringify( );
```

A filename can be provided for "Save As" downloads by adding a `Content-Disposition` field to the header:

```
print "Content-type: application/pdf\n\n";
print "Content-Disposition: inline; filename=foogum.pdf\n";
print $pdf->stringify( );
```

ttfont( )

`$font = $pdf->ttfont(tt_filename)`
`$font = $pdf->ttfont(tt_filename, lazy)`

This method includes a font dictionary based on a TrueType font. All of the font glyph and metric information is wrapped up in a single file in TrueType fonts; the *filename* parameter points to the *.ttf* file containing this information. If the `lazy` flag is set, the TrueType font is not embedded in the document. Not embedding the font assumes that the "Latin1" encoding is intended, and that the user agent is able to substitute an appropriate font if the TrueType font in question is not available. (It probably also assumes a Microsoft bias.)

update( )

`$pdf->update( )`

If you have created a new PDF object from an existing PDF document with the `open( )` method, the `update( )` method writes any changes you have made to the document back to the source file.

PDF::API2::Page

Page objects are created using the `page( )` constructor method of the top-level document object. The methods defined in this module can be used to change the attributes of the page itself or add content to the page with the `gfx( )`, `text( )`, and `hybrid( )` constructor methods.

artbox( )

`$page->artbox(width, height)`

The "art box" can be set to designate the bounding box of the area that encloses all of the meaningful content on the page.

bleedbox( )

`$page->bleedbox(width, height)`

By default, the "bleed box" is the same as the "crop box." When printing a PDF that has content that bleeds off the page, you may sometimes want to print crop marks and have some of the printed content bleed past the crop marks. This method may be used to set the bounding box of this bleed area.

cropbox( )

`$page->cropbox(width, height)`

This method sets the bounding box for this page. Any elements that extend over the margins of the page are cropped.

gfx( )

`$gfx = $page->gfx( )`

This method creates a new PDF::API2::Gfx object associated with this page. This object can be used to add a "content stream" of graphics drawing commands to the page.

hybrid( )

`$hybrid = $page->hybrid( )`

Use the hybrid( ) method to create a new object that can contain both textual and graphical information. You can call any of the PDF::API2::Text or PDF::API2::Gfx methods on a hybrid content object.

mediabox( )

`$page->mediabox(width, height)`

This method sets the bounding box for this page.

text( )

`$text = $page->text( )`

This method returns a new PDF::API2::Text object that can be used to draw text on a page.

trimbox( )

`$page->trimbox(width, height)`

As with the "bleed box," you may wish to specify a trim size that is smaller than the bounding box of the document in some printing applications.

PDF::API2::Content

The Content object represents a content stream dictionary. You don't directly instantiate a Content object; rather, it is subclassed by the Gfx, Text, and Hybrid objects. All of the methods in this class may be applied to any of these three types of PDF content.

compress( )

`$content->compress( )`

If this method is called on a block, the Flate algorithm is applied to the content in the block when the document is saved to a file or written to a string buffer.

restore( )

`$content->restore( )`

This method restores the previously saved graphics state of the content object.

save( )

`$content->save( )`

This method saves the current graphics state of the object. The graphics state includes the current transformation matrix and current stroke and fill color information. The graphics state is pushed onto a stack; you can pop it off with the restore( ) method.

fillcolor( )

`$content->fillcolor(color)`
`$content->fillcolorbyname(colorname, as_cmyk)`

This method sets the fill color, which can be specified by one of the following means:

Grayscale:	`$content->fillcolor(0);`
RGB hex notation:	`$content->fillcolor("#FF0000");`
CMYK hex notation:	`$g->fillcolor("%FF000066");`
HSV hex notation:	`$g->fillcolor("!FF8723");`
X11 color name:	`$content->fillcolorbyname("AliceBlue", 0)`

flatness( )

$content->flatness($value)

The flatness tolerance parameter (expressed as a number between 0 and 100) gives the PDF user agent an indication of the allowable margin of error when drawing curves. This parameter is taken into account when the vector curves are scan-converted before they are drawn to the raster display. Smaller values take more computation time to render, but appear smoother. The default value is 0.

linecap( )

$content->linecap(*cap_style*)

The cap style is a code that determines how the ends of lines are drawn (see Figure 12-5). Acceptable values are:

0   Square butt cap
1   Rounded cap
2   Projected square cap

The default value is 0.

Figure 12-5. The linecap styles

linedash( )

$content->linedash(*@dash*)

This method sets the style for dashed lines. The @dash array is a list of values (expressed in user space units) representing the length of the dashes and the spaces between the dashes. Three examples are shown in Figure 12-6. The top line is the result of (20,20), the middle is (20,5), and the bottom is (20,10,5,15).

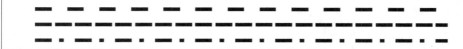

Figure 12-6. Line dashes are specified with a list of alternating dashes and spaces

linejoin( )

`$content->linejoin(join)`

This method sets a code that determines how line joints are drawn. The join value can be:

0   Miter join
1   Round join
2   Bevel join

linewidth( )

`$content->linewidth(width)`

This method sets the width of the stroke.

rotate( )

`$content->rotate(degrees)`

This method rotates the content object around its origin by the specified number of degrees.

scale( )

`$content->scale(x_scale,y_scale)`

This method scales the object in the x and y dimensions by the provided fractions or multiples.

skew( )

`$content->skew(x_skew,y_skew)`

This method applies a skew transform to the content object. The x axis is skewed by $x_skew degrees, and the y axis is skewed by $y_skew degrees.

strokecolor( )

```
$content->strokecolor(color)
$content->strokecolorbyname(colorname, as_cmyk)
```

These methods set the stroke color. The color argument is the same as for `fillcolor( )`. If the second form is used, the *colorname* should be an X11 color name, which is represented as CMYK color if $as_cmyk is true.

transform( )

```
$content->transform(%transforms)
```

This method allows you to combine multiple transformations into a single function call. The *%transforms* hash can contain any of the following key/value pairs, using anonymous arrays for transforms with multiple arguments:

```
$content->transform( -translate => [100,100],
                     -rotate => 45,
                     -scale => [.5,.75],
                     -skew => [10,10] );
```

You need to use the transform method if you want to apply more than one transformation to a content object. Otherwise, if you apply a `translate( )` followed by a `rotate( )`, for example, the rotation would trounce the translation.

translate( )

```
$content->translate($x,$y)
```

This method moves the content object (i.e., the text or graphic) to the provided global coordinate .

Figure 12-7 shows an image being manipulated with the translate, scale, rotate, and skew transformations. The `transform( )` method can be used to string together several transformations.

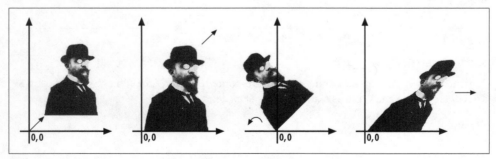

Figure 12-7. Translate, scale, rotate, skew transformations

PDF::API2::Gfx

A Gfx object is used to draw lines, curves, and shapes on a page. It is created using the gfx( ) constructor of the Page object. All of the drawing commands use a local coordinate system that is subject to transformation with any of the PDF::API2::Content methods. All of these methods can also be used with a hybrid graphics/text object (created with the Page->hybrid( ) constructor).

arc( )

`$gfx->arc(x, y, rx, ry, start, end, move)`

This method draws an elliptical arc centered at (x, y) that sweeps between the provided starting and ending angles (in degrees). The radii along the x and y axes can be adjusted with rx and ry. If *move* is 0, the arc is drawn from zero degrees; if it is 1, the starting point is moved to a point on the curve at the starting angle.

circle( )

`$gfx->circle(cx, cy, r)`

This method draws a circle centered at (cx, cy), with a radius of r.

clip( )

`$gfx->clip(nonzero)`

This method sets the clipping path to the current path using the nonzero winding rule (see Chapter 10).

close( )

`$gfx->close( )`

This method closes a path. It draws a straight line segment between the end point and the start point, if they are not already the same point.

curve( )

`$gfx->curve(x1, y1, x2, y2, x3, y3)`

This method draws a quadratic Bezier curve from the current point to $(x3, y3)$, using $(x1, y1)$ and $(x2, y2)$ as the two control points.

ellipse( )

`$gfx->ellipse(cx, cy, rx, ry)`

This method draws an ellipse centered at (*cx, cy*), with a radius of *rx* in the x dimension and *ry* in the y dimension.

endpath( )

`$gfx->endpath( )`

This method destroys the current path. If you do not end the path, subsequent drawing commands are appended to the current path.

fill( )

`$gfx->fill(nonzero)`

This method causes the path to be filled, using the nonzero winding rule if $nonzero is true. The current fill color (set with `fillcolor( )`) is used.

fillstroke( )

`$gfx->fillstroke(nonzero)`

Calling this method is equivalent to calling both the `fill( )` and `stroke( )` methods.

image( )

`$gfx->image(imgobj, x, y)`
`$gfx->image(imgobj, x, y, scale)`
`$gfx->image(imgobj, x, y, w, h)`

This method adds a previously created Image object (read in from a file with the `PDF::API2->image( )` constructor) to a graphic. The image is placed with its lower left-hand corner at the specified coordinate, and may be scaled by defining a scaling ratio or providing another coordinate for the upper-right corner of its bounding box.

line( )

`$gfx->line(x, y)`

This method draws a line from the current point to (*x, y*).

move( )

`$gfx->move(x, y)`

This method moves the current point to (*x, y*) without creating a new line segment.

poly( )

`$gfx->poly(x1,y1,x2,y2...)`

This method draws a polygon consisting of straight line segments connecting all of the points in the argument list.

rect( )

`$gfx->rect(x1,y1,w1,h1,[...])`

This method draws a rectangle with its lower left corner at the coordinate (*x1*, *y1*) and a bounding box of (*$w1* × *$h1*). Multiple rectangles may be drawn within the same method call by adding more sets of dimensions as parameters.

rectxy( )

`$gfx->rectxy(x1,y1,x2,y2)`

This method draws a rectangle with its lower left corner at the coordinate (*x1*, *y1*) and its upper right corner at (*x2*, *y2*).

stroke( )

`$gfx->stroke( )`

This method is used to stroke a path after it has been constructed. Note that you must call the fill( ) method if you want the path to be filled. The current stroke color (set with strokecolor( )) is used.

PDF::API2::Text

Text is drawn on a page using the Text object. You can create a new Text object with the Page->text( ) constructor. All of the following methods can also be used with a hybrid graphics/text object (created with the Page->hybrid( ) constructor).

charspace( )

`$text->charspace(spacing)`

This method sets the amount of space between individual characters.

cr( )

`$text->cr(linesize)`

This method moves to the next line of text. If `linesize` is not specified, the current leading value determines how much space is left between baselines. Note that the line size (or leading) must be negative if you want the text to be read top to bottom.

font( )

`$text->font(font_obj, size)`

This method indicates the font and size to be used to render the text. The `font_obj` argument is a previously created Font object, as returned by the corefont( ), ttfont( ), or psfont( ) method.

hspace( )

`$text->hspace(hscale)`

This method controls the horizontal scaling of the displayed text. The `hscale` parameter should be a multiple or fraction that indicates how much wider (or narrower) the text should be with respect to its original width.

lead( )

`$text->lead(leading)`

This method sets the leading (the amount of space between the baseline of one line and the baseline of the next) for a block of text. Note that the leading direction is in the global coordinate system—that is, for text running down the page, use a negative value.

nl( )

`$text->nl( )`

This method is the same as cr( ), except that the current leading is always used to advance the line.

text( )

`$width = $text->text(string)`

This method adds a string of text to the text block at the current point, subject to all transformations currently in effect.

text_center( )

`$text->text_center(string)`

This method sets the alignment of the text block to center. The specified string is centered around the current point.

textln( )

`$text->textln(string1, ..., stringn)`

This method renders several lines of text strings by inserting a carriage return between each line. The leading must be set (with `leading( )`) for this to be effective.

text_right( )

`$text->text_right(string)`

This method indicates that the specified string should be drawn right-aligned to the current point.

text_utf8( )

`$text->text_utf8(utf8_string)`

This method adds a string encoded in the UTF-8 Unicode character encoding to a Text object.

wordspace( )

`$text->wordspace(spacing)`

This method sets the amount of space between words.

PDF::API2::Outline

An Outline object provides the user agent with a linked table of contents that may be displayed alongside the document and used for navigation. In Adobe's Acrobat Reader, outlines are displayed in a frame called the Bookmark frame; this section sticks with the term "outline."

To create an outline, you must first create a root outline entry with the `outlines( )` constructor, which returns a new PDF::API2::Outline object. Once the root is created, add outline entries with the `outline( )` method; this also returns Outline objects. You can create a hierarchy of outline entries using the `outline( )` method. Example 12-5 creates a PDF document with 20 pages, divided into 5 sections of 4 pages each. As each page is created, a new outline entry is added, and the entry is linked to the page with the dest( ) method.

Example 12-5. Adding an outline to a PDF document

```perl
#!/usr/bin/perl -w
#
# Example 12-5. Create a bookmark frame

use strict;

use PDF::API2;      # Used to generate the PDF output

# Create a new top-level document

my $pdf = PDF::API2->new( );

# Initialize the root of the outline tree

my $outline_root = $pdf->outlines( );

# Use Helvetica throughout

my $font = $pdf->corefont('Helvetica');
my ($page, $text);

# Create four sections

foreach my $s (1..4) {

    # Add an entry for each section. Each section has
    # suboutline entries

    my $section = $outline_root->outline( );
    $section->title("Section $s");

    # Add five pages for each section

    foreach my $n (1..5) {

        # Draw some text on the page

        $page = $pdf->page( );
        $page->mediabox(612, 792);
        $text = $page->text( );
        $text->transform( -translate => [306, 396]);
        $text->font($font, 36);
        $text->text_center("Section $s, page $n");

        # Add an outline entry for the page,
        # title it, and link it.

        my $outline = $section->outline( );
```

Example 12-5. Adding an outline to a PDF document (continued)

```
        $outline->title("Page $n");
        $outline->dest($page);

    }
}

print $pdf->stringify();
exit;
```

The result (as displayed in Adobe's Acrobat Reader) is shown in Figure 12-8.

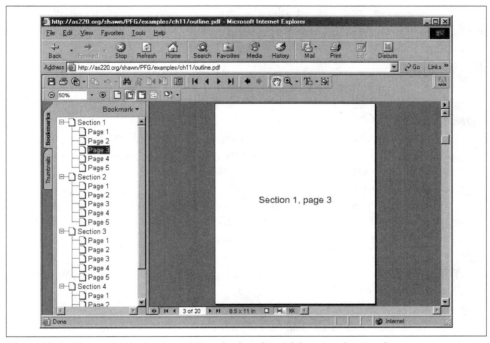

Figure 12-8. The outline (or bookmarks) as displayed in Adobe's Acrobat Reader

dest( )

$outline->dest(*page*)

This method sets the target page for the outline entry. When the outline entry is clicked, the given page is displayed.

outline( )

`$suboutline = $outline_root->outline( )`

This method returns a new PDF::API2::Outline object that can be used to create an outline entry (bookmark). The outline root is either a top-level Outlines object (created with `PDF::API2::outlines( )`) or another suboutline.

title( )

`$outline->title(text)`

This method sets the string that is displayed as the name of the outline entry (bookmark).

References

Several additional modules are provided in the PDF::API2 distribution. They are:

PDF::API2::Lite
> This module provides a simplified, procedurally oriented interface to the PDF::API2 module. This can be useful for easily writing PDF files. If you are reading and modifying PDF files, you can't really use the Lite module.

PDF::API2::Annotation
> The Annotation object allows you to associate annotation dictionaries with a section of a PDF page. An annotation is a kind of floating note or comment window that can be activated by a mouse click.

PDF::API2::Barcode
> The Barcode object provides a set of ready-made functions for drawing barcodes in various formats.

PDF::API2::Color
> A Color object is used to easily manipulate PDF colors with an object-oriented interface.

PDF::API2::Pattern
> A Pattern object can be used to fill a region. The pattern can be a gradient or a tiled image.

Appendixes

Serving Graphics on the Web

When creating graphics, it's good to keep in mind that not all web browsers handle all "standard" HTML features in the same way. At various times, different browsers have had their own idiosyncratic interpretations of the ALT tag, client-side image maps, the usemap attribute, GIF89a animation, image spacing attributes, transparency, inline PNG/XBM/Progressive-JPEG images, the lowsrc tag, borders on image links, alignment tags, and scaling tags. In short, many features that should have a standard implementation have had different levels of compliance to the standard on different browsers.

You can retrieve a good deal of information about the user agent that is looking at your web page. You may want to know which browser the client is using (accessible through the HTTP_USER_AGENT environment variable), or the MIME types that the client accepts. Some web servers offer options for modifying the image request negotiation process to accommodate different browser capabilities, so browsers that can't see PNG files are automatically sent a GIF version instead, for example. Consult your web server's documentation for these features.

The Server and CGI

Hopefully, you have access to some sort of web server. When people talk about a "web server," they are generally referring to two things: a program that accepts a request for resources (HTML pages, images, applets, DOM objects, etc.) and returns resources, as well as the actual collection of resources to return (and, I guess, the computer where everything lives, if you want to get picky). When we talk about a web server here, we refer only to the program that does the serving; we assume that there is also a corresponding collection of web pages and images to be served.

The requests made to and responses returned by the web server must be in the standard form described by the HyperText Transfer Protocol (HTTP). Web servers are an inherently simple concept that in practice may be very simple programs or very complicated affairs. The popular Apache web server falls somewhere in between.

Apache takes a modular design approach; it has a very fast, simple core set of operations that may be extended with other modules. Whichever web server you run, the basic capabilities of handling requests and returning resources are the primary function of the server.

When a web browser requests an image from a server, the request is in the form of a URL, just like any other HTTP request. This URL points to a file that resides on the same computer as the web server, in its collection of resources. Generally the web server points to a specific root directory, which it uses to determine the location of the requested image. For example, the URL:

```
http://www.shemp.net/splashscreen.png
```

points at a file in the Portable Network Graphics (PNG) format located in the web server's root directory. If this URL is requested by a client (and it exists), the web server determines a MIME (Multipurpose Internet Mail Extensions) type for the file and sends back an HTTP header to the client. The web server then reads the data in the file pointed to by the URL and immediately follows the header with a stream of data from the file.

Certain MIME types are said to be *registered*, i.e., clients implementing the HTTP protocol should at least recognize them as valid MIME types. Some of the registered MIME types that we are interested in are:

text/html	HTML documents
image/gif	GIF image files
image/jpeg	JPEG image files
image/png	PNG image files
image/svg+xml	SVG files
application/x-shockwave-flash	SWF files
application/postscript	PostScript files
application/pdf	PDF documents

The HTTP header consists of the case-insensitive string "Content-type:" followed by one of the content types listed above, followed by two "Internet standard" newlines (a carriage return followed by a linefeed):*

```
Content-type: image/gif

(...image data...)
```

An image may be generated dynamically by a program or script run on the server. All a script has to do is generate an appropriate HTTP header, then generate valid image

---

* Technically, two "Internet standard" linefeeds are \r\n\r\n, but because of widespread use of two plain newlines (\n\n) in HTTP headers produced by CGI scripts, most browsers accept either form. If you are writing a CGI script using the CGI module, it's best to avoid the issue and use the header( ) method.

data. When a web client makes a request for a dynamically generated image, the web server simply runs the script specified by the URL (if it is a valid script and if the web server has been properly configured to run external scripts), retrieves the output from the script, and passes it back to the client. These scripts are generally called CGI scripts because they adhere to the Common Gateway Interface, which is simply a standard way that the web server and external scripts can communicate. There is a module for Perl that makes this communication relatively painless.

The CGI.pm Module

The CGI.pm Perl module is a collection of object-oriented routines for creating HTML forms, parsing form submissions, and writing valid HTTP headers and HTML responses. In other words, it is a tool that helps you take input from and write output to the Common Gateway Interface. Using the CGI module simplifies the process of implementing CGI scripts and helps you avoid common pitfalls and write more readable Perl code. The CGI module is used by several examples in this book to parse queries and print HTTP headers in a standardized way. CGI.pm was written by Lincoln Stein and is available on CPAN.

The methods of the CGI module are made available to your script with the use function, the same as with any other module. The new method creates a new CGI object. Thus, CGI scripts using the CGI module have the following lines somewhere near the beginning of the script:

```
use CGI;
my $query = new CGI;   # create a new CGI object
```

Once you have instantiated a CGI object, you can use it to parse input to your CGI script or to create output destined for the web server.

Parsing CGI input with CGI.pm

Input to a CGI script usually, but not always, comes from a user filling out a form. In any case, the input (generally called a *query string*) is always encoded in a standard format. A form submission using the GET method with three input fields, for example, would send a query string in the following format:

```
http://www.shemp.net/script.cgi?field1=data1&field2=data2&field3=data3
```

Rather than writing all new code (with potential bugs or security holes) each time you write a CGI script, you can use the param method to access each of the query parameters with an OO-style syntax. To access the value for the field named field1, for example, use:

```
use CGI;
my $query = new CGI;
my $field1value = $query->param('field1');
```

If `field2` were a collection of values returned from a scrolling list in a form, simply assign it to an array. CGI parses the query and returns a list of values:

```
my @field2values = $query->param('field2');
```

To retrieve a list of all of the parameter names from the query, call `param` without an argument:

```
# returns ('field1', 'field2', 'field3')
my @params = $query->param( );
```

To provide default values for the parameters that are overridden if the value is specified by the user's form submission, supply the default values as a hash when creating the query object:

```
my $query = new CGI( name => 'Anonymous',
                     address => 'No address provided' );
```

You can also get the unparsed query string (URL and all) with the `query_string` method:

```
$qs = $query->query_string( );
```

Generating HTTP headers with CGI.pm

The `header` method provides a simple way of writing HTTP headers in which you don't have to worry about the exact format of the header. You can print a header for any sort of MIME type (or create your own type) by specifying the -type attribute in the call to `header`. To write an HTTP header for an image file, use one of the following:

```
use CGI;
my $query = new CGI;
print $query->header(-type => 'image/gif');    # for a GIF, or
print $query->header(-type => 'image/png');    # for a PNG, or
print $query->header(-type => 'image/jpeg');   # for a JPEG
```

If the content type is the only parameter being sent to `header( )`, you may omit the left side of the hash and just include the content type string.

The `header` method also allows you to include any field that is defined by the HTTP standard in the header. You can easily include an `expires` field, for example, that tells the browser when to remove the image from its cache. Usually, the output of CGI scripts is not cached by browsers, but you can control this behavior with:

```
print $query->header(-type    => 'image/png',
                     -expires => '1d');
```

This removes the image from the cache tomorrow. The expiration value can indicate seconds, minutes, days, months, years, or a specific date:

`'5s'`   in five seconds

`'5m'`   in five minutes

'5d'   in five days

'5M'   in five months

'5y'   in five years

'Wednesday, 21-Oct-03 12:00:00 GMT'
          at a very specific time

To make sure that your image is not cached, use a negative value ('-1s') or specify 'now' for -expires.

To include a "refresh" field within an HTTP header, use the -Refresh attribute, where the assigned value is the number of seconds the browser should wait before reloading the page:

```
print $query->header(-type    => 'image/png',
                     -Refresh => '5s');
```

To redirect the browser to another URL after a certain period of time, you can specify an optional URL within the refresh value:

```
print $query->header(
    -type    => 'image/png',
    -Refresh => '5s; URL=http://www.shemp.net/image2.png');
```

This was a common trick before the widespread use of animated GIF89a images as a form of simple animation.

The CGI module provides many other methods for writing CGI output, such as a clean, object-oriented way to create the HTML for fill-out forms. These methods are beyond the scope of this introduction; visit the CGI.pm home site referenced at the end of this chapter if you wish to explore its other capabilities.

Increasing Server Performance

Dealing with graphics can be a computationally intensive procedure. Generating graphics for a medium like the Web in a short enough time span that the user experience can still be called "interactive" is even more intensive. Luckily, images destined for the Web are generally small and optimized for quick transfer and display rates, but often at the expense of a longer encoding time. In addition to the actual RAM and processor resources necessary to generate web graphics, there is the additional overhead of the web server and the Perl interpreter itself. The load multiplies with the number of simultaneous hits received by your server.

But perhaps I am painting too bleak a picture. In fact, most computers used as web servers today can easily handle a moderate load of requests for image-generating CGI scripts. And for busier web sites or sites with more intensive graphics-serving needs, there are a few options for enhancing your web server to meet the demand.

Limit the number of simultaneous requests

When it comes to web server performance, the most valuable system resource is RAM. An image generation script typically takes anywhere from 1 MB to 32 MB of system resources. The amount of physical RAM on your system determines how many simultaneous requests your server can take before it has to use whatever disk space has been allocated for virtual (swap) memory. Once processes start using the swap, performance quickly drops off and your server becomes quite unresponsive. To head off this problem, you should configure your web server to limit the maximum number of requests to be processed simultaneously. Requests beyond this limit will have to wait, which is preferable to an excessive number of requests bogging down the server.

Figure out how much RAM is typically used by one web server process for your specific application, and limit the number of users so that the maximum number of requests fit within the amount of physical RAM on your system.

Install mod_perl

If you are writing scripts in Perl and running the popular Apache web server, a fairly painless way to limit the amount of memory taken up by each process (thereby allowing your server to process more simultaneous requests) is to install *mod_perl* on your server. *mod_perl* allows you to write Apache modules directly in Perl; for CGI developers, this means that the Perl interpreter can be "embedded" within the web server, so that multiple HTTP requests can avoid the performance cost of restarting an external instance of the interpreter with each request. *mod_perl* also allows you to preload commonly used modules that may be shared among multiple web server processes for an additional memory savings. Well-behaved CGI programs should run without modification on a *mod_perl*-enabled web server.

mod_perl does not provide any specific mechanisms for optimizing the process of generating images for the Web. It merely reduces the amount of overhead needed to serve many requests for web resources generated dynamically by Perl scripts by making the Perl interpreter persistent. For information about installing and running *mod_perl*, check out the Perl-Apache integration project link listed in the "References" section of this chapter.

Image farming

If you have more than one computer available, consider "farming out" some of the work to other machines so that your main web server isn't bogged down. The actual SRC attributes of the images within the HTML page may be modified to point to the new URL, or the request for the image may be redirected by the server to the appropriate machine, so the actual "passing of the buck" is opaque to the web page requesting the image. The following IMG tag, for example, calls a CGI script that generates a PNG image as its output:

```
<IMG SRC="http://www.shemp.net/image1.cgi">
```

If the computer at *www.shemp.net* later becomes a popular site and you decide to farm out the task of producing this image to another computer on your network named *images.shemp.net*, you could move the CGI program to the new server and change the SRC attribute to:

```
<IMG SRC="http://images.shemp.net/image1.cgi">
```

Alternately, you could move the CGI program to the new server and replace the file *image1.cgi* with a shell script (or batch file) that prints a short HTML file with a Location HTTP header redirecting the request to the new server. The following Unix-style shell script does the job:

```
#!/bin/sh
echo 'Location: http://www.as220.org/as220.gif';
echo;
```

The redirection document must be some sort of executable file, because the server identifies the file *image1.cgi* as an executable program and attempts to execute it.

Probably the most important enhancement for serving images is not a hardware or software solution at all. Simply make sure that you use the WIDTH and HEIGHT attributes of the IMG tag properly, so that the layout of the page by the browser is not at all dependent on the speed of execution of a CGI script.

Web Graphics and the Browser

Too see how a web browser processes and organizes images internally, let's look at the model used by the Mozilla web browser, which is the "open source" release of the Netscape browser. This is a good object of study because the browser's code is freely available under the Netscape Public License, and the code is amply documented at Mozilla headquarters (*http://www.mozilla.org*).

Mozilla is written in C++, and is designed as a modular structure with well-defined tasks handled by different modules. Image management is handled by an "image library" that manages the flow, decoding, and eventual display of images. The Image Library takes the following steps in displaying an image:

1. A URL is requested by the code that handles the layout of the page. This request can be initiated by the parsing of an IMG element or by one of the user interface options, such as the Show Images button on the navigation bar. This request is made with the GetImage( ) function.

2. The Image Library maintains a cache of previously requested and decoded images. With each image request, the Image Library looks for the image in the cache and, if it finds it, draws the previously requested image from the cache. If the image is not in the cache, the Library opens a data stream to get the image data, create a new image object, decompress and decode the data, and store the object in the cache according to the pragmas associated with the file. A request

to the Image Library returns an ImageReq data structure that consists of the decoded image data.

3. The Image Library provides an interface for the integration of multiple image decoders (in the future, this model will most likely be superseded by a COM-like component model). Each decoder must implement five functions that allow it to communicate with the Image Library:

init( )
> This function allocates all necessary resources and data structures.

write_ready( )
> This function is needed with some image file formats to determine the maximum number of bytes to read ahead. It exists primarily as a workaround for supporting older platforms.

write( )
> This function handles the decompression, color table management, and dithering tasks.

complete( )
> This function lets the observer know that the image has been decoded.

abort( )
> This function is called when a request is aborted or at the end of a successful decode. It cleans up the resources and structures used by the decoder.

4. The decoding process is straightforward:

   a. The header info for the image is parsed and information such as the dimensions of the image is extracted.

   b. If this is the first time the image has been loaded, the Image Library adds the five functions for the appropriate image decoder to its function table.

   c. The target dimensions are computed, taking into account adjustments indicated in the IMG tag.

   d. The decoded data is resized to the target dimensions as it is read line by line.

   e. The transparency mask (if any) is scaled to the target dimensions.

   f. If the color depth of the image exceeds that of the browser, the image is dithered to best match the client.

5. An "observer" is created with each request to the Image Library. The observer provides status information on the progress of the image request and notifies the layout module of such info as when the image has been decoded or when a complete frame of a multi-image animation has loaded. This allows the browser to update the screen as the request is being processed.

6. The actual display of the image on the screen is handled by separate display code that handles the decisions necessary to render pixmaps on different platforms.

Currently, all of the decoded images in a single HTML page are stored in memory at the same time, even though they may not all be displayed on the screen at once. This is one of the factors that contribute to the relatively large footprint of most browsers.

Now that we've looked at the underpinnings of graphics and the web browser, let's look at the HTML elements that couch images and control their placement and sizing.

Presenting Images in HTML

As of the Version 3.2 HTML specification, the only way to include an image in an HTML document was with the IMG tag. The 4.0 HTML standard introduced another means of including images: the OBJECT tag. The OBJECT element is intended as a more open solution to the problem of inserting inline media into web documents.

The IMG element embeds an image in the body of a document (it cannot be used in the head section). The element consists of a start tag without an end tag, without any "content" as such. It is formed according to standard HTML syntax, which is to say it should look like this in its simplest form:

```
<IMG src='someimage.png'>  # include an inline png
```

In Perl, you may use the HTML::Element module to create image tags. This module is designed to let you build the nodes of an HTML syntax tree with method calls. It can be used as in the following example:

```
use HTML::Element;        # use this module

# Set attributes when creating the element...
my $img = new HTML::Element 'img', src => 'someimage.gif';

# ...or add them later with the attr() method
$img->attr('alt','This is Some Image!');

# Use as_HTML() to print the element as an html tag
print $img->as_HTML;
```

The SRC Attribute

The SRC attribute indicates the Uniform Resource Locator (URL) of the image. This can be an absolute or relative address, and it may refer to a file to be read as data or to a script to be run to create the proper image output. The syntax in either case is the same:

```
<IMG SRC = "images/staticfile.gif">
<IMG SRC = "cgi-bin/dynamicscript.cgi">
```

In the first case, the browser reads the file at the given URL (in this case, a local file), interprets the image data within that file, and displays that data in-line at the proper place in the document. In the second case, the browser requests the CGI script at the given URL, the web server invokes the script, and whatever output is generated from the script (whatever is written to STDOUT) is sent to the web browser for inclusion in the web page. The browser doesn't really care what language the script is written in, just that it adheres to the Common Gateway Interface and sends back valid image data. If the script fails for some reason, the image data coming back is not in a valid image format, and the browser displays a broken image icon.

One problem with creating images on the fly via the Common Gateway Interface is the reporting of errors. A broken image icon does not tell us very much. Did the script crash? Is the network unreachable? Do we have an incompatible browser? It's hard to tell from the stone-faced broken image icon. In Chapter 2, we implemented the BrokenImage package to generate a more informative broken image icon.

Another way to get around this problem is to print "wrapper" HTML around your image, so that your script is not just printing out a stream of image data (or *not* printing out a stream of image data, as the case may be). With this approach you can print an appropriate error message in HTML. On the server side, it is generally a good idea to use the Perl CGI::Carp module to neatly report CGI error messages in your server log file.

The following trivial script reads in a binary image file and prints it to STDOUT. When this is called from a web browser as a CGI script, it has the same result as if *someimage.gif* had been included as the source file in the SRC attribute. The script is called from a single line of HTML:

```
<IMG SRC = "someimage.cgi">
```

Here is the code for the script:

```
#!/usr/local/bin/perl

# someimage.cgi
# A trivial script for passing an image to a web browser.
#
open INFILE, "someimage.gif";
undef $/;                          # Set the file input separator
binmode(STDIN);
my $input2 = <INFILE>;             # Now the whole file is in $input

print STDOUT "Content-Type: image/gif\r\n\r\n";
binmode(STDOUT);                   # For our Win32 friends
print STDOUT $input2;              # Write the image data to STDOUT
```

Let's say we want to check if the image file exists, and print an appropriate message if it does not. Adding the following to the above script doesn't work the way we want it to:

```
open INFILE, "someimage.gif" or die "Image not found";
```

This is because the browser is expecting some sort of MIME header, and gets the string "Image not found" if the file does not exist. We can get around this by doing the image inclusion as a Server Side Include (SSI), or using a "wrapper" script that generates the entire HTML page. The wrapper method is also useful when you want to generate a page that contains text and images generated based on data provided by the user (perhaps from a form). In the case of a page with mixed text and images, you would indicate the wrapper script in the ACTION attribute of the form tag, and the script would embed the call to the image generation script in an IMG tag, as in the following HTML page:

```
<HTML>
<HEAD>
<TITLE>Example start page</TITLE>
</HEAD>
<BODY>
<FORM METHOD=POST ACTION="wrapper.cgi">
Enter up to 20 characters, no spaces:
<INPUT TYPE=TEXT NAME="sometext">
<INPUT TYPE="submit" VALUE="Submit"><br>
</FORM>
</BODY>
</HTML>
```

The wrapper script could look something like this:

```
#!/usr/local/bin/perl

# wrapper.cgi
# Generate a response to a form submission.

use CGI;

# Get the parameter passed into the script

my $query = new CGI;

print $query->header(-type => 'text/html');

print <<EndHeadSection;
<HTML>
<HEAD>
<TITLE>An example of a wrapper script</TITLE>
</HEAD>
<BODY>
EndHeadSection

# Do some basic range checking

if ((length($text) > 20) || ($text =~ /\s/)) {
    print "<H2>20 chars max with no spaces, please...</H2>";
} else {
    # The makeimage.cgi script creates the GIF image
    print "<H2>Here's your text as a GIF:</H2>";
    print "<IMG SRC=\"makeimage.cgi?text=$text\">";
    print "<BR>";
}
```

```
# Note that the action string in the form tag refers to this very script

print <<EndBodySection;
<FORM METHOD=POST ACTION="wrapper.cgi">
Enter up to 20 characters, no spaces:
<INPUT TYPE=TEXT NAME="sometext">
<INPUT TYPE="submit" VALUE="Submit"><br>
</FORM>
</BODY>
</HTML>
EndBodySection
```

And the image generation script (using the GD Perl module described in Chapter 2) could look like:

```perl
#!/usr/local/bin/perl

# makeimage.cgi
# Generate an image given a string.

use strict;
use CGI;
use GD;

my $query = new CGI;

# Get the parameter and its length
my $text = $query->param('text');
my $length = length($text);

# Each character is 9 pixels wide and 15 pixels high
my $image = new GD::Image(9*$length,15);
$image->colorAllocate(0, 0, 0);        # allocate a black background
my $yellow=$image->colorAllocate(255, 255, 0);     # the text color

# Draw the string on the image
$image->string(gdGiantFont, 0, 0, $text, $yellow);

# Let the CGI module print the content-type header
print $query->header('image/gif');

# Write the image to STDOUT as a GIF
binmode(STDOUT);
print $image->gif();
```

This method can be awkward, and is one of the reasons that the Common Gateway Interface can be so clunky to use. It works, however, which is why CGI will remain useful for quite a while. With the advent of HTML 4.0 and the OBJECT tag, image data can be included directly within the HTML document as part of the object's DATA attribute. While this alleviates the need for wrapper scripts in many cases, it is generally not a good practice in this sort of application because the resulting pages will be visually unreadable.

The WIDTH and HEIGHT Attributes

The WIDTH and HEIGHT attributes may be added to an IMG tag to make the loading of web pages more efficient. When a web browser is loading and displaying a page, it must load all of the image files and extract information about their dimensions from the information encoded in the files. If the page contains complicated layout elements (such as tables), it may take quite a bit of time for a browser to load and compose an entire page. If the WIDTH and HEIGHT attributes are provided, however, the browser can compose the page as it loads, and fill in the images as they load. The attributes are simply included within the IMG tag (the order doesn't matter).

```
<IMG SRC="someimage.gif"  HEIGHT=200  WIDTH=300>
```

These attributes can also be used to scale an image by providing dimensions that are different from the actual dimensions of the image. To scale the image above to half its size, for example, use:

```
<IMG SRC="someimage.gif"  HEIGHT=100  WIDTH=150>
```

In general, it is not good practice to reduce the size of an image with the WIDTH and HEIGHT attributes; in this case, the entire 200×300 image is loaded over the network, and then it is scaled by the browser to 100×150. It is much better to create a smaller image in the first place to reduce the network load. Browsers can't necessarily be depended upon to do an adequate scaling job, either.

To create a horizontal line that is 4 pixels high and 150 pixels wide, start with an image that is a single pixel of color:

```
<IMG SRC="onepixel.gif"  HEIGHT=4  WIDTH=150>
```

You can also specify a scaling percentage, such as:

```
<IMG SRC="someimage.gif"  HEIGHT="50%"  WIDTH="50%">
```

where the percentages indicate a fraction of the *current browser window's* width and height. This method will almost certainly distort the original image, so be sure to test it under different circumstances before using it.

Many HTML authoring applications provide options for automatically assigning the WIDTH and HEIGHT tags while the page is created. For those of you who like to use a plain-old text editor or when updating legacy HTML documents, the following script may be useful. With the HTML module (from CPAN), it parses an HTML document, determines the dimensions of each of the local images referenced by the document, and changes the IMG tag's WIDTH and HEIGHT attributes to reflect the actual dimensions of each image. Note that the script does not check to see if these attributes have already been set; previously defined values for these parameters are replaced by the actual dimensions of the image.

```
#!/usr/local/bin/perl -w

# AddImgInfo.pl
```

```
# This script tries to add width and height information to the
# img tags in the document given as a parameter on the command line.
# It outputs the modified web page to a file called modified.filename.

use HTML::TreeBuilder;
use Image::Magick;
use strict;

my $filename = $ARGV[0];
my $p = HTML::TreeBuilder->new;

if ($filename) {
    my $html = $p->parse_file($filename);
    open OUTFILE, ">modified.$filename";
    $html->traverse(\&analyzeHtml);
    close OUTFILE;
} else {
    print "You must specify a filename.\n";
}

# This routine defines our callback action.
#
sub analyzeHtml {
    my ($node, $startbool, $depth) = @_;

    if (ref $node) {
        # In this case, the node is some sort of markup tag; use the startbool
        # flag to determine if it is a start tag or end tag
        #
        if ($startbool) {
            if ($node->tag eq 'img') {
                # In this case we have an image tag on our hands.
                # Use the Ping() method to find the information
                # and add it to the end of the attribute string...
                #
                my $info = Image::Magick->Ping($node->attr('src'));
                if ($info) {
                # Ping() returns the info as a comma-delimited string
                    #
                    my ($width, $height, $filesize, $format) = split /,/, $info;
                    $node->attr('width', $width);
                    $node->attr('height', $height);
                }
            }
            print OUTFILE $node->starttag;
        } else {
            print OUTFILE $node->endtag;
        }
    } else {
        # In this case the node is just text; print it as is.
        #
        print OUTFILE $node;
    }
```

```
      print OUTFILE "\n";        # add a new line
      return 1;                  # continue analyzing the children of this node
   }
```

These scripts use the Ping( ) method of the Image::Magick module, which is described in Chapter 3. The Ping( ) method returns information about an image's file type and geometry without decoding the entire file. Another way to find information about the dimensions of an image is with the Image::Size module, which also recognizes many file formats.

```
use Image::Size;
my $filename = "someimage.png";

# Use the imgsize method to find the dimensions of the image
my ($x, $y) = imgsize($filename);

# The html_imgsize returns the geometry as a string
# ready to be included in an HTML tag...
# Returns the string 'HEIGHT=y WIDTH=x'

my $size = html_imgsize($filename);
```

Layout and Spacing Attributes

The HTML 3.2 specification defined four tags that allowed you to control the space around an image and how the image is aligned with other elements on the page. These were the ALIGN, BORDER, HSPACE, and VSPACE tags. The HTML 4.0 specification brings with it a paradigm shift in the way HTML authors look at the visual presentation and layout of web pages. All four tags are deprecated in the official 4.0 spec in favor of style sheets. However, it will take a while for programs implementing the 3.2 specification to be completely subsumed by HTML 4.0, so this chapter includes a discussion of using these tags and leaves the explanation of style sheets to other books.

The ALIGN attribute tag specifies how the image should be positioned on the page with respect to the elements around it. The default value for the ALIGN tag is bottom. Both Netscape and Microsoft have created their own proprietary extensions to the ALIGN tag, which we will not go into here. The HTML 3.2 specification defines the following alignment options (shown in Figure A-1):

bottom
    This indicates that the bottom of the image should be aligned with the baseline of the text or objects surrounding it.

middle
    This indicates that the vertical center of the image should be aligned with the baseline of the text or objects immediately before it. Note that Netscape and Internet Explorer implement this differently; Netscape aligns the image with the text's baseline, and IE aligns the image to the absolute middle of the line of text.

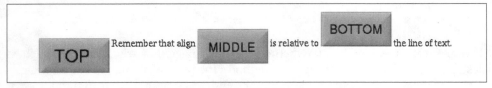

Figure A-1. The top, middle, and bottom alignment options

`top`

> This indicates that the top of the image should be aligned with the baseline of the text or objects surrounding it.

`left`

> This indicates that the image should be pushed to the left margin of the current text flow, and any text or other objects should wrap around it. This is useful for effects such as starting a paragraph with a drop cap, as in Figure A-2.

Figure A-2. The left and right alignment options

`right`

This indicates that the browser should push the image to the right margin of the current text flow and wrap any text or other objects around its left side. This can be used to quickly create layouts that have a newspaper feel, as in Figure A-2.

The BORDER attribute allows you to set the width, in pixels, of the space around the image. If the image is within a link element, the border is whatever color the browser has defined as a link color. In many of the more artsy sites, having square, clunky, colored borders around the images would ruin the design of the page. If, for example, you are designing a page with several interlocking transparent images that act as hyperlinks, you can turn off the image borders by assigning 0 to BORDER. Keep in mind, though, that users often use colored borders as visual clues as to what is a link and what is not, so be sure to provide some indication of whether an image is a link if you remove its border (and by this I don't mean JavaScript mouseovers saying CLICK ME!).

The ALT Attribute

You might be surprised by how many people use text-only web browsers. In addition to being useful, low-overhead tools in the command-line world (for browsing the Web via a Telnet session, for example) and their widespread use on Free-nets and BBSes, text-based browsers have a user base that should not be ignored. There is nothing in the HTML specifications saying that the World Wide Web must be a graphically oriented place. In fact, it's just the opposite—the HTML 4.0 specification distributed by the World Wide Web Consortium *requires* that the ALT tag be used to provide alternate representations for those users in the text-based world. Quoting from the specification:

> Several non-textual elements (IMG, AREA, APPLET, and INPUT) require authors to specify alternate text to serve as content when the element cannot be rendered normally. Specifying alternate text assists users without graphic display terminals, users whose browsers don't support forms, visually impaired users, those who use speech synthesizers, those who have configured their graphical user agents not to display images, etc.
>
> The alt attribute must be specified for the IMG and AREA elements. It is optional for the INPUT and APPLET elements.

Generally, the ALT tag should be used only to provide *useful* information. In other words, if you have a bunch of little red balls acting as bullets, it is not adding any useful information to place "little red ball" in the ALT field. In some circumstances, however, you may want certain images to be displayed on both graphics-capable and text-only browsers. The graphical browser could simply display the image, and the text browser could use an alternative representation rendered as ASCII art.

ASCII art is an esoteric pastime on Usenet and the Web; it is the art of arranging characters in the ASCII character set to simulate the shades and nuances of the pixels of an image. Of course, not all images can be rendered successfully as ASCII art; photographs in particular are difficult to identify in ASCII art form unless they are sufficiently large. Some images translate surprisingly well, however, particularly very graphic images like logos or other graphic elements. Figure A-3 is an example of a web page that uses ASCII art.

Figure A-3. ASCII art can replace traditional image formats (kind of)

When the ALT tag is used by a text-only browser, the ALT text is plopped into the document in place of the image. However, you cannot embed HTML within the ALT text string. Thus, the following HTML tag:

```
<IMG SRC="gum.gif" ALT="
AAAAAAAAAAAA
BBBBBBBBBBBB
CCCCCCCCCCCC
DDDDDDDDDDDD
">
```

would, if you viewed it from a text-only browser, produce the output:

```
AAAAAAAAAAAA BBBBBBBBBBBB CCCCCCCCCCCC DDDDDDDDDDDD
```

And if you attempted to add an HTML linefeed with <BR> elements to the end of each line within the ALT text string, you would get:

```
AAAAAAAAAAAA<BR> BBBBBBBBBBBB<BR> CCCCCCCCCCCC<BR> DDDDDDDDDDDD<BR>
```

The solution is to wrap the image element up in a <PRE> tag, which maintains the exact formatting of the ALT text, and render it in a fixed-width font (which, if you're using a text-only browser, is the standard font anyway). The HTML code:

```
<PRE>
<IMG SRC="gum.gif" ALT="
AAAAAAAAAAAA
BBBBBBBBBBBB
CCCCCCCCCCCC
DDDDDDDDDDDD
">
</PRE>
```

renders the desired output of:

```
AAAAAAAAAAAA
BBBBBBBBBBBB
CCCCCCCCCCCC
DDDDDDDDDDDD
```

The Gimp has a plug-in that uses the AA-Lib ASCII art library to save an image as an ASCII approximation. To use the plug-in, the image must be in grayscale mode and you must select Save As from the File menu. Save the image with the extension *.ansi*, or choose AA (ASCII art) from the Save Options list in the Save dialog. The AA save file plug-in provides you with many options (see Figure A-4):

Text file

This option causes the image to be broken down into 2×2 blocks of pixels. Each block is represented by the ASCII character that most closely matches its luminance. This results in a text file where each line has half as many characters as the image's width in pixels. The same is true for the number of lines in the file. Thus, a 300×200 pixel image is translated into a text file of 100 lines, with each line containing 150 characters.

Pure html

This performs the same operation as the Text file option, but it also includes HTML code before and after the image text (the HTML, BODY, and PRE tags). Note that this option is intended for ASCII art that is to be used directly within the body of an HTML document, not necessarily within an ALT tag.

Netscapeized html

This option does the same as Pure html, but it attempts to render the image more accurately by setting the COLOR attribute of the FONT tag to various grayscale levels to add depth to the rendition.

HTML <IMG ALT= tag

This option automatically wraps up the ASCII art object in an IMG element with an ALT tag and PRE tags.

Other options

The plug-in provides several other options that are optimized for particular applications. For example, you can create an ASCII art object that is meant to be viewed with a pager such as *more* or *less*; you can also customize ASCII art to be printed as ANSI escape sequences (suitable for startup screens), to be printed on a laser printer, to be sent to an IRC channel, or to be included in a manpage.

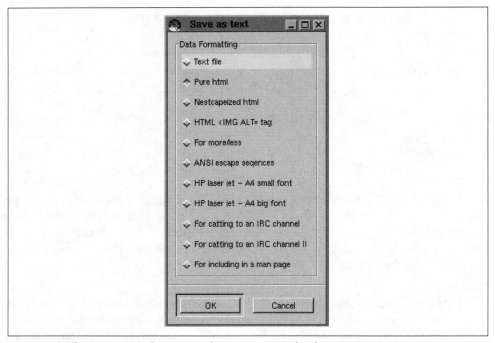

Figure A-4. The Gimp's AA plug-in provides many options for the aspiring ASCII artist

The resulting ASCII image is always larger than the source image. The actual "resolution" of the resulting image depends on the font that is used by the display client to render the text. There is really no means to control the way that the image is finally viewed (ASCII art is a particularly inexact art), but there are a few rules of thumb to follow:

- The AA plug-in subsamples the source image into 2×2 blocks of pixels. A standard terminal window (which most viewers using a text-only browser use) is 80 characters wide. Thus, your starting image should be no more than 160 pixels wide (actually 159 pixels due to rounding errors) if you want the final image to stay within the confines of the average user's screen. The typical depth of a standard default terminal window is 25 lines or so.

- Using a font that is anything other than square results in an ASCII art image being displayed malproportioned (see Figure A-5). In reality, there are few square fonts, though most text-only displays use fixed-width fonts. A typical fixed-width font has a width of 6 pixels and a height of 12 pixels. Thus, the height is twice the width, which maybe accounted for by scaling the source image by 50% before saving as ASCII art to correct the aspect ratio.

Figure A-5. The aspect ratio of an ASCII art image usually has to be adjusted

- You will also have problems with the ASCII art image being larger than the source image. Because each ASCII character represents a 2×2 block, and each ASCII character is (for a 6×12 font) 6 screen pixels wide, the ASCII image is rendered 3 times larger than the source image. (Of course, if different font sizes are used, this ratio is different.) For the 6×12 font, you can get an ASCII image that is almost exactly the same size as the source image by resizing the image to 33% its size before saving. However, this may not be sufficient resolution to achieve legible output, so be sure to experiment.

- The AA plug-in translates the *inverse* of the image, so the ASCII art image must be viewed as white text on a black background in order to give an accurate representation. To reverse this effect, simply invert the image before saving it.

These rules of thumb, along with the Gimp's AA plug-in, should get you on the road to becoming a true ASCII artist.

Background Images

Most HTML authoring books warn against the gratuitous use of fancy background patterns for web pages. The general consensus is that a textured marble background does not add any *content* to a document, and can, for some users, render actual content unreadable. It seems that most web authors are aware of this problem, and the novelty of psychedelic swirling background patterns has given way to a more clever design sense that takes the user into account.

Animated image formats (such as GIF89a) may also be used as background images. This is not necessarily a Good Thing, simply because it is a feature that can be easily abused.

The OBJECT Tag

Starting with HTML 2.0, the architects of the HTML specifications realized the need for a more robust means to insert media into documents. The IMG tag used to be the only official way to insert inline images; Netscape extended the language with the EMBED tag, Microsoft introduced the DYNSRC attribute for inline AVI movies, and Sun brought the APPLET tag for including code within a document. None of these decisively addresses the need for including generic inline media, possibly in several alternate formats. The OBJECT tag is meant to serve this purpose. It can also be used as an alternative to the IMG tag.

The OBJECT tag can be used in conjunction with an IMG tag to provide backward compatibility, or if the user agent does not have the capability to render the data type, as in:

```
<OBJECT data="MonkeyMovie.avi" type="application/avi">
    <IMG SRC="MonkeyStill.png" ALT="Monkeys sitting around.">
</OBJECT>
```

Most importantly, the OBJECT tag has replaced the APPLET tag, which is deprecated in HTML 4.0. The primary use of the OBJECT tag is for implementing complex media objects that cannot be instantiated only on the server side. For just representing inline images, it is still perfectly acceptable to use the plain old IMG tag.

References

- *The Official Guide to Programming with CGI.pm*, by Lincoln D. Stein. John Wiley & Sons, 1998.

- Online CGI.pm documentation: *http://www.genome.wi.mit.edu/ftp/pub/software/ WWW/*

- The Perl-Apache Integration Project: *http://perl.apache.org*

- *HTML & XHTML: The Definitive Guide*, by Chuck Musciano and Bill Kennedy. O'Reilly & Associates, 2002.

Gimp Reference

The first section in this appendix is a reference for the register( ) method of the Gimp::Fu module described in Chapter 5. It provides more detail on the parameters and data types used when registering Gimp plug-ins in the Procedural Database (PDB). The bulk of the appendix is a quick guide to the Gimp's user interface. The discussion in Chapter 5 assumes that the reader has some familiarity with this interface.

The Gimp::Fu register( ) Method

The register( ) method takes a list of 12 parameters:

name
> The name of this script, as it is to appear in the PDB. This name can be used by other plug-ins to call this script. If the name of the script does not begin with "perl_fu_", "plug_in", "extension_", or "file_", then "perl_fu_" is prepended to the provided name. To circumvent this behavior, prepend a single plus sign (+) to the name.

blurb
> A short description of the script. This blurb appears in the user input window generated by Gimp::Fu. It is best to format all of your documentation in Perl's POD format. The blurb argument defaults to =pod(NAME).

help
> A longer description of the script. This blurb appears when the help button is selected within the user input window generated by Gimp::Fu. The help argument defaults to =pod(HELP).

author
> Your name and some sort of contact information. The author argument defaults to =pod(AUTHOR).

copyright

The name of the script's copyright holder. The copyright argument defaults to =pod(AUTHOR).

date

The last modified date, e.g., "2003-8-16". The date argument defaults to =pod(DATE).

menu_path

A string describing the location of the script in the Gimp's menu hierarchy, e.g., "<Image>/Filters/Misc/Foo Filter". The string should begin with "<Image>" for the image menu structure, "<Toolbox>" for the toolbox menu structure, "<Save>" or "<Load>" if the script is a file format writer/reader, or "<None>" if the script should not have a menu entry.

image_types

A string listing the types of images accepted by this script, e.g., "*", "RGB*", "GRAY, RGB". If the script appears in the toolbox (i.e., if it does not operate on an existing image), use an empty string ("").

[parameters]

A reference to an array of parameter descriptions. Each parameter description entry is another anonymous array with five elements: [*type*, *name*, *description*, *default_value*, *extra_args*].

The *type* element is one of the types listed below. The name for each parameter should be all lowercase letters, and should use underscores instead of spaces. The *default_value* is the initial value for the parameter. The *extra_args* can be a list of extra arguments for parameter types that require additional values such as PF_SLIDER or PF_SPINNER.

Some valid parameter list elements are:

```
[ [ PF_COLOR, "Color", "Text color", [255, 0, 0] ],
  [ PF_TOGGLE, "Copy?", "Work on a copy?", 1 ],
  [ PF_DRAWABLE, "Drawable", "The drawable" ],
  [ PF_STRING, "Text", "Some text", "HamHam" ],
  [ PF_SPINNER, "Angle", "Rotate angle", 45, [0, 360, 5] ],
  [ PF_SLIDER, "Compression", "Compression Level", 7,  [0, 9, 1] ]
]
```

[ret_values]

A reference to an array describing the values returned by the script, if any. Each parameter description entry is another anonymous array with three elements: [*type*, *name*, *description*]. Note that a script should return an image only if it creates a new image (or a list of images if more than one is created). If a script merely changes the input image, it should return undef, and the ret_values array should be empty [ ].

[features]
> This argument allows you to optionally specify a list of feature requirements that Gimp::Fu should check for when the script is invoked. See the Gimp::Features manpage for more info.

\&code
> This argument is either a subroutine reference or an anonymous subroutine that performs the work of the plug-in.

The parameter types are as follows:

PF_INT8, PF_INT16, PF_INT32, PF_INT, PF_FLOAT, PF_STRING, PF_VALUE
> All of these parameter types are represented as strings in Perl.

PF_COLOR, PF_COLOUR
> A color parameter is represented as an anonymous array containing three elements, one for each of the red, green, and blue channels. For example, red is [255, 0, 0] and "peach puff" is [255, 218, 185].

> In the user input dialog, a color preview button is created that opens the GTK color picker when clicked.

PF_IMAGE
> A Gimp image, which is actually a numeric image ID.

PF_DRAWABLE
> A Gimp image, which is actually a numeric image, channel, or layer ID.

PF_TOGGLE, PF_BOOL
> A Boolean value. The parameter is represented in the user input dialog as a toggle button, with the description of the parameter used as the button label.

PF_SLIDER
> This parameter type is used to pass an integer or floating-point number as a parameter, to be selected by the user via a horizontal sliding scale. This parameter type requires you to specify a number of attributes for the sliding scale, which should be set using the extra_args element of the parameter description. The attributes of the slider are:

range_min
> The minimum value for the range.

range_max
> The maximum value for the range.

step_size
> The amount of space between each discrete value over the range of the slider. This is the amount added to or subtracted from the current value when the slider is moved to the left or the right.

page_increment

This provides for a coarser manipulation of the slider. The page_increment is the amount that the current value should be incremented or decremented with each mouse click within the slider.

page_size

This argument controls the visible portion of the slider. It is mainly used for operations such as panning across a larger area when only a portion of the total range should be visible. Since this argument is optional, it is best to leave this option out if you do not need it.

An example of the slider in use:

```
[ PF_SLIDER,                 # parameter type
  "randomness",              # parameter name
  "degree of randomness",    # description
  100,                       # default value
  [0, 100, 1, 10] ]          # extra arguments
```

Note that default values are used if any of the extra arguments are not specified.

PF_SPINNER

The spinner operates the same as PF_SLIDER, but it is represented onscreen as a "spin button" instead of a slider adjustment.

PF_RADIO

This parameter type results in the creation of a radio button group from which the value may be selected. A radio button group is a collection of buttons, only one of which may be selected.

The radio type takes a default value and a list of option/value pairs. For example:

```
[ PF_RADIO,                  # parameter type
  "randomness",              # parameter name
  "degree of randomness",    # description
  75,                        # default value
  [ None => 0,
    Some => 25,
    Half => 50,
    "A Lot" => 75,
    Total => 100 ] ]         # extra arguments
```

This example creates a radio button group with five buttons in it, labeled "None", "Some", "Half", "A Lot", and "Total". The value associated with the particular button is used as the parameter value.

PF_FONT

This parameter type should be used if you need the user to select a font. The Gimp::Fu user input dialog provides you with a button that brings up a font selection dialog when clicked. The default value should be in the 13-field XLFD (X Logical Font Descriptor) format.

PF_BRUSH, PF_PATTERN, PF_GRADIENT

If one of these types is provided as a parameter, it is passed in as a string containing the name of the brush, pattern, or gradient.

PF_CUSTOM

This parameter type is provided for developers who wish to use a Gtk widget not listed above to obtain the initial parameters from the user. See the Gimp-Perl documentation for its use.

PF_FILE

This parameter type is used to obtain a filename. A text entry field is provided, along with a "Browse" button that brings up a file selection dialog box.

PF_TEXT

This parameter type allows for the entry of a text string, but provides a larger form element and "Load" and "Save" buttons that allow you to load text from a previously created file.

The Gimp Interface

The following sections describe each group of functions in brief, and provide information such as command key combinations for the various tools where appropriate. The Gimp interface is broken down as follows:

The Gimp toolbox

This section describes the tools available in the floating toolbox (and from the <Image> → Tools menu).

The toolbox menu hierarchy

This section describes the menus accessible via the toolbox and the functions associated with them.

The image menu hierarchy

This section describes the menus associated with an image window. This menu group is accessed by clicking the right mouse button within the image window.

The Toolbox

Figure B-1 shows the Gimp's toolbox. Each tool has a Tool Options dialog box associated with it that may be accessed by double-clicking on the tool's icon. These options vary from tool to tool; generally they provide access to parameters, and may put the tool in different modes that affect its behavior.

The selection tools

All of the selection tools operate in a similar manner. To start drawing a selection, hold down the left mouse button and drag the mouse to define the selection area. To

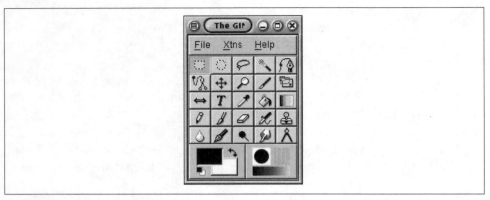

Figure B-1. The Gimp toolbox

cancel a selection while drawing it, hold down the right mouse button while drawing and release the left button. To add to the existing selection, hold down the Shift key before drawing the selection. To subtract from the current selection, hold down the Control key before drawing the selection.

To create a selection area that is the union of two selections, hold down the Shift and Control keys before drawing the second selection. To constrain the selection image (for a perfect square or circle, for example), hold down the Shift key while drawing the selection. To draw an area that is centered on the initial click point, hold down the Control key while drawing the selection.

Once an area is selected, it may be moved by holding down the Alt key, clicking on the selection area with the left mouse button, and dragging it to the desired position.

The Tool Options dialog for each selection tool allows you to specify whether you want to "feather" the selection area, which will result in a smoother selection.

The first six tools in the toolbox are the selection tools:

The rectangular selection tool
> Allows you to select a rectangular region.

The elliptical selection tool
> Allows you to select an elliptical region.

The hand-drawn selection tool
> Allows you to draw an arbitrary region. The tool will automatically connect the first point and the last point on the path when you release the mouse.

The magic wand tool
> Selects a region based on all of the contiguous pixels of the same color as the pixel that was clicked. The Tool Options dialog box offers a Sample Merged option that, if on, will cause the magic wand to operate on all visible layers. If Sample Merged is off, the selection is made only on the current layer.

Bezier selection tool

Allows you to define a selection area with curves or lines using a Bezier drawing tool similar to those found in most drafting programs. You can adjust the curves of the selection after it has been drawn by moving the handles associated with each point on the curve.

The intelligent scissors tool

This is similar to the hand-drawn selection tool, but it is easier to use in that it will attempt to guess the outlines of the region that you are attempting to select. This selection region is then converted to a Bezier selection region, which may be further tweaked to get it just right.

The move tool

The move tool will move a layer or a selection, depending on which keys are held down when the tool is used:

No keys

The tool will move the current layer when the mouse is clicked and dragged.

Shift + Up, Down, Left, or Right cursor keys

The tool will move the current layer in the direction specified by the cursor key by 25 pixels.

Control + Up, Down, Left, or Right cursor keys

The tool will move the current layer in the direction specified by the cursor key by 1 pixel. Useful for minute adjustments.

Alt + Up, Down, Left, or Right cursor keys

The tool will move the current selection in the direction specified by the cursor key by 1 pixel.

Alt + Shift + Up, Down, Left, or Right cursor keys

The tool will move the current selection in the direction specified by the cursor key by 25 pixels.

The magnifying glass tool

Clicking on a coordinate with the magnifying glass will increase the magnification of the current view and center the window on the clicked point. The Tool Options dialog provides options that will resize the window to fit the image.

The crop tool

The crop tool allows you to select part of an image and discard the rest.

The transform tool

The transform tool can be in one of four tool modes: Rotation, Scaling, Shearing, and Perspective. The tool mode is set via the transform tool's Tool Options dialog box.

Rotation mode
> The transform tool will act as a free rotation tool on the current selection. Hold down the Control key to constrain the rotation angle to 15 degree increments.

Scaling mode
> The transform tool will scale (enlarge or shrink) the current selection. Hold down the Control key to constrain scaling to the y dimension, or the Shift key to constrain to the x dimension. Holding down both the Shift and Control keys will make the scaling proportional.

Shearing mode
> The transform tool will "shear" the image, i.e., shift all the pixels in a plane.

Perspective mode
> The transform tool will allow you to shift the pixels of the image to get a perspective effect.

The flip tool

Use the Tool Options dialog to determine whether the flip tool will reflect the image on the horizontal or vertical axis.

The text tool

This tool allows you to place text on the image, with the upper left corner of the text box at the clicked point. Once the text is placed on the image, it ceases to be editable text and becomes an image of text. The text dialog box allows you to specify a font and the vertical size of the text in pixels. The color of the text will be the current selected color.

The color picker

The color picker tool sets the current selected color to the color of the clicked pixel. It also brings up a dialog with the values for the red, green, blue, and alpha channels of the color.

The bucket fill tool

The bucket fill tool behaves differently depending on whether there is a current active selection. If there is an active selection, the bucket tool will fill the selection with the foreground color. If there is not an active selection, it will fill the contiguous area around the clicked pixel with the foreground color. If the Shift key is held down in either case, the background color is used for the fill.

The Tool Options dialog for the bucket tool has a number of options of note:

Fill Opacity

Allows you to specify a percentage value for the opacity of the fill.

Fill Threshold

A range of values used to determine whether a pixel is part of the area to be filled. A pixel is part of the area if it is within this many values of the clicked pixel.

Mode

Allows you to choose a paint mode.

Fill Type

If this option is set to Color Fill, the tool will use the foreground or background color to fill. If it is set to Pattern Fill, it will use the current active pattern to fill.

Sample Merged

If this option is selected, the area to be filled will be determined using the merged image of all the visible layers. Otherwise it will perform on the current layer (the default setting).

The blend tool

The blend tool, also called the gradient tool, allows you to fill an area with a gradient. The start and end points of the gradient are determined by mouse movements; click on the starting point and drag the mouse to the end point. The Tool Options dialog provides the following gradient controls of note:

Opacity

A percentage value specifying the overall transparency of the gradient.

Offset

A percentage value indicating the point at which to start the gradient. A value of 20, for example, would start the gradient a fifth of the way through.

Mode

The paint mode to be used to apply the gradient.

Blend

Allows you to specify whether the colors in the gradient should run from the foreground to the background color or vice versa, from 100% opaque foreground color to 100% transparent foreground color, or to apply a custom gradient provided by the Gradient Editor.

Gradient

Allows you to choose from one of nine gradient types: Linear, Bi-linear, Radial, Square, Conical (Symmetric or Asymmetric), or Shapeburst (Angular, Spherical, or Dimpled).

Repeat

Allows you to specify whether the gradient should repeat if it does not fill the entire area.

The pencil tool

The pencil tool draws pixels in the current selected color with the current selected brush. Unlike the paintbrush tool, the pencil draws in a single solid color. If you draw fast with the pencil tool, you may find that the Gimp has trouble keeping up with the cursor and will hedge the line a bit by simplifying the pencil line and making it more choppy. You can avoid this behavior by holding down the Alt key while you draw, which stores the cursor events in a buffer that will let the Gimp catch up without losing information. To draw a straight line between two points, hold down the Shift key when drawing.

The paintbrush tool

The paintbrush is similar to the pencil tool, except it draws in the currently selected brush using all the colors of the brush. You can use the Alt and Shift keys with the paintbrush as you would with the pencil tool. In addition, the Tool Options dialog offers a Fade Out option that specifies the distance in pixels you can paint before the paint "runs out," and you must release the mouse and click again to start a new brushstroke. The default value for Fade Out is 0, which indicates that the brush has an infinite supply of paint.

The eraser tool

The eraser tool behaves differently on images with an alpha channel. If the image does not have an alpha channel, the eraser will draw the background color with the currently selected brush. If the image has an alpha channel, the eraser will draw in a transparent color with the current brush. The Alt and Shift keys operate the same as for the pencil tool.

The airbrush tool

The airbrush tool paints using the current brush like the paintbrush tool, but the paint is applied gradually in a semi-transparent spray. The Rate and Pressure tool options let you control how quickly the paint flows and how quickly the transparency of the spray decreases. The Alt and Shift keys operate the same as for the pencil tool.

The clone tool

The clone tool allows you to paint using the current brush filled in with the currently selected pattern or with a region of pixels within the same image. The clone tool's icon is a stamp and stamp pad.

The convolver tool

The convolver tool is similar to the Smudge tool in Adobe Photoshop; it allows you to soften sharp edges in an image. The Tool Options dialog allows you to control the pressure (intensity) of the action, and whether the area under the cursor should be blurred or sharpened.

The ink tool

The line drawn by the ink tool varies in thickness with the speed of the tool. The ink tool was specially designed for use with drawing tablets.

The dodge and burn tool

In traditional photography, overexposing selected parts of a photograph is called burning, and underexposing areas is called dodging. Burning will lighten an area touched by the tool, and dodging will darken the area.

The smudge tool

The smudge tool picks up some of the color under the tool and simulates the smudging of wet paint.

The measure tool

The measure tool can be used to measure the distance between two points on the canvas. The Shift key can be used to add additional points to the line.

The Toolbox Menu Hierarchy

The toolbox menus are available at the top of the floating toolbox. A few of the options have equivalent menus associated with the image window, such as New or Open from the File menu. The commands accessible from these menus generally create new images or perform administrative functions such as setting user preferences or starting services. Typically these menus are referred to by the notation <Toolbox> → menu → submenu.

The file menu

New
> Starts a new image. This dialog allows you to specify a new width and height and the initial background color.

Open
> Opens an existing image.

Acquire

These options allow you to acquire a source image from a screenshot, a scanner, or some other external device. The screenshot snaps an image of a single window or the whole screen, and it returns a new Gimp image with the screenshot. The "include decorations" option controls whether window trimmings (such as window names and close boxes) are to be included in the screenshot.

Preferences

Provides a dialog box that gives access to the user's preferences for the display, user interface, memory usage, and default colormap settings, as well as the paths to Gimp resources such as plug-ins, palettes, and gradients (see Figure B-2). This information is stored in the *.gimprc* file in the *.gimp* subdirectory of the user's home directory.

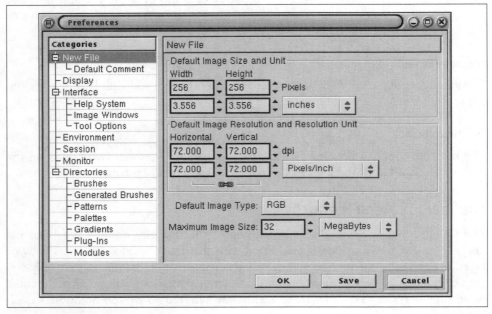

Figure B-2. The Preferences dialog

Dialogs

Provides access to the Gimp's dialog boxes:

Layers, Channels, Paths

A dialog with three tabs that acts as an index to the layers, channels, and paths in the image (see Figure B-3).

Tool Options

Brings up a window that is used to control the preferences for the currently selected tool (see Figure B-4).

Figure B-3. The Layers, Channels, and Paths dialog

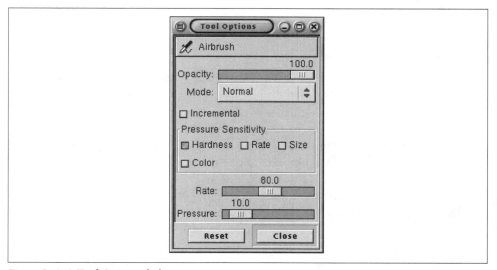

Figure B-4. A Tool Options dialog

Brushes

Selects a brush from the brush collection, or sets the paint mode, opacity, and spacing of a brush.

Patterns

Selects a pattern from the pattern collection to be used by the fill tools or other tools that use patterns.

Palettes

Selects a palette from the palette collection, or creates a new palette.

Gradient Editor

Selects a built-in custom gradient, or creates a new custom gradient for use by the blend tool.

Input Devices

The Gimp supports input devices such as graphics tablets. This menu allows you to select from a list of available devices.

Device Status

Each input device can be assigned different settings for the selected tool, foreground color, brush, pattern, and gradient.

Document Index

Provides a history of all documents previously opened with the Gimp.

Recent Documents

Provides a handy list of the most recently opened documents.

Quit

Quits the Gimp.

The Xtns menu

Module Browser

Displays a list of all the installed modules, which are reusable interface features such as the Color Selection dialog.

PDB Browser

Opens a window that contains information culled from the Gimp's internal Procedural Database (see Figure B-5). It is a very handy tool for writing plug-ins and scripts, or even just gleaning hints about the usage of some obscure function. Each of the Gimp's internal functions, as well as plug-ins, scripts, and extensions, are all listed in the browser. You may pull out groups of functions with the Search by Name and Search by Blurb buttons.

Parasite Editor

A parasite is a Gimp internal data structure that allows a plug-in to save its state between invocations. The Parasite Editor lets you access and set the values of various parasites (see Figure B-6).

PDB Explorer

An alternative to the PDB Browser.

Plug-in Details

Provides a flat list of all of the installed plug-ins.

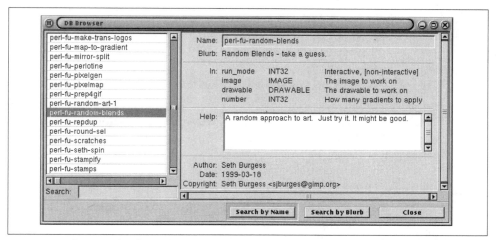

Figure B-5. The Procedural Database Browser

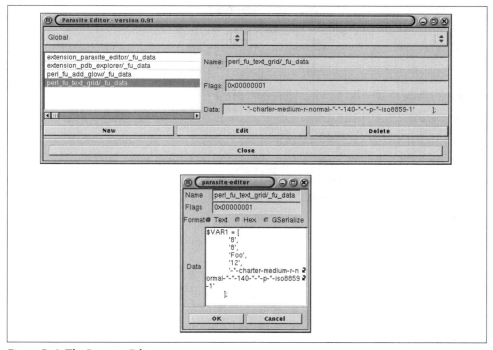

Figure B-6. The Parasite Editor

Unit Editor

The Gimp's *.unitrc* file contains definitions for all of the available unit settings (point, pixels, inches, etc.). This option allows you to add units to this file.

Animation

    Animation Optimize

        This plug-in applies various optimizations to a Gimp layer-based animation.

    Animation Playback

        This plug-in allows you to preview a Gimp layer-based animation.

    Animation UnOptimize

        This plug-in "reconstructs" a Gimp layer-based animation that has been optimized with Animation Optimize. This can make the animation much easier to work with.

Perl

    Provides access to the Perl control center and the Perl server (see Figure B-7). The control center is a dialog that lists all Perl plug-in error messages. The Perl server allows you to run standalone scripts that communicate with the Gimp (see Chapter 5 for more about standalone scripts).

Figure B-7. The Perl control center

Render

    This menu is home to scripts that render special effects or generate graphics from data (such as buttons for web pages).

Script-Fu

    Console

        Provides a command-line interface to the SIOD (Scheme In One Day) Scheme interpreter on which Script-Fu is built. You can type a Scheme instruction on the "Current Command" line, and the interpreter will execute it. Try (+ 2 2) and see what you get.

    Server

        Allows you to select a port for the Gimp to communicate with Script-Fu scripts, and to specify an optional log file that will capture errors and messages generated by scripts. The default Script-Fu port is 10008.

    Refresh

        Allows you to add scripts to the Gimp while it is running. The refresh option will reread the list of available scripts and register new entries.

Web Browser

Contains bookmarks to online Gimp documentation resources such as the FAQs, Gimp News, the plug-in registry, the manual, tutorials, and the bug report page. The Open URL option allows you to type in a specific URL with which the Gimp will launch an external web browser such as Netscape.

Help

Provides access to the Gimp's built-in help dialogs. The About menu brings up a dialog box with a scrolling message bar featuring the names of all the Gimp developers. The Tip of the Day item brings up a dialog box with an often helpful tip of the day. This box also pops up when the Gimp is first started.

The Image Menu Hierarchy

These menus are available by clicking the right mouse button within an image window. In general, the commands accessible via these menus operate on the image (or on a layer of the image, or on a selection area) from which they were called. These menus are typically referred to by the notation <Image> → menu → submenu.

The File menu

New

Starts a new image. The dialog allows you to specify a new width and height and the initial background color. This is functionally equivalent to the New option under the Toolbox → File menu.

Open

Opens an existing image. This is functionally equivalent to the Open option under the Toolbox → File menu.

Save

Saves the current image.

Save As

Saves the current image and specifies a filename and format. Some image formats require a certain type of image (to save as a GIF, for example, the image must be in Indexed mode). Only the formats applicable to the current image will be shown in the file type selector of the Save As dialog. If the "By extension" option (the default) is selected, the Gimp will attempt to guess the file format based on the filename extension provided (e.g., given the name *quahog.png*, it will try to save as a PNG file).

Recent Documents

Equivalent to the Recent Documents option under the Toolbox → File menu.

Mail Image

A somewhat gratuitous (but actually kind of nice) feature, the Mail Image option will mail the current image (either Uuencoded or as a multipart MIME message) to a specific email address.

Print

Prints the image to a PostScript file or printer.

Close

Closes the image.

Quit

Quits the Gimp.

The Edit menu

Undo

Undoes the last action. Note that most actions and commands are undoable, even those that you wouldn't necessarily expect (such as moving guidelines). The number of levels of Undo may be set in the Preferences dialog box (the default is 5 levels).

Redo

Performs the opposite of an Undo (i.e., redoes the action that was last undone). Note that this must be done immediately after an Undo for it to have an effect.

Cut

Removes the selection from the image and places it in the paste buffer, from which it may be retrieved with the paste command. Note that anything currently in the paste buffer will be lost. If a selection is cut from a layer with an alpha channel, the selected area will be replaced with 100% transparent pixels. If the layer does not have an alpha channel, the selected area will be replaced with the current background color.

Copy

Places a copy of the selected pixels in the paste buffer. Anything previously in the paste buffer will be lost.

Paste

Places a copy of whatever is in the paste buffer (from a previous cut or copy) on the image.

Paste Into

Places a copy of whatever is in the paste buffer on the image. Paste Into will also position the pasted image within the current selection area and crop the pasted image to the selection.

Paste as New

Creates a new image from the paste buffer.

Buffer

> *Cut Named*
>
> > Performs the same action as Cut, but allows the user to associate a name tag with the paste buffer. This allows you to maintain many offscreen paste buffers from which to pull image pixels with Paste Named.
>
> *Copy Named*
>
> > Performs the same action as Copy, but allows the user to associate a name tag with the paste buffer.
>
> *Paste Named*
>
> > Performs the same action as Paste, but allows the user to choose the paste buffer from which to paste. Only selections cut or copied with Cut Named or Copy Named will show up in this list.

Clear

> Removes the selected area from the image. If a selection is cleared from a layer with an alpha channel, the selected area will be replaced with 100% transparent pixels. If the layer does not have an alpha channel, the cleared area will be replaced with the current background color.

Fill with FG Color

> Fills the selected area with the currently selected foreground color.

Fill with BG Color

> Fills the selected area with the currently selected background color.

Stroke

> Draws an antialiased line that follows the border of the currently selected area with the currently selected brush. For example, this command may be used in conjunction with the circular selection tool to draw circles.

Repeat and Duplicate

> Pastes multiple copies of the selection into the current layer. Offsets for each copy may be set.

Copy Visible

> Copies an image consisting of the current visible layers flattened into a single layer. Useful for obtaining a flattened image from a multilayered file without flattening the source image.

The Select menu

Invert

> Selects the negative area around the current selection (you can think of it as "omitting" the currently selected area from a larger selection).

All

> Selects the entire image.

None

Deselects any areas that are currently selected.

Float

Creates a "floating selection" from the current selection. A floating selection is a movable selection area that occupies a layer of its own. The anchor command from the Layers and Channels dialog box will merge a floating selection with the layer it was originally associated with.

Feather

A feathered selection is a selection with a "soft edge." The pixels of the selection region grow progressively more transparent toward the edge of the selection. The Tool Options dialog for each of the selection tools allows you to specify the number of pixels that are feathered. A feathered selection blends in with a background better than an unfeathered selection.

Sharpen

Removes the fuzziness from the edges of a selection, resulting in a sharp-edged selection area.

Shrink

Contracts the current selection area by a given number of pixels in each direction.

Grow

Expands the current selection area by a given number of pixels in each direction. Along with Shrink, this allows very fine control over the extent of a selection area.

Border

Creates a new selection area that consists of the specified number of pixels surrounding the border of the current selection area.

Save to Channel

Creates a "selection mask" that will appear in the Layers and Channels dialog box. This is essentially a way to save selection regions for later use.

By Color

Allows you to select all of the pixels in the image of a certain color or within a certain range of colors.

Round

Rounds off the corners of a rectangular selection.

To path

Converts a selection to a path that will show up in the Paths dialog and may be edited.

The View menu

Zoom In

Increases the magnification of the image displayed in the current window.

Zoom Out

Decreases the magnification of the image displayed in the current window.

Zoom

Provides a list of magnification ratios at which you may view the image (ranging from 16:1 to 1:16).

Dot for dot

Displays the image with each screen pixel representing a single pixel of the image.

Info Window

Provides information about the image in the current window, including its size, display ratio, color mode, the color depth at which it is currently displayed, and the number of bits used for the red, green, and blue channels of the image.

Toggle Selection

Turns the "marching ants" of a selection on or off, but keeps the selection area active.

Toggle Rulers

Turns the rulers on or off.

Toggle Status Bar

Turns the status bar on or off.

Toggle Guides

Guide lines may be added to an image by clicking on the ruler and dragging a guide into place. This option turns these guides on or off.

Snap to Guides

Causes selections to "snap" to a guide line when moved close to it. This is useful for aligning several selection areas.

New View

Opens another window on the same image. Changes made to this new view will be reflected in all other open views. The Close command closes a view (window). When the last view on an image is closed, the Gimp will ask you if you wish to save the image if you have not already done so.

Shrink Wrap

If Shrink Wrap is selected, the size of the window of the current view will expand if you zoom in on the image, so the entire image will fit within the window.

The Image menu

Mode

RGB

Converts the image to RGB mode (the default mode for a new image), which allows millions of colors. Each pixel is saved as individual red, green, and blue values.

Grayscale

Converts the image to grayscale mode. In grayscale mode, each pixel is one of 256 shades of gray. Grayscale images may be saved directly as GIF files.

Indexed

Converts the image to Indexed mode, with a color table of user-defined size. In Indexed mode, each pixel in the image is stored as an index to a color table. When converting an RGB image to an Indexed image, the color quantization is performed intelligently (i.e., the Gimp will make good guesses as to what colors to use in the color table), and dithering may be applied to create a better image. Most filters will not work directly on Indexed mode images because they must often generate new colors that are not necessarily in the color table (the Blur filter does this, for instance). You can view the resulting color table by selecting the Dialogs → Indexed Palette dialog box.

Compose

Assembles three (or four) images that are the result of a Decompose action (see below) into a single new image created by using the individual images as the appropriate channels. The mapping of images to channels may be specified by the user within the Compose dialog box.

Decompose

Separates each channel of the current layer into a separate image file. The image may be decomposed in several different color spaces: RGB, HSV, CMY, CMYK, or Alpha. In CMYK color space, for example, the Cyan, Magenta, Yellow, and Black channels are each copied into their own separate image.

Canvas Size

Resizes the borders of the image, but does not scale the pixels.

Scale

Resizes the image and scales the pixel data to fit the new image dimensions. The new size may be indicated in absolute pixels, or in proportion to the image's original size.

Duplicate

Creates a copy of the image with layers and channels preserved.

Histogram

Brings up a dialog box with a histogram graph showing the frequency of intensity values of pixels in each channel of the current selection. The horizontal axis of the histogram is the intensity value (in the range 1 to 255). The vertical "spikes" represent the number of pixels in the image with that particular intensity level. The histogram window also shows specific information such as the mean, standard deviation, and the actual number of pixels with a certain intensity level.

Save palette

Allows you to save the color table of an Indexed mode image as a palette that will appear in the Palettes dialog box.

Colors

This menu option provides access to a number of commands for manipulating the color levels in an image. All of these commands are applied to the currently selected area.

Color Balance

Allows you to control the values of the red, green, and blue channels relative to the current values. The values can be adjusted individually for the shadow, midtone, and highlight areas of the image.

Hue-Saturation

Allows you to control the hue (the color's place in the spectrum) and saturation (the intensity of the color) of all the colors in the current selection. Note that this works only for RGB mode images.

Brightness-Contrast

Allows you to control the brightness and contrast of the currently selected area by adjusting a sliding scale that indicates a range of −127 to 127 levels in relation to the current brightness and contrast.

Threshold

Calls up a dialog box with a histogram showing the frequency of intensity values in an image. Selecting an intensity value (or range of values) will display only those pixels of the given intensity.

Levels

Displays a histogram like that of the Threshold command, and lets you control the minimum and maximum values for each individual channel of the image. The Levels command is useful for accentuating the highlighted and shadowed areas of an image.

Curves

Brings up a dialog box that provides a fine degree of control over the color and brightness levels of the currently selected area. You can define custom curves for each of the red, green, blue, and alpha channels in the image.

Desaturate

Removes the color information from the selected area, but keeps the image in RGB mode.

Invert

Inverts all of the pixels within the current selection. For color images, "inversion" means that the value of each channel (R, G, B) is subtracted from the maximum value (255).

Posterize

Quantizes the color values within the current selection to a given number of color levels. This is used mostly as a special effect.

Equalize

Equalize is a color filter that may be used to correct an image that is either over- or underexposed.

Color Enhance

Stretches the saturation range of the image to create more contrast between colors.

Normalize

This filter is a variation of Auto-Stretch Contrast that performs the "stretching" of values a bit more intelligently.

Auto-Stretch Contrast

This is an enhancement technique that finds the minimum and maximum values of each of the red, green, and blue channels for a selected area and "stretches" them so that they span the full range of values. It is a good tool for enhancing muddy photos or scans of poor quality.

Auto-Stretch HSV

This is an enhancement technique that finds the minimum and maximum values of Hue, Saturation, and Value for a selected area and "stretches" them so that they span the full range of values.

Alpha

Add Alpha Channel

Adds an alpha channel to the image. An image must have an alpha channel if it is to have transparency.

Clear Alpha

Clears the alpha channel.

Threshold Alpha

Allows you to specify an alpha channel threshold in the range 0 to 255.

Transforms

Offset

Shifts the current layer by a given amount in the x and y directions. The image will wrap around if the appropriate option is set.

Rotate

This is another rotate tool that allows you to rotate either the entire image or the currently selected layer by 0, 90, 180, or 270 degrees clockwise.

Autocrop

Crops the unused background from the edges of an image. That is, it will crop the image to the bounding box of the actual content of the image.

Guillotine

Chops up the image into a series of smaller images. The images will be chopped according to the current guide settings.

Zealous Crop

Crops the unused background from the edges and middle of an image.

The Layers menu

Layers, Channels, Paths

Opens the Layers, Channels & Paths dialog box.

Layer to Image Size

Resizes the image canvas to the current layer size.

Stack

> *Previous Layer*
>
> Selects the layer underneath the current layer.
>
> *Next Layer*
>
> Selects the layer above the current layer.
>
> *Raise Layer*
>
> Moves a layer up one level in the layer stack. The background layer can be neither raised nor lowered.
>
> *Lower Layer*
>
> Moves a layer down one level in the layer stack.
>
> *Layer to Top*
>
> Moves a layer to the top of the layer stack.
>
> *Layer to Bottom*
>
> Moves a layer to the bottom of the layer stack.

Rotate

Rotates the selected layer by 90, 180, or 270 degrees.

Anchor Layer

Merges a floating selection with the layer the selection was originally associated with.

Merge Visible Layers

Combines all visible layers into a single layer. The position of the resulting layer in the layer stack will be the same position as the lowest original visible layer. All layers not marked as visible will remain as separate layers.

Flatten Image

Combines all visible layers into a single layer and discards all nonvisible layers. This command takes alpha information into account when combining layers, but it removes the alpha channel from the final image. The result is an image with a single layer and no alpha channel.

Mask to Selection

Retrieves a previously saved selection mask and marks it as the current active selection region.

Add Alpha Channel

Adds an alpha channel to only the currently selected layer.

Alpha to Selection

Creates a new selection region consisting of the alpha channel for the current layer.

Align Visible Layers

Aligns all of the visible layers based on a variety of parameters.

Center Layer

Moves the selected layer so that it is centered horizontally and vertically within the image canvas.

The Tools menu

This menu provides access to all the tools in the toolbox.

The Dialogs menu

This menu is the same as the Dialog menu under the Toolbox hierarchy, with the additional options:

Error Console

If open, the error console displays any Gimp error messages. If not open, error messages will be displayed in popup dialogs.

Undo History

Displays a list of the previous actions that can be undone. You can also preview the undo before actualizing it.

The Filters menu

All of the filters available from this menu will be applied to the currently selected area. Most of the filters have custom dialog boxes that allow you to modify many input parameters.

Repeat Last
> Reapplies the last action chosen from the Filters menu with the same parameters.

Re-show Last
> Reapplies the last action chosen from the Filters menu, but allows you to reset the input parameters.

Filter all Layers
> Applies any filters to all layers in the image.

The rest of the menu offers a number of plug-in filters, as shown in Figure B-8.

Figure B-8. The Filters menu organizes all of the currently installed filter plug-ins

The Guides menu

Center Guides
> Adds two guidelines, one at the vertical and one at the horizontal center of the image.

Guide Grid
> Adds a user-defined grid of guides to the image.

Remove Grids
> Removes any previously set guides.

To Selection
> Creates a new selection based on the current guides.

The Script-Fu menu

One important thing to remember when applying scripts is that they often cannot be undone all at once. Scripts are sequences of commands that can be undone individually when you select Undo. Often, more commands are performed than your Undo buffer will hold (the default is five levels of Undo). When possible, it is best to apply scripts to a copy of your original image (usually the script will offer this as an option).

Version 1.0 of the Gimp was distributed with a separate Script-Fu menu hierarchy for scripts written in Script-Fu. This menu structure will probably become less relevant in the future, as scripts should really be placed next to their functional counterparts (e.g., a script that combines other images should go in the <Image> → Filters → Combine menu rather than <Image> → Script-Fu → Combine). This is not to say that you cannot create new subgroups within the menu hierarchy; it's just that the criteria for organizing the workflow should not necessarily include the language in which the plug-in was written. Figure B-9 shows some of the scripts written in Script-Fu.

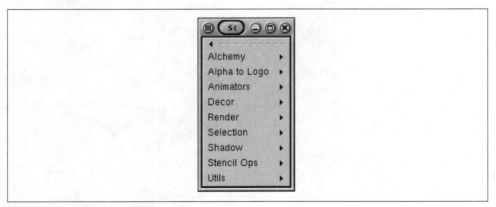

Figure B-9. The Script-Fu menu is the repository for all scripts written in Scheme

Image::Magick File Formats

Table C-1 shows the various file formats supported by Image::Magick. The headings indicate whether the file format provides support for multiple images in a single document and for binary large objects (BLOBs), whether it is a raw format, and whether Image::Magick can decode and encode files in this format.

Table C-1. ImageMagick file formats

File format	Mult. images?	BLOBs?	Raw format?	Decoder?	Encoder?	Description
afm		✓		✓		TrueType font
art	✓	✓		✓		PF1: 1st Publisher
avi	✓	✓		✓		Audio/Visual Interleaved
avs	✓	✓		✓	✓	AVS X image
bie		✓		✓	✓	Joint Bi-level Image Experts Group interchange format
bmp	✓	✓		✓	✓	Microsoft Windows bitmap image
cmyk	✓	✓	✓	✓	✓	Raw cyan, magenta, yellow, and black bytes
cmyka	✓	✓	✓	✓	✓	Raw cyan, magenta, yellow, black, and matte bytes
cut	✓	✓		✓		DR Hallo
dcm		✓		✓		Digital Imaging and Communications in Medicine image
dcx	✓	✓		✓	✓	ZSoft IBM PC Multi-page Paintbrush
dib	✓	✓		✓	✓	Microsoft Windows bitmap image
dpx	✓	✓		✓		Digital Moving Picture Exchange
epdf		✓		✓	✓	Encapsulated Portable Document format
epi		✓		✓	✓	Adobe Encapsulated PostScript Interchange format
eps		✓		✓	✓	Adobe Encapsulated PostScript
eps2		✓			✓	Adobe Level II Encapsulated PostScript
eps3	✓	✓			✓	Adobe Level III Encapsulated PostScript

Table C-1. ImageMagick file formats (continued)

File format	Mult. images?	BLOBs?	Raw format?	Decoder?	Encoder?	Description
epsf		✓		✓	✓	Adobe Encapsulated PostScript
epsi		✓		✓	✓	Adobe Encapsulated PostScript Interchange format
ept		✓		✓	✓	Adobe Encapsulated PostScript with TIFF preview
fax	✓	✓		✓	✓	Group 3 FAX
file	✓	✓		✓		Uniform Resource Locator
fits		✓		✓	✓	Flexible Image Transport System
fpx		✓		✓	✓	FlashPix format
ftp	✓	✓		✓		Uniform Resource Locator
g3		✓		✓	✓	Group 3 FAX
gif	✓	✓		✓	✓	CompuServe Graphics Interchange format
gif87		✓		✓	✓	CompuServe Graphics Interchange format (version 87a)
gradient		✓		✓		Gradual passing from one shade to another
granite		✓		✓		Granite texture
gray	✓	✓	✓	✓	✓	Raw gray bytes
h		✓		✓	✓	Internal format
h5	✓			✓	✓	Hierarchical Data Format
hdf	✓			✓	✓	Hierarchical Data Format
histogram		✓			✓	Histogram of the image
htm		✓			✓	Hypertext Markup Language and a client-side image map
html		✓			✓	Hypertext Markup Language and a client-side image map
http	✓	✓		✓		Uniform Resource Locator
icb	✓	✓		✓	✓	Truevision Targa image
icm		✓		✓	✓	ICC Color Profile
ico		✓		✓		Microsoft icon
icon		✓		✓		Microsoft icon
iptc		✓		✓	✓	IPTC Newsphoto
jbg	✓	✓		✓	✓	Joint Bi-level Image Experts Group interchange format
jbig	✓	✓		✓	✓	Joint Bi-level Image Experts Group interchange format
jp2		✓		✓	✓	JPEG-2000 JP2 File Format Syntax
jpc		✓		✓	✓	JPEG-2000 Code Stream Syntax
jpeg		✓		✓	✓	Joint Photographic Experts Group JFIF format
jpg		✓		✓	✓	Joint Photographic Experts Group JFIF format
label		✓		✓		Text image format
logo		✓		✓	✓	ImageMagick Logo

Table C-1. ImageMagick file formats (continued)

File format	Mult. images?	BLOBs?	Raw format?	Decoder?	Encoder?	Description
map		✓	✓	✓	✓	Colormap intensities and indices
matte	✓	✓	✓		✓	MATTE format
miff	✓	✓		✓	✓	Magick image format
mng	✓	✓		✓	✓	Multiple-image Network Graphics
mono		✓		✓	✓	Bi-level bitmap in least-significant-byte-first order
mpc				✓	✓	Magick Persistent Cache image format
mtv	✓	✓		✓	✓	MTV Raytracing image format
mvg		✓		✓	✓	Magick Vector Graphics
netscape		✓		✓		Netscape 216 color cube
null		✓		✓		Constant image of uniform color
p7	✓	✓		✓	✓	Xv thumbnail format
pal		✓	✓	✓	✓	16bit/pixel interleaved YUV
pbm	✓	✓		✓	✓	Portable bitmap format (black and white)
pcd		✓		✓	✓	Photo CD
pcds		✓		✓	✓	Photo CD
pcl		✓			✓	Page Control Language
pct		✓		✓	✓	Apple Macintosh QuickDraw/PICT
pcx		✓		✓	✓	ZSoft IBM PC Paintbrush
pdb	✓	✓		✓		Pilot Image format
pdf	✓	✓		✓	✓	Portable Document format
pfb		✓		✓		TrueType font
pfm		✓		✓		TrueType font
pgm	✓	✓		✓	✓	Portable graymap format (gray scale)
picon		✓		✓	✓	Personal Icon
pict		✓		✓	✓	Apple Macintosh QuickDraw/PICT
pix	✓	✓		✓		Alias/Wavefront RLE image format
plasma		✓		✓		Plasma fractal image
pm		✓		✓	✓	X Windows system pixmap (color)
png		✓		✓	✓	Portable Network Graphics
pnm	✓	✓		✓	✓	Portable anymap
ppm	✓	✓		✓	✓	Portable pixmap format (color)
preview		✓			✓	Show a preview of an image enhancement, effect, or f/x
ps	✓	✓		✓	✓	Adobe PostScript
ps2	✓	✓			✓	Adobe Level II PostScript

Table C-1. ImageMagick file formats (continued)

File format	Mult. images?	BLOBs?	Raw format?	Decoder?	Encoder?	Description
ps3	✓	✓			✓	Adobe Level III PostScript
psd		✓		✓	✓	Adobe Photoshop bitmap
ptif		✓		✓	✓	Pyramid encoded TIFF
pwp	✓	✓		✓		Seattle Film Works
ras	✓	✓		✓	✓	SUN Rasterfile
rgb	✓	✓	✓	✓	✓	Raw red, green, and blue bytes
rgba	✓	✓	✓	✓	✓	Raw red, green, blue, and matte bytes
rla		✓		✓		Alias/Wavefront image
rle		✓		✓		Utah Run length encoded image
sct		✓		✓		Scitex HandShake
sgi	✓	✓		✓	✓	Irix RGB image
shtml		✓			✓	Hypertext Markup Language and a client-side image map
stegano	✓	✓		✓		Steganographic image
sun	✓	✓		✓	✓	SUN Rasterfile
svg	✓	✓		✓	✓	Scalable Vector Gaphics
text	✓	✓	✓	✓	✓	Raw text
tga	✓	✓		✓	✓	Truevision Targa image
tif	✓	✓		✓	✓	Tagged Image File Format
tiff	✓	✓		✓	✓	Tagged Image File Format
tile	✓	✓	✓	✓		Tile image with a texture
tim	✓	✓		✓		PSX TIM
ttf		✓		✓		TrueType font
txt	✓	✓		✓	✓	Raw text
uil		✓			✓	X-Motif UIL table
uyvy		✓	✓	✓	✓	16bit/pixel interleaved YUV
vda	✓	✓		✓	✓	Truevision Targa image
vicar		✓		✓	✓	VICAR rasterfile format
vid	✓	✓		✓	✓	Visual Image Directory
viff	✓	✓		✓	✓	Khoros Visualization image
vst	✓	✓		✓	✓	Truevision Targa image
wbmp		✓		✓	✓	Wireless Bitmap (level 0) image
wpg	✓	✓		✓		Word Perfect Graphics
x		✓		✓	✓	X Image
xbm		✓		✓	✓	X Windows system bitmap (black and white)

Table C-1. ImageMagick file formats (continued)

File format	Mult. images?	BLOBs?	Raw format?	Decoder?	Encoder?	Description
xc		✓	✓	✓		Constant image uniform color
xml	✓	✓		✓		Scalable Vector Gaphics
xpm		✓		✓	✓	X Windows system pixmap (color)
xv	✓	✓		✓	✓	Khoros Visualization image
xwd		✓		✓	✓	X Windows system window dump (color)
yuv		✓	✓	✓	✓	CCIR 601 4:1:1
8bim		✓		✓	✓	Photoshop resource format

APPENDIX D

ActionScript Reference

Most ActionScript books and tutorials assume that you will be using the Flash software to construct your SWF files. Macromedia provides a handful of tutorials and an ActionScript Dictionary reference on its support web site, which isn't as well organized as it could be. This appendix presents a slightly better-organized ActionScript reference that is geared toward writing scripts by hand (i.e., without the Flash user interface). The tables in this appendix cover only ActionScript Version 5, as this is what the latest version of Ming supports. For a reference to newer or deprecated versions, refer to Macromedia's Flash support site.

The reference is organized in three sections:

- Operators and control structures
- Actions, functions, and properties
- Objects

Operators and Control Structures

ActionScript basic operators and control structures are broken down into the following tables:

Table D-1, "Arithmetic operations"
Table D-2, "Assignment operations"
Table D-3, "Logical operations"
Table D-4, "Comparison operations"
Table D-5, "Bit operations"
Table D-6, "Other operators"
Table D-7, "Control structures"

Table D-1. Arithmetic operations

Operator	Description
( )	Parentheses
*	Multiply
/	Divide
%	Modulo
+	Add
-	Subtract
- -	Decrement
++	Increment

Table D-2. Assignment operations

Operator	Description
=	Assignment
*=	Multiplication assignment
/=	Division assignment
%=	Modulo assignment
+=	Addition assignment
-=	Subtraction assignment
&=	Bitwise AND assignment
|=	Bitwise OR assignment
^=	Bitwise XOR assignment

Table D-3. Logical operations

Operator	Description
!	Logical NOT (you can also use the keyword not)
~	Bitwise NOT
&	Bitwise AND
&&	Logical AND (you can also use the keyword and)
?:	Conditional
|	Bitwise OR
||	Logical OR (you can also use the keyword or)
^	Bitwise XOR

Table D-4. Comparison operations

Operator	Description
!= , <>	Inequality
==	Equality
<	Less than
>	Greater than
<=	Less than or equal to
>=	Greater than or equal to
eq	String equal
ge	String greater than or equal to
gt	String greater than
le	String less than or equal to
lt	String less than
ne	String not equal

Table D-5. Bit operations

Operator	Description
<<	Bitwise left shift
<<=	Bitwise left shift and assignment
>>	Bitwise right shift
>>=	Bitwise right shift and assignment
>>>	Bitwise unsigned right shift
>>>=	Bitwise unsigned right shift and assignment

Table D-6. Other operators

Operator	Description
.	The dot operator, which allows you to call methods of an object or access its properties
[ ]	Array element access operator
//	Single-line comment delimiter
/* */	Multi-line comment delimiters

Table D-7. Control structures

Structure	Description
if (*condition*) { } else { }	If the condition is true, perform the first block; otherwise, perform the else block (if any).
for (*init; condition; next*) { }	A for loop, just like Perl's for loop.
for (*variable* in *object*) { }	Evaluate the block for each property of *object*. The variable will reference each property with each iteration.
while (*condition*) { }	Loop while the condition is true.
do { } while (*condition*)	Same as a while loop, but the condition is tested at the end of each iteration.

Table D-7. Control structures (continued)

Structure	Description
break	Break out of a while or for loop.
continue	Skip over the rest of the body of the loop for this iteration and go to the next condition test.

on (mouseEvent) { }	Perform the block of code when one of the following mouse events is encountered:
	
	`press` `rollOut`
	`release` `dragOut`
	`releaseOutside` `dragOver`
	`rollOver` `keyPress`

onClipEvent(movieEvent) { }	Perform the block of code when one of the following movie events is encountered:
	
	`load` `mouseUp`
	`unload` `keyDown`
	`enterFrame` `keyUp`
	`mouseMove` `data`
	`mouseDown`

Actions, Functions, and Properties

The actions and properties described in this section can be thought of as methods and properties of the top-level movie. ActionScript also provides built-in functions for evaluating various expressions. These are described in the following tables:

Table D-8, "ActionScript actions"
Table D-9, "ActionScript functions"
Table D-10, "ActionScript properties"

Table D-8. ActionScript actions

Action name	Parameters	Description
call	`frame`	Switch the context from this script to the script attached to the specified frame.
delete	`object`	Delete (undefine) the specified object or variable.
duplicateMovieClip	`movie_clip, new_name, depth`	Create a new instance of the given MovieClip, place it at `depth`, and label it with new_name.
fscommand	`command, argument_string`	Pass a command and list of arguments to the system that is running the SWF user agent.
function	`name { code_block }`	Define a function.

getURL	`url , window`	Load a MovieClip from an external URL. The optional `window` parameter can be one of the following values:
		
		`_self`
		  The current frame in the current window.
		`_blank`
		  A new window.
		`_parent`
		  The parent of the current frame.
		`_top`
		  The top-level window.

Table D-8. ActionScript actions (continued)

Action name	Parameters	Description
gotoAndPlay	`frame`	Go to a particular frame and play the movie.
gotoAndStop	`frame`	Go to a particular frame and stop the movie.
loadMovie	`url, target`	Load an external movie from the specified URL. The target can be a path to an existing object in the movie (which will be replaced) or the depth at which the movie clip should be placed.
loadVariables	`url, level`	Load variable data from a text file or CGI script. The data will be read into text fields at the given level. The file at `url` should be in MIME encoded format, e.g.: `var1=value1&var2=value2...`
nextFrame	-	Go to the next frame.
nextScene	-	Advance to the first frame of the next scene and stop.
play	-	Play the movie.
prevFrame	-	Go to the previous frame.
prevScene	-	Advance to the first frame of the previous scene and stop.
print	`target, bounding_box`	Print the frames of the target MovieClip. The bounding box can be one of the following: *bframe* Use the bounding box of each frame. *bmax* Use the bounding box of the largest frame. *bmovie* Use the bounding box of the frame labeled "#b".
printAsBitmap	`target, bounding_box`	Same as print, but takes into account color effects and transparency.
removeMovieClip	-	Remove an attached or duplicated MovieClip from the timeline.
return	`expression`	Return a value at the end of a function.
startDrag	`target, lock, left, right, top, bottom`	This method allows the target to be dragged around the frame by the user. All of the parameters are optional. The lock parameter is a Boolean: `true` Position the target centered on the pointer. `false` Position the target at the location of the mouse click. The left, right, top, and bottom parameters can be used to specify a rectangle to which the dragging movement is constrained.
set	`variable, expression`	Give the variable the value of `expression`.
stop	-	Stop the movie.
stopDrag	-	The method "drops" a dragged target and no longer allows the clip to be dragged around the frame by the user.
stopAllSounds	-	Stop playing sounds.
toggleHighQuality	-	Turn on (or off) antialiasing in the movie.

Table D-8. ActionScript actions (continued)

Action name	Parameters	Description
trace	`expression`	Evaluate the expression and display it as a text field on the stage for debugging purposes.
unloadMovie	`target`	Unload a previously loaded movie.
var	`variable = initial_value`	Declare a variable with an optional initial value.
with	`(object)` `{ code_block }`	Execute the block of code with all properties and actions referring to the given object.

Table D-9. ActionScript functions

Function name	Parameters	Description
Boolean	`expression`	Convert the given expression into a Boolean.
escape	`expression`	Escape all special characters in the expression (i.e., replace special characters with corresponding entities).
eval	`string`	Evaluate a string, returning a value or reference.
getProperty	`name, property`	Return the value of the property associated with the MovieClip of the specified name.
getTimer	-	Return the number of milliseconds elapsed since the movie began.
getVersion	-	Return the version information associated with the movie.
isFinite	`expression`	Return false if the expression is not a finite number.
isNaN	`expression`	Return true if the expression is not a number.
parseFloat	`string`	Convert a string into a floating-point numerical value.
parseInt	`string`	Convert a string into an integer numerical value.
random	`number`	Return a random integer between 0 and the given number.
setProperty	`target, property, expression`	Set a property of a target to the value of an expression.
String	`expression`	Return the expression as a String object. If `expression` is a MovieClip, the path to the MovieClip is returned in "slash notation."
targetPath	`MovieClip`	Return the path to the MovieClip in dot notation.
typeof	`expression`	Return a string describing whether the result of the expression is a String, MovieClip, Object, or function.
unescape	`string`	Decode all escape entities in the string.
updateAfterEvent	`event`	Force the display to be updated after a particular event is handled. This is used for creating a flicker-free animation effect.
void	`expression`	Evaluate the expression and always return an undefined value.

Table D-10. ActionScript properties

Property name	Description
_alpha	A number representing the opacity of the object, from transparent to opaque (0..100).
_current_frame	The number of the frame currently displayed (read-only).
_droptarget	Return the path to the MovieClip on which the last dragged item was dropped (read-only).
_focusrect	If true, the associated button will be outlined with a yellow rectangle when the button has focus.
_height	Get or set the height of a MovieClip, in displayed pixels.
maxscroll	The maximum value that is allowable for use with the scroll property. This takes into account the displayed height of the text field (read-only).
_name	Get or set the name of an object.
_parent	Return a reference to the parent of the current movie (read-only).
_quality	Set the degree of antialiasing and bitmap smoothing:
	LOW No antialiasing, no bitmap smoothing
	MEDIUM No bitmap smoothing, antialiasing using a 2x2 grid
	HIGH Antialiasing using a 4x4 grid, smoothing on static bitmaps
	BEST Antialiasing and bitmap smoothing always applied
_root	Return a reference to the root movie (read-only).
_rotation	Get or set the rotation (in integer degrees) of the object.
scroll	Get or set the topmost line number of a text field. This can be used to jump to a particular section of text in the text field.
_soundbuftime	A delay (in seconds) used to give the user agent time to buffer sound objects before the movie begins playing. The default is 5.
_target	Return the pathname as a string (read-only).
this	Return a reference to the current movie (read-only).
_totalframes	Return the number of frames in the movie (read-only).
_url	Return a string containing the URL of the movie (read-only).
_visible	Get or set the visibility of the object
_width	Get or set the width of a MovieClip, in displayed pixels.
_x	Get or set the x coordinate of the movie
_xmouse	Return the x coordinate of the mouse position (read-only).
_xscale	Get or set the horizontal scale of the object as a percentage.
_y	Get or set the y coordinate of the movie.
_mouse	Return the y coordinate of the mouse position (read-only).
_yscale	Get or set the vertical scale of the object as a percentage.

Objects

ActionScript provides the predefined objects described in the following tables:

Table D-11. Array object methods

Method name	Parameters	Description
new Array	`value_list`	Returns a new empty Array object, or an Array object initialized with a list of values.
Array.concat	`value_list or Array`	Adds a list of values to the end of an array and returns a new Array object with the concatenated values.
Array.join	`separator`	Returns a string constructed by concatenating each value of the Array object, separated by an optional separator string. A comma is the default separator.
Array.length	-	Returns the number of elements in the array.
Array.pop	-	Returns and removes the last element from the array.
Array.push	`value_list`	Adds a list of values to the end of the array and returns the new length.
Array.reverse	-	Returns a new Array object that is in the reverse order of the original.
Array.shift	-	Returns and removes the first element from the array.
Array.slice	`start_index, end_index`	Returns a new array that is a subrange of the target array. The returned array contains the value at the start index but not the value at the end index. Use a negative index to count from the end of the array.

Table D-11. Array object methods (continued)

Method name	Parameters	Description
Array.sort	order_function	Sorts the array in place. If the order function is not specified, elements will be sorted using the less-than (<) operator. The order_function should be a function that takes two arguments (a and b) and returns −1 if a should appear before b, 0 if a equals b, and 1 if a should appear after b.
Array.splice	start_index, delete_count, value_list	Inserts a list of values into an array at the specified starting index. The delete_count argument specifies how many elements (counting from the start_index) should be deleted when the new values are inserted.
Array.toString	-	Returns the array as a string. This has the same effect as calling the default *join* method.

Table D-12. Boolean object methods

Method name	Parameters	Description
new Boolean	expression	Returns a new Boolean object, initialized with the given expression (if any). If the expression is a number, it is initialized to true if the value is nonzero. If the expression is a String, the value will be true if the String evaluated as a number is nonzero. If it is any other object, the value will be true if the object is not equal to null.
Boolean.toString	-	Returns the string "true" or "false".

Table D-13. Color object methods

Method name	Parameters	Description
new Color	-	Returns a new Color object.
Color.getRGB	hex_color	Returns the numeric value of the object in the form 0xRRGGBB.
Color.getTransform	-	Returns the value of the last color transform performed.
Color.setRGB	hex_color	Sets the color of the object by specifying an RGB hexadecimal triplet in the form 0xRRGGBB.
Color.setTransform	color_transform	Sets a color transform, which is created with the generic Object constructor. Set the following properties:

ra The percentage for the red component.
rb The offset for the red component.
ga The percentage for the green component.
gb The offset for the green component.
ba The percentage for the blue component.
bb The offset for the blue component.
aa The percentage for alpha.
ab The offset for alpha.

All percentages are in the range −100 to 100, and offsets are in the range −255 to 255.

Table D-14. Date object methods

Method name	Parameters	Description
new Date	–	Returns a new Date object.
Date.getDate	–	Returns the number of the current day of the month in local time relative to the user agent.
Date.getDay	–	Returns the number of the current day of the week in local time relative to the user agent.
Date.getFullYear	–	Returns the current (four-digit) year in local time relative to the user agent.
Date.getHours	–	Returns the current hour in local time relative to the user agent.
Date.getMilliseconds	–	Returns the current millisecond in local time relative to the user agent.
Date.getMinutes	–	Returns the current minute in local time relative to the user agent.
Date.getMonth	–	Returns the current month as a number (0 = January) in local time relative to the user agent.
Date.getSeconds	–	Returns the current second in local time relative to the user agent.
Date.getTime	–	Returns the number of milliseconds since midnight January 1, 1970 in universal time.
Date.getTimezoneOffset	–	Returns the number of minutes between local time and UTC.
Date.getUTCDate	–	Returns the number of the current day of the month in universal time.
Date.getUTCDay	–	Returns the number of the current day of the week in universal time.
Date.getUTCFullYear	–	Returns the current (four-digit) year in universal time.
Date.getUTCHours	–	Returns the current hour in universal time.
Date.getUTCMilliseconds	–	Returns the current millisecond in universal time.
Date.getUTCMinutes	–	Returns the current minute in universal time.
Date.getUTCMonth	–	Returns the current month as a number (0 = January) in universal time.
Date.getUTCSeconds	–	Returns the current second in universal time.
Date.getYear	–	Returns the current year in local time. The return value is in non-Y2K-compliant form (i.e., 2000 = 100, etc.).
Date.setDate	day	Sets the number of the current day of the month in local time.
Date.setFullYear	year	Sets the current (four-digit) year in local time.
Date.setHours	hour	Sets the current hour in local time.
Date.setMilliseconds	millisecond	Sets the current millisecond in local time.
Date.setMinutes	minute	Sets the current minute in local time.
Date.setMonth	month_number	Sets the current month as a number (0 = January) in local time.
Date.setSeconds	second	Sets the current second in local time.

Table D-14. *Date object methods (continued)*

Method name	Parameters	Description
Date.setTime	`milliseconds`	Sets the local time by specifying a number of milliseconds since midnight January 1, 1970 in universal time.
Date.setUTCDate	`day`	Sets the number of the current day of the month in universal time.
Date.setUTCFullYear	`year`	Sets the current (four-digit) year in universal time.
Date.setUTCHours	`hour`	Sets the current hour in universal time.
Date.setUTCMilliseconds	`millisecond`	Sets the current millisecond in universal time.
Date.setUTCMinutes	`minute`	Sets the current minute in universal time.
Date.setUTCMonth	`month_number`	Sets the current month as a number (0 = January) in universal time.
Date.setUTCSeconds	`second`	Sets the current second in universal time.
Date.setYear	`year`	Sets the local year minus 1900.
Date.toString	-	Returns the local date and time as a string in the format: `Sun Mar 17 12:49:08 GMT-0500 2002`
Date.UTC	`year, month, date, hour, minute, second, millisecond`	Returns the number of milliseconds from midnight January 1, 1970 to the specified date in universal time. Only the year and month are required arguments. Note that this is a class method, not an object method.

Table D-15. *Key object methods (note that the Key object does not have a constructor method)*

Method name	Parameters	Description
Key.getAscii	-	Return the ASCII value of the pressed key.
Key.getCode	-	Return the key code (see Table D-16) of the pressed key.
Key.isDown	`Key constant`	Return true if the specified key is pressed.
Key.isToggled	-	Return true if Caps Lock or Num Lock is enabled.

Table D-16. *Key code constants*

Constant name	Key code
Key.BACKSPACE	8
Key.CAPSLOCK	20
Key.CONTROL	17
Key.DELETEKEY	46
Key.DOWN	40
Key.END	35
Key.ENTER	13
Key.ESCAPE	27
Key.HOME	36
Key.INSERT	45

Table D-16. *Key code constants (continued)*

Constant name	Key code
Key.LEFT	37
Key.PGDN	34
Key.PGUP	33
Key.RIGHT	39
Key.SHIFT	16
Key.SPACE	32
Key.TAB	9
Key.UP	38

Table D-17. *Math object methods (note that the Math object does not have a constructor method)*

Method name	Parameters	Description
Math.abs	n	Return the absolute value of a number.
Math.acos	n (in the range −1.0 to 1.0)	Return the arccosine of a number.
Math.asin	n (in the range −1.0 to 1.0)	Return the arcsine of a number.
Math.atan	n	Return the arctangent of a number.
Math.atan2	y, x	Return the arctangent of y/x in radians.
Math.ceil	n	Return the closest integer that is greater than or equal to n.
Math.cos	n	Return the cosine of n.
Math.exp	n	Return the value of e (Math.E) to the power of n.
Math.floor	n	Return the closest integer that is less than or equal to n.
Math.log	n	Return the natural logarithm of n.
Math.max	a, b	Return the larger of a and b.
Math.min	a, b	Return the smaller of a and b.
Math.pow	a, b	Return a raised to the b power.
Math.random	-	Return a random number between 0.0 and 1.0.
Math.round	n	Return the nearest integer to n.
Math.sin	n	Return the sine of n.
Math.sqrt	n	Return the square root of n.
Math.tan	angle (in radians)	Return the tangent of an angle.

Table D-18. *Math object constants*

Constant name	Description
Math.E	The base of natural logarithms = 2.71828.
Math.LN2	The natural logarithm of 2 = 0.693147.
Math.LN10	The natural logarithm of 10 = 2.302585.
Math.LOG2E	The base-2 logarithm of e = 1.442695.

Table D-18. Math object constants (continued)

Constant name	Description
Math.LOG10E	The base-10 logarithm of e = 0.43429.
Math.PI	Pi = 3.14159.
Math.SQRT1_2	The square root of 1/2.
Math.SQRT2	The square root of 2.

Table D-19. Mouse object methods (note that the Mouse object does not have a constructor method)

Method name	Parameters	Description
Mouse.hide	-	Make the cursor invisible.
Mouse.show	-	Make a previously hidden cursor visible.

Table D-20. MovieClip object methods

Method name	Parameters	Description
new MovieClip	-	Return a new MovieClip object.
MovieClip.attachMovie	clip_name, new_name, depth	Attach a MovieClip to the current object. This method gives the attached movie a new name and places it at the specified depth.
MovieClip.duplicate-MovieClip	target_path, new_name, depth	Duplicate a MovieClip, give the copy a new name, and place it at the specified depth.
MovieClip.getBounds	target_path	Return the dimensions of the MovieClip, using the coordinate space of the target. The return values will be wrapped up in an object with the properties xMin, xMax, yMin, yMax.
MovieClip.getBytes-Loaded	-	Return the number of bytes of the MovieClip that have been loaded so far.
MovieClip.getBytesTotal	-	Return the number of bytes in the MovieClip.
MovieClip.getURL	url , window	Load a MovieClip from an external URL. The optional window parameter can be one of the following values: _self The current frame in the current window. _blank A new window. _parent The parent of the current frame. _top The top-level window.
MovieClip.globalToLocal	point	Convert a point from a global coordinate to the MovieClip's coordinate system. The point parameter is a generic object with x and y properties.
MovieClip.gotoAndPlay	frame_number	Start playing the MovieClip at the specified frame.
MovieClip.gotoAndStop	frame_number	Stop the movie after going to the specified frame.
MovieClip.hitTest	target, or x, y, shape_flag	Return true if the MovieClip overlaps the given target or the given coordinate. If shape_flag is false, only the bounding box of the MovieClip will be used to determine the intersection.

Table D-20. MovieClip object methods (continued)

Method name	Parameters	Description
MovieClip.loadMovie	`url, target`	Load an external movie from the specified URL. The target can be a path to an existing object in the movie (which will be replaced) or the depth at which the movie clip should be placed.
MovieClip.loadVariables	`url`	Load variable data from a text file or CGI script. The file at `url` should be in MIME encoded format, e.g.: `var1=value1&var2=value2...`
MovieClip.localToGlobal	`point`	Convert a point from the MovieClip's coordinate system to the global coordinate system. The point parameter is a generic object with x and y properties.
MovieClip.nextFrame	-	Go to the next frame.
MovieClip.play	-	Play the movie.
MovieClip.prevFrame	-	Go to the previous frame.
MovieClip.remove-MovieClip	-	Remove an attached or duplicated MovieClip from the Movie-Clip's timeline.

MovieClip.startDrag	`lock, left, right, top, bottom`	Allows the MovieClip to be dragged around the frame by the user. All of the parameters are optional. The lock parameter is a Boolean:
		
		`true`
		    Position the MovieClip centered on the pointer.
		`false`
		    Position the MovieClip at the location of the mouse click.
		
		The left, right, top, and bottom parameters can be used to specify a rectangle to which the dragging movement is constrained.

MovieClip.stop	-	Stop the movie.
MovieClip.stopDrag	-	"Drops" a dragged MovieClip and no longer allows the clip to be dragged around the frame by the user.
MovieClip.swapDepths	`depth or target_path`	Swaps the depths of the MovieClip and the object at the specified depth or with the specified target.
MovieClip.unloadMovie	-	Unloads a previously loaded movie.

Table D-21. MovieClip object properties

Property name	Description
MovieClip._alpha	The value of the alpha channel (transparency) of the movie. A number from 0 to 100.
MovieClip._currentframe	The number of the currently displayed frame.
MovieClip._droptarget	The path to the object that was the last target of a startDrag action.
MovieClip._framesloaded	The number of frames of the movie that have loaded so far.
MovieClip._height	The height of the movie.
MovieClip._name	The name of the movie.
MovieClip._rotation	The current rotation factor of the movie.

Table D-21. *MovieClip object properties (continued)*

Property name	Description
MovieClip._target	The target pathname of the movie (read-only).
MovieClip._totalframes	The number of frames in the movie.
MovieClip._url	The URL of the movie (read-only).
MovieClip._visible	The visibility of the movie.
MovieClip._width	The width of the MovieClip.
MovieClip._x	The current x coordinate of the upper left corner of the MovieClip.
MovieClip._xmouse	The current x coordinate of the mouse.
MovieClip._xscale	The current horizontal scale factor.
MovieClip._y	The current y coordinate of the upper left corner of the MovieClip.
MovieClip._ymouse	The current y coordinate of the mouse.
MovieClip._yscale	The current vertical scale factor.

Table D-22. *Number object properties*

Property name	Parameters	Description
new Number	-	Return a new Number object.
Number.MAX_VALUE	-	A constant for the largest number that can be represented (1.79E+308).
Number.MIN_VALUE	-	A constant for the smallest number that can be represented (5e−324).
Number.NaN	-	A constant representing "Not a Number."
Number.NEGATIVE_INFINITY	-	A constant representing negative infinity.
Number.POSITIVE_INFINITY	-	A constant representing positive infinity.

Table D-23. *Generic object methods*

Method name	Parameters	Description
new Object	-	Return a new generic Object.
Object.toString	-	Return the object as a String.

Table D-24. *Selection object methods*

Method name	Parameters	Description
new Selection	-	Create a new Selection object.
Selection.getBeginIndex	-	Return the index of the beginning of the selection within a text field, or −1 if there is no selected text. Indices are 0-based.
Selection.getCaretIndex	-	Return the index of the insertion cursor within a text field, or −1 if there is no cursor.
Selection.getEndIndex	-	Return the index of the end of the selection within a text field, or −1 if there is no selected text.

Table D-24. Selection object methods (continued)

Method name	Parameters	Description
Selection.getFocus	-	Return the name of the text field that has focus, or null if none.
Selection.setFocus	`target_name`	Set the focus to the text field with the specified name.
Selection.setSelection	`start_index, end_index`	Select the given region of a text field.

Table D-25. Sound object methods

Method name	Parameters	Description
new Sound	-	Return a new Sound object.
Sound.attachSound	`name`	Attach a previously created sound with the given name to the Sound object.
Sound.getPan	-	Return the current pan setting. The pan is an integer from −100 (left) to 100 (right).
Sound.getVolume	-	Return the current volume setting, an integer between 0 and 100.
Sound.setPan	`pan`	Set the current pan setting. The pan is an integer from −100 (left) to 100 (right).
Sound.setVolume	`volume`	Set the current volume setting, an integer between 0 and 100.
Sound.start	-	Play the sound.
Sound.stop	-	Stop playing the sound.

Table D-26. String object methods

Method name	Parameters	Description
new String	`string`	Return a new String object initialized with the given string.
String.charAt	`index`	Return the character at a particular (0-based) index.
String.charCodeAt	`index`	Return the Unicode value (a 16-bit number) of a character at a particular index.
String.concat	`value_list`	Return a new String object that is a concatenation of all the elements in the value list. Each value can be a string or an expression (which will be evaluated and converted into a string).
String.fromCharCode	`char_list`	Return a new String object that is composed of the given character codes.
String.indexOf	`substr, start`	Return the index of the first occurrence of substr with the String. If start is specified, the search will start at that index.
String.length	-	Return the number of characters in the String.
String.slice	`start, end`	Return a new String object that contains a substring of the original. The substring starts at index start and ends at index end − 1.

Table D-26. String object methods (continued)

Method name	Parameters	Description
String.split	separator	Return an array of substrings that are bounded by the given separator (just like Perl's split function).
String.substr	start_index, length	Return a new String object containing the substring beginning at the start index. Length, if specified, will determine the length of the substring. Otherwise, the remainder of the string will be returned.
String.substring	from_index, to_index	Return a new String containing the substring between the two indices.
String.toLowerCase	-	Convert all characters in the String to lowercase.
String.toUpperCase	-	Convert all characters in the String to uppercase.

Table D-27. XML object methods

Method name	Parameters	Description
new XML	-	Create a new XML object that can be used to generate and parse XML trees or create discrete XML tags.
XML.appendChild	child_node	Attach a child node to the object.
XML.cloneNode	node	Return a copy of the node.
XML.createElement	tag_name	Create a new XML element with the given tag name.
XML.createTextNode	xml_text	Create a new XML element from the preformatted XML text.
XML.haschildNodes	-	Return true if the XML object has child nodes.
XML.insertBefore	child_node, target_node	Add the child node to the XML object's list of children before the target node.
XML.load	url	Load an external XML file at the specified URL, parse it, and fill the XML object with the document's tree.
XML.onLoad	success	This function is called when an XML document has been loaded using XML.load. Override this function by assigning your own function. The success parameter will be passed to the function, indicating whether the document successfully loaded.
XML.parseXML	string	Create an XML tree by parsing the XML text contained in the string.
XML.removeNode	child_node	Remove the child node from the XML object.
XML.send	url, window	Send the XML object (as a formatted XML document) to the specified URL using the POST method. The optional window parameter can be one of the following values: _self The current frame in the current window. _blank A new window. _parent The parent of the current frame. _top The top-level window.

Table D-27. XML object methods (continued)

Method name	Parameters	Description
XML.sendAndLoad	`url, target_xml`	Send the XML object (as a formatted XML document) to the specified URL using the POST method and store the XML response in the target XML object.
XML.toString	-	Return the XML object as a formatted XML string.

Table D-28. XML object properties

Property name	Description
XML.attributes	Return an associative array that can be used to reference or change any of the attributes of the XML object.
XML.childNodes	Return an array of the child nodes of the object.
XML.docTypeDecl	Return (or set) the string that is the XML document type declaration for the XML object.
XML.firstChild	Return the first child in the XML object's list of children.
XML.lastChild	Return the last child in the XML object's list of children.
XML.loaded	Return true if a call to XML.load has completed successfully.
XML.nextSibling	Return the next child of the object, or null if none.
XML.nodeName	Return the tag name of the node (or null if a Text Node).
XML.nodeType	Return the type of the node, where 1 = an XML element and 3 = a Text Node.
XML.nodeValue	Return the text string of a Text Node.
XML.parentNode	Return the parent of the node.
XML.previousSibling	Return the previous child of the object, or null if none.
XML.status	Return whether a load action was successful. Return values can be:
	0 Document loaded and parsed.
	-2 A CDATA section was missing an end tag.
	-3 An XML declaration was missing an end tag.
	-4 The document declaration was missing an end tag.
	-5 A comment was missing an end tag.
	-6 An XML tag was malformed.
	-7 Out of memory.
	-8 An attribute was not properly terminated.
	-9 A start tag was missing an end tag.
	-10 An end tag was missing a start tag.
XML.xmlDecl	Return or set the Declaration section of the XML object.

Table D-29. XMLSocket object properties

Property name	Parameters	Description
new XMLSocket	-	Create a new XMLSocket object.
XMLSocket.close	-	Close a connection created with XMLSocket.connect.
XMLSocket.connect	`host, port`	Open a connection between the movie and a TCP port on a host computer (specified by a domain name or IP address).

Table D-29. XMLSocket object properties (continued)

Property name	Parameters	Description
XMLSocket.onClose	-	This function is called when a socket is closed. Override this function by assigning your own function.
XMLSocket.onConnect	-	This function is called when a socket connection is opened with XMLSocket.connect. Override this function by assigning your own function. The success parameter is passed to the function, indicating whether the socket was successfully opened.
XMLSocket.onXML	object	This function is called when XML data has been received from a connected server. Override this function by assigning your own function. The object parameter is an XML object containing the received XML tree.
XMLSocket.send	object	Send data to a connected server, terminated with a null (\0) delimiter. The object can be an XML or other object, which is transformed to a string before it is sent.

Index

Symbols

< > (angle brackets)
    << and >>, enclosing PDF object
        definitions, 302
    <!-- and -->, in SVG comments, 177
    in XML tags, 177
@ (at sign), first character in primitive string
        for Draw( ) (Image::Magick), 105
. (dot)
    . (dot) operator, accessing object methods
        or properties, 420
    .= (string assignment) operator, 164
% (percent sign), %% and %! in PostScript
        comments, 297

Numbers

8-bit indexed images
    creating, 36
    creating from PNG files, 37
16-bit grayscale images, 37
24-bit color images
    converting to 8-bit color images, 44
    creating, 36
48-bit truecolor images, PNG file format
        and, 37
216-color web-safe palette, converting image
        colormap to, 98

A

<a> tag, SVG, 193
AA-Lib ASCII art library, 381
abort( ), 370
absolute coordinate space in SVG, 185

ActionScript, 215, 418–436
    actions, 421
    control structures, 420
    DoAction tags (SWF), 219
    event loops in Astral Trespassers
        game, 243
        movement of gun, aliens, and bullet,
            controlling, 244
    functions, 423
    objects, 425–436
        Array object methods, 425
        Boolean object methods, 426
        Color object methods, 426
        Date object methods, 427
        Key code constants, 428
        Key object methods, 428
        Math object methods, 429
        Mouse object methods, 430
        MovieClip object methods, 430
        MovieClip object properties, 431
        Number object properties, 432
        Object methods, 432
        Selection object methods, 432
        Sound object methods, 433
        String object methods, 433
        XML object methods, 434
        XML object properties, 435
        XMLSocket object properties, 435
    operators, 418–420
    properties, 424
    Sprites, operating on, 250
    SWF::Action module, 240, 272
    XMLSocket object, 285
ActiveState Win32, GD in standard Perl
        distribution, 26
Adam7 (PNG) interlacing, 13

We'd like to hear your suggestions for improving our indexes. Send email to *index@oreilly.com*.

C

C language
    Gimp functions, calling, 155
    libgd library, 26
    Ming library (see Ming)
caching, controlling for browser, 366
callback methods (XMLSocket class), 285
can_do_ttf( ) (GD::Graph), 131
can_read( ) (IO::Select), 283
can_write( ) (IO::Select), 283
carriage returns, 364
    inserting into PDF text, 357
Cascading StyleSheets (CSS), 211
case-sensitivity in XML tags and
        attributes, 177
Catalog dictionary object in PDF, 302
CDATA tags, 204
centered text, 265
    drawing four lines of in SVG
        (example), 190
    in PDF files, 357
CGI scripts, 363–369
    biorhythm server (example), 125–130
    CGI.pm module, implementing
        with, 365–367
        generating HTTP headers, 366
        parsing CGI input, 365
    converting astral_trespassers.swf to, 246
    image generation (makeimage.cgi), 374
    increasing server performance
        for, 367–369
        image farming, 368
        installing mod_perl, 368
CGI::Carp module, 372
ChangeColor( ) function (JavaScript), 206
Channel( ) (Image::Magick), 97
channels (RGB primaries), 5
char( ), 53
character data (CDATA) tags, 204
character id (SWF tags), 224, 226
characters( ) (XML::Writer), 198
Charcoal( ) (Image::Magick), 108
charspace( ) (PDF::API2::Text), 355
charts
    data, handling with
        GD::Graph::Data, 120
    legends for, 133
        fonts, 133
    mixed, 120
    pie charts
        attributes of, 141
        example, 122–125
    (see also graphs)

charUp( ), 54
chat server (Perl), communicating with SWF
        client, 283–285
Chop( ) (Image::Magick), 88
circle( ) (PDF::API2::Gfx), 353
circles
    bouncing ball application (example), 203
    drawing, 29
    drawing in Image::Magick, 103
    drawing with SWF::Shape module, 257
    SWF files, drawing with Ming, 273–277
clients (SWF), communicating with Perl
        backend, 282–288
clip( ) (PDF::API2::Gfx), 353
clipping JPEG image with PDF::API2
        module, Gfx object, 335
clipping layer, 220
Clone( )
    GIF animation, use in, 74
    Image::Magick, 92
clone( ) (Image), 48
clone tool (Gimp), 394
clonepage( ) (PDF::API2), 343
close( ) (PDF::API2::Gfx), 353
CLUT (Color Lookup Table), 7
CMYK color space, 6
    converting RGB to, 6
color, 5
    background
        rotated images in Image::Magick, 90
        setting for movie, 248
    brushes, using, 45
    CMYK color space, 6
    color and transparency attributes,
        Image::Magick, 95–97
    color depth, 7
    Color object methods (ActionScript), 426
    color tables, images with, 7
    display items in SWF, 253
    for Draw( ) in Image::Magick, 103
    enhancing contrast in
        Image::Magick, 112
    entries to gradient object, adding, 269
    fill color for PDF document pages, 349
    in graphs, 142–144
        colour_list( ), 143
        hex2rgb( ), 144
        importing rgb, hue, and luminance
            functions, 143
        predefined color names and hex values
            for, 142
        read_rgb( ), 144
        rgb2hex( ), 144
        sorted_colour_list( ), 144

J

JavaScript
  DOM, use in, 205
  SVG animation, creating, 204–208
    document events, 204
    element events, 204
    functions, 206
JFIF file format (JPEG File Interchange
    Format), 15
Joint Pictures Expert Group (see JPEG file
    format)
jpeg( ), 39
JPEG file format, 3, 15
  color depth, 7
  color reduction, 8
  compression, 10
    custom system, 12
    lossy, 11
  creating images from, 36
  library, downloading, 26
  MIME type, 364
  Progressive JPEGs, 14
  transparency and, 9
justified text, 265

K

Key code constants, ActionScript, 428
Key object methods, ActionScript, 428
keyboard events, tracking with buttons, 259
keys (legends) for graphs, 133
Kids attribute, PDF Pages object, 303
Kimball, Spencer, 145

L

Label( ) (Image::Magick), 105
labelFrame( )
  SWF::Movie module, 247
  SWF::Sprite module, 249
labels
  graph axes, setting fonts for, 134
  pie charts, 124
    setting fonts, 132
  text fields, setting for, 267
layers
  Gimp Layers menu, 409
  handling in Gimp, 159–162
lead( ) (PDF::API2::Text), 356
leading in PDF documents, 356
legends for graphs, 133, 141
Lehmann, Marc, 148
Lempel-Ziv-Welch compression (see LZW
    compression algorithm)
Length attribute for PDF pages, 304

libgd C library, 26
libgimp, 156
  objects used to call functions, 157
licenses
  GNU Public License, 145
  LGPL (Lesser GNU Public License), 238
line( ) (PDF::API2::Gfx), 354
line style array (SWF tags), 224, 228
line styles, 45
  gdStyled and gdStyledBrushed
    constants, 44
  shape stroking, 259
  SWF shapes
    changes in, 230
    StraightEdge Records, 232
linecap( ) (PDF::API2::Content), 350
linedash( ) (PDF::API2::Content), 350
linefeeds, 364
linejoin( ) (PDF::API2::Content), 351
lines
  drawing in PostScript, 295
  drawing with Draw( )
    (Image::Magick), 104
  drawing with PDF Gfx object, 334
  drawing with PostScript::Elements
    module, 328, 331
  drawing with SWF::Shape module, 258
  graphs with, 139
  spacing in text fields, 266
linewidth( ) (PDF::API2::Content), 351
links
  images within link elements in
    HTML, 379
  SVG linking elements, 180, 193
    xmlns namespace attribute, 191
  XLink standard, 176
little-endian byte order, 221, 226
loading SWF documents, creating preloader
    for, 276–279
loadMovie( ) (SWF::Sprite), 280
local palette for GIF animation files, 78
locked files, SWF, 219
logarithmic spiral using the Golden
    Mean, 255
logical operators, ActionScript, 419
logos for graphs, 141
long tags (SWF), header records for, 225
Loop Extension, 77
loops
  browser iterations through GIF animation
    files, 77
  event loops in ActionScript, 243, 244
  infinite, in Image::Magick, 77
lossless compression, 11
lossy compression, 11

MatteFloodfill( ), 98
Transparent( ), 99
transparent( ), 44
Transparent( ) (Image::Magick), 95, 99
trigonometric functions overloaded by
PDL, 163
Trim( ) (Image::Magick), 90, 91
trimbox( ) (PDF::API2::Page), 349
trueColor( ), 27, 36, 44
truecolor images, 7
converting to 16 colors, with and without
dithering, 8
creating from PNG files, 37
saving as pseudocolor images, 7
trueColorToPalette( ), 27, 44
TrueType fonts, 26
drawing string onto image, 55
FreeType font rendering library for, 26
<tspan> tags, SVG, 189
anchors and, 194
ttfont( ) (PDF::API2), 347
twips, 223
LINESTYLE element, width in, 228
RECT structure fields, 226
two's complement notation, 222
Type attribute in PDF dictionaries, 302

U

undef, destroying image objects, 68
Undo and Redo commands, Gimp, 160
Unicode
in SVG <text> element, 190
text in SVG images, 208–210
UTF-8 character encoding in PDF, 357
units, SVG, 180
unpack( )
converting binary structure to strings of
1's and 0's, 223
converting little-endian binary values to
integers, 222
unsigned integers (in SWF), 221
converting from bit values in SWF, 222
reading from SWF tags, 237
update( ) (PDF::API2), 341, 347
updating drawables, 161
URLs
browser requests for images from
servers, 364
indicating for images with SRC
attribute, 371
use function, 365
user agents
HTTP USER AGENT, 363
for SVG, 176

user coordinate system in SVG, 180
user input, tracking with buttons, 259

V

<value-of> element (XSLT), 212
vector file formats, 3, 17–20
PostScript, drawing with Elements
module, 328
PostScript, rendering in, 296
SVG, 175–194
XML images with, 17–20
SWF, 218
vectors, RBG colors represented as, 6
Verbruggen, Martien, 117
versions
PostScript Document Structuring
Conventions, 297
SWF, 247
vertical lines, indicating for SWF shapes, 232
vertices( ), 61
View menu (Gimp images), 405
viewer, PostScript, 291
viewers
Adobe, for SVG files, 177
Apache Batik, for SVG documents, 177
GhostView PostScript viewer, 315
viewing SVG documents, 176–179
views in SVG, 179
Visual Image Directory (thumbnails), 70
VSPACE tags (HTML), 377

W

W3C (World Wide Web Consortium), 175
SVG Test Suite, 176
warning codes, Image::Magick, 69
Wave( ) (Image::Magick), 116
wbmp( ), 40
WBMP (Wireless Bitmap) and GD files, 27
web browsers (see browsers)
web servers, 363
(see also servers)
web-safe palette (216-color), converting
image colormap to, 98
whitespace
delimiting tokens in PDF documents, 301
line spacing in SWF::TextField
module, 266
spacing attributes in HTML, 377
between words in PDF text, 357
width
bitmaps, 263
bounding box for text field, 266
lines in PDF document contents, 351

About the Author

Shawn Wallace is a writer and trumpet/mandolin/accordion player from Providence, RI. His past efforts for O'Reilly include *Programming Web Graphics*, documentation for WebBoard, and two chapters for the Perl Resource Kit. By day Shawn is the managing director of AS220, an artist community in downtown Providence. Concurrent with the writing of this book, he created a piece of musical theatre called "Dylan Thomas in America: A Monkey Robot Opera," which chronicled a collaboration between Dylan Thomas and Igor Stravinsky that never happened.

Colophon

Our look is the result of reader comments, our own experimentation, and feedback from distribution channels. Distinctive covers complement our distinctive approach to technical topics, breathing personality and life into potentially dry subjects.

The animal on the cover of *Perl Graphics Programming* is a red colubus monkey (*Procolobus badius*). This equatorial African species has a blackish back, long dark tail, tan belly, and a red crown on its head. Males (20 pounds) are larger than females (13 pounds) and have more bushy hair. They usually live in troops of 30–80 individuals, with a hierarchy based on dominant males. These monkeys rest for long periods of time, a trait sometimes attributed to their unique diet and digestive system. The red colubus eats only leaves, and digests tough plant cells in the same way that many hoofed animals do: it has a four-chambered stomach in which bacterial fermentation breaks down cellulose and releases nutrients.

While leopards and chimpanzees prey on red colubus monkeys, humans pose the largest threat. These monkeys do not fear hunters, and their bright color, loud alarm calls, and dormant nature make them an easy target. The most critically endangered among the approximately 18 species and subspecies in Africa today are the Iana River red colubus (Kenya) and the Bouvier's red colubus (Republic of Congo). In the year 2000, the Miss Waldron's subspecies (Ghana, Ivory Coast) was declared extinct, making it the first primate species eradicated in the twentieth century.

Emily Quill was the production editor and copyeditor for *Perl Graphics Programming*. Linley Dolby and Jane Ellin provided quality control. Ellen Troutman wrote the index.

Ellie Volckhausen designed the cover of this book, based on a series design by Edie Freedman. The cover image is a 19th-century engraving from the Royal Natural History. Emma Colby produced the cover layout with QuarkXPress 4.1 using Adobe's ITC Garamond font.

David Futato designed the interior layout. This book was converted to FrameMaker 5.5.6 by Joe Wizda with a format conversion tool created by Erik Ray, Jason McIntosh, Neil Walls, and Mike Sierra that uses Perl and XML technologies. The text font is Linotype Birka; the heading font is Adobe Myriad Condensed; and the code font is LucasFont's TheSans Mono Condensed. The illustrations that appear in the book were produced by Robert Romano and Jessamyn Read using Macromedia FreeHand 9 and Adobe Photoshop 6. The tip and warning icons were drawn by Christopher Bing. This colophon was written by Philip Dangler.

Other Titles Available from O'Reilly

Perl

Learning Perl, 3rd Edition

By Randal Schwartz & Tom Phoenix
3rd Edition July 2001
330 pages, ISBN 0-596-00132-0

Learning Perl is the quintessential tutorial for the Perl programming language. The third edition has not only been updated to Perl Version 5.6, but has also been rewritten from the ground up to reflect the needs of programmers learning Perl today. Other books may teach you to program in Perl, but this book will turn you into a Perl programmer.

Mastering Regular Expressions, 2nd Edition

By Jeffrey E. F. Friedl
2nd Edition July 2002
484 pages, ISBN 0-596-00289-0

Written by an expert in the topic, this book shows programmers not only how to use regular expressions, but how to think in regular expressions. Updated with a wealth of new material, the second edition explains how to use regular expressions to code complex and subtle text processing that you never imagined could be automated. Included are such key topics as avoiding common errors and optimizing expressions. The book covers many new features added to Perl—a language well endowed with regular expressions—as well as other languages such as Java, Python, and Visual Basic that include support for this powerful tool.

Embedding Perl in HTML with Mason

By Dave Rolsky & Ken Williams
1st Edition October 2002
320 pages, ISBN 0-596-00225-4

Mason, a Perl-based templating system, is becoming more and more popular as a tool for building websites and managing other dynamic collections. While using Mason is not difficult, creating Mason-based sites can be tricky, and this concise book helps you navigate around the obstacles. The book covers the most recent release of Mason, 1.10, which has many new features including line number reporting based on source files, sub-requests, and simplified use as a CGII. It also explores using Mason for dynamic generation of XML documents.

Perl & XML

By Erik T. Ray & Jason McIntosh
1st Edition April 2002
224 pages, ISBN 0-596-00205-X

Perl & XML is aimed at Perl programmers who need to work with XML documents and data. This book gives a complete, comprehensive tour of the landscape of Perl and XML, making sense of the myriad of modules, terminology, and techniques. The last two chapters of Perl and XML give complete examples of XML applications, pulling together all the tools at your disposal.

Mastering Perl/Tk

By Steve Lidie & Nancy Walsh
1st Edition January 2002
768 pages, ISBN 1-56592-716-8

Beginners and seasoned Perl/Tk programmers alike will find *Mastering Perl/Tk* to be the definitive book on creating graphical user interfaces with Perl/Tk. After a fast-moving tutorial, the book goes into detail on creating custom widgets, working with bindings and callbacks, IPC techniques, and examples using many of the non-standard add-on widgets for Perl/Tk (including Tix widgets). Every Perl/Tk programmer will need this book.

Perl Cookbook

By Tom Christiansen &
Nathan Torkington
1st Edition August 1998
794 pages, ISBN 1-56592-243-3

The *Perl Cookbook* is a comprehensive collection of problems, solutions, and practical examples for anyone programming in Perl. You'll find hundreds of rigorously reviewed Perl "recipes" for manipulating strings, numbers, dates, arrays, and hashes; pattern matching and text substitutions; references, data structures, objects, and classes; signals and exceptions; and much more.

O'REILLY®

To order: *800-998-9938* • *order@oreilly.com* • *www.oreilly.com*
Online editions of most O'Reilly titles are available by subscription at *safari.oreilly.com*
Also available at most retail and online bookstores.

How to stay in touch with O'Reilly

1. Visit our award-winning web site

http://www.oreilly.com/

★ "Top 100 Sites on the Web"—PC Magazine
★ CIO Magazine's Web Business 50 Awards

Our web site contains a library of comprehensive product information (including book excerpts and tables of contents), downloadable software, background articles, interviews with technology leaders, links to relevant sites, book cover art, and more. File us in your bookmarks or favorites!

2. Join our email mailing lists

Sign up to get email announcements of new books and conferences, special offers, and O'Reilly Network technology newsletters at:

http://elists.oreilly.com

It's easy to customize your free elists subscription so you'll get exactly the O'Reilly news you want.

3. Get examples from our books

To find example files for a book, go to:

http://www.oreilly.com/catalog

select the book, and follow the "Examples" link.

4. Work with us

Check out our web site for current employment opportunities:

http://jobs.oreilly.com/

5. Register your book

Register your book at:

http://register.oreilly.com

6. Contact us

O'Reilly & Associates, Inc.
1005 Gravenstein Hwy North
Sebastopol, CA 95472 USA
TEL: 707-827-7000 or 800-998-9938
      (6am to 5pm PST)
FAX: 707-829-0104

order@oreilly.com
For answers to problems regarding your order or our products. To place a book order online visit:

http://www.oreilly.com/order_new/

catalog@oreilly.com
To request a copy of our latest catalog.

booktech@oreilly.com
For book content technical questions or corrections.

corporate@oreilly.com
For educational, library, government, and corporate sales.

proposals@oreilly.com
To submit new book proposals to our editors and product managers.

international@oreilly.com
For information about our international distributors or translation queries. For a list of our distributors outside of North America check out:

http://international.oreilly.com/distributors.html

adoption@oreilly.com
For information about academic use of O'Reilly books, visit:

http://academic.oreilly.com

O'REILLY®

To order: *800-998-9938* • *order@oreilly.com* • *www.oreilly.com*
Online editions of most O'Reilly titles are available by subscription at *safari.oreilly.com*
Also available at most retail and online bookstores.